THE AMERICAN WOMAN

THE AMERICAN WOMAN

Her Past, Her Present,
Her Future

MARIE RICHMOND-ABBOTT
Eastern Michigan University

HOLT, RINEHART AND WINSTON
New York   Chicago   San Francisco   Dallas
Montreal   Toronto   London   Sydney

Acknowledgments

Quotations from poems on pp. 64–66 are from the following sources: From *To Be of Use,* selections by Marge Piercy from "She Leaves" and "Councils" reprinted with permission of author and Doubleday, 1973, New York, N.Y. From *Hard Loving,* selection by Marge Piercy from "The Friend" reprinted with permission of author and Wesleyan University Press, 1969, Middletown, Conn. From *The Dream of a Common Language,* the selection from "Phantasia for Elvira Shatayev" by Adrienne Rich reprinted with permission of W. W. Norton & Company, Inc., New York, N.Y. From *Selected Poems* by Gwendolyn Brooks, the selection from "The Mother" reprinted with permission of Harper & Row, Publishers, New York, N.Y. From *The Floor Keeps Turning,* the selection from "Mothers, Daughters" by Shirley Kaufman reprinted with permission of University of Pittsburgh Press, 1970, Pittsburgh, Pa. From *Between Wars and Other Poems* by Anne Halley, the selection from "Dear God, the Day Is Gray" reprinted with permission of University of Massachusetts Press, 1965, Amherst, Mass. From *Monster* by Robin Morgan, the selection from "Monster" reprinted with permission of Random House, Inc., 1972, New York, N.Y. Extract p. 66 from *Women in Drama: An Anthology* edited by Harriet Kriegel. Copyright © 1975 by Harriet Kriegel. Reprinted by arrangement with The New American Library, Inc., New York, N.Y. Table 4.1, p. 83, "The Definition of Sex Stereotypes via the Adjective Check List" by John E. Williams and Susan M. Bennett, reprinted with permission of *Sex Roles, A Journal of Research,* Vol. I, No. 4, 1975, by Plenum Publishing Corporation, New York, N.Y.

Library of Congress Cataloging in Publication Data

Main entry under title:

The American woman.

    Includes bibliographical references and index.
    1. Women—United States—Addresses, essays, lectures. 2. Women—United States—Social conditions—Addresses, essays, lectures. I. Richmond-Abbott, Marie.
HQ1426.C63   301.41'2'0973   78-31520
ISBN 0-03-046536-2

9 0 1 2   090   9 8 7 6 5 4 3 2 1

Contributors

Daryl Hafter received her Ph.D. in History from Yale University in 1964. She teaches Women in History and French History at Eastern Michigan University and has recently taught the interdisciplinary course in women's studies and served as Assistant Coordinator of the program. She has just completed research on Philip de la Salle and the French silk industry under an American Philosophical Society grant.

Karen Sinclair received her Ph.D. in Anthropology from Brown University in 1976. She has done field work in the Caribbean and, under a Fulbright Scholarship, in New Zealand. She teaches Sex Roles and an interdisciplinary women's studies course at Eastern Michigan University, and has recently participated in an NEH funded seminar dealing with the development of curricula for women's studies courses.

Nadean Bishop is serving her second term as Coordinator of women's studies at Eastern Michigan University. She teaches a course on Women in Literature and the interdisciplinary women's studies course, and was involved in an NEH funded seminar to write new women's studies course materials. Her recent publications include work on Matthew Arnold and original poetry as well as a review of the "Total Woman" books (*Human Behavior*, April 1977).

Marie Richmond-Abbott received her B.A. from Duke University in History and her Ph.D. from Florida State University in Sociology. She teaches Family, Sociology of Sex Roles, and the interdisciplinary women's studies course at Eastern Michigan University. Her recent publications include an examination of power structures in families, done through a field study of Cuban immigrants (*Journal of Marriage and the Family*, May 1976), and a review of the "Total Woman" books and their sociological implications (*Human Behavior*, April 1977). She is currently doing research on a sample of 2,000 single-parent families to examine sex role attitudes and behavior and to assess the implication of these behaviors for custody decisions and counseling.

Barbara Ellen Brackney received her Ph.D. in Clinical Psychology from the University of Michigan in 1975. She is currently an Assistant Professor at Eastern Michigan University where she teaches Psychology of Women and is active in the women's studies program. Dr. Brackney also has a private practice, specializing in feminist psychotherapy. Her research interests center presently on sex differences in body image as reflected in a recent article in *Sex Roles*, "The importance of inner and outer body parts attitudes in the self-concept of late adolescents," (in press).

v

Gwen Reichbach is an Assistant Professor in Home Economics at Eastern Michigan University where she teaches Consumer Affairs and Home Management and has also taught the interdisciplinary women's studies course. Ms. Reichbach has also worked with lawyers in the area of costs of childrearing and has been accepted as an expert witness in family finance in the Circuit Court of Washtenaw County.

Mary F. McCarthy received her M.A. in Economics from Columbia University and has completed further graduate study at the University of Chicago and the University of Michigan, including a Ford Foundation Faculty Research Seminar Fellowship. She has been a member of the faculty at Eastern Michigan University in the Department of Economics since 1959, currently holding the rank of Assistant Professor. She has taught Economics of Women several times and is actively involved in women's affairs.

Marjorie Lansing received her Ph.D. from the University of Michigan and is currently a Professor of Political Science at Eastern Michigan University. She has been involved with women's studies for ten years, during which time she has delivered papers at several international conferences. In 1976 she lectured on the equal rights of women in Singapore and Jakarta for the U.S. Information Service. She is a political activist, having attended the Democratic National Convention as a delegate in 1976 and run statewide in Michigan for a Congressional post. She is a member of Who's Who among American Women and International Women's Who's Who. Among her publications are various empirical studies relating to the political behavior of women, such as a chapter on American women in *Women around the World: A Study in Comparative Politics,* ABC-CLIO Press, 1975.

Robert Hefner and Meda Rebecca Robert Hefner is a Professor in the Department of Psychology at the University of Michigan. Meda Rebecca received her Ph.D. from the University of Michigan in 1978, focusing on sex roles in psychology. She is now an Assistant Professor at the State University of New York, College at Geneseo. Along with other research on sex roles, Drs. Hefner and Rebecca have just completed three years of work on an NIE grant to develop a model for sex role transcendence. A summary of their major findings is found in *The Journal of Social Issues,* Spring 1976. In addition, Robert Hefner is currently working on sex roles in contemporary China and Meda Rebecca is doing work on career development in adult women.

Preface

Our purpose in writing this book was to develop an interdisciplinary text dealing with all aspects of the contemporary American woman. All of us who have worked in women's studies programs over the last few years have searched for material from other disciplines to supplement the information that is available in our own. Such material, however, is frequently compartmentalized and fragmented. Often we had to search for and compile material from books and journals in the various disciplines and put numerous articles on library reserve to fulfill students' needs. This imposed an unrealistic burden on us as instructors, and despite our efforts, we did not believe that the students were getting an integrated or comprehensive view of women's studies. We thus recognized an intense need for a text that would bring together the diverse material on women. In particular, we wanted more than a collection of readings; we wanted a text with broad coverage and a common reading level, which contained suggestions for further reading or class discussion.

Out of this need came *The American Woman.* It was written by nine women and one man who are specialists in their particular area; most of the women have also jointly taught an interdisciplinary women's studies course. This book is intended for use in interdisciplinary women's studies courses or, as an integrating text in more advanced courses on, for example, the sociology of women or sex roles. It is also useful as a text in any course where sexism is treated.

The book presents an overview of the status of present-day American women. The first part assesses historical and cross-cultural factors that have shaped their present status; the second section examines the stereotypes, socialization, and roles that perpetuate that status; and the final part describes specific areas in the society where women suffer institutional discrimination. The book concludes by exploring what alternatives women may have to their present condition.

In developing the text, we discovered that three important themes run through all the material: women's development of an identity separate from husband, family, or tribal unity; women's unity with other women; and women's participation in society. We can see the changes in the status of women by following these themes through the chapters.

In Chapter 1 we find that the development of women's identity and the increase in women's participation in society have been a matter of peaks and valleys rather than a straight-line progression. In the Middle Ages many noblewomen and some peasants were able to exert a fair amount of political influence, earn masterships in trades, and participate quite fully in society. However, by the thirteenth or fourteenth century onward, and particularly with the advent of the nineteenth century's Napoleonic Code, many of these rights were taken away. Although restrictions upon women existed in the American frontier days, they were relaxed because of the need for female participation in society. Only as the country became settled were the more conventional restrictions reimposed. However, by this time women were developing a unity, first centered around the antislavery movements and later around their own desire to vote and participate more fully in society. Finally, we see this unity and participation being carried forward in the present women's movement.

In Chapter 2 we compare the status of women in other cultures present and past with that of women in the United States. In particular, we learn that while women basically realized their identity through membership in a tribe, or national unity, they had a strong unity with other women. The bonds they formed in this regard enabled them to achieve a uniquely female power, such as in cases where they used "female" magic to achieve their ends. We also see that in most cultures women are interwoven into the societal structure so that they are active members of the productive system even though they may be unable to exercise direct political influence.

Chapter 3 reveals how literature has frequently imposed a stereotyped identity on women. Writers have variously shown women as the pure, mothering Madonna, the evil temptress Eve, or a combination of the two: the pure, but sexual, Venus. The various forms of literature, however, such as drama, poetry, and fiction, have recently been a vehicle through which women search for their own identities. Literature has also been a medium by which they share their thoughts and questions with other women. We can see in particular the search by Black women for a sense of their special place. As women have increasingly contributed to literature, their beliefs have also had a greater impact on the values of their society.

Chapter 4 describes the stereotypes of women now operating in American society and their perpetuation in the popular media. We learn how stereotypes for American women have developed out of a unique blend of western cross-cultural traditions and our own American tradition. These stereotypes have imposed upon American women a "shadow set of values" different from those that the culture prescribes for men. Such shadow values make it possible for a woman to succeed in the feminine sphere but difficult for her to achieve success through wider participation in society. Cultural stereotypes have imposed rigid boundaries, such as those of the "nice girl," on women who wish to have an approved feminine identity. These stereotypes perpetuate negative self-feelings and dependency in women in much the same way that racial stereotypes have perpetuated negative attitudes and actions among Blacks. We can also see how these stereotypes of women have been used to perpetuate a linking of their identity to men and to emphasize women's need for men's protection and approval. Women are allowed participation in society only as a support system for the male culture. The description of popular songs and literature shows how female stereotypes continue today and reveals a continuing fear that women will develop a separate identity from men and move out of their rigidly defined roles to participate more fully in society.

Chapter 5 describes in great detail how girls are socialized to accept commonly held stereotypes of their abilities and potential. The chapter begins by examining the differences between inherited and learned behavior for males and females. It shows us how most differences in abilities and behavior between the sexes are learned differences started by such things as parental expectations and reinforced by everything from television to the elementary-school classroom. The chapter looks at the subtle messages conveyed by language, teachers, toys, and clothing, and the more explicit ones conveyed by books and television, to show how this cultural training affects young girls. In particular, we see the difficulties a young girl faces in developing a full, positive identity and a sense of unity with other girls.

Chapter 6 on adolescence continues the description of women's developing identity and the problems that come when women are forced to choose between achieving societal success or winning approval for feminine behavior. It points out the special identity problems of many young women: Black women, lesbians, and women who choose to dedicate themselves to academic or sporting success. Again we see that it is difficult for the adolescent female to firm up an independent identity. Not only is she caught in the bind of choosing between femininity and success, but she must also choose between being a "nice" girl or a "bad" girl. She has little unity with other women and may even compete with them for the approval of men. She may end up withdrawing from competition for success and full participation in society so that she can gain male approval.

Chapter 7 describes how this budding identity of young women may then be submerged when they marry and form a family. The traditional marriage is typically a "his" and "her" marriage and has not been good for women's self-esteem or mental health. The chapter surveys recent changes, such as lowered birthrates and greater participation by married women in the labor force, and how these have affected marital roles. It looks particularly at the dual-career family and the attendant problems and benefits for mothers who work outside the home. The chapter examines three kinds of families, which have special structures, strengths, and weaknesses: the working-class family, the Black family, and the single-parent family. In the Black family women have retained a stronger sense of individual identity and have developed a supportive unity with which they face adverse circumstances. In the working-class family women have a similar, though less positively valued, unity, and in the female single-parent family, are developing more of a sense of unity as roles change. Although there are certainly difficulties in the single-parent situation, many women have found new fulfillment and self-realization in being able to cope with and control their own destinies. The chapter concludes by looking at some alternatives to traditional family structures: singlehood, lesbian relationships, cohabitation, and communal living arrangements.

The final section of the book describes women's participation in two important areas which influence their status: the economic and political spheres. Chapter 8 examines women's role in the world of work. It looks at such questions as why women work and why they are working today in greater numbers. We learn that in spite of a plethora of laws that ban discrimination against women, they are still usually paid less than men for the same work, are kept out of the most prestigious and high-paying jobs, and suffer from underemployment and unemployment. The chapter also discusses women's role as homemaker: the value of this production economically, the problems for women when this value is not realized, and the increasing problem of displaced homemakers. The chapter ends with predictions about the future of women in the economic world. Throughout we can see where women's uncertainty about their own identity and potential have influenced their possibilities for occupational success. We can also see how increasing emphasis on their unity—in unions, in political coalitions fighting for rights, and in other areas of society—will enable them to expand and strengthen their increasing participation in society.

Chapter 9 shows us how women have attempted to influence their position in society by gaining the vote and participating in the political arena. The chapter details the long and painful political process through which women gained equal suffrage. It goes on to describe what factors have been influential in determining whether or not women have used their hard-earned right to vote. We learn that in spite of some gains few women are today participating in policy-making positions in the government, although women have had some effect on public policy with proposed legislation such as the Equal Rights Amendment. The chapter discusses the implications of this amendment and the possibilities for its enactment. It concludes by showing us that women must consciously participate in the political process if they wish wider influence in society. They must unite in this effort if they wish to support their own interests and influence their position in the culture.

In conclusion, Chapter 10 gives us a theoretical look at the possibilities for women in the future. It attempts to show us that we must look beyond predictions for women's role in specific areas, such as family or the world of work, to answer larger questions. What do women really want to be in terms of their personality characteristics and identity? What kind of a society do they want to live in? How are they going to achieve that identity and that type of society? The chapter then examines two possibilities for more equalitarian sex-roles in the future; androgyny and the transcendence of sex roles. It points out that we must think beyond a mere blending of masculinity and femininity; rather we must creatively examine new ways of behaving for both sexes. It describes the cultural patterns that could be established in American society (segregation, assimilation, pluralism, etc.) and how each of these patterns could facilitate or retard changes in sex roles. We see that in some of these patterns women have a greater possibility to develop individual identities and to participate more fully in society than they do in other choices. The important message that the chapter leaves with us is that we must submit the available choices to creative analysis and make decisions about what type of cultural patterning of sex roles this society will have and how we can achieve change.

Thus, this text gives an overview of the status of women in our contemporary society. It shows us the historical and cross-cultural roots of that status, the present cultural and institutional patterns that perpetuate it, and examines the future possibilities for changing it. We hope that our readers will come away with a greater understanding of the contemporary American woman.

My overwhelming debt of gratitude is to all the contributors to this volume, without whose hard work and persistence this book could never have been written. All of these people took time from their busy schedules to contribute their expertise. Not only did they do an admirable job of developing the content, but they pushed to meet deadlines and were willing to compromise individual style for common reading level. I greatly appreciate all of their effort, their good humor and their patience with their sometimes picky editor.

I would also like to thank those who helped us develop and refine our ideas in many hours of conversation. Outstanding among these is Margaret Rossiter, who has been the inspiration for the women's studies program at Eastern Michigan University. In addition, I would like to thank our typists, Maureen Anderson and Linda Greig, who frequently worked under time pressure but were still able to edit and correct. Without the help of all of the above, this book would never have been completed.

Special thanks also go to my husband, Richard Abbott, who urged me to stop complaining about not finding material which fit my women's studies course and to produce a book of my own. I appreciate his encouragement, his scholarly criticism and editing, and his patience in my endeavor. My thanks, too, to my children, Charlie and Kim, for allowing their mother the necessary working periods of calm and quiet.

December 1978   Marie Richmond-Abbott
                                                Eastern Michigan University

Contents

Preface   vii

1   **An Overview of Women's History**   1
Daryl M. Hafter

2   **Cross-Cultural Perspectives of American
Sex Roles**   28
Karen Sinclair

3   **Women in Literature**   48
Nadean Bishop

4   **Stereotypes of Men and Women in the
American Culture**   71
Marie Richmond-Abbott

5   **Early Socialization of the American Female**   96
Marie Richmond-Abbott

6   **The Psychology of Female Adolescence:
Identity and Conflict**   133
Barbara Brackney

7   **Women's Roles in the Family**   163
Gwen Reichbach

8   **Women's Economic Roles, Problems, and
Opportunities**   186
Mary F. McCarthy

9   **Women in American Politics**   227
Marjorie Lansing

10   **The Future of Sex Roles**   243
Robert Hefner and Meda Rebecca

Index   265

CHAPTER 1

An Overview of Women's History*

Daryl M. Hafter

THE EUROPEAN EXPERIENCE

Why should we learn about the history of women? What does the past have to do with women today? Our idea of what women are like and what they should do is the result of ideas planted in society long ago. Whether male or female, we accept these assumptions of what is natural and normal behavior without realizing that many of them come from a past hundreds of years old. We have rejected the plumbing and heating standards normal a thousand years ago, but our notions about women are shaped by thinkers reacting to conditions that have long since passed. To free ourselves for lives that fulfill our highest potential, we must find the way to reject these stereotypical ideas. To do this, we must first understand where they originated. A brief look at the history of women will help us to see women's roles in perspective. The contradictory images of women as simultaneously "sinful" and "pure," and "passive" and "bossy," come from cultural standards of the past. They are not the inevitable product of women's nature. By reviewing the past we will also see that, even when under suspicion and deprived of legal rights, women played a part in history that was essential to the well-being of society.

By tracing the extent to which women were able to assert themselves, we can also assess important facts about the dynamics of political control in various periods. Although this use of women's history as a social indicator is in its infancy, we can generalize about the transition from medieval to

*The author would like to thank Professor Margaret L. Rossiter, whose aid and inspiration were tantamount to collaboration.

1

modern state forms. In the European Middle Ages, when decentralized governments left much power to noble families, women were able to exert influence. Noblewomen wielded power through their families. Working women took advantage of a lack of skilled labor, and acquired trades. Women in all economic brackets could benefit from the relatively unstructured nature of government and administration. Rules prohibiting women's participation in public activity were not spelled out until kings began to impose centralized control over their territories. Then, as administration was made more formal, laws were written to keep women in the role of minors.

An interesting confirmation of this theory suggests that seventeenth-century French families with new wealth, who wanted to be accepted into aristocratic circles, asserted that women should have more privileges. To them, women's influence was symbolic of decentralized political control. The development of political structures in the United States shows a similar trend. In frontier days women participated widely in activities that the law forced them to abandon when the country became more populous and centralized. Ideology justifying both forms of behavior has a long history.

Classical Alternatives

Although the world of the ancient Greeks seems very far away in time, the basic alternative views of women originated with them: women are equal to men or inferior to them. Aristotle defined women as inferior and considered them to be biologically imperfect. He wrote: "We should look upon the female state as being, as it were, a deformity, though one which occurs in the ordinary course of nature."[1] From this definition it follows that Aristotle believed women should obey their husbands, be modest and silent, and marry spouses who were twenty years older than they. Aristotle generalized from the conditions in the Athens of his time, when women had few legal rights, were always under the guardianship of a male relative, and spent their days doing household industry inside dark, small houses.

Plato, on the other hand, wrote that excellence and intelligence were traits that men or women might have, depending on their education. Plato had as his model the women of Sparta, who were encouraged to develop athletic skills and a sense of dignity. This thinker perceived that it was basically to produce legitimate heirs that the women of his day married and became dependent: in his ideal state there would be no marriage, and children would be claimed by the entire community.[2] Throughout history those who have supported equal rights for women have quoted Plato's words.

The Christian Era: Woman as Temptress or Virgin Mary

In the Christian Era women's role kept its dual nature. Christianity acted to dignify women by insisting that the souls of all human beings were equal in worth. Salvation was possible for men and women: Women could practice a chaste, holy life as nuns, and they could become saints. Christianity also preached that marriage was a friendship, not an exploitive relationship. But at the same time the Christian Church was very suspicious of women.

Reacting against the freedom that he saw around him in the late Roman Empire, Saint Paul advised in his Letter to the Corinthians: "Women must keep quiet at gatherings of the church. They are not allowed to speak; they must take a subordinate place, as the Law enjoins. If they want any information let them ask their husbands at home."[3] This passage provides the basis for the restrictions against women's becoming priests in many churches today. Saint Paul also laid the foundation for relations between husbands and wives. He wrote to the Colossians: "Wives, be subject to your husbands; that is your proper duty in the Lord. Husbands, love your wives, do not be harsh to them."[4] Because they gave the persistent attitudes of society religious sanction, these words of Saint Paul justified the curtailment of women's legal rights and set a pattern for women's subordinate position in marriage throughout history.

In the law codes of the Middle Ages, for instance, women's rights in all spheres were severely limited. However, many factors intervened to help overcome these barriers. In the early Middle Ages (the eighth through the eleventh centuries) when governments were weak, some noblewomen managed to exert control through their position in the aristocratic families. This was especially true when their husbands went off to engage in wars or crusades, leaving the women to manage the estates and defend them on their own. Some of these women were even representatives at town assemblies.[5] Individual noblewomen like Eleanor of Aquitaine and Blanche of Castile, the mother of King Louis IX of France, showed that women could rule with wisdom and firmness. For the most part, the influence of all these noblewomen receded as the kings gained greater control over the legal institutions of their countries.

A similar pattern can be seen in women's participation in the church. Stressing the equalitarian theme of the early church, women officially in charge of abbeys before A.D. 800 were able to give penance to monks as well as nuns. They also presided over monasteries, taught boys and girls, and acted as vigorous administrators. Women had been key participants in the early church, and they continued in this role as long as the ecclesiastic units were controlled locally. In his attempts to bring vast areas of Europe under his active control, Emperor Charlemagne (crowned in 800) reorganized the church and insisted that clerics become instruments of government. Since clerical women were considered unsuited to this political purpose, they lost many important functions they had performed earlier. Thus, as the church increased its centralized control over the religious orders, nuns were strictly segregated and permitted to teach only girls. Since nuns staffed the early grades where children learned to read, boys in this system went through school untainted by contact with women or reading primers. This has led one historian to conclude that there may have been more women than men who could read after the ninth century A.D. These women, of course, were expected to obey their illiterate husbands and be subservient to them.[6]

Women were also important in the development of popular religion and the urban friar movements that stressed chastity and care of the poor. Given the restrictions imposed on women in regular nunneries, it is not surprising that many women expressed religious commitment by joining less restricted groups. Sometimes these spontaneous communities were considered heretical or were thought to be filled with nonbelievers.

The idea that women should be put on a pedestal and transformed to exemplify all good qualities, even when they were not nuns, inspired the cult of courtly love among worldly nobles. This ideal served to free wealthy women from ordinary standards of morality. From a positive standpoint, noble ladies were understood to have the right to choose their lovers and to enjoy lovemaking. They wrote poetry and participated fully in cultural activities like singing in company and playing musical instruments to accompany their songs. Even though the Middle Ages as a whole was not prudish, this freedom only benefited noblewomen. It was a substitute for legal and political influence, not a means of gaining it.

One path to economic rights, still only a measure of personal not political power, came from the working classes. As merchants and craftsmen in towns fought for the right to control their own inheritances, they established this right for their wives as well. Women in the late Middle Ages (the twelfth through the fourteenth centuries) were permitted to join guilds and earn masterships in a variety of trades. There is evidence that they even became wealthy merchants in Italy and England.[7]

"Did Women Have a Renaissance?"

The Renaissance and Early Modern periods (the fifteenth through the seventeenth centuries) were mixed in terms of the freedom women had. In fact, one scholar was moved to ask, "Did women have a Renaissance?" Her suspicions that women's status fell after the Middle Ages are based in part on the restrictions on women's sexuality and in part on the restrictions on her political rights. One can see the change in women's liberty in the behavior of the princely courts. In Renaissance Italy the courts were led mostly by men; earlier, during the Middle Ages, there had been many courts headed by noblewomen. Women's right to initiate a loving relationship, even if it was not approved by the church, was winked at during the earlier period. The Renaissance ideal of a chaste, nonsexual woman conflicted with the earlier view. A very influential book that set cultural standards of behavior,

The Courtier, emphasized that women should only think of married love and urged men to idealize love so that it was no longer considered frankly sexual.[8]

During the Renaissance (the fourteenth through the sixteenth centuries) classical scholars who called themselves humanists focused interest on Greek and Roman antiquity. Their desire to revive the cultural and artistic standards of the Golden Age induced them to praise the sort of restricted life that Athenian women had lived. And in their intellectual games these scholars took up the Aristotelian idea that heaven was spiritual and good, but the "lower" substances and activities on earth were less praiseworthy. On earth creatures were subject to decay and passion; sexual love might be tolerated within marriage, but abstinence was preferable. Contact with women carried with it the possibility of sin, since man's more earthly physical nature was likely to respond to them.[9]

Women were not totally excluded from the cultural life of the Renaissance courts. The ideal of education stated that what was truly human should be cultivated, and this applied to women's intellectual capacities too. Some noblewomen were trained in Latin and Greek and were brought up just as their brothers had been, by tutors. A few women like Marguerite of Navarre, sister of Francis I, king of France, participated in the discussions of court salons. Some received university training in the liberal arts and the professions. That there were such exceptional intellectuals as Louise Labé, a sixteenth-century French poet descended from a family of rope makers, shows that middle-class women could gain literary distinction. But in general women were advised to undertake "a certain pleasing affability [which] is becoming above all else, whereby she will be able to entertain graciously every kind of man."[10] At the same time young men were told to become proficient in the use of weapons, horseback riding, general knowledge, psychology of governing, as well as manners.

Some women did manage to act as rulers of small Italian duchies or the larger countries elsewhere in Europe. In Italy Caterina Sforza ruled a small duchy, vigorously standing off enemies until she was conquered; Isabel of Spain reorganized the kingdom and laid the groundwork for a modern, centralized nation; Elizabeth I of England ruled with supreme statecraft in dangerous political and military situations. Aside from such women, few females enjoyed any degree of political power and influence. In some Renaissance courts, they became patrons of the arts—but they did not single out women's activities for promotion. As the male rulers' power increased over the institutions of the state, and noblemen trained themselves to become the princes' lieutenants, the importance of aristocratic families declined. The wives and daughters of these families lost their influence outside the home. Even aristocratic women were thought of as handmaidens to the princes, and less and less as political personalities to be dealt with in their own right.[11]

An Unexpected Work Force

The shrinking of noblewomen's rights and importance had a parallel in the declining status of working women who made up the vast majority. Tradeswomen had been learning skills as apprentices and acquiring their own workshops throughout the Middle Ages. From the fourteenth century onward, they were gradually expelled from legal participation in guilds. As the population of Europe grew, men took over the prized role of guildmaster, and even they found access to the mastership more difficult. Only the wives, daughters, and some widows of masters benefited from the guild rules that gave the masters a legal monopoly over most crafts. Women unrelated to masters were thrown into the large group of workers who had to accept the lower day rates or piece rates. Sometimes they were no longer permitted to do even the jobs they had traditionally held. Silk weaving had been considered women's work until the sixteenth century in parts of France; from that time on, women were forced to do the less rewarding tasks associated with the weaving trade. Printing, which in England had been a women's occupation, became exclusively male. Clothing manufacture in Switzerland passed into the hands of male tailors. These restrictions did not exempt women from heavy physical labor, though. Denied the chance to learn trades, many joined the ranks of the unskilled laborers, carrying construction materials, acting as porters of water or market goods, ferrying clumsy boats across rivers, and working as miners. In these jobs they worked alongside men, usually earning half as much in pay.[12]

Even as their economic opportunities became more restricted, women's contribution to the family economy became more important. We are now beginning to understand just how important that contribution was. Most unmarried women earned their own dowries by working as industrial or agricultural servants. They saved their pitiful wages for as long as seven to eight years before they were able to marry childhood sweethearts. It has been a revelation to historians that these young, uneducated girls traveled far from their homes to get work and managed against great odds to put together enough money at the end of their service to buy a small farm or purchase the machines needed to support the family. Often these small sums were the only cash the poor family would ever have; if it were not for the girls' work and thrift, their families would have been utterly destitute. But even after marriage, chances were overwhelming that husbands could not earn enough to support their families. The wives expected to contribute to the family income by spinning, lace making, farming, hiring themselves out as day workers, or, if the worst came to the worst, becoming temporary prostitutes. Once again, the meager sums these women earned, sometimes as little as two cents a day for fourteen hours of lace making, were crucial in keeping the families together. In times of desperation the wives resorted to theft, smuggling, and begging and taught their children how to get private or church charity. One historian has called this way of life "an economy of makeshifts."[13] Ultimately, it was the wife who made it work or not.

When we think of the role of women in preindustrial societies, the picture in our minds is of cottage industries existing in self-sufficient farms. Although this view is too neat to be historically accurate, it is true that when the home itself was the work unit, the value of women's labor was never questioned: It had central importance in producing articles for home consumption and sale. While every member had to contribute to the family's support, the tasks themselves were divided into men's or women's activities. Despite the division of labor, women frequently helped out with the men's jobs at harvest time or during a busy industrial season because the workplace and home were one.

Popular literature warned workingmen not to marry wives without trades; women had to be able to undertake their own support. This is why the closing of guilds to women was damaging. Their opportunities for lucrative employment were sharply curtailed, but society's notion that they should support themselves in marriage remained. This contradiction of the real facts and the ideal no doubt led greater numbers of women to practice the economy of makeshifts in the period after the sixteenth century.[14]

These facts showing the curtailment of women's opportunities in economic, political, and cultural life during the Renaissance cast the earlier Middle Ages in a perspective that differs from that with which we usually view it. The status of women seems to have declined toward the onset of the modern era. By contrast, the Middle Ages appear to have given women some freedoms of opportunity that have not yet been regained. It is often hard to fathom the idea that history has not always been the story of steady progress and that the modern age is not necessarily the "best." Tracing the ups and downs of women's history brings home this uncomfortable fact.

Was the Reformation a Reform for Women?

There is no simple graph line for women's status in the period of religious turmoil that followed the Renaissance. Many women participated in the Protestant Reformation in ways that were unique for the age. In England some wrote theological tracts and marched to public gathering places shouting religious slogans. In France and Switzerland literate women entered into religious discussions with priests and studied the Scriptures. Church authorities called these women "learned beyond their sex." The compliment was partly a reprimand, implying that education for women should be limited to an appropriately low level. This was not the case with Protestants, who encouraged women to become literate in order to read the Bible with their husbands. Some women went further and tried to preach and gain converts to the Reformed faith. But here they ran into the disapproval of the Protestant clergy. Women were to read the Bible, teach their children, and be pious. But if they tried to take an active part in church affairs, they would have been condemned—as was Renée of Ferrara, whose activism inspired one pastor to complain to Calvin: "She is turning everything upsidedown in our ecclesiastical assembly. . . . Our Consistory will be the laughingstock of papists and Anabaptists. They'll say we're being ruled by women."[15]

Underscoring that the Protestants maintained traditional views of women's limitations does not tell the whole story. The Protestants did establish novelties that bettered women's status in marriage. They enforced standards of good behavior between husbands and wives, bringing either to public trial for mistreating the other. Permitting the minister to have a wife raised the status of marriage and appeared to condone sexuality within the proper bonds. But there were other characteristics of the new faith that suggested that women may have lost more than they had gained. Saints of both genders had been suppressed as the Protestants stressed the importance of monotheism. This affected the spiritual life of women more than men because women could no longer look to Mary or the other female saints as comforting objects of devotion. In childbirth they had to invoke a masculine God who exacted obedience rather than dispensed mercy. The closing of nunneries removed the one traditional arena where women could administrate for themselves and undertake religious and intellectual activities without reference to society's prescribed docile role for females. Though they were taught to read, the Protestant women on the Continent failed to become the strong cultural leaders that the outstanding Catholic women were in earlier times.[16]

Women Gain and Lose Rights in the French Revolution

Perhaps this lack of progress was to be expected, since the Reformation was ideologically conservative when it came to women. A better measure of women's rights might be sought in the period of the French Revolution. The slogan of the Revolution was Liberty, Equality, Fraternity. At first, women, as well as men, were attracted to the promise of government response to their problems. The notebooks in which the French were invited to air their complaints for the benefit of the legislators record a number of women's demands. They wanted more education and the opportunity to work gainfully. Some expressed the desire for laws that would give them rights over their earnings, their inheritances, their possessions, and their children. In the first expectant months of the Revolution, women effectively participated in political activities. The most noted of their actions was the bread march to Versailles, in which working-class and middle-class women together petitioned the king for cheaper and more abundant provisions. Later they participated in other marches and demonstrations, following the inspired radical woman playwright, Olympe de Gouges. She urged them to act as the patriotic women of ancient Rome and make donations of their jewels to the hard-pressed state.[17]

A few political clubs were founded for a mixed membership, and many more were established exclusively for women. Political education trained the more active Parisian women to hold demostrations and write their own revolutionary newspapers. Although the male legislators had not indicated that women's rights would be secured by the Revolution, Olympe de Gouges's Declaration of the Rights of Woman and of the Citizen demanded political participation, equal rights to property, and divorce laws.

In gratitude for women's efforts as soldiers and war workers in the Revolutionary wars, the French government awarded some important rights to women. (This event reminds us that in England and the United States suffrage was granted to women as a direct result of World War I.) The years 1792 and 1793 saw the establishment of divorce laws. Divorced parents were given custody of children on the basis of gender, instead of having them automatically assigned to the father. Wives could share in family property, girls might inherit, as could children who were born illegitimate. Later, public schools were established for boys and girls. But these laws marked the high point of influence in favor of women. By 1793 political factions turned sharply against the participation of women in public affairs. Leaders of the women's movement were descredited. Women on the conservative side, living in the provinces, were blamed for committing counterrevolutionary acts and for sheltering the discredited Catholic clergy. The women's activism was attacked as political factions purged the assembly. Even so, the French woman emerged from the Revolution with a number of important legal rights.[18]

If these laws had remained on the books in France, the history of women's rights would probably have been very different. Some of the work of nineteenth-century women's rights groups in England and the United States would already have been achieved. But the era of liberal ideals and political activism was followed by the Napoleonic period. This was a time of conservative morality and standards for the institution of marriage and family. Napoleon believed strongly in the preservation of private property and male inheritance. The laws entitling women to share in family property were nullified by the Napoleonic Code, which cut women out of these benefits. Once again the wife was to be subservient to her husband and had to obey him without fail. By 1815 women in France were not allowed to divorce. There was no longer an example of female rights that could serve as a model for spreading a new standard of equality. Opponents of legal benefits for women could claim that they would never work, since no one could point to a society that gave such freedom to women.[19]

THE AMERICAN EXPERIENCE

A Labor Shortage Encourages Businesswomen

The overturning of legal rights was a blow to French women who had known a glimmering of something better, but it also had profound implications for the lives of women elsewhere. The conservatism of the early nineteenth century ushered in restrictive conditions that set women's rights back throughout the western world. In the United States, acceptance of the Victorian Era put American women even more solidly under the yoke of male supremacy than some of their European sisters. The reasons for this strange occurrence in "the land of the free" show another peculiar zigzag in the history of women's status and tell us a great deal about ourselves as twentieth century Americans.

When the American colonies began to prosper in the eighteenth century, the old legal restrictions against the women's autonomy that existed in Europe were ignored. It is true that English Common Law, which governed the colonies, imposed the same legal restrictions on American women as on the British. Women were under the control of their husbands; their earnings legally belonged to the men as did their children and all their worldly goods. The married woman was called a *femme couverte*, in law, that is, a woman "covered" by her husband's identity. When two individuals married, they became one legal person—and that person was the husband. The wife could not appear in court, enter into a contract, or inherit without the approval of a male relative or guardian. But lack of population and a weak central government combined with the informality of frontier conditions to let people ignore legalities. The economic needs of the colonists encouraged women to participate in a wide variety of business and trades.[20]

Women became innkeepers, peddlers, seamstresses, and shoemakers. Of course, the greatest number of women performed jobs that were considered women's work. In colonial newspapers they advertised for jobs caring for children, laundering, cooking, and teaching. Other women became pharmacists, barbers, blacksmiths, and gunsmiths—all jobs that were considered men's. Some women became printers and often kept up the family printing press. Congress chose Mary Katherine Goddard, of a prominent printing family, to print the official copy of the Declaration of Independence in 1776. The business that most women and men were involved in was farming. Many women have been recorded as being the active managers of large plantations, especially when their husbands died or were absent for long periods. One of the most successful of these women was Eliza Lucas Pinckney, who managed her own family plantation as well as that of her husband. She experimented with plants and was the first to begin the production of indigo in South Carolina. Of course women engaged in trade, whether they dealt in manufactured goods, agricultural products, or homemade articles, found themselves required to make contracts, sue, or defend themselves at law. Even though the law did not sanction these acts, before the end of the 1700s some women managed to act as their own lawyers and to be the executors of male relatives' estates.[21]

Healing and nursing were other tasks that colonial women did. Midwives were the usual medical assistants in childbirth. Women, as well as male barbers, performed tooth extractions. Women trained by their mothers with old herbal remedy books provided most of the medical help for the colonists. In fact, there were few male doctors in the colonies. The professionalization of medicine in the nineteenth century, which shut women out of medicine, is another example of an early opportunity that was forfeited to men as the country became more settled.[22]

These restrictions must have been particularly irksome to women who remembered their participation in the American Revolution. Picking up the traces of home life without husbands, and acting as nurses, spies, and soldiers, the female participants in the struggle experienced an acceptance and rough equality that they were to lose afterward. It was ironic that a war fought under enlightened slogans of liberty and equality should be followed by a shrinkage of freedoms for American women. In part this was due to the increased influence of English common law, published between 1765 and 1769 in a handy format as Blackstone's *Commentaries.* The book was influential in formulating American law after the Revolution; unfortunately for women, it helped to pass into American law the formula, made stronger than it had been earlier, that married women were not legal persons. Single women who were over twenty-one, and widows, had the legal rights of a citizen, but a married woman's legal individuality was merged into that of her husband. As the population of the United States grew and frontier conditions evolved into settled communities, laws were made stricter. The new nation was eager to establish its legitimacy among nations and tried to impose conventional behavior on its population. There was an attempt to revoke the pre-Revolutionary freedoms that women had appropriated.[23]

Of course, the physical conditions of the New World continued to be primitive until well after the Revolution. These conditions imposed on American women needs that differed from those of their European sisters, and played a part in shaping the American character. The "woman of fashion," for instance, was an ideal that Americans could not afford to adopt. In the early eighteenth century there were few dressmakers and hairdressers capable of recreating the styles popular in European capitals. If colonial upper-class women had their hair fixed in an elaborate style, the high price of that hairdo made them keep it untouched for weeks. Since the hair was stiffened with flour, it attracted vermin—hence the need for a pick and a cage to wear when sleeping, to discourage rats and mice. During the Revolution it was considered unpatriotic to ape the British upper class. Afterward, even in families that were comfortable, wives had to participate in soap making, textile work, food preserving, and gardening along with the servants. The need to work may have discouraged constricting fashions somewhat. So rare were stays and hoopskirts in America that men could not understand what their charm for women could possibly be. One man wrote of a young Virginia woman who tried the outfit in 1773:

> She was pinched up rather too near in a long pair of new fashioned Stays, which, I think, are a Nuisance both to us and themselves. For the late importation of stays which are said to be now most fashionable in London, are produced upwards so high that we can have scarce any view at all of the Ladies Snowy Bosoms; & on the contrary, they are extended downwards so low that whenever Ladies who wear them, either young or old have occasion to walk, the motion necessary for walking must, I think cause a disagreeable Friction of some part of the body against the lower Edge of the Stays which is hard and unyielding. I imputed the Flush which was visible in her Face to her being swathed by Body & Soul & Limbs together.[24]

As we will see, this sensible attitude to women's clothes changed when the norms of society changed. When women's work was considered necessary and customary, their clothing had to be comfortable enough to work in. When women were supposed to be decorative and idle, their clothing kept them so.

Frontier conditions made demands not only on what women should wear and what they should do but on educational ideals for them as well. A surprising number of colonial women could read (if not write). This degree of education was favored, especially following the Puritan emphasis on Bible reading. In line with the standards of the day it was thought that women should be able to read, write, and figure, but not be so learned that they got into philosophical arguments or theological discussions. In this the Old World and the New World agreed perfectly. Women who were too well educated would be considered "masculine women." As one book put it, these subjects "lie out of a Lady's Way: They fly up to the Head, and not only intoxicate weak Brains, but turn them."[25] Even cultivated colonial men who did not personally object to having their daughters learn Latin and Greek warned them not to let others know of their studies because "it is scarcely reputable for young ladies to understand Latin and Greek."[26]

However, those who held such ideas could not ignore the fact that many American women would be faced with the task of educating their children by themselves. Families frequently moved from the civilized enclaves of New York or South Carolina into the western wilderness. There families would be isolated from schools as well as stores and medical help. The children's learning would be completely dependent on their mothers' knowledge and skill. Therefore, to provide sons with at least a smattering of the serious knowledge men ought to have, American women needed to be familiar with natural science, philosophy, and other "masculine" subjects. This was

Thomas Jefferson's justification for permitting his daughter to study. Once again we see that an abstract ideal of feminine behavior was altered by the conditions early America presented.

The Cult of True Womanhood

Because of this eighteenth-century freedom, the fate of women in later years presents a dilemma. American women, who in the eighteenth century were the most active and responsible individuals, turned into the most intellectually confined and domestic creatures in the nineteenth century. Foreigners especially remarked on the extraordinary docility of American wives. The Frenchman Alexis de Tocqueville, who traveled here in 1830, found American women much more independent and self-assertive than Europeans *before* marriage, taking trips unescorted, addressing strangers, and engaging in public festivities. But after marriage the opposite was true.

> In America the independence of woman is irrevocably lost in the bonds of matrimony: if an unmarried woman is less constrained there than elsewhere, a wife is subjected to stricter obligations. The former makes her father's house an abode of freedom and of pleasure; and latter lives in the home of her husband as if it were a cloister.[27]

De Tocqueville attributed this change to the particular sort of education and character formation that prevailed in the United States. Given a better education than French girls because a democracy required educated citizens, American women understood the constraints that marriage imposed on freedom. Having exercised their willpower as girls and strengthened it, they were in a better posisiton to curb their personal desires and whims voluntarily after marriage. Americans too believed that women willingly accepted the social restrictions that enforced conformity to a domestic ideal in marriage; for, as de Tocqueville put it, "in the United States the inexorable opinion of the public carefully circumscribes woman within the narrow circle of domestic interests and duties, and forbids her to step beyond it."[28]

Another foreign visitor, Harriet Martineau, noticed the same pattern of behavior, but she assigned different causes to it. Martineau, an Englishwoman, is considered one of the early sociologists. She charged that American women were subservient to men because economic and political institutions forced them into dependence. Women were given an education inferior to men's. Their economic opportunities were limited to careers as seamstresses, governesses, or teachers—all low-paying jobs. And most damning of all for a country that had recently fought a Revolution under the principles of citizen representation, American women were denied the vote and the opportunity to participate in the political life of the country. Martineau accused Americans of being false to their own standards, of presenting themselves as a country of democracy and opportunity while they withheld these ideals from half the population.[29]

What had happened to America in the brief space of time between the end of the Revolutionary War and the visits of these observers? Why had the self-sufficient and forceful women of the colonial era transformed themselves into shrinking violets? Were the physical conditions of life so different in thirty or so years? Or had the ideals of society changed so drastically that only the docile woman appeared normal?

The reasons for the change in female behavior are very complex and only partly understood. Possibly America's desire to appear a seasoned society influenced her to adopt many more English customs than before, just as she had introduced more strictly English laws earlier. And in England a new standard of feminine behavior was developing, which fostered idleness, passivity, and gentility. Influential Americans imported this feminine ideal across the Atlantic, along with fashion magazines and European products. In effect, middle-class women were now being encouraged to act like aristocrats, scorning work and occupying themselves with activities that had nothing to do with the marketplace. This new ideal took into account the commercial wealth that was flowing to middle-class merchants who were engaged in the conspicuous consumption of large houses, staffs of servants, and costly furnishings. Having a wife who did not work was possibly the most visible means of all to prove that a man had "arrived," since only middle- and upper-class Americans could afford a nonsalaried wife.

This new standard found ready acceptance in the new United States. Wanting above all not to appear provincial and lacking in social graces, Americans too began training women to be "ladies." Many factors in the new country lent themselves to the "cult of true womanhood," as Barbara Welter has called it.[30] As in England, the home was ceasing to be a productive unit where the family's income was earned. With the construction of factories, productive work was increasingly done outside the home, and factory work came, in time, to be considered men's work. This idea made a profound difference in attitudes toward women. It became the norm for husbands to be the sole breadwinner in the family, at least in theory. Therefore the husband's work, which was done outside the home, was given credit and respect. Wives were caught in a situation of double jeopardy. If they worked in the home, their efforts were depreciated (they were "only housewives"); if they worked outside the home, they were accused of taking a man's job.

Social pressure for women to stay in the domestic sphere arose from other aspects of economic life in America too. As Americans spread across the country, they brought with them an aggressive business style that fostered economic opportunism. It became the wife's place to offset the "opportunism, greed, uncertainty and impersonality that marked the dark side of the coin of Jacksonian 'individualism.' "[31] The sheltered woman became a foil for the amoral economic activity and frontier violence fostered by the new society.

A cult of true womanhood grew, establishing the ideals of passivity, purity, domesticity, and piety for women. As men seemed to gain more license to act immorally, women became more and more insistently the moral guardians of society. Their function was to provide a peaceful and clean island for husband and children in the midst of a dog-eat-dog world.

Religion too approved of the domestic, pious woman who kept out of temptation by clinging to the home and never disagreeing with her husband. America had been founded on religious precedents. Some historians believe these spiritual origins to be the unique element in our society. This provides another rationale for the desecularization of women, taking them away from bad influences. A New England religious movement called the second Great Awakening tried to bring Americans back to their spiritual origins by encouraging personal conversions. Stressing the individual's own unworthiness and fostering obedience, the Great Awakening reinforced society's ideal for women. Men emerged from this conversion experience with confidence in their salvation and took over the reins of activity in the external world. In marriage women were imbued with the same psychological dependence that religion fostered. Even the Bible told them to "be silent" and "obey their husbands."[32]

To some extent it may be that the genteel white American woman became society's hostage to atone for the cruel institution of slavery. Unable to wish away the indignities of that "peculiar institution," American consciousness may have needed to create an exaggerated counterweight in the form of ideal white womanhood. Farm labor became slaves' work and taboo for white women to perform. By keeping its white women innocent and pure, Southern society could claim that innocence and purity were its ideals rather than the human exploitation it saw daily. An aura of hypocrisy arose from this situation, further widening the gap between myth and reality. In the South, the myth of the idle belle helped to keep women from gaining participation in an adult world of mutual trust. Hypocrisy about the sexual relations forced on Black women degraded everyone in the community. Kept from bringing humane and moral conditions into effect, the white woman of the South perceived a bond of frustration with the Black slave women.[33]

The Women's Rights Movement Begins

Ironically, one of the first movements toward women's rights grew out of women's preoccupation with the moral guardianship of society. Moral guardianship was considered a ladylike concern. By taking this approach, women could criticize institutions without descending into the dirty aspects of politics. This idealistic focus of the women's rights movement lasted until the Civil War. Although a high-minded rationale persisted from 1865 to 1890, reformist women were drawn into contact with political parties and had to choose between tactical gains or long-term achievements that might seem impractical. During the progressive era, the notion that women could "clean up" government justified their participation in politics. Both the strengths and weaknesses of the women's rights movement stemmed from its original emphasis on morality.

Beginning this process, the first antislavery societies were outgrowths of Christian concerns. Blacks themselves, notably such brave women as Sojourner Truth and Harriet Tubman, set an example by rescuing slaves and encouraging freedmen. Gradually pioneers like Angelina and Sarah Grimké, raised in a slave-holding family in South Carolina, came to draw the parallel between restrictions suffered by Blacks in the South and women throughout the United States. Sarah Grimké was one of the first Americans to show how the trivializing of women actually undermines their moral influence. Women, she argued, were trained to remain in their "appropriate sphere" for fear of not appealing enough to prospective husbands. "Fashionable women regard themselves, and are regarded by men, as pretty toys or as mere instruments of pleasure." As a result, they developed "vacuity of mind, the heartlessness, the frivolity which is the necessary result of this false and debasing estimate of women."[34] Writing in 1838, Sarah Grimké expressed this surprisingly modern hope:

> I do long to see the time, when it will no longer be necessary for women to expend so many precious hours in furnishing "a well spread table," but that their husbands will forgo some of their accustomed indulgences in this way, and encourage their wives to devote some portion of their time to mental cultivation, even at the expense of having to dine sometimes on baked potatoes, or bread and butter.[35]

For this early feminist, educated women whose realm was not limited to kitchen and home would be effective in getting slavery abolished.

In American history there was an important link between the antislavery movement and the struggle for women's rights. Many women with no other political involvement belonged to antislavery societies where they wrote pamphlets, signed petitions, and listened to speakers. In 1848 the women of the American delegation to a World Anti-Slavery Convention in London were refused seating as delegates because of their gender. Two of these women, Lucretia Mott and Elizabeth Cady Stanton, began to consider making a frontal attack to promote women's rights. They decided to hold a meeting in Seneca Falls, New York, where Mrs. Stanton lived to "discuss the social, civil and religious rights of women." Rephrasing the Declaration of Rights in their own declaration, and initiating the succession of meetings that became the woman suffrage movement, the first convention in 1848 was a momentous event for the future.[36]

At first the women's rights movement was the heir of church clubs and antislavery societies that had functioned as women's only organ of action outside the home. Idealistic and filled with Christian morality, the early workers had to learn strategy and organization. Leaders like Susan B. Anthony were faced with public prejudice against women who spoke in public and traveled alone. It was a back-breaking job to gather signatures for a petition asking the New York state legislature to permit women to control their own earnings, have guardianship of children in cases of divorce, and vote. Susan B. Anthony traveled in unheated carriages, taking full charge of local arrangements and requesting a small bit of money so that she could pay for her stay in the next town. Anthony and Stanton worked as a team, marshaling information, formulating policy, and encouraging others. They were helped by a host of women, among them Lucy Stone, Ernestine Rose, Abbey Kelly Foster, and many others.[37]

Women's cooperation in volunteer groups gathered momentum during the Civil War. In the North the volunteer movement addressed itself to the serious problems of supplying nurses and medical supplies where the army needed them. Dorothea Dix, Clara Barton, and others helped to establish a sanitary commission which flourished on donations collected by women and provided nursing care and such social services as notifying relatives of wounded men. Dr. Mary Edwards Walker worked as the first female military surgeon for the Union Army. Another novelty occured as women were encouraged to enter war production. Even at that early date, women who were shirtmakers for the army complained that they were being exploited. In national politics Anna Dickinson was permitted to become a spokeswoman for the Republican party. She was "the young elephant sent forward to try the bridges to see if they were safe for older ones to cross."[38] Stanton and Anthony mobilized the older abolitionist groups in the National Women's Loyal League. Cooperation in these wartime efforts added to the women's experience in political activity and stimulated the women's suffrage movement after the war.

The Civil War was responsible for even greater change in the status of Southern women. During the fighting, women had to manage the plantations and deal with drastic shortages of food and other necessities. Afterward, many Southern women had to substitute for their husbands who returned home disabled or psychologically broken. Their diaries reveal their mixed feelings about trying to appear as the helpless, fragile women that Southern culture continued to require. At the same time they were forced to become strong and hardworking simply to keep a bare livelihood for their families. For Black women the post-Civil War era was even more difficult after a campaign of vilification had been led against them. They also bore the brunt of a depressed economy and a dislocated community.[39]

Jobs and Votes for Women

Economic developments in the post-Civil War era brought new social problems. While women in cultural clubs and suffrage groups continued to advocate the vote for women, the growth in the number of women working in factories and sweatshops created the need for reforms in working conditions. The earliest factory girls had been native white Americans working in the model mills in Lowell, Massachusetts. By the 1830s their places had been taken by Irish immigrants accustomed to longer hours and lower wages. As factory work became more exploitive, the workday lengthened to twelve or fourteen hours, workers were fined if they sang or talked, and the wage by the early 1900s was eight dollars a week. Some middle-class women tried to improve the working conditions for these women by bringing pressure to bear on state legislators. But even Jane Addams, who founded Hull House as a shelter for working-class immigrants, came to believe that the direct action of the strike was needed. After the Civil War women had made some tentative steps toward joining men's unions like the Knights of Labor or organizing their own. Although these efforts had symbolic meaning, the real beginning of women's entrance into organized labor did not come until the twentieth century. The year 1909 saw the first large-scale sustained strike of women. The striking women were shirtwaist makers in New York. They were helped by funds gathered by the Women's Trade Union League and by the courage and spirit of the thousands of workers who suffered police brutality and poverty. The strike was not an industry-wide triumph, but it showed everyone that working women were capable of organizing.[40]

Economic disabilities like those that prompted the shirtwaist strike lent further weight to the idea that women should gain the vote. In earlier decades women claimed the right to cast ballots because it was their democratic right or because their votes could aid the antislavery movement. After the Civil War, new circumstances changed the issues with which the reformers had to deal. The campaign for the Fourteenth Amendment presented the women's suffrage forces with a new dilemma: Should they support the Amendment to give the vote to newly freed Black men, as Lucy Stone and her husband urged, or should they insist that women, both Black and White, be enfranchised too. The National Women's Suffrage Association was split into two groups by this controversy. Further fragmenting came when some southern women urged women's suffrage as a means of outvoting the newly enfranchised Black males. An equally prejudiced motive lay behind some northern groups' support of women's votes in order to counterbalance the political influence of poor immigrant city men. These refugees were criticized for the contradictory faults of being too radical and of being too easily led by corrupt political bosses. Essentially the nativists faulted the immigrant's foreign origins.[41]

The women's suffrage movement restored itself to its original broad-minded stance when it turned from restrictive purposes to democratic ones. Responding to the Progressive Movement, women's suffrage groups claimed that women should be allowed the chance to "clean house" in Washington, D.C. since government is a household in the large. While this view of women's political stance linked suffrage to reforms like child labor laws, factory legislation, and pure food, it also insisted that women were to be above the political arena. In 1913 a New Jersey Quaker, Alice Paul, criticized the National American Women's Suffrage Association's practice of nonpartisanship. Alice Paul's founding of the Congressional Union began a more militant strategy that was continued until the Nineteenth Amendment granting woman suffrage was passed in 1920. She asserted that Woodrow Wilson had it within his power to see that woman suffrage became law, but that he found it more expedient to withhold active support. Gradually, lobbying on the state level by the National American Woman Suffrage Association and campaigning in the nation's capital made their mark, and some politicians began to fear retaliation if they did not support the suffrage idea. The cause was aided by the nation's sense of gratitude for the energetic efforts woman suffrage groups had made on behalf of war work during World War I. Until the last moment, when a narrow margin in the Tennessee legislature made the Nineteenth Amendment a certainty, the women maintained a desperate effort. The reform had taken "a century of struggle" to achieve.[42]

Why Wasn't the Nineteenth Amendment Enough?

Many factors contributed to the inevitable decline of zeal after the Nineteenth Amendment was passed. The differences among the various women's groups, which had been glossed over during the long campaign for the vote, now came to the surface. Some reformers channeled their energies into the cause of world peace promoted by Jane Addams and others in the Women's International League for Peace and Freedom. Others, exhausted by the suffrage campaign, gave way to the trend of the times toward personal enjoyment. Professional women united to form the National Confederation of Business and Professional Women's Clubs but would not at first join the National Woman's party in supporting the Equal Rights Amendment, which was first introduced into Congress in 1923. Women's concerted action was further hindered by the continuing activities of antisuffrage groups, which played on the public's belief that with the Nineteenth Amendment women were too emancipated. Laws passed after 1920 prohibiting women from sitting on juries and holding office showed the influence of these conservative groups.[43]

Social feminism was responsible for continued investigation of poor working conditions and the founding of the Women's Bureau in 1919, along with many other reforms. However, the trend toward conservatism, which the whole country experienced, tended to put a damper on social reforms; by 1925 the impulse of progressivism had waned. Accusations by conservative groups that feminist leaders had communist tendencies increased the women's sense of defensiveness.[44]

The suffragists' idealism was itself responsible for disillusion. They had thought that women would actively vote and provide blocs for promoting reform. That few women came to the polls, and that their voting pattern resembled that of men, were the disheartening reality. The leaders of the National American Woman's Suffrage Association disbanded the organization and formed the League of Women Voters to be its successor. The league was intended to educate the new voters to public issues. It held itself above partisan politics, as the National American Woman Suffrage Association had, and although it fostered many reforms, the league did not act as a compelling lobby on the range of women's issues. Nor did it cooperate with the Woman's party's advocacy of the Equal Rights Amendment. Especially harmful to the cause of women's political power was the fact that women failed to vote for women's issues. The political parties thought they would have to push through extensive laws on such social welfare issues as child labor, aid to poor mothers, voting reforms, and ethical practices for government employees. At first responsive to the threat of a bloc of women voters, politicians stopped supporting women's issues by the mid-1920s when the bloc failed to materialize. The essential problem was that, despite the coming of flappers, women and men continued to hold the conventional belief that wives should concern themselves with domestic duties and leave decisions about politics to the men. The dramatic campaign to gain suffrage had temporarily obscured this fact, but later, political and economic practice brought it home.[45]

In both world wars women had been encouraged to enter skilled jobs in factories, and after those wars they were transferred to less lucrative work to make way for the returning soldiers. Social pressure kept most women from protesting these demotions; the male-dominated unions did not stand up for the women. In order to justify their "retirement" from jobs, it was necessary to reverse the propaganda that had encouraged women to help the war effort. Other nations did the same thing, but the American mentality had a more intense experience of genteel ladies to fall back on. The "role of true womanhood" was updated to convince women that their place was in the home as psychologist, educator, and nurturer of the children. With the labor-saving devices invented to wash clothes and dishes, sweep floors, and refrigerate food came new social customs providing activities that would consume time in a ladylike way in cultural, social, and reforming clubs.[46]

It is true that in the 1920s and 1930s a number of women entered universities and became career professionals. But the waning of the women's movement combined with other cultural pressures to preserve the ideal of domesticity for most. This does not mean that many women were not employed fulltime. As in the past, the husband's low salary or disability kept many a married woman at work. Single women and widows also worked because of necessity. By the early twentieth century a white-collar revolution had come to provide many office jobs for women. Typewriters, telephones, and the need for clerical workers opened the doors of business to respectable work for women. The notion that this was just employment to occupy the few years before marriage justified low wages. In the field of education, which became dominated by women, their unmarried status was ensured by laws requiring women to give up their jobs if they married.[47]

Job discrimination against women in the 1930s, the decade of the depression, was one indication that American ideals had still not become egalitarian. Even Mrs. Samuel Gompers expressed the popular view that working wives should retire and free their salaries for male heads of households. In contrast, as the Democratic party put the New Deal into operation, some women became influential in party activities and policymaking. Particularly with the encouragement of Eleanor Roosevelt, who continually brought women's issues to the administration's attention, aspects of social welfare were recognized as issues that were important to women. Many women flocked to Washington, D.C., to staff the new agencies.[48]

Was World War II a Giant Step for Women?

The uncertain nature of women's political influence was felt once World War II began. Although they were put on committees to encourage war efforts, women complained that they were never seriously brought into the decision-making process. They were not allowed to make policy regulating women's military service, to encourage women to enter war industry, not to help plan the distribution of consumer goods and rationing. A glaring result of the failure to take women's problems and needs seriously was the fiasco over federal support of day-care centers. Only in 1943, when it became evident that the time women lost from work to supervise children had a direct effect on the war effort, was federal money for day-care centers appropriated. When the war ended, day-care funding quickly stopped. Congress reflected the nation's continued belief in women's traditional domestic role. The wartime debate on whether the government should provide working women with child care was resolved in favor of the argument that women contributed more to society by rearing their children at home.[49]

After congratulating women on their outstanding work in every sector of the economy, American opinion reverted to the 1930s ideal which held that women should not seek employment ouside the home. Advertising media effectively glamorized the role of the housewife, creating an artificial set of values, according to Betty Friedan.[50] But, unlike the post-1918 generation of women, many women who had entered the work force for the first time during World War II, remained full-time employees afer the war. By 1945 the proportion of women employed rose from 25 percent to 36 percent of the labor force. Although female employment declined immediately after the war, as returning soldiers reclaimed skilled jobs, women continued to make up a large proportion of the labor force. The employment of married women and those over thirty-five was a novel feature of the postwar era. The historian William Chafe has pointed out the gulf between what most Americans thought women should do and what they actually did. While almost half of the women spent their days at work outside the home, people continued to picture the typical wife in the home, cooking, making the house comfortable for the family, and attending PTA meetings. Most married women who worked identified themselves essentially as housewives. They believed that their stint in the work force was a temporary break in their normal lives: Statistics showed otherwise.[51] By 1977, almost half of the female population worked, accounting for 41 percent of the total labor force.

How Much Past in the Future

The ideals that had become a part of American culture in the early 1800s were so deeply rooted, though, that it required the social challenges of the 1960s to bring them into question. There is no better example of living history than the twentieth-century acceptance of these nineteenth-century standards. People who had long since rejected the fashions and plumbing of the Victorian era lived by its behavioral norms. The movement for black equality was the first to challenge the differences between the American ideals of democracy and equality, and the reality of discrimination. Using techniques of civil disobedience learned in the fight for black civil rights, the antiwar movement of the 1960s was the next radicalizing element in the development of women's consciousness of their subservience. Reacting against their use in the antiwar movement as coffee makers, typists, and sexual trophies, activist women began to redefine society. Like Sarah Grimké when she talked about the slaves, these women perceived that they were being discriminated against as a class and that no amount of camaraderie with the radical males would earn them equality.[52]

As they discussed ways to restructure society and began to form feminist organizations, many of their ideas echoed the writings of critics in the past. It is a measure of women's subordination that the radical analyses had been ignored and buried. In her discussion of the causes of middle-class women's unhappiness in *The Feminine Mystique,* Betty Friedan returned to some of the ideas of Mary Wollstonecraft, an early nineteenth-century English feminist writer. As Shulamith Firestone wrote her Marxist critique of the family, she developed some of the ideas that Charlotte Perkins Gilman had discussed earlier. The contemporary movement for equal rights is supported by a wide network of organizations whose politics range from liberal to radical; all of these groups dedicated to changing the norms of women's status in the United States.

By going back to examine some of the origins of prejudice against women, we can see how each historical period passed on its bias to the next. If we wonder where the notion of women's passivity came from, we can see how Aristotle's definition of women fed into the Christian doctrine requiring women to be silent and obedient. Tracing this notion to the Renaissance, we realize why the question of political rights for women was not raised during the Middle Ages and why women were merged into the legal person of their husbands when they married. To view American history in terms of these earlier themes gives us a new insight on the independent, active colonial women on one hand and the domesticated wives of the nineteenth century on the other. We can tell how early expectations that women should be subservient kept them from entering college and persist in barring women from jobs with responsibility. It remains to be seen whether women's history can become a story of past events and attitudes and cease to be a controlling mechanism for women's activities today. Only then will we be able to go beyond the restraint of history as destiny.

NOTES

1. "Generation of Animals," trans. A. L. Peck (Cambridge, Mass.: Harvard University Press, 1943), p. 406, quoted in *Women from the Greeks to the French Revolution,* ed. Susan G. Bell (Belmont, Calif.: Wadsworth Publishing Co., 1973), p. 18. See Vern L. Bullough and Bonnie Bullough, *The Subordinate Sex: A History of Attitudes toward Women* (1973; reprint ed., New York: Penguin Books, Inc., 1974), for a lively introduction to the subject. Chapter 2 discusses women in ancient Greece.

2. Sarah Pomeroy, *Goddesses, Whores, Wives, and Slaves: Women in Classical Antiquity* (New York: Schocken Books, Inc., 1976), Chaps. 1–2.

3. I Cor. 14:34–35, quoted in Bell, *Women,* p. 82.

4. Ibid. Col. 3:18–19, quoted in Bell, *Women,* p. 82.

5. Jo Ann McNamara and Suzanne Wemple, "The Power of Women through the Family in Medieval Europe: 500–1100," in *Clio's Consciousness Raised,* ed. Mary Hartman and Lois W. Banner (New York: Harper & Row, Publishers, 1974), pp. 103–111

6. Jo Ann McNamara and Suzanne F. Wemple, "Sanctity and Power: The Dual Pursuit of Medieval Women," in *Becoming Visible: Women in European History,* ed. Renate Bridenthal and Claudia Koonz (Boston: Houghton Mifflin, 1977), pp. 100–101.

7. A. Abrams, "Women Traders in Medieval London," *Economic Journal,* no. 26 (June 1916), pp. 276–285; Henri Hauser, *Ouvriers du temps passé* (Paris: Felix Alcan, 1909), pp. 48, 142–143, 153, 156–157; Dayton Phillips, *Beguines in Medieval Strasburg* (Ann Arbor, Mich.: Edwards Bros., Inc., 1941), pp. 21–23.

8. Joan Kelly-Gadol, "Did Women Have a Renaissance?," in Bridenthal and Koonz, *Becoming Visible,* pp. 141–161.

9. Ibid., p. 159.

10. Quoted ibid., p. 150.

11. Ibid., pp. 159–161. Carolyn C. Louges notes scholarly discussions of women's influence in the family and the larger community in the review essay "Modern European History," *Signs: Journal of Women in Culture and Society* 2, no. 3 (spring 1977): 633–635. The view that women exerted influence through their dowries is found in Stanley Chojnacki, "Dowries and Kinsmen in Early Renaissance Venice," *Journal of Interdisciplinary History* 5 (1974–1975): 571–600.

12. Liliane Mottu-Weber, "Apprentissages et Économie genevoise au Début du xviiie Siècle," *Schweizerische Zeitschrift fur Geschichte* 20 (1970): 340–341; Natalie Zemon Davis, "City Women and Religious Change," in *Society and Culture in Early Modern France* (Stanford: Stanford University Press, 1975), pp. 65–95.

13. Olwen H. Hufton, *The Poor of Eighteenth-Century France, 1750–1789* (Oxford: Clarendon Press, 1974), pp. 69–127; and "Women and the Family Economy in Eighteenth-Century France,"

French Historical Studies 9 (1975): 1–22; Theresa M. McBride, *The Domestic Revolution: The Modernization of Household Service in England and France, 1820–1920* (New York: Holmes & Meier Publishers, 1976).

14. This conclusion stems from my paper "Issues in the Position and Training of Women in the Silk Industry at Lyons, 1700–1810," read at the Third Berkshire Conference on the History of Women, June 1976.

15. Cited in Davis, "City Women," Zemon Davis, ibid., p. 84.

16. Ibid., pp. 68, 75–76, 87–91; Pearl Hogrefe, *Tudor Women: Commoners and Queens* (Ames, Iowa: Iowa State University Press, 1975). Many active and influential women in England from the late fifteenth through the sixteenth centuries show women's accomplishments in secular life.

17. For this discussion of the French Revolution I have relied on Ruth Graham, "Loaves and Liberty: Women in the French Revolution," in Bridenthal and Koonz, *Becoming Visible*, pp. 238–254. See also Scott Lytle, "The Second Sex (September, 1793)," *Journal of Modern History* 27 (1955), 1:14–26.

18. Graham, "Loaves and Liberty," pp. 244–245.

19. Ibid., pp. 251–253.

20. Linda Grant DePauw, *Founding Mothers: Women in America in the Revolutionary Era* (Boston: Houghton Mifflin Company, 1975), pp. 24–44; Barbara Mayer Wertheimer, *We Were There: The Story of Working Women in America* (New York: Pantheon Books, Inc., 1977), pp. 7–25.

21. DePauw, *Founding Mothers*, pp. 28–35; Elizabeth A. Dexter, *Colonial Women of Affairs* (Boston and New York: Houghton Mifflin company, 1931), pp. 1–57, 98–125.

22. Dexter, *Colonial Women*, pp. 58–77; DePauw, *Founding Mothers*, pp. 17–20, 41–42.

23. Linda Grant DePauw, "Land of the Unfree: Legal Limitations on Liberty in Pre-Revolutionary America," *Maryland Historical Magazine* 68 (1973): 355–368.

24. Cited in DePauw, *Founding Mothers*, p. 65.

25. Ibid., p. 205.

26. Ibid., p. 209.

27. *Democracy in America*, quoted in *Root of Bitterness: Documents of the Social History of American Women*, ed., Nancy F. Cott (New York: E. P. Dutton & Co., Inc., 1972), p. 119.

28. Ibid., p. 120.

29. *Society in America* (Garden City, N. Y.: Doubleday & Company, Inc., Anchor Books 1962), pp. 291–308.

30. *Dimity Convictions: The American Woman in the Nineteenth Century* (Athens, Ohio: Ohio University Press, 1976), pp. 21–41.

31. Introduction, in Cott, *Root of Bitterness*, p. 12; Caroll Smith-Rosenberg, "Beauty, the Beast and the Militant Woman: A Case Study in Sex Roles and Social Stress in Jacksonian America," *American Quarterly* 23 (October 1971): 562–584.

32. Kathryn Kish Sklar, *Catharine Beecher: A Study in American Domesticity* (New Haven: Yale University Press, 1973), pp. 28–33, 59–72, 78–89.

33. Mary P. Ryan, *Womanhood in America from Colonial Times to the Present* (New York: New Viewpoints, 1975), pp. 180–190; Anne Firor Scott, "Women's Perspective on the Patriarchy in the 1850's," in *Our American Sisters: Women in American Life and Thought*, ed. Jean E. Friedman, and William G. Shade, 2nd ed. (Boston: Allyn and Bacon, Inc., 1977), pp. 149–162.

34. "Letters on the Equality of the Sexes," in Cott, *Root of Bitterness*, p. 182.

35. Ibid., p. 183.

36. Eleanor Flexner, *Century of Struggle: The Woman's Rights Movement in the United States* (New York: Atheneum Publishers, 1974), pp. 71–77.

37. Ibid., pp. 78–94.

38. Quoted ibid., p. 108. See pages 105–112 for information on Northern women's contributions during the Civil War.

39. Ann Firor Scott, *The Southern Lady: From Pedestal to Politics, 1830–1930* (Chicago: Univer-

sity of Chicago Press, 1970); Gerda Lerner, ed., *Black Women in White America: A Documentary History* (New York: Vintage Books), pp. 94–212, 240–252.

40. Flexner, *Century of Struggle*, pp. 240–247.

41. Aileen S. Kraditor, *The Ideas of the Woman Suffrage Movement, 1840–1920* (New York: Columbia University Press, 1965; Doubleday & Company, Inc., Anchor Books, 1971), pp. 105–184.

42. Ibid., pp. 185–209; J. Stanley Lemons, *The Woman Citizen: Social Feminism in the 1920's* (Urbana: University of Illinois Press, 1973), pp. 10–14.

43. William H. Chafe, *The American Woman: Her Changing Social, Economic, and Political Roles, 1920–1970* (New York: Oxford University Press, 1972), pp. 25–38; Lois W. Banner, *Women in Modern America* (New York: Harcourt Brace Jovanovich, Inc., 1974), pp. 131–141.

44. Chafe, *American Woman*, pp. 51–53.

45. Ibid., pp. 33–36.

46. Ruth Schwartz Cowan, "A Case Study of Technological and Social Change: The Washing Machine and the Working Wife," in Hartman and Banner, *Clio's Consciousness*, pp. 245–252; and "The 'Industrial Revolution' in the home: Household Technology and Social Change in the Twentieth Century," *Technology and Culture* 17 (January 1976): 1–23.

47. Banner, *Women*, pp. 155–159; Chafe, *American Woman*, pp. 53–63.

48. Chafe, *American Woman*, pp. 39–46, 64.

49. Ibid., pp. 151–173.

50. *The Feminine Mystique* (1963; reprint ed., New York: Dell Publishing co., Inc., 1974), pp. 197–223.

51. Chafe, *American Woman*, pp. 181–195.

52. Jean E. Friedman, "Contemporary Feminism: Theories and Practice," in Friedman and Shade, *Our American Sisters*, pp. 430–444.

REVIEW QUESTIONS

1. What was Aristotle's view of female nature? Did Plato agree with him?
2. How did these ideas from the Classical Era influence the Christian idea of women and what they should do?
3. In what ways did women achieve status and political power in the Middle Ages?
4. Did women's status continually improve from the days of ancient Greece to the current time?
5. What influence did the growing influence of kings have on women's power in Renaissance and Early Modern (fifteenth- to seventeenth-century) Europe?
6. Was Protestantism "good" for women? Is there a clear-cut answer to this question?
7. To what extent was the French Revolution a women's revolution?
8. How did colonial American women ignore restrictive English laws?
9. Why did nineteenth-century American life embrace the cult of true womanhood? How much of this was a native American pattern; how much reflected international influences?
10. What elements of the cult of true womanhood can we find in attitudes toward women during the twentieth century?
11. Why did the passage of the Nineteenth Amendment fail to make voters of the majority of American women?
12. Did women have different employment patterns after World War I and World War II?

SELECTED READINGS

Bridenthal, Renate, and Claudia Koonz, eds. *Becoming Visible: Women in European History.* Boston: Houghton Mifflin Company, 1977.

A first-rate anthology of readable studies focusing on women's hidden role throughout history. The authors present fresh material that opens many new windows;—authoritative scholarship is expressed in a lively way. European trends are related to larger themes in women's studies.

Banner, Lois W. *Woman in Modern America.* New York: Harcourt Brace Jovanovich, Inc., 1974.

A brief survey of women's activities in America from the 1890s to the present. This well-illustrated book is an appealing short account that incorporates recent scholarship.

Chafe, William H. *The American Woman: Her Changing Social, Economic, and Political Roles, 1920–1970.* New York: Oxford University Press, 1972.

This first-rate work covers a period that is relatively unexplored. Chafe's prose is always balanced, as is his treatment of controversial issues. Every chapter brims with original insight.

Cott, Nancy, ed. *Root of Bitterness: Documents of the Social History of American Women.* New York: E. P. Dutton & Co., Inc., 1972.

A treasure house of documents that illuminate every aspect of women's life. Well chosen and introduced, these short pieces teach us about the realities of the past in a vivid and immediate way.

Davis, Natalie Zemon. *Society and Culture in Early Modern France.* Stanford: Stanford University Press, 1975.

Employing through original research, these essays provide a unique picture of the cultural life of Europe in the fifteenth through the seventeenth centuries.

DePauw, Linda Grant. *Founding Mothers: Women in America in the Revolutionary Era.* Boston: Houghton Mifflin Company, 1975.

Written for young people, this account of American women's accomplishments embodies a significant scholarly argument. Interesting examples show how women rose above the restrictive law in the Revolutionary era. Social and legal focus.

Flexner, Eleanor. *Century of Struggle: The Women's Rights Movement in the United States.* New York: Atheneum Publishers, 1974.

The indispensable basic scholarly work on women's suffrage, education, and involvement in the club movement and early labor unions during the period 1820–1920. Presented in a readable form.

Friedman, Jean E., and William G. Shade, eds. *Our American Sisters: Women in American Life and Thought,* 2nd ed. Boston: Allyn and Bacon, Inc., 1977.

An anthology of provocative contemporary articles on women's cultural and political history. The second edition does not contain the same articles as those in the first edition.

Sklar, Kathryn Kish. *Catharine Beecher: A Study in American Domesticity.* New Haven: Yale University Press, 1973.

> Superbly researched, elegantly written, this study sheds light on many of the larger trends in nineteenth-century American life.

CHAPTER 2

Cross-Cultural Perspectives on American Sex Roles

Karen Sinclair

There is much interest in the role women are to play in contemporary society. Involved in the discussion are questions about the inherent suitability of the female to the world outside the domestic sphere. The work of anthropologists has taught us to expect a great deal of diversity in the tasks that women perform. Yet, on the other hand, we face the troubling conclusion that, despite this variation, which seems to defy biologically based roles, women are, in most cases, "the second sex." Their endeavors are, in almost all social contexts, deemed less important than those of the males of the society. Here, too, we must attempt to explain this universal subordination of women. In this chapter we will examine the roles women assume, the positions they hold, and the means by which, despite their apparent subordination, they may impose their will upon a world of men.

The question of female power has been addressed only in recent years. For almost a century anthropologists were men, who talked to male informants.[1] We now know that there is often a female view of most societies that does not necessarily accord with masculine judgment. Moreover, women have different roles in different types of societies. Such variation is not random but appears to be systematic: Hunting and gathering societies provide for somewhat greater autonomy than do agricultural societies.[2] In instances where men are absent, for example, because of military pursuits, women quickly gain control of resources.[3] Women, in short, gain in stature when they contribute to, and maintain control over, the group's production and when they have an opportunity to form links with other women. In the pages that follow, we will examine the range of positions that women occupy as we try to explore the commonalities of the female experience in a variety of cultural settings.

Ruby Leavitt has written:

According to a popular myth in the patriarchal cultures of the West, the biological act of giving birth to a child has always limited women's activities, and thus, because of either this limitation or her innate inferiority, woman has contributed little or nothing to the development of human society. Another widely articulated myth is that women have achieved their highest status in the Western industrialized world. But when we go back to our human beginnings and then look at the role and status of women in some non-Western societies, we find that neither myth has any substance.[4]

Such a statement represents not merely the views of a feminist anthropologist but also the position taken by others (with a few exceptions to be discussed below) who have explored the position of women in society. In the nineteenth century it was generally thought that the course of civilization passed through a stage of "mother-right" or matriarchy (a social system where authority is in the hands of women) on its path toward the development of the "monogamous patriarchal family."[5] The armchair anthropologists of the time based their ideas in part on the reports of travelers and missionaries, which were biased, incomplete, and inaccurate. Nevertheless, the evidence, such as it was, established the fact that the status of women in non-western societies exhibited a great deal of variation. Furthermore, in far-off places women enjoyed prerogatives denied their western counterparts. When these nineteenth-century gentlemen found evidence of high female status, they theorized that this represented a lower form of social life.

In the early years of this century anthropologists abandoned these speculative and biased schemes. Instead, today anthropologists maintain that all cultures seek to cope with basic human problems and, in so doing, arrive at a variety of solutions. It is not surprising, then, that we also find a great diversity in the positions and occupations of women. Such demonstrated variety has important implications for the study of the female role: for if women occupy a wide range of statuses and perform diverse tasks, we cannot argue that they are biologically unsuited to the more challenging positions in society. In a study of three New Guinea societies the anthropologist Margaret Mead attempted to disprove the notion that certain personality traits were consistent with an ideal male or female innate temperament.

She undertook the study of these three New Guinea cultures—the Arapesh, the Mundugumor, and the Tchambuli—in the early 1930s, a time of social ferment and reevaluation in our own society. Many American women had gone to work during World War I. After the war when men returned to the labor force, women were reluctant to part with the advantages and financial independence they had achieved. Male proponents of the entrenched division of labor argued that women belonged in the home where they could carry out the tasks for which they were biologically suited. They suggested that women were incapable of handling the emotional and physical strains of the world of work and masculine affairs. Moreover, women's continued absence from the home was held responsible for the threatened demise of the American family and the promotion of juvenile delinquency.[6] Mead's goal was to show, through the study of other cultures, that sex roles and biology were not necessarily bound together. She writes:

> Two of these tribes [Arapesh and Mundugumor] have no idea that men and women are different in temperament. They allow them different economic and religious roles, different skills, different vulnerabilities to evil magic and supernatural influences. The Arapesh believe that painting in colour is appropriate only to men and the Mundugumor consider fishing an essentially feminine task. But any idea that temperamental traits of the order of dominance, bravery, aggressiveness, objectivity, malleability, are inalienably associated with one sex (as opposed to the other) is entirely lacking. This may seem strange to a civilization which in its sociology, its medicine, its slang, its poetry, and its obscenity accepts the socially defined differences between the sexes as having an innate basis in temperament and explains any deviation from the socially determined role as abnormality of natural endowment or early maturation.[7]

Indeed, among the Arapesh and the Mundugumor certain personality traits are deemed desirable for both sexes. For the Arapesh, tender, nurturing behavior is appropriate for both men and women. Unlike our own society, the Arapesh believe the man who displays such characteristics is both reasonable and well adjusted. The Arapesh man or woman with an aggressive, domineering personality is the deviant. A similar pattern exists for the Mundugumor, although it emphasizes different temperamental traits. Here both sexes are aggressive, with rivalry and hostility characterizing even the most intimate relationships. Mead demonstrates that amongst this fierce, belligerent people the division of labor is quite unlike our own.

> What work the men do can easily be done alone. They make yam gardens and they cut down sago palms. . . . The women do everything else. The men can quarrel and refuse to speak to each other; they can move their houses, most of which are flimsy . . . ; they can sulk by their firesides, or plot revenge with a new set of associates—the work of the household goes on uninterrupted. . . . Cheerfully and without overexertion, the strong well fed women conduct the work of the tribe. They even climb the coconut trees—a task from which almost all primitive New Guinea exempts women.[8]

Yet despite the fact that women play a critical role in subsistence,[9] men dominate ceremonial life. This is quite important for it suggests an asymmetry in the evaluation of men and women. Regardless of women's economic importance, it is male activities that are given value. Reasons for this differential importance placed on men's work and women's work will be examined in the following pages. For now, it is enough to note the different stress placed on male and female endeavor, even within a social context that emphasizes temperamental similarity.

Mead's final case, the Tchambuli, provides us with an example of temperamental differences between the sexes that runs counter to our expectations. In this society, as among the Mundugumor, subsistence rests with women, who tend to be businesslike and efficient in the conduct of their affairs. The men, while permitted to engage in some marketing, are ultimately answerable to their wives. Tchambuli males devote themselves to art and to their vanity, spending much time and energy in the preparation of their curls and on general appearance. Women, who themselves wear only sparse jewelry, view the preening, fauning actions of the opposite sex with "kindly tolerance and appreciation." We have here, then, men and women who exhibit behavior quite different from our traditional ideals of masculinity and femininity.

Mead's three societies help to illustrate the plasticity, rather than the rigidity, of human behavior. Individuals are patterned by their culture, and biological or genetic universals would appear to have a minor impact when contrasted with the diversity of cultural rules and expectations.

Nevertheless, women do play subordinate roles in most societies. Even among the Tchambuli, where women's activities are critical to the economic maintenance of the tribe, it is the artwork of the men that is given cultural value. The universal importance of men, regardless of their activities, and the pervasive subordination of women, whatever their contribution, must be explained. We will now examine some possible explanations for the preeminence of men.

In the years following Mead's study anthropologists have demonstrated, with a wide range of examples from all over the world, the variation and diversity of men's and women's roles. Yet consistently, in all societies, we find a division of labor based on sex. In other words, regardless of whether members of one sex wear skirts or trousers, or which sex is responsible for the economic maintenance of the group, there are, universally, differences in the occupations, personalities, and responsibilities characteristically attributed to men or to women. Rosaldo has noted that there are indeed limits to the variations that we may find, for persistently "it is women, and not men, who have the primary responsibility of raising children; this fact seems to make it unlikely that women will be a society's hunters, warriors, or the like. Differences in physical constitution, and especially in endurance and strength, may also lead to characteristic differences in male and female activities."[10] The fact that it is women who bear and, in most societies, rear children, along with the generally acknowledged difference in strength and endurance between men and women, has been used by anthropologists of various persuasions as the foundation for explanations of the lower status accorded to women.

One anthropologist who has received much attention in the popular press for his theory about the origins of sexual asymmetry has been Lionel Tiger, who wrote *Men in Groups* in 1969. In this work Tiger maintains that the hunting of large animals, an activity that many anthropologists feel is ultimately responsible for the development of complex social forms, depends upon strength, endurance, and, most importantly, cooperation. Since women were both ill equipped physically for the rigors of hunting and confined to the home arena by their childbearing responsibilities, only males developed the cooperation necessary for far-ranging hunting expeditions. While it is possible that male cooperation was essential for the development of hunting, and that male strength and stature led to an ethic of man the protector, Tiger goes much further than this. He claims that thousands of years of male bonding have produced a different genetic and chemical structure in the brains of men and women that will manifest itself in the behaviors of the two sexes. Thus males possess an inherent tendency to cooperate, while women, lacking such an inclination, are doomed to solitary lives without similar female ties. While men bond, women, according to Tiger, remain unfastened to the social moorings.[11]

Recent research has raised serious questions about Tiger's conclusions.[12] Slocum has demonstrated the importance of women's gathering activities in contemporary hunting and gathering populations. She also suggests an earlier stage of small-game hunting, accomplished by both men and women, that probably preceded big-game hunting. Moreover, she argues that the socialization of children produces a mother-child bond that is at least as important as Tiger's male bond; the cooperative and communicative skills essential for successful socialization of the young would have significant implications for the development of more eloborate social patterns.[13]

Although it is important to note the counterarguments to Tiger's thesis, the relative importance of men or women to the development of society is, for the time being at least, speculative. The more important issues have been articulated by Lamphere and Rosaldo:

> Although it seems likely that the development of big game hunting and warfare promoted an ethic of male dominance, it is difficult to see why biases associated with man's earlier adaptations should remain with us today. The question then becomes: why, if our social worlds are so different from those of our ancestors, has the relation of the sexes continued to be asymmetrical, and how is it that social groups, which change radically through time, continue to produce and reproduce a social order dominated by man?[14]

The question of female subordination has recently been addressed by Ortner and Rosaldo. Male dominance finds expression not only in the power and authority accorded to men but also in the importance and value placed on male activity and the secondary significance granted to female endeavors. Both Ortner and Rosaldo seek the underlying reasons why this might be the case and each, in her own way, ties women's subordinate status to their childbearing capacities. This is not especially surprising; since women are universally relegated to a secondary position, the reason must lie outside the realm of particular cultural rules and prescriptions. As Ortner writes, "We are up against something very profound, very stubborn."

Ortner maintains that women everywhere are identified with the natural world. The perceived closeness of women to nature means that there will be certain symbolic associations attached to femininity and, more importantly, women will be symbolically opposed to men, who are identified with culture. Since culture is man's tool for transcending nature, men achieve a symbolic transcendence over women.

Ortner points to female physiology and social roles as evidence for her contention. Physically women are more closely allied to nature than are men. Their bodies, operating on a menstrual cycle, are geared for reproduction. In fact, most of their organs exist for the perpetuation of the species. Unlike men, who are relatively free of natural time cycles, women are constrained by a rhythm over which they have no control. Quoting Simone de Beauvoir, Ortner notes that "the female is more enslaved to the species than the male, her animality is more manifest."[15] While men gain their status by mastering nature, whether through technology or ritual,[16] women derive their position by moving in accordance with natural law. As a result, women in their creative feats produce mortal replicas; man's creativity, on the other hand, is geared toward the immortal and everlasting.

In her child-rearing capacity a woman's association with children, who in early years are more "natural" than "social" creatures, further divorces her from the cultural world of men. Yet it is because she is a socializer, transforming "natural" children into "cultured" adults that a woman's position resists easy classification. The symbolic ambiguity of woman as socializer—as a mediator between nature and culture—lends further complications to her position. Anthropologists have noted that articles in a cultural repertoire that cannot be classified are seen as contaminants or pollutants. Ortner suggests that women, who are viewed both as being more closely identified with nature while also being mediators between nature and culture, cannot be readily categorized. Thus women are often believed to be polluting and contaminating. It is not surprising, then, that many societies perceive a menstruating woman as a source of danger and insist on her banishment during this treacherous time. Nor is it an accident, according to Ortner, that prohibitions that surround a woman will be concerned with her feminine, natural functions; women who have just given birth are often segregated from their peers.

While Ortner suggests that women's subordination is related to their identification with nature, Rosaldo finds the source of feminine inferiority in women's predominantly domestic orientation. Because of childbearing responsibilities, women spend most of their years immersed in the concerns of the home. Men, on the other hand, free of this "enduring, time consuming and emotionally compelling" commitment,[17] work outside the domestic sphere in the public arena. It is the contrast between these two spheres, the private (domestic) world of women and the public world of men, with their different orientations, that provides a necessary framework for the analysis of male and female roles. Rosaldo thus offers an explanation of why, regardless of women's contribution to subsistence, it is men's work that is viewed as more compelling. Men's labors take place in the public arena, where they command attention and are more consistent with the explicit values of the culture, while women's work is relegated to the domestic sphere and hence lacks the persuasive authority granted to men's endeavors. There is, of course, a paradox here: Whether a culture places importance on men's activities as warriors, businessmen, artists, or politicians, women, in their childbearing role, are critical for the biological survival of the group. In many of the examples discussed below, it is clear that despite the public lack of recognition of women, and the ritual and the bravura that surround the more spectacular undertakings of men, there is often private uneasiness over the crucial importance that underscores women's contribution to society.

The actual creative importance of childbearing and rearing can be found in the different means of marking adulthood for boys and girls. Many anthropologists have pointed out that for most cultures it is a common assumption that girls become women with little difficulty. A young girl grows up under the auspices of her mother, or some other female surrogate, and, as a child, can witness what will be expected of her as an adult. Hence her childhood and adult roles have a continuity that is lacking for boys, who grow up in a domestic world of women, only to have to find their place in the public sector of male responsibility. Here, at male adolescence, the division between the public and the private can be seen. In many cultures, becoming a man is an event distinguished by elaborate ritual and, not infrequently, an element of danger. The discontinuity between childhood and adulthood is emphasized; the contrast between the world of men and that of women is marked and exaggerated. Quite commonly a young man's new status is forged in a ritual of purification, which frees him from the pollution associated with the domestic world of women he now leaves behind. In addition, these rituals take place under the guidance of men. The underlying logic seems to suggest that while women create human beings, only men can make men. Since the social hierarchy and authority orderings of so many societies fall into the hands of men, it is no wonder they take a strong interest in refashioning recruits into their midst. Such rituals provide examples of the basic correctness of Rosaldo's and Ortner's contentions.

The two explanations, taken together, provide us with a framework to examine the role of women in a variety of social contexts. Rosaldo has allowed us to see that there is not merely a difference in the jobs men and women perform but a qualitative distinction in the worlds they occupy. Ortner has offered us compelling reasons why the world of women is devalued and so often seen as tainted and dangerous.

The question of the devaluation of women is, however, quite often one of degree. We will see that while in some societies women are viewed as trecherous contaminants, in others they are able to maintain a reasonable amount of autonomy and command a measure of respect.

Devaluation of women may be expressed in a variety of ways: There may be explicit rules that limit female participation in the major activities of the society, or there may be religious or symbolic notions that suggest women's impurity. In the highlands of New Guinea cultural ideology maintains that male and female principles are not only conceptually dissimilar but, in fact, are opposed to one another. By their very nature women are perceived as dangerous to men. As Ortner leads us to expect, women's natural functions pose a threat to the society of men. The barriers between the public world of men and the private world of women remain strong and impenetrable. The extreme case provided by New Guinea illustrates that, underlying the tension and hostility between men and women, what is really at issue is a question of power.

The Mae Enga are horticulturists who keep pigs and fowl in the western highlands of New Guinea.[18] Men reside together in the men's house, while married women live with their unmarried daughters and infant sons. As early as age five, a young boy, usually of his own accord, will leave his mother and move into the men's house. Quite early in life he is taught, and apparently learns well, the unsavory consequences of keeping female company.

In the world view of the Mae Enga, women are seen as pollutants of the worst kind—by their very being they can ruin the crops of the tribe, thwart a war effort, or strike down a virile young warrior. The physiological differences between men and women are believed to make men vulnerable to feminine abuse of power. As Meggitt points out, young men learn magic in their attempts to protect themselves from the all-pervasive contamination of the womanly presence:

> Females they say are basically different from males for their flesh is laid on vertically along their bones and horizontally across them. Thus they mature more quickly than do males and are ready for marriage earlier. Whereas youths are still vulnerable because they are not fully adult, adolescent girls have already acquired through the menarche their most dangerous attribute—their ability to pollute males. Young men should therefore employ magic to hasten their own growth and to protect themselves from the perils of contamination. Above all, they must recognize the need to avoid unnecessary encounters with women, including their own mothers and sisters.[19]

In this culture women's powers are indeed awesome: Contact with menstrual fluid, it is believed, produces a blackening of the blood and a corruption of the vital juices. While men may protect themselves by learning black magic to counter these influences, they enhance their security by isolating the offending sex during especially dangerous periods—menstruation and childbirth. Even babies, who have been contaminated by contact with uterine blood, are kept in ritual isolation for several months.

Meggitt explains these extreme beliefs about feminine pollution by pointing out that the Mae Enga, a warrior people, select their brides from enemy groups. Hence the threat that these women, as daughters of an enemy, may pose to the group is elaborated symbolically in the beliefs surrounding female impurity. Indeed their potential political disloyalty is transformed into ideological notions of feminine treachery. Under such circumstances intermarriage between feuding groups brings about a cessation of hostilities. Thus, even if the women themselves are undesirable, they are seen as necessary for the perpetuation of the group. Women are therefore not the outcasts that the cultural ideology would hold them to be. Their position, as both dangerous but essential, makes them somewhat of an enigma. There is then another dimension to the contamination associated with female sexuality: If it is dangerous, it is also powerful. The separation of men from women—ostensibly to afford security for men—may in fact only enhance the power of women. Rosaldo points out that:

> the very symbolic and social conceptions that appear to set women apart may be used by women as a basis for female solidarity and worth. When men live apart from women they in fact cannot control them, and unwittingly they may provide them with the symbols and social resources on which to build a society of their own.[20]

The Mae Enga allow us to see that both a woman's power and danger lie in her sexuality. Even in a society where women are socially insignificant and culturally despised, they are biologically necessary. This is the flaw in the masculine claim for absolute power and authority. Ultimately their control over any society depends on its continuity, which can be assured only through women. Dennich points out the paradox: "Exaggerated values of male supremacy are linked with mechanisms of female suppression. The more omnipotent the males are construed to be, the more this omnipotence is threatened by ostensibly insignificant females."[21] In societies where hostility between the sexes is characteristic of domestic relations, rules limiting and circumscribing women will be more numerous and more explicit. Hostility toward, and fear of, women are most likely to be found in those areas directly concerned with sexuality and procreation—that is, those areas which are mysterious to men and over which they have no control.

In many societies men attempt to gain such control in the initiation of young boys into men's cults. Quite often the symbolism suggests the death of the novice and the rebirth of the adult male. The rituals signify that men are responsible for creating the important members of society, while women produce merely the raw material. Bruno Bettelheim, a psychoanalyst, has seen in Australian aborigine initiation an attempt by men to usurp the feminine life-giving role. He points out that while the tone of the ceremony suggests death and rebirth, specific aspects of female anatomy associated with childbirth (the womb and the vulva, for example) are mimicked in this all-male company.[22] Mead has suggested that the association between female-ness and fertility produces a sense of male inferiority that must be compensated. She writes:

> The basic theme of the initiatory cult, however, is that women, by their ability to make children, hold the secrets of life. Men's role is uncertain, undefined, and perhaps unnecessary. By a great effort man has hit upon a method of compensating himself for his basic inferiority. Equipped with various mysterious noise making instruments, whose potency rests upon their actual forms being unknown to those who hear the sound . . . they can get the male children away from the women, brand them as incomplete, and themselves turn boys into men.[23]

A slightly different turn is to be found among the Wogeo, another Melanesian group. As with other groups in the area, men and women live separate existences. Yet, although women are ostensibly without any political power and are confined to the domestic sphere, they too have predictable weapons in their arsenal should a man overstep himself. Hogbin, the ethnographer, writes: "The husband, because he is the stronger, may beat his spouse, but he does so at his peril. All she has to do by way of retaliation is to touch his food when next she menstruates and thereby inflict him with a fatal illness."[24] Ideally, men and women are believed to be dangerous to one another. The social consequences, nevertheless, are not very different from what they are for the Mae Enga, for such beliefs reinforce the isolation of women from all that is publicly significant. The major difference is to be found in the belief among the Wogeo that menstrual bleeding is purifying. While women menstruate of their own accord, men must induce bleeding to ensure their disinfection. This is really only a variation on what we have seen earlier: If women are suspect for what they do naturally, men will mimic them, and thus have access to their power, by artificial means. However, the point remains the same: Naturally and biologically women possess powers and abilities that men may only envy or imitate ineffectively.

The Melanesians provide us with an extreme case that, nevertheless, emphasizes the potency of female sexuality. However, if women obey the rules and proscriptions set down for them, they are generally viewed as benign. A wife and mother is rarely seen as a threatening force.[25] But should a woman move into the masculine domain, or deviate from cultural expectations, she can expect to be harrassed and stigmatized. In two dramatic cases taken from Africa and India, the consequences of not following the rules may be seen.

The Nupe of Nigeria are a patrilineal* group of agriculturalists. Like many African groups, they hold a belief in witchcraft that pervades almost all

---

*A system of kinship reckoning in which descent is traced through a line of ancestors in the male line. (Keesing, *Cultural Anthropology,* New York: Holt, Rinehart and Winston, 1976, p. 564.)

aspects of their lives. The Nupe specify that a witch is a woman and, in the minds of Nupe men, the reverse also holds: to be a woman is to be a witch.[26] Men, on the other hand, are the self-annointed protectors of village safety; it is their task to undertake periodic reform and purification of village land. If women are the scourge of society in their roles as witches, men, for their part, are responsible for the well being of the social order. What have Nupe women done to deserve such a stigma? Simply this: they flout their husband's demands to stay home and raise children, and choose, instead, to assert themselves and to trade in the nearby market towns. The financial and moral independence of such an extradomestic occupation summons forth masculine accusations of illicit sexual activities and suspicions that the women are subverting the best interest of the social group by practicing abortion and contraception. Moreover, their trading activities provide them with an additional income. Their less wealthy husbands frequently find themselves in the humiliating position of having to request a loan from their wives to dispense with the business of the male descent group properly. Such a position only highlights the Nupe man's lack of control and the dilution of male prerogatives. In such a situation the only course open to men is to brandish their anger in witchcraft accusations. "In so doing they acknowledge their women's real power while labelling it illegitimate and wrong."[27] Thus, in a society where women constantly remind men of female independence, they are cast in the role of outcasts and evildoers.

In India a similar fate awaits a woman who, by an accident of fate, no longer derives her identity from the men that surround her. Among high-caste Brahmins a woman's status is defined by her relationship with the crucial men in her life. A woman is controlled first by her father and later, upon marriage, by her husband. His family's control over the newly married bride is so complete that her obedience is guaranteed by keeping her housebound under the watchful and tyrannical eye of her new mother-in-law. Denied any formal social significance at first, a young woman may hope to gain some power as her sons mature, marry, and bring daughters-in-law to reside under her supervision. However, all her plans will go awry should her husband predecease her. A Brahmin woman's daily prayers should contain an invocation that she die before her husband. Should she find herself a widow, she must tolerate the suspicions of all around her that she is responsible (either through the use of magic or poison) for the death of her husband. For the rest of her days she will bear the stigma of poisoner. Harper maintains that since Brahmin women derive their status only through men, a woman without a husband has no social definition, she no longer fits, and therefore her position as outcast only reflects her marginality on the social scene.[28]

The extreme case proves the larger point that there is in fact a great deal of similarity in the ways in which women are treated all over the world. Women are daughters, sisters, wives, and mothers. Their main status flows from and through their relationships with men. It is only when women refuse to stay neatly confined in these categories that trouble results. Initiation and other similar markings of male adulthood permit manhood to be an achieved status. On the other hand, "womanhood is an ascribed status; a woman is seen as 'naturally' what she is."[29]

Rosaldo has suggested that the ascribed nature of woman's position is connected to her association with home and children, while the achieved nature of manhood is related to the actual achievements necessary to perform effectively on a wider stage. It would seem likely, then, that there would be more status equality in those societies where there is not a very rigid boundary between public and private worlds: in other words, in societies where men and women perform similar kinds of activities.

The !Kung bushmen of the Kalihari desert are a hunting and gathering people who live in a society where egalitarian impulses appear to dominate. Draper maintains that in this small-scale society, where both men and women contribute to subsistence, women do have a considerable degree of influence and independence.[30] Here the division of labor between men and women is not rigid, and physical aggression is forbidden by cultural norms. The existence or nonexistence of sexual equality in these contexts is very important. For, as Lamphere writes, "in those small scale band societies, many feel a case can be made for sexual equality. On the other hand, if these societies are not egalitarian, then more highly stratified complex societies are unlikely to be, thus strengthening the case for universal subordination."[31]

The introduction of agriculture has had devastating effects on the status of women. Draper has demonstrated that once traditional foraging yields to a sedentary existence, the position of !Kung women decreases markedly. While women are homebound, men take over more of the public decision making; without the constraints of high mobility, there is an accumulation of wealth which is managed by men, not women. Surplus and private property are now exclusively handled by males. Moreover, the differential wealth of men creates a system of ranking and stratification that leads to male public activities and the increasingly private preoccupations of the women. Draper writes: "As households and possessions become private, I believe women are becoming private as well. . . . In contrast, both men and women are equally 'public,' mobile, and visible. I believe that exposure of women is a form of protection in the bush setting."[32]

While it is true that in the bush setting there is more equal sharing of public life, and hence of major decision making, the subordination of women is still a fact of life. Draper, for example, attributes the apparent equality of bush women to the absence of a defined male leader and to cultural values that prohibit aggression and thereby avoid the expression of male physical dominance. Although it is true that there is more equality in a hunting and gathering context, this equality is far from absolute. It is not enough for women to produce food and thereby make a major contribution to subsistence—they must be able to control their production. Since women and food are so often used by men in exchanges, especially in hunting and gathering societies, the case for the equality of women is weakened. As Rubin maintains, "the traffic in women" (the exchange of women in marital alliances between men) suggests that at the very root of social organization female subordination is assured.[33] Although women do have more power in those societies where the domestic and public spheres are not strongly differentiated, a close examination of these contexts indicates that female subordination would appear to be a universal. This does not mean that women are consistently powerless; on the contrary, knowing the structure well, they are often able to manipulate it quite effectively and insinuate their own interests without upsetting the apparent balance of male supremacy.

To gain power in most male-dominated societies, women must rely on a subtle manipulation of the social structure. While an individual's attempt to rebel against the strictures and demands of the feminine condition may prove successful, a more productive battle against male dominance can be waged by a group of women acting in concert. Women who come together in extradomestic groups not only relieve their own isolation but are able to influence, in indirect ways, the events that occur around them. The degree of influence a woman may wield depends on her stage in the life cycle. Quiet, demure, and passive young daughters and new wives will eventually have considerable autonomy and power in decision making as their sons marry and they can assume the role of domineering mother-in-law.

In her study of rural Taiwan Wolf has shown how women use gossip and scandal to exert pressure on men.[34] While a wife may have little actual influence on her husband's actions, she can manipulate village public opinion by careful use of her own feminine network. Few men, in any social context, are willing to subject themselves to public scorn and ridicule. Indeed female cohesiveness is a powerful tool protecting the interests of women. One of the most effective groups of women is the Bundu of West Africa. The Bundu is a woman's organization in Sierra Leone. The girls enter at puberty, at which time a clitorectomy is performed, and the young women are taught the secrets of the organization. The shared ordeal, and good times, of this period provide a basis for lifelong solidarity that is marked by ready assistance and cooperation among its members. Although only some Bundu members achieve political prominence, Hoffer points out the important fact that the general status of all women is enhanced. In this context the actual existence of a group of women with institutionalized practices and rituals that are not accessible to men adds an additional dimension to female identity; women are not merely extensions of the important men around them. The Bundu affords protection against all manner of male abuse as Hoffer demonstrates:

> Bundu law enhances the status of all women by protecting them, for example, from degrading acts such as male voyeurism. . . . Should he make sexual advances to an uninitiated girl, he risks illness and death unless he goes to the Bundu leader, confesses, pays a fine and submits to ritual cleansing. Husbands are wary

of offending their wives in marital disputes. There is always the chance that the abused wife, or her mother, will use "medicine" known to Bundu women to harm him, especially to render him impotent.[35]

Groups of women can also be effective in providing for their kinsmen. In her study of black urban life in the United States, Stack has documented the importance and significance of female networks in economic exchange.[36] The cooperation and mutual assistance of women assure that an existence will be maintained despite the lack of financial resources. Moreover, the moral support afforded by these interlocking chains of women gives sustenance in an otherwise hostile environment.

Female solidarity can offer an assault on male domination in even the most challenging of circumstances. In Muslim Africa the position of women is devalued both by social conditions and a religious ideology that supports the social structure. The Somali, a group of nomadic pastoralists, offer evidence of the variety of ways women may express their disaffection with the status quo. In addition to the rigors of pastoral life, Somali women have to contend with a situation in which marital customs heavily favor men, divorce is easily obtained, and polygyny (plural wives) is a masculine prerogative. Furthermore, religious authority is exclusively in the hands of men. Viewed at best as passive spectators, women are not permitted into the mosques where men worship. In general, women are viewed as "weak, submissive creatures."[37]

To make matters worse, women also suffer periodic possession by *sar* spirits. During these interludes the spirit enters the body of the sick woman, which it then uses to express its demands. Lewis reports that it is not uncommon for a man to return home only to discover that his wife has become a victim of spirit possession in his absence. However, a cure is readily available for a suitable fee. A female shaman will interpret the demands made by the intruding spirit. The husband must then decide whether or not to give in to these claims. This is not an easy decision, for costly and luxurious items are frequently the only things that will satisfy these avaricious spirits. Quite coincidentally, these demands may occur just at the time a husband is considering taking an additional wife. The husband protests but generally gives in, as public opinion, buttressed by a Koranic justification for the existence of the *sar*, works to the benefit of the stricken woman.

Lewis points out that such possession episodes permit a redress for the female in the face of real or imagined male neglect. At the same time, men can yield without losing face, because it is the spirits, and not the normally passive women, who are issuing these strident demands. Here, too, a feminine subculture is able to mount an effective attack on the dominant society of men. But, as Lewis points out, while there can be no ignoring the note of protest involved in such activities, they are not meant to endanger the present order. Such crises highlight the contradiction, seen earlier in Melanesia, between the low social position accorded to women and their strong, but officially unrecognized, biological commitment to the society. As Lewis writes:

It seems possible that this tolerance by men of these cults, as well as the license and blessing also accorded to women more generally, may reflect a shadowy recognition of the injustice of this contradiction between the official status of women and their actual importance to the society. If, in short, women are sometimes, even in traditional tribal societies, explicitly envious of men, the dominant sex, in turn, also, acts in ways which suggest that it recognizes that women have some ground for complaint.[38]

In this case affliction, in the form of spirit possession, allows women to protest the harsh circumstances of existence. At the same time, it also provides the basis for feminine solidarity that will ameliorate and soften their dependence upon men. The organizations of women, whether formal or informal, have the effect of enhancing the status of particular individuals while also promoting the general cause of womanhood.

Many of the societies discussed in this paper have come into contact with western industrialization, with a resulting reevaluation of the role of women. As women have entered the wage labor force in increasing numbers, their status has not improved. In those societies where their efforts provided, in traditional times, the major contribution to subsistence, their status has actually declined. In surveying the situation, Bossen has commented that "the global trend toward female equality may be more apparent than real."[39] Although we saw above that women who participate in production are more likely to approach, if not achieve, equality, a consideration of women in modernizing contexts reveals that the relationship between status and productivity is involved and complex.

When western technology is introduced, it is often accompanied by western values; men, at the expense of women, are introduced to the more sophisticated agricultural techniques and trained and educated for the more demanding urban jobs. Such circumstances work against the improved position of women. Young men leave their native villages to seek advancement in the cities; women are left behind in the unproductive hinterlands. Even where women now assume the major responsibility for family sustenance, their position often actually suffers. Using the newly introduced techniques, men increase their production while expending less energy. By contrast, women's work with the hoe "is exhausting, boring, and relatively less productive."[40] While local governments may do research toward the improvement of cash crops (men's work), family crops are not supported in a similar manner. Men thus participate in the wider economic context, while women are relegated to a life of enforced leisure and idleness in the impoverished indigenous economy. The result is increased status and prestige for men, while women suffer a status decline from main producer to family assistant.

Remy has written of Nigeria: "Capitalist economic development has either introduced or reinforced structural inequalities within the Nigerian economy. But while economic options for men have widened, and they have assumed new roles which permit varying degrees of personal autonomy, the same is not true for women."[41]

In varying degrees similar circumstances have devalued the position of women in diverse settings. Women not only lose economic autonomy but suffer in their interpersonal relationships as a result of their new dependence on men. The condition of women has not been enhanced by the introduction of an economic system that we in the United States take for granted.[42]

The apparent strides that women have made in this country should not blind us to the affinity we share with women in all cultural settings. Rosaldo's and Ortner's theoretical statements are relevant for us today. The isolation of a suburban housewife is much the same as that of many women discussed here. Moreover, although there is a large percentage of women in the labor force in this country, it is men who make decisions and who enjoy status and prestige. A woman's position is all too commonly a derived position. While we live in one of the most technologically advanced societies in the world, the distinction between public and domestic orientations remains quite strong. As Rosaldo suggests, true equality will be achieved not only when women join men in the public arena, but "when men themselves help to raise new generations by taking on the responsibilities of the home."[43]

In this chapter we have seen that the position women occupy in society varies from one social group to another. Thus simple appeals to biology would not seem to be adequate in defining the place that women should assume in contemporary America. Women may be traders, farmers, gatherers. In every society female identity is buttressed by an ideology that suggests that what women do is both absolute and inevitable. But, despite this variety, women in many parts of the world have much in common: They are, for the most part, isolated, and their work is undervalued. It is this universal aspect of women's position that has proved so compelling, for, in spite of the apparent diversity in the status of women, there is an unmistakable pattern of underlying subordination. There is an important lesson here however: As women overcome their isolation, and as they begin to do work that is culturally valued, we may expect to see the rise, if not the preeminence, of the female in American society.

NOTES

1. Naomi Quinn, "Anthropological Studies on Women's Status," in *Annual Review of Anthropology*, ed. Bernard J. Seigel (Palo Alto: Annual Reviews Inc., 1977), pp. 181–225.

2. Ernestine Friedl, *Women and Men* (New York: Holt, Rinehart and Winston, 1975).

3. P. R. Sanday, "Female Status in the Public Domain," in *Women, Culture, and Society*, ed. Louise Lamphere and Michelle Rosaldo (Stanford: Stanford University Press, 1974), pp. 189–206; J. K. Brown, "Economic Organization and the Position of Women among the Iroquois," *Ethnohistory* 17 (1970): 131–167.

4. "Women in Other Cultures," in *Woman in Sexist Society,* ed. Vivian Gornick and Barbara K. Moran (New York: Basic Books, Inc., 1971), pp. 393–427.

5. Ibid., p. 345.

6. H. R. Hays, *From Ape to Angel* (New York: Capricorn Books, 1964), p. 346

7. *Sex and Temperament* (1935; reprint ed., New York: Dell Publishing Co., Inc., 1969), p. 18.

8. Ibid., p. 179.

9. The technical processes whereby food and other physical means of life are produced and consumed. Keesing, *Cultural Anthropology* (New York: Holt, Rinehart and Winston, 1976), p. 568.

10. Michelle Rosaldo, "Women, Culture and Society: A Theoretical Overview," in *Women, Culture and Society,* ed. Louise Lamphere and Michelle Rosaldo (Stanford: Stanford University Press, 1974), pp. 17–42.

11. Lionel Tiger, *Men in Groups* (New York: Vintage Books, 1969).

12. M. Martin and B. Voorhies, *Females of the Species* (New York: Columbia University Press, 1975), pp. 162–165; Sally Slocum, "Women the Gatherer: Male Bias in Anthropology," in *Toward an Anthropology of Women,* ed. Rayna Reiter (New York: Monthly Revised Press, 1975), pp. 26–50.

13. Introduction, Lamphere and Rosaldo, *Women, Culture and Society,* p. 7; Martin and Voorhies, *Females of the Species,* pp. 165–166, 172–176.

14. Lamphere and Rosaldo, *Women, Culture and Society,* p. 7.

15. Sherry Ortner, "Is Female to Male as Nature Is to Culture," in Lamphere and Rosaldo, *Women, Culture and Society,* pp. 67–87.

16. E. Kessler, *Women: An Anthropological View* (New York: Holt, Rinehart and Winston, 1976), p. 13.

17. Rosaldo, "Women, Culture and Society," p. 24.

18. M. J. Meggitt, "Male-Female Relations in the Highlands of Australian New Guinea," *American Anthropologist* 66, no. 4, part II (1964): 204–224.

19. Ibid., p. 207.

20. Rosaldo, "Women, Culture and Society," p. 39.

21. Dennich, "Sex and Power in the Balkans," in Lamphere and Rosaldo, *Women, Culture and Society,* pp. 243–262.

22. Bruno Bettelheim, *Symbolic Wounds: Puberty Rites and the Envious Male.* (Glencoe, Ill.: The Free Press, 1954).

23. Margaret Mead, *Male and Female* (New York: William Morrow and Company, Inc., 1975).

24. Ian Hogbin, *Wogeo: The Island of Menstruating Men* (Scranton, Pa.: Chandler Publishing Company, 1970), p. 86.

25. Rosaldo, "Women, Culture and Society," p. 32.

26. Nadel, "Witchcraft in Four African Societies," *American Anthropologist* 54 no. 1 (1952): 18–29.

27. Rosaldo, "Women, Culture and Society," p. 34.

28. Edward Harper, "Fear and the Status of Women," *Southwestern Journal of Anthropology* 25 (1969): 81–95.

29. Rosaldo, "Women, Culture and Society," p. 28.

30. Patricia Draper, "Contrasts in Sexual Egalitarianism in Foraging and Sedentary Contexts," in Reiter, *Toward an Anthropology of Women,* pp. 77–109.

31. Louise Lamphere, "Review Essay: Anthropology," *Signs* 2, no. 3 (Spring 1977): 612–627.

32. Draper, "Contrasts in Sexual Egalitarianism," p. 108.

33. Gail Rubin, "The Traffic in Women: Notes on the Political Economy of Sex," in Reiter, *Toward an Antrhopology of Women,* pp. 157–210.

34. Margery Wolf, "Chinese Women: Old Skills in a New Context," in Lamphere and Rosaldo, *Women, Culture and Society,* pp. 157–172.

35. Carol Hoffer, "Bundu: Political Implications of Female Solidarity in a Secret Society," in *Being Female,* ed. Raphael (The Hague: Mouton, 1975), pp. 155–163.

36. Carol Stack, *All Our Kin* (New York: Harper & Row, Publishers, 1975).
37. I. M. Lewis, *Ecstatic Religion* (London: Penguin Books Ltd., 1971), p. 73.
38. Ibid., p. 88.
39. Bossen, "Women in Modernizing Societies," *American Ethnologist* 2, no. 4 (November 1975): 587–601.
40. Leavitt, "Women in Other Cultures," p. 409.
41. Remy, "Underdevelopment and the Experience of Woman: A Nigerian Case Study," in Reiter, *Toward an Anthropology of Women*, pp. 358–371.
42. Anna Rubbo, "The Spread of Capitalism in Rural Colombia: Effects on Poor Women," in Reiter, *Toward an Anthropology of Women*, pp. 333–357.
43. Rosaldo, "Women, Culture and Society," p. 42.

REVIEW QUESTIONS

1. In many societies women are seen as inferior and dangerous. Why do women accept this public view of themselves? If they are indeed believed to be so dangerous, why don't they spend their time terrorizing, rather than acquiescing to, the surrounding men? In other words, why don't they translate their symbolic potency into actual power?
2. Margaret Mead suggests that through the process of initiation men can make men. She further suggests that this is, in fact, an attempt to compensate for the male's inability to produce children. In other words, the ritual process of initiation may be seen as a form of womb envy. Do you agree? Can a case be made for such feelings in our own society?
3. Several authors have noted that the transition from childhood to adulthood is much smoother for females than for males. Why do you think this might be the case? Is it true in our own culture?
4. At times women air their distress by joining religious movements that permit them to vent their frustration. What often results is a strong feeling of female solidarity. But why do these women stop here? Once organized, why do they not effect an economic and social revolution?
5. The widespread existence of religious movements that concentrate on female ecstasy suggests not only common experiences among women but common solutions to their distress. Do similar strategies exist in our society today?
6. Men are isolated in the men's house where they perform duties and rituals that are culturally prescribed as male activities, and women are in the menstrual huts at times when they are most womanly (i.e., during menstruation, childbirth). Why is it that men perceive it as an honor to go to the men's house, while they view women as banished to the menstrual huts in order to protect men? In other words, since there is often masculine and feminine solidarity, why is one viewed as an honor to be earned, while the other is seen as a stigma to be overcome?

SELECTED READINGS

Friedl, Ernestine. *Women and Men: An Anthropologist's View.* New York: Holt, Rinehart and Winston, 1975.

An excellent, analytic discussion of the relationship between men and women. Dr. Friedl is particularly illuminating in her discussion of hunting societies. The book is presented with an evolutionary perspective, examining women in hunting, agricultural, and peasant societies.

Hammond, D., and A. Jablow. *Women in Cultures of the World.* Menlo Park, Calif.: Cummins Publishing, 1976.

A lively discussion of the position of women in the family and in the economy. The authors illustrate the variety of female experience with many relevant, well-chosen examples.

Harper, Edward. "Fear and the Status of Women," *Southwestern Journal of Anthropology* 25 (1969): 81–95.

This article documents the poison complex in India. It provides a clear example of women's derived status and illustrates that women without men are seen as powerful and dangerous.

Hogbin, Ian. *Wogeo: The Island of Menstruating Men.* Scranton, Pa.: Chandler Publishing Company, 1970.

This monograph provides an excellent case study of a Melanesian society. Hogbin demonstrates the power and effectiveness associated with menstruation in Wogeo society. Men are so impressed by menstruation that they undergo multilation to induce similar experiences.

Kessler, E. *Women: An Anthropological View.* New York: Holt, Rinehart and Winston, 1976.

A survey of women in a variety of cultural settings. Presented in an evolutionary framework, the materials are documented by life histories and personal accounts.

Lamphere, Louise, "Review Essay: Anthropology," *Signs* 2, no. 3 (Spring 1977): 612–627.

An excellent, concise statement of recent issues in, and contributions to, the anthropology of women.

Lamphere, Louise, and Michelle Rosaldo, eds. *Women, Culture and Society.* Stanford: Stanford University Press, 1974.

An anthology of excellent analytic essays that deal with women in a cross-cultural and historical perspective. Among the many important contributions to feminist scholarship in this volume are Sherry Ortner's article and Michelle Rosaldo's theoretical overview.

Lewis, I. M. *Ecstatic Religion.* London: Penguin Books Ltd., 1971.

Lewis provides many interesting examples of women in ecstatic religious movements. He makes the important point that ecstasy can be an impressive weapon against male domination.

Martin, M., and B. Voorhies. *Female of the Species.* New York: Columbia University Press, 1975.

A thorough discussion with many good examples of women in various societies. The authors adopt an evolutionary framework and present an excellent discussion of the implications of various subsistence patterns for women.

Reiter, Rayna, ed. *Toward an Anthropology of Women.* New York: Monthly Revised Press, 1975.

A good collection of essays on a variety of feminist concerns. Among the essays of particular interest are those by Gayle Rubin, Sally Slocum, and Patricia Draper.

CHAPTER 3

Women in Literature

Nadean Bishop

A radical critique of literature, feminist in its impulse, would take the work first of all as a clue to how we live, to how we have been led to imagine ourselves, how our language has trapped as well as liberated us; and how we can begin to see—and therefore live—afresh. (Adrienne Rich, "When We Dead Awaken: Writing as Re-Vision")

Literature deals with human beings in conflict, whether conflict with society, with other human beings, or within the self. Thus the quest for identity is sharpened by two functions of literature, as a reflection of what is and as a model for what may be. Literature as mirror reveals the realities of women's lives as described by women and men writers. Literature as searchlight illuminates a world of possibility where the acculturation of sex-role stereotyping described elsewhere in this text may be left behind.

Women's identity is a major motif of the three major classifications of literature: drama, fiction, and poetry. In ancient literature written by men this identity is other-defined and often stereotypical, based on men's perceptions. In more recent literature by women the focus is more often on an individual woman's quest for her own identity, but the mirror still reflects societal expectation and reality. Women's mutuality or unity with other women is less apparent in older literatures, especially in drama, but becomes more frequent and more significant in representations of contemporary women. Women's participation in society is revealed with greatest impact in contemporary fiction, but all literatures give some insight into how women live and how women serve vital functions in the wider world.

Men were the only ones taught to read and write in most countries before 1760, and thus men were the ones creating literature. Both the mirror put up to reality and the searchlight probing the future related predominantly to men. The ancient Greeks pictured women as either idealized homemakers or seductive sirens; Renaissance poets wrote of love from a man's perspective; epics told of sea adventures and male explorations in which the only woman was the wife back home; More's Utopia, like Plato's, dealt with male preoccupations like governing and commerce.

Though the world of writing and publishing has traditionally been dominated by men, we discover that the master writers are often able to rip off the blinders of sex stereotyping and encompass the feminine worlds and sensitivities as well as the male arenas and characteristics. Thus William Shakespeare's Desdemona and Juliet and Kate can speak like believable women and express sentiments to which women readers respond with recognition. Similarly Henrik Ibsen can capture the frustration of Nora trapped in the doll's house. But most of what was written and published in the past was from a male perspective that omitted or belittled women. Only occasionally could women find accurate reflections of their own outer reality, and even more rarely could they find replicas of their inner reality.

As we turn to examine first drama, then fiction, and finally poetry, we will examine the changes that came when women began writing of their identity, bonding with other women, and participation in society. We will first look at drama to see how men presented women in the past and how women in modern times have written of their own lives in plays. Drama has four golden periods: the fifth century B.C. in Greece, the Renaissance in Europe, the nineteenth century in Scandinavia and England, and the twentieth century in England and America. The patterns of female roles that evolved in ancient tragedy provided a major starting point for the treatment of women in all other literatures. The women of Shakespeare's theater show how the dramatist adapts to changing notions of what is appropriate for women. Strong, independent women protagonists emerge in the plays of Ibsen in the nineteenth century, only to be answered with neurotic, dependent women in the backlash led by Strindberg. Twentieth-century plays by men continue this antiwoman tradition but are countered in dramas by women. Drama is largely conservative and reflects reality instead of projecting new images and role models, but throughout history the satiric portraits and startlingly accurate versions of reality helped to awaken women to their actual conditions.

Fiction began to be written in the late eighteenth century as a response to the "new literacy" when women were taught to read. Many of the major novelists of the nineteenth century were women, and yet the fiction written by women in the twentieth century has largely been excluded from the canon of literature. An examination of the images of women in representative novels will show some stereotypes being exploded and some new roles and identities being created. A survey of novels written in the 1970s shows that too many women are still in socially accepted prisons and stereotypes. These negative pictures of women have the psychological advantage of allowing women the recognition that they are not alone in their frustration.

The same sense of relief comes from reading poetry written by contemporary women that probes their hostilities and motivations. After years of being condemned for writing "confessional" poetry, women have established their own feminist presses and marketed their own poetry and have found critical affirmation of a new kind of self-exploration. The phases of consciousness and self-defined identity among poets will be shown to parallel the stages in the feminist movement in America and will conclude the chapter on a note of hope for the future.

WOMEN IN DRAMA

Early Drama by Men

The earliest dramatic representations of women occur in the ancient Greek tragedies written during the Golden Age of Greece in the fifth century B.C. These plays, written by Aeschylus, Sophocles, and Euripides, show intense moral conflict usually centered around family relationships. Repeatedly a woman figure appears in one of two guises: the Good Mother or the Devouring Mother. Psychoanalyst Eric Neumann in his book *The Great Mother* shows that these antithetical mother figures dominate primitive art and religion as well as drama. In the psychoanalytic view they appeal powerfully to every man because of the crisis in his own early years when the nursing mother gave totally of love and nourishment until the time for separation and the development of individuality. The breast was no longer available, and mother was characterized as withholding. This was followed by the oedipal period when the boy desired his mother as a love-object but was forced to counteract that attachment for fear of castration by the father. Thus the Devouring Mother image arises to protect the male psyche from mother fixation.

Such figures in drama that take on attributes of unusual power because of their roots in the unconscious are called archetypes. As psychoanalyst Carl Gustave Jung describes them, they are notable for being found in every culture in every age and for causing an extraordinary rush of recognition. Examples of these two facets of the Great Mother from ancient Greece will help set up the basic stereotypes of women in literature through the ages.

The Good Mother is exemplified by Hecuba, widow of the patriarch of Troy, in *The Trojan Women* by Euripides. Hecuba has suffered the horror of seeing the body of her son, Hector, dragged around the walls of Troy by Achilles, and now, as Troy is plundered, she must also witness the murder of her grandson and wrap his battered body for burial. As archetypal mother, she accuses Helen of Troy of causing all the heartbreak of the Trojan War, making her one of the negative facets of mother: the Devouring Mother, the seductress who through her beauty causes the deaths of many warriors. Their wrangling interaction is typical of the lack of unity or mutual support between women in Greek tragedy.

A harsher portrait of the Terrible Mother who wreaks her revenge on another woman is in *Medea* by Euripides. Medea, a barbarian princess noted for her sorcery, helps her husband capture the golden fleece from her father by slaughtering and dismembering her own brother. After years of marriage and two children, Jason casts her aside to marry the beautiful princess. Medea sends a poison robe to the bride-to-be which consumes her and her father. Then Medea kills her own children to spite Jason and flees in a dragon-drawn chariot with their bodies. The playwright constructs a horrifying woman archetype onto whom all males in the audience can unload their hostilities toward women and emerge from the theater purged of negative emotions. Unfortunately, this split identity for women has persisted as if it were describing a real type of woman instead of a psychologically constructed bogey. Versions of this Devouring Mother are seen in contemporary literature as the castrating bitch, such as Martha in Edward Albee's *Who's Afraid of Virginia Woolf* and the ego-sucking mother in *The Effect of Gamma Rays on Man-in-the-Moon Marigolds* by Paul Zindel.

This dichotomy of the good and evil woman figures can be recognized in another guise in the theology of the medieval church. The Virgin Mary was used as an ideal of woman: chaste, pure, tender, compassionate, subordinate. The Blessed Virgin was used by priests to intimidate women who deviated from their role as nurturant subordinate beings who should be devoid of original impulse or erotic feelings. The opposite was Evil Eve, counterpart of the Devouring Mother, who, because of her seductive sensuality, brought sin into the world by eating the forbidden fruit. Domesticity was sanctified, and fidelity in marriage was the virtue most praised in the drama of the Middle Ages and Renaissance.

When we move to the Renaissance we find drama was changed by the elevation to the throne of Queen Elizabeth, "a woman in a position of unusual power and visibility, who demonstrated to all that women were politically competent."[1] Because of her example and patronage, the women in the plays of Shakespeare are "intelligent, interesting, self-willed. As a rule, the women of his comedies are witty, charming, bright, and self-possessed. They frequently control their own property and rule their own lives; they command those who serve them authoritatively."[2] Following the death of Elizabeth, Shakespeare's women become more sinister. As Harriet Kriegel describes them in *Women in Drama:* "They are demonic in *King Lear* (1605–1606), power hungry in *Macbeth* (1606), and irresponsible to the point of losing an empire for the satisfaction of sensual desire in *Anthony and Cleopatra* (1607)."[3] A backlash against forceful women characterizes drama of the next two centuries, with few positive portrayals of women until the era of liberation and self-realization in the mid-nineteenth century.

Modern Drama by Men

Henrik Ibsen was one of the first major modern playwrights to deal extensively with the problems of women. His *A Doll's House,* published in 1879, shows a marriage based on deception. Nora pretends to be a helpless female, dependent on her husband for every idea. In reality she has been doing handcrafts secretly to repay a loan undertaken for forging her father's signature to pay for a year's recuperation for her tubercular husband. When her husband discovers that she is about to be blackmailed by a bank employee, he upbraids her mercilessly instead of understanding her loving sacrifice. Though he offers to forgive her when the employee removes the threat, Nora has seen him in his true light and leaves the marriage to seek a life of independence. Nora slamming the door gives us the first forceful dramatic portrait of a woman's self-liberation, but Ibsen does not make the future seem rosy—simply better than the stultifying marriage. In *Pillars of Society* Ibsen drew on the career of a leading feminist of the day to depict Lona Hessel, who fights for equality against the outwardly respectable male leaders.

Hedda Gabler shows a forceful phallic woman caught up in thwarted passion and blackmail and an unwanted pregnancy. Her identity crisis is complicated by her jealousy of a modest and self-sacrificing schoolmate. She cannot tolerate life at the command of the lustful Judge Brack or with the guilty association with Lövborg's botched suicide in a brothel, so she takes her own life. Ibsen's sympathetic championing of women, even conflicted women like Hedda, was repugnant to his contemporary August Strindberg, who created one of theater's most despicable women in *The Fathers.* Laura drives her cavalry officer husband insane by causing him to question his paternity of their talented daughter. He has sought a Madonna-Mother figure and instead finds a mistress-whore in the sexual act, which shatters his trust and thrusts him successively into a rage and finally into a fatal stroke.

The male presentation of the identity of women characters in this archetypal split mode is crippling in many ways. Male viewers expect women to function as pure and holy mother figures or as vamps and punishers. Women find it more difficult to accept themselves as a very human mixture of good and evil, to accept their sexuality as healthy, and to accept their own experiences of being sometimes dependent and sometimes independent. If drama shows the only positive role for a woman as that of taking care of some man and the only negative role as dominance or duplicity against a man, then life's possibilities are drastically limited.

George Bernard Shaw broke out of these stereotypic patterns and gave the world women characters who are independent, intelligent, sometimes sinning, but thoroughly human. Even his Saint Joan is not a plaster saint or an innocent victim but a boisterous country girl of great military genius caught up in the power struggle between the medieval church and the nationalism of secular status. Her naiveté in such matters is balanced by her awesome faith and courage. Shaw's Eliza Doolittle, unlike the star of *My Fair Lady*, is a rational and intelligent woman who rejects Professor Higgins' treatment of her as a thing and marries a man of her own class who will treat her as a human being and help with the flower shop. Not only does Shaw refuse to make his women characters the servants or seducers of men on whom they are dependent; he shows men as well as women as having difficult moral decisions in a world corrupted by greed and industrial power. Though most of Shaw crackles with the urbanity of the upper-class drawing room, *Major Barbara* shows the poverty of the Salvation Army clientele and the recognition by Major Barbara of the dishonesty of trying to buy her faith.

"After Shaw, the rational woman all but disappears from drama," Kriegel contends. She goes on to show the disappearance of strong women from contemporary American drama by men and the predatory destructiveness of the ones portrayed:

> Eugene O'Neill essentially deals with psychological types beset by psychic demons, women who are destructive to others as well as to themselves. Tennessee Williams offers a devastating view of American society through his pitiful women, beings who have no control over their destinies, who are maimed and mutilated by the world, who are overwhelmed by loneliness and weakness. . . . Albee's women are castrating; in LeRoi Jones' *Dutchman*, the white woman is pathologically destructive; in Kopit, mothers gobble fathers and sons whole.[4]

Modern Drama by Women

If American male dramatists have thus portrayed women as parasites and predators, can we look to American women dramatists for corrective portraits of full rounded, self-identified women characters? Not always. Fewer women artists have been successful in writing for the theater than for any other literary form. Part of the reason for this is the cliquish male exclusivism in controlling the instruments of production. Part is the unwillingness of producers to risk capital on works by unknowns, and particularly unknown women. A few women have emerged as major playwrights, but not all of their characterizations of women are exemplary or inspiring role models. Moreover, many plays by women show women fighting other women.

A famous example is Clare Boothe's *The Women,* a devastating 1936 satire of the bitchiness and pettiness of a group of upper-class New York women. The *New York Times* reviewer at its opening said Miss Boothe "succeeded by spraying vitriol over the members of her sex," and lines condemning women spring often from the lips of the forty-four women in their frantic movements through the hairdresser's, powder room, fitting rooms, kitchens. The central figure has lost her husband to a seductress, regrets it, and claws her rival in her struggle to get her husband back. The women reveal intense self-loathing against a background of dependency on men: "There's only one tragedy for a woman—losing her man." "But Mother dear, I don't want to be a girl. I hate girls. They're so silly." "Practically nobody ever misses a clever woman."[5] Freud in 1933 defined women as masochistic and narcissistic, and *The Women* reinforces this view. But it also shows the reality of women's existence in the 1930s, and these conditions are highlighted in feminist revivals of the play. Wages were so low and conditions so oppressive for women that security with any man was preferable to the poverty and despair of being on one's own.

The bitterness of poverty is also shown in an avant-grade 1969 all-female drama called *Rites,* written by Maureen Duffy. What is notable, however, is the solidarity of the women and the fact that the hatred is now directed at men and society. London working-class women in a public washroom replace the elegant snobs of Clare Boothe's fashionable powder room. The head matron expresses the gut reactions of the lower class in such matters as the perception of a woman's body as a commodity in the sexual market. Men are the others, the enemy; and the women who come to the lavatory build bonds and coalitions on their mutual feelings of being used and needing to retaliate. They find a girl who has slashed her wrists in the john and work to rescue her, all the while muttering against men when she whispers a man's name as she revives: "Bastard men. Get a man, she says, I'll get him right where I want him. He thinks because I'm flat on my back he's got me but I've got him; caught, clinched as if I had my teeth in him."[6] Ultimately their frustration erupts in the violent rites of the title.

Between these two bitter extremes are many dramas by women filled with believable whole women, captured in moments of trauma or stasis. Progressively these plays show more women with self-defined identities and more unity among women. Two of the best representatives of these are among the 125 dramas written by Black women in America since 1916 when Angelina Grimké's *Rachel* was first produced.[7]

In 1959 Lorraine Hansberry's *A Raisin in the Sun* became the first play by a Black woman produced on Broadway. The three women characters are real and strong, and each one represents a type of Black womanhood in contemporary America. Mama is the Black matriarch of the past who works in other people's kitchens to supply the cramped apartment shared by her son, her daughter-in-law Ruth, her young grandson, and her daughter Beneatha. Ruth is a hard-working mother and self-sacrificing wife who is employed as a domestic. Bennie represents the new Black woman—aspiring toward medical school, seeking her roots in a relationship with an African intellectual—who hopes to rise above her mother's hard life and her sister-in-law's role as dutiful wife. Mama blows up when her son is swindled out of all her husband's insurance money except what she put as a down payment on a house;

but then she challenges him to become a man, and he achieves maturity by resisting the temptation to sell out to the racists who do not want the family to move into their all-white neighborhood. This well-written drama highlights the crushing effects of poverty and racism, but the ultimate message is antifeminist: The need for a black woman to make her man feel proud overrides her need for autonomy and self-expression.

If *A Raisin in the Sun* shows the search for identity in the 1950s, *Wine in the Wilderness* by Alice Childress provides insight into the level of consciousness among Black women in the late 1960s. Tommy, a Black woman of thirty from the working class, is brought to the studio of a Black artist in the middle of a riot to pose for his three-panel portrait of Black womanhood. She falls for him and thinks he wants to make her his ideal when in reality he sees her as the "real messed-up woman." After they make love, she discovers her mistake and converts the artist to seeing the woman who has made it against great odds as the true ideal. She describes herself as "Tomorrow-Marie, cussin' and fightin' and lookin' out for my damn self 'cause ain't nobody else 'round to do it."[8] Bill accepts her love and eulogizes her as the play closes: "Look at Tomorrow. She came through the biggest riot of all, . . . somethin' called 'slavery,' and she's even comin' through the 'now' scene, . . . folks laughin' at her, even her own folks laughin' at her. And look how . . . with her head high up like she's poppin' her fingers at the world."[9] Most of the dramas written by Black women in the last fifteen years show the misery and reflect the anger legitimately felt against reality, but *Wine in the Wilderness* gives hope by showing one woman who knows who she is.

Women's emerging identity as represented in drama may be illustrated by considering plays by two prominent American women playwrights, one writing tragedies and one writing comedies. Lillian Hellman, a crusader in her autobiography, views women as victims and victimizers in her dramas and rarely gives a positive image of a woman. In *The Children's Hour* (1934) two young teachers have their boarding school closed by the vicious lie of a problem child who accuses them of lesbianism while trying to cover her own misdeeds. After losing a libel suit and the support of Karen's doctor fiance, the two are crushed and miserable. Martha kneels by Karen's chair and in her distraught condition says she is guilty of having thought of Karen in "that way"; She then immediately runs out and shoots herself. The student's grandmother, discovering the lie about the teachers' lesbianism, ironically enters just after Martha's suicide to offer restoration of their reputations, and money. In *The Little Foxes* Hellman's money-hungry Southern belle allows her husband to die so she can take charge of the family wealth.

Women are often portrayed as hapless homemakers by the popular writer of sparkling comedies Jean Kerr. Her *Mary, Mary* is a farce focusing on the meeting of a divorcing couple to arrange their tax return. They discover they still like each other better than any of the rivals who keep popping in and out. *Please Don't Eat the Daisies* shows the suburban wife and mother coping with home repairs, a commuting husband, an obstreperous son who is kept in a cage, and other frustrations of mothering. *Finishing Touches* portrays a faculty wife nursing her husband through the male menopause and flirtation with a sensuous coed.

Broadway plays by women authors, whether in serious mode like those of Lillian Hellman or in comic mode like Jean Kerr's, have strong roles for female protagonists, but these women are rarely shown deviating far from stereotypic norms. Off-Broadway and experimental dramas by women, by contrast, often show outstanding portraits of women breaking stereotypes and icons while shaping their own identities. Two of the best of these draw on the lives of women of the past. E. M. Broner's *The Body Parts of Margaret Fuller* (1976) uses the life story taken from the journals of the author of *Women in the Nineteenth Century* as the vehicle through which the women actors explore their own identities. Megan Terry's *Approaching Simone* (1970) gives a surrealistic and poetic version of the life of the French Marxist philosopher Simone Weil who becomes a martyr as she starves herself in sympathy for the sufferers of the Hitler era.

It appears that more strong heroines will emerge and will reach the theater audience in spite of male domination of the productions. We must not, however, despair that so few strong heroines have yet appeared, because accurate dramatic portrayals of the present role of women may well motivate women to reconsider their own identities and life choices. The parallel is television. Women are outraged at the limiting views of women as sex objects as in "Charlie's Angels," warm-as-apple-pie mommies as in "The Brady Bunch," or ploddingly patient domestics as in "The Courtship of Eddie's Father." Their letters and their consciousness-raising complaints to daughters watching with them have brought change: a woman attorney on "Rockford Files" and a string of independent women such as Alice and Rhoda and Mary Tyler Moore. Contemporary theater for the stage will probably be changed in much the same direction as women make their opinions known.

WOMEN IN FICTION

Differences between Fiction Written by Men and Women

Unlike drama, which had its roots in very ancient times, fiction was not born until the last part of the eighteenth century. As chronicled by Ian Watts in *The Rise of the Novel,* this new literary form, which includes novels and short stories, arose in response to the needs of middle-class women and their maids who were just learning to read. Perhaps it is logical, therefore, that several women rank among the major novelists of the next hundred years: Jane Austen, Charlotte and Emily Brontë, and George Eliot.

These earliest women novelists, as Elaine Showalter describes them in *A Literature of Their Own,* were content to imitate prevailing modes of writing of the dominant male tradition, internalizing its standards and views on social roles. But in the second stage (1880–1920), which she terms *feminist* in contrast to the earlier *feminine stage* (1840–1880), women were free to experience more of the world and thus write about a wider range of experiences. The transition to the third *female* stage (which began in the 1920s but entered a new phase of self-awareness in about 1960) was marked by the emergence of a "female aesthetic":

> By 1910 advanced women like Dorothy Richardson could move freely in social atmospheres previously closed to them; they could enjoy a masculine range of sexual and professional experiences. But the possession of quantitatively more experience did not lead to picaresque or even naturalistic fiction. Instead women writers found the world sexually polarized in psychological terms. They had fought to have a share in male knowledge; getting it, they decided that there were other ways of knowing. And by "other" they meant "better"; the tone of the female aesthetic usually wavered between the defiant and the superior.[10]

The "better" way of knowing had to do with self-discovery, "a turning inward freed from some of the dependency of opposition." Virginia Woolf was the pioneer in this mode which has dominated the creative landscape for women writers since, a model who urged the woman novelist to be "subjective, and yet to transcend her femaleness, to write exquisitely about inner space and leave the big messy brawling novels to men."[11]

Showalter reminds us that "there is clearly a difference between books that happen to have been written by women, and a 'female literature' which purposefully and collectively concerns itself with the articulation of women's experience, and which guides itself 'by its own impulses' to autonomous self-expression."[12] But some generalizations about the differences between novels by men and novels by women can be made. For one thing, novels by women have a vision of social justice for peoples of other races, sects, and class. Ellen Moers in her splendid book *Literary Women* speaks of women authors in the "epic age"—one age of participation in society from the Brontës to Virginia Woolf—as having one major characteristic: "an involvement in social causes, including those of women like themselves, but also of the working classes, male and female, and of slaves."[13] She finds close connections between feminism and radicalism and shows a strong women's subculture formed internationally through letters and visits among these women authors.

Textbooks organizing fiction around images of women highlight how different the views of male writers are from those of females. Mary Anne Ferguson's *Images of Women in Literature,* for example, shows how many male writers, from Chekhov through James to Mailer, persist in seeing women in negative terms as stereotypes: "the submissive wife," "mother-angel or 'Mom'," "the bitch," "the seductress-goddess," "the sex object." Women writers like Dorothy Parker and Doris Lessing and Tillie Olsen more often see women in terms of their capacities for work, thought, and social action.

Persistent female conflicts about their identity and their position in society are shown in the analysis of contemporary novels by women undertaken by Patricia Spacks in *Contemporary Women Novelists*. For example, in *Delta Wedding* Eudora Welty portrays the women of the Mississippi Delta in the 1920s as unquestioning of their dependence in spite of the fact that the intricate social structure is superficially controlled by females. No one challenges the notion that "life consists of having babies, taking care of one's men, demonstrating hospitality, exchanging gifts, dancing, playing the piano, cooking or arranging that cooking be done."[14] By contrast, Doris Lessing persistently portrays women who constantly seek independence. Martha Quest rebels against her mother's way of life and the expectations of her society. Anna Wulf in *The Golden Notebook*, the feminist classic of the twentieth century, strives to achieve the status of "free woman" and the goal of self-knowledge. The middle-aged protagonist of *The Summer before the Dark* struggles painfully toward the knowledge of how to defy others and how to become invisible when male attentions are unwanted.

Oppression of Women in Fiction about Blacks, the Aged, and Lesbians

The search for identity and casting off of oppression are especially striking in fiction about black women, old women, and lesbians. The mirror to reality often shows violence and defeat in novels about black women: Lutie in Ann Petry's *The Street* finally commits suicide as her only response to a squalid life of poverty. Sula, the eponymous heroine of Toni Morrison's classic novel, escapes from a girlhood that was blighted by the horrors of seeing her own mother burn to death and causing the drowning of a young boy whom she tossed playfully into the river. When she returns from college looking like a movie star, the townspeople in the Bottoms curse her as a witch and ostracize her so that she dies a lingering death quite alone. One inspiring part of this novel, however, is the adolescent bonding between Sula and Nel, which gives them protection from the threatening world. Survival becomes a dominant motif as Alice Walker tells us in describing her woman-centered fiction: "I am preoccupied with the spiritual survival, the survival whole of my people. But beyond that, I am committed to exploring the oppressions, the insanities, the loyalties, and the triumphs of black women."[15] But sheer physical struggles for survival may minimize the chance for chance, as Barbara Smith asserts:

> Unable to depend on fathers, brothers, or husbands to run interference between them and the outside world, black women have been responsible for creating their own lives. It should always be kept in mind, however, that this "indepen-

dence" is double-edged. It can either contribute to the building of remarkable strength in Black women or it might never allow a woman to get beyond the most bitter struggle for material survival.[16]

The plight of the aged woman is captured by Tillie Olsen in "Tell Me a Riddle." As the grandmother's vitality recedes, with the progression of terminal cancer, she reluctantly visits each of her children and reconsiders the choices of a lifetime, having denied herself the literature and culture she craved, for the demands of family and unfeeling husband. She retreats into the memorized poetry of her girlhood as enduring solace for the hardships of the early years and the pain of her dying. Independence of mind increasingly compensates for physical disability and ultimate total dependency. While nursing her, her granddaughter captures the essence of her spiritual beauty and catches the message early enough to resist a life of self-abnegation and regret.

Lesbians form another group who have oppression in common with blacks, the poor, and the aged. In *The Lesbian Image* (1975) Jane Rule does a skillful job of marshaling historical background combined with literary examples to demonstrate the struggle for freedom for women who love women. She takes, chapter by chapter, the literary life of lesbians and bisexuals over two centuries, including Virginia Woolf, Vita Sackville-West, Gertrude Stein, Elizabeth Bowen, Edith Wharton, and May Sarton. The lesbian life is shown by two representative fictional portrayals: one, *Patience and Sarah,* by Isabel Miller, a tale of persecution and courage in pioneer days, and the other, *Rubyfruit Jungle,* by Rita Mae Brown, a rollicking modern adventure of lesbian life. Many recent novels, such as Lisa Alther's *Kinflicks* (1976) and Erica Jong's *How To Save Your Own Life* (1976), include chapters recounting a lesbian affair as part of the discovery of sexual identity or as part of the breaking away from a bad marriage. One of the major novels of this decade, *Small Changes* (1973), by Marge Piercy, shows a wide spectrum of possible life-styles including marriage, a commune, a women's theater company, promiscuous sex, and celibacy by choice, and in the end shows a lesbian relationship as the most egalitarian and fulfilling. The two women alternately viewed in the book exemplify extremes on the dependence/independence continuum and pass each other in moving to the opposite extreme.

Women's Identity in Recent Novels

A study of fifty novels by American women published between 1972 and 1976 led Laura Adams to conclude that modern women protagonists "lack the imagination to create stronger, more independent alter egos and the power to develop into them." Expecting to find that the feminist movement has shaped fictive characters who can be role models, regretfully Adams reports: "the more I read the more I am plunged back into that pre-feminist women's world of despair and madness, restrictions and stereotypes."[17] Adams put these very recent books by women into three categories: (1) growing up female, (2) the suffering single, and (3) the mad and/or miserable wife.

Novels of the growing-up-female genre involve initiation into womanhood, usually sexual in nature, through stages from menstruation, to dating, to necking, to petting above and then below the waist, to going-all-the-way. Having succumbed, girls feel helpless to refuse sex, with an extreme case being Sasha Davis in *Memoirs of an Ex-Prom Queen*. After being deflowered at fifteen in 1945 on the night of her coronation, she accepts her role as sex object and by age twenty-six has had twenty-five lovers. All the girls find more guilt than pleasure in sex but realize it is a source of power. Five of the young women in the growing-up novels seduce a professor in their desire for control over the authoritarian, the father, figure. As these women make their lives focus on a man or men they lose touch with the community of women. Few have more than one woman friend, usually gained in college, and all see their mothers as natural enemies.

The second group of novels, centering on the suffering single, offers even less in terms of self-definition, solidarity among women, and an expanding range of roles. The losers, who have avoided matrimony and motherhood, blame themselves instead of society. Gail Parent's *Sheila Levine Is Dead and Living in New York* (1972) takes a comic look at the suffering single. Like several other protagonists of this type, Sheila Levine is fat, very Jewish, and well-educated, she has an abortion, and she has been in analysis. After nine years of waiting to become Mrs. Prince Charming, Sheila decides on suicide, only to find this is a great turn-on for one of her male hangers-on, who enthusiastically joins in arranging the process. She botches this too and must settle for a new job and apartment with the same frayed self-image.

The Odd Woman (1974) by Gail Godwin comes closest of the suffering-single books to showing growth in self-definition and self-worth. Jane Godwin at thirty-two has a Ph.D. from Columbia and is willing to chuck her career to go to England with her married lover on his Guggenheim. When he lets her know he only wants her for sex, she walks out on him, stands up to a shrewish friend from college, and gains a sense of identity from her family.

Forty of the fifty novels deal with the mad and/or miserable wife, as described by Adams:

Her marriage is moribund and since she has no identity apart from that as wife and mother she is in the throes of an identity crisis. Precipitated by her husband's or her own infidelity, her pregnancy, a death in the family or her own boredom, this crisis may have one or more of these outcomes: (1) having taken a lover, she realizes that by contrast her husband isn't so bad after all and decides to put up with him; (2) abandoned by her lover and husband, she is faced with reconstructing her life, which we never get to see acted out; (3) she goes into analysis and is made worse because her psychiatrist wishes to see her conform to what is destroying her; (4) if pregnant, she aborts if she is ending the marriage or keeps it and reconciles with her husband; (5) she goes back to school or gets a job, but this is rarely a positive experience.[18]

Erica Jong's *Fear of Flying* (1973) is one of the livelier and sexier versions of this genre. After a cross-country fling with a psychiatrist who dumps her in Paris when the time comes for him to rejoin his family, Isadora has a crisis and panic ending in a dialogue with herself which concludes: "If no man loves me I have no identity." In Jong's sequel, *How To Save Your Own Life,* Isadora dissolves her marriage with recriminations for her husband's methodical dullness and deceptions in not admitting his love affairs while giving her loads of guilt about hers. She has an exotic lesbian affair with a married friend but then, *à la* Snow White, is awakened from her torpor by the kiss of a young blond god. Fantasy fades into endless bliss in the glass villa by the California seacoast.

Lisa Alther's *Kinflicks* is the funniest and most substantial of all these novels. Ginny Babcock moves through transformations from cheerleader, who smooches the football hero in the trunk of the car, to highbrow college intellectual, to radical lesbian, to rural commune leader, to wife of a snowmobile salesman. A romp through extraordinary territory, the novel ends in an unlikely mystical union with a meditating draft evader before a heartrending reconciliation with her dying mother.

Very few of the fifty novels show any feminist consciousness, partly because they tell of the authors' lives growing up in the 1940s and 1950s. A few women writers, however, are postulating new myths for our future. Some of these come in the androgynous visions of science fiction writers like Ursula LeGuin in *Left Hand of Darkness* and Joanna Russ in *The Female Man.* In *Call Me Ishtar* (1973) Rhoda Lerman brings back to earth in human form the ancient goddess Ishtar, Mother/Harlot/Maiden, Wife, Queen of Heaven, Angel of Death, Whore of Babylon, and Mother of the Gods. Ishtar works to encourage modern women to be as she was, incorporating the best of both male and female principles: "I am God and a Woman and so are all of you."

Marge Piercy's *Woman on the Edge of Time* (1976) displays a utopia of a hundred years from now to which a poor mental patient named Connie Ramos can escape through her sensitivity to mind projection. There Luciente shows Connie what life can be like when sex-role stereotypes disappear, and men and women, young and old, can love one another, rear test-tube babies together in threesomes, develop maximum artistic potential together, and build a true community of love.

We have seen how fiction reveals modes of coping with reality, whether the poverty of the Black ghetto or the oppression of lesbians or the stereotypes of marriage and motherhood. Novels also relieve the loneliness of those oppressed and develop a sense of shared knowledge. By rejecting the distorting mirrors of male writers and looking to the all-too-revealing mirrors and probing searchlights focused by contemporary women writers, women of twentieth-century America may find new visions for themselves.

POETRY BY WOMEN

Poetry as Self-Exploration

Poetry, in contrast with the more conservative drama and fiction, is consistently on the edge of change in women's consciousness, possibly because poetry is at many points a private voice, a hidden space in which the author can be absolutely honest about personal emotion. The act of writing personal poetry often yields information from the unconscious which, by being objectified, can be dealt with. Adrienne Rich speaks of poetry as asbestos gloves: "It allowed me to handle materials I couldn't pick up barehanded." She goes on to explain: "Instead of poems about experiences I am getting poems that *are* experiences, that contribute to my knowledge and my emotional life even while they reflect and assimilate it."[19]

This act of discovery of identity on the part of the poet is communicated to the reader in such power that reverberations from the id respond to the newness of the material. If the poet has done her work well, the will to change on the part of the growing woman poet is transmitted to the reader. Thus very personal poems may become the most public and political kind if the woman reading reacts with growth to the woman writing.

Women have not always written poems of self-discovery, and not all women poets today break out of the objective subject matter and the distancing style. Gertrude Stein and Marianne Moore come to mind as women artists, accepted by the male publishing establishment, who wrote no personal poetry but preferred the objective mode. Even when Marianne Moore writes a poem entitled "Marriage," she loads it with barbed insults to women from Bartlett's. Truth emerges as counterpoint to the hurtful myths, but the voice is always depersonalized.

Most of the poetry of Elizabeth Barrett Browning was objective descriptions and narratives, and this kind of poetry made her more famous than Robert when they met. When their romantic escape and deep love was put into personal poetry in the *Sonnets from the Portuguese,* she created for women what Florence Howe calls "one of the most devastating traditions we have had to live with; the lovesick woman, prostrate before her heroic, accomplished love."[20] In her later life she did write one feminist masterpiece, *Aurora Leigh,* which shows a strong woman negotiating an equalitarian marriage to allow her freedom to develop her own potential.

Emily Dickinson revolutionized poetry by her flashing personal poems about death and love and self-discovery. Buried in a dresser drawer until after her death, they revealed a genius at self-exploration. Muriel Rukeyser is typical of the women poets of the early twentieth century who expressed their womanhood in ways that exhibited their differences from men. In "Kathe Kollwitz" she asks: "What would happen if one woman told the truth about her life? / The world would split open." Part of the truth revealed in the letters and diaries of Kathe Kollwitz, which Rukeyser uses in this poem, is her sense that the artist must utilize both male and female portions of her personality: The artistic mind must be bisexual. Certainly the full range of emotional and creative responses should become more accessible to both men and women. Many women poets see this as happening as a result of probing their feelings about their uniquely female functions. For example, in "The Poem as Mask" Rukeyser uses a cesarean section as a metaphor of the stripping away of masks in unifying her self-image around her womanliness, concluding, "the fragments join in me with their own music." Throughout her long life as a poet we see Rukeyser plunging toward the center of self to bring up truths to help other women.

Let there be no mistake. Women are not the only poets probing for inner truth. Whitman, Pasternak, Lowell, all sounded the depths of their being for personal truths. But women poets much more often than men grapple with their feelings as Edna St. Vincent Millay does in "Renascence," recreating the pain of death and the emergence, in rebirth, to full womanhood. Marianne Moore calls what we are after "the raw material of poetry in / all its rawness" and sees it as genuine.

Many contemporary American women poets have progressed through the inhibition of self-revelation described by Jong:

It was as though I disdained myself, felt I had no right to have a self. . . . Once I confessed to my vulnerability, I was able to explore it, and from that everything followed. I stopped writing about ruins and nightingales. I was able to make poetry out of the everyday activities of my life: peeling onions, a trip to the gynecologist, a student demonstration, my own midnight terrors and dreams— all the things I would have previously dismissed as trivial. Because of my own history, I think women poets have to insist on their right to write like women.[21]

Poetry Moving from Anger to Oppression to Solidarity among Women

Let us turn now to some of the self-images expressed by contemporary American women poets who have suffered through their quest for self-knowledge and have emerged with battle scars and some answers. My recent analysis of a hundred volumes of poetry by contemporary American women poets showed that the personal poetry written in the last fifteen years replicates the stages of the women's movement in relationship to men. Simply put, the five stages are: (1) resentment in which bitterness is turned inward and made self-punishing, (2) anger expressed outwardly and directed appropriately toward evils in society, (3) revolution to alter the oppressive structures, (4) self-acceptance, and (5) mutuality.

Resentment was most often expressed toward the life-denying roles into which some males thrust women. Marge Piercy's "The Friend" concludes:

> I love you, I said.
> that's very nice, he said
> I like to be loved,
> that makes me happy.
> Have you cut off your hands yet?

The role of housewife is similarly described as deadening, as in Lynn Strongin's "Van Gogh" in which she speaks of "our fate / which we must find less bitter than it seems." As the housewife grows middle-aged, resignation replaces resentment.

Sometimes the resentment builds against one's own family as well as against chauvinists. The ultimate taboos, hating one's mother and hating one's children, spring forth in many poems of women writing today. The wrangling rattles one's teeth in Shirley Kaufman's "Mothers, Daughters":

> She's cruel,
> as if my private meanness
> found a way to punish us.
> We gnaw at each other's
> skulls.

And those who decide for whatever reason that they cannot have another child must suffer too with Gwendolyn Brooks in "The Mother." As she writes:

> Abortions will not let you forget.
> You remember the children you got
> that you did not get.

Too often the resentments are turned inward to infect the woman with self-hatred. The lowest point of this period of resentment comes when self-loathing permeates every day's most menial chore, as Anne Halley moans in "Dear God, the Day Is Gray":

> I, walking here,
> still loathe the labors I would love
> and hate the self I cannot move.

Relief from this kind of depressing self-image came in a period of focusing the anger out onto appropriate subjects. Adrienne Rich and other radical feminists label this phase "the refusal of the self-destructiveness of male-dominated society." Rich goes on: "Both the victimization and the anger experienced by women are real, and have real sources, everywhere in the environment, built into society. They must go on being tapped and explored by poets, among others. We can neither deny them, nor can we rest there. They are our birthpains, and we are bearing ourselves."[22]

In "A Just Anger" Marge Piercy affirms the advantage to directing anger outward when she speaks of a good anger acted upon as "beautiful as lightning / and swift with power." The violence of male-created war is attacked by Denise Levertov through expressions of hatred felt toward the perpetrators of brutality and then through poignant descriptions of the victims, such as the mother who lost an arm and "cannot hold her baby and caress it at the same time / ever again." Levertov and Rukeyser went to Vietnam to work for peace. Piercy and many others of the younger poets fought for peace in the movement at home.

In "Rape" Adrienne Rich expresses healthy anger at the biases of police who treat victims of rape as provocateurs. Bigotry of all kinds caught the white heat of the poets' anger in these years of learning to express hostility outward. As Judy Grahn puts it: "It's the question of male domination that makes everybody angry." This anger against controlling males led to the women's revolution, the bonding together of women. While the women's revolution brought political action against the oppression that women felt in many areas, the women achieved a sense of solidarity. The anger and the solidarity are expressed by Robin Morgan in "Monster" when she lists the outrages like rape and beatings and burnings and then rages before the invocation:

> I want a women's revolution like a lover.
> I lust for it, I want so much this freedom,
> this end to struggle and fear and lies.[23]

The poets express with great tenderness the joy of bonding with other women, healing the alienation and loneliness, and gradually finding self-acceptance. As Adrienne Rich phrases it in "Phantasia for Elvira Shatayev":

> We will not live
> to settle for less
> We have dreamed of this
> all of our lives.

The conclusion to Marge Piercy's poem on divorce titled "She Leaves" is the challenge given to women who have been subordinate too long:

> You have loved him as his mother always told him
> he deserved to be loved.
> Now love yourself.

The result of self-acceptance and self-love is the ability to reach out to men in healing and mutuality. As a former revolutionary, Piercy speaks in "Councils" about ground rules for hearing one another:

♀ Thus saying what we feel and what we want,
   what we fear for ourselves and each other
   into the dark, perhaps we could begin
   to begin to listen.

♀ Perhaps we should start by speaking softly.
   The women must learn to dare to speak.

♂ The men must bother to listen.

Rich sees the need for men to grow and change but rejects the idea that women must sacrifice their own growth to nurture men:

Just as woman is becoming her own midwife, creating herself anew, so man will have to learn to gestate and give birth to his own subjectivity—something he has frequently wanted woman to do for him. We can go on trying to talk to each other, we can sometimes help each other, poetry and fiction can show us what the other is going through; but women can no longer be primarily mothers and muses for men; we have our own work cut out for us.[24]

In her introduction to *Rising Tides,* Anais Nin summarizes succinctly the value that poetry by women can have for other women: "The skillful, the clarified expression of our joys and sorrows, our angers and rebellions, makes them sharable and therefore less destructive. Words as exorcism of pain, indispensable to communion, the opposite of war."[25]

This swift excursion through literature convinces us of the need for community and commune among women against the destructive stereotypes that society and male writers have constructed. From the ancient classical drama, which showed women as either idealized for being nourishing mothers or condemned as devouring witches, to the most recent novels, which demand stereotyped motherhood, literature has been shown to be an accurate mirror of the way society views women. Happily, drama and fiction and poetry have the other dimension of suggesting new potentialities both for coping with the real world and moving toward a better world. The progression in this chapter has been from the more depressing mirrors to the more hopeful searchlights. Emphasis has been less on the societal changes that literature by women caused, such as the public outcry against slavery after Harriet Beecher Stowe's *Uncle Tom's Cabin* was published, and more on the ability of literature to reflect reality and to inspire more positive roles for women. By dealing with the literature from the most ancient drama, to the fairly recent novels, to the most contemporary poetry, we have been able to chronicle the past and look with hope toward the future.

NOTES

1. Harriet Kriegel, ed., *Women in Drama: An Anthology* (New York: Mentor Basic Books, Inc., 1975), p. xx.
2. Ibid., p. xxi.
3. Ibid., p. xxii.

4. Ibid., p. xxxi.

5. Clare Boothe, *The Women,* in *Plays by and about Women,* ed. Victoria Sullivan and James Hatch (New York: Vintage Books, 1974), p. x.

6. Maureen Duffy, *Rites,* in Sullivan and Hatch, *Plays by and about Women,* p. 373.

7. Sullivan and Hatch, *Plays by and about Women,* p. xiv.

8. Alice Childress, *Wine in the Wilderness,* in Sullivan and Hatch, *Plays by and about Women,* p. 420.

9. Ibid., p. 421.

10. Elaine Showalter, *A Literature of Their Own* (Princeton, N.J.: Princeton University Press, 1977), p. 257.

11. Ibid., p. 265.

12. Ibid., p. 4.

13. Ellen Moers, *Literary Women: The Great Writers* (Garden City, N.Y.: Doubleday, 1976), p. xiii.

14. Patricia Spacks, *Contemporary Women Novelists* (Englewood Cliffs, N.J.: Prentice-Hall, 1977), p. 10.

15. Alice Walker in *Interviews with Black Writers,* ed. John O'Brien (New York: 1973), p. 192.

16. Barbara Smith, "Doing Research on Black American Women," *Radical Teacher* 3 (1976): 25.

17. "The Way We Are Now: New Novels by Women" (Paper presented at MMLA, 1975), p. 1.

18. Ibid., p. 5.

19. Quoted in *The Norton Introduction to Literature: Poetry,* ed. J. Paul Hunter (New York: 1973), p. 482.

20. "Feminism and the Study of Literature," *Radical Teacher* 3 (1976): 10.

21. Erica Jong, "The Artist as Housewife/The Housewife as Artist," *Here Comes and Other Poems* (New York: New American Library, 1975), p. 261.

22. "When We Dead Awaken: Writing as Re-Vision," in Hunter, *Norton Introduction to Literature* p. 510.

23. "Monster," in *Monster* (New York: Random House, 1972), p. 82.

24. Rich, "When We Dead Awaken," p. 511.

25. *Rising Tides,* ed. Laura Chester and Sharon Barba (New York: Pocket Books, 1973), p. xxxi.

REVIEW QUESTIONS

1. Define *archetypes* and give examples for the Good Mother and the Devouring Mother from ancient Greek tragedy.

2. Describe how the women in Shakespeare's plays differed according to whether the play was written during or after the reign of Queen Elizabeth.

3. Contrast the women characters in plays by Henrik Ibsen and August Strindberg.

4. Describe one play by a woman that has negative stereotypes of women and one that has positive images.

5. Give an example of each of these categories of modern novels by women: growing up female, the suffering single, and the mad and miserable wife.

6. Contrast a novel by a male author that you have studied in school with one of the recent novels by women described in this chapter in terms of the presentation of women characters.

7. Describe the five stages of poetic expression as they parallel stages in the women's liberation movement.

8. Discuss the alternatives to the stereotypic roles for women, given by dramas, novels, and poetry, which point toward the future for women.
9. Are new possibilities for women more often shown in drama, poetry, or fiction?
10. Which contemporary novels that you have read stress the differences between males and females, and which show their roles and expectations to be more alike than in past years?
11. Think of five women characters in plays or novels who have careers outside the home and discuss their relative ego strength compared with that of five who are homemakers.
12. Contrast the portrayals of women in TV commercials with those of women in plays or novels you have read.
13. Compare the heroines of recent movies you have seen with the heroines of plays and novels discussed in this chapter.
14. In what ways are the women of minority races or low economic status portrayed in the fiction, poetry, drama you have read?
15. Contrast the novels which show the author's view of the way a woman really lives her life with novels in which new visions for a better world are expressed.

SELECTED READINGS

FOR THE TEACHER

Ellmann, Mary. *Thinking about Women.* New York: Harcourt Brace Jovanovich, 1968.

This lively, eclectic book deals with stereotypes about women and their impact on women and on society.

Heilbrun, Carolyn. *Towards a Recognition of Androgyny.* New York: Harper & Row, 1973.

Using literary examples from nineteenth- and twentieth-century novels and plays, Professor Heilbrun shows the movement toward nonstereotypic behavior on the part of both men and women. This is a major theoretical work tracing a theme through literature.

Millett, Kate. *Sexual Politics.* Garden City, N.Y.: Doubleday, 1970.

This famous and controversial book gives a history of the women's movement in terms of literary images, focusing on the negative images portrayed in Norman Mailer, D. H. Lawrence, and Jean Genet.

Moers, Ellen. *Literary Women: The Great Writers.* Garden City, N.Y.: Doubleday, 1976.

These very insightful essays weave the connections among women writers of the past and present, showing dominant themes and major influences.

Rule, Jane. *Lesbian Images.* Garden City, N.Y.: Doubleday, 1975.

Chapters on twelve novelists and their lesbian characters and/or actions follow a very comprehensive survey of lesbian attitudes and literature.

Showalter, Elaine. "Literary Criticism." *Signs* 1, no. 2 (Winter 1975): 435–460.

This review article summarizes the major critical themes in literature by women and describes the best of the original criticism written in the last five years.

Showalter, Elaine. *A Literature of Their Own: British Women Novelists from Brontë to Lessing.* Princeton, N.J.: Princeton University Press, 1977.

These brilliant essays tell of the growth and changes in the writings of major women novelists of Britain.

Spacks, Patricia, ed. *Contemporary Women Novelists.* Englewood Cliffs, N.J.: Prentice-Hall, 1977.

Spacks introduces critical essays on recent women novelists written by a dozen eminent critics.

Washington, Mary Helen, ed. *Black-Eyed Susans.* Garden City, N.Y.: Doubleday, Anchor Books, 1975.

Short stories written by Black women authors to describe the spectrum of contemporary life-styles and attitudes. Edited and introduced with insight by the Director of Afro-American Studies at the University of Detroit.

Williams, Ora. *American Black Women in the Arts and Social Sciences.* New York: Scarecrow Press, 1973.

This bibliography gives sources where the professor can find the most recent critical writings on work by black women artists.

FOR STUDENTS

Drama:

Kriegel, Harriet, ed. *Women in Drama: An Anthology.* New York: New American Library, 1975.

This anthology includes two Greek plays, examples from Ibsen, Strindberg, and Shaw, and two plays by modern women. The introduction is particularly strong.

Sullivan, Victoria, and James Hatch, eds. *Plays by and about Women.* New York: Vintage Books, 1974.

This collection of eight plays, including *The Children's Hour, The Women,* and *Wine in the Wilderness,* gives a good overview of modern theater by women.

Fiction:

Alther, Lisa. *Kinflicks.* New York: Knopf, 1976.

The larger-than-life story of a Florida girl who grows through hilarious stages to the point at which she can break from those who have unreasonable expectations of her, and venture on a life of her own.

Eliot, George. *Middlemarch.* New York: Signet Books, 1964.

A classic of Victorian days showing the escape of Dorothea Brooke from a loveless marriage and the new life she builds for herself.

Lessing, Doris. *The Summer before the Dark.* New York: Knopf, 1973.

A middle-aged woman finds all her children gone and shapes a career for herself in which she finds autonomy and a lover but the same function: taking care.

Piercy, Marge. *Woman on the Edge of Time.* New York: Knopf, 1976.

A futuristic kingdom without sex-role stereotyping is contrasted with the life of a poor inmate of a mental hospital.

Poetry:

Chester, Laura, and Sharon Barba, eds. *Rising Tides: Twentieth Century American Women Poets.* New York: Pocket Books, 1973.

This collection stresses the poetry about women and their feelings and includes photographs and life histories of each of the women poets.

Howe, Florence, and Ellen Bass, eds. *No More Masks!: An Anthology of Poems by Women.* Garden City, N.Y.: Doubleday, Anchor Books, 1973.

This collection stresses the modern and revolutionary poems of younger poets classified by subject matter. The introduction by Florence Howe is superb.

Iverson, Lucille, and Kathryn Ruby, eds. *We Become New: Poems by Contemporary American Women.* New York: Bantam, 1975.

Rich, Adrienne. *Poems: Selected and New, 1950–1974.* New York: Norton, 1975.

The poet's selection from eight previous volumes amounts to a comprehensive and progressively more self-revealing collection.

CHAPTER 4

Stereotypes of Men and Women in the American Culture

Marie Richmond-Abbott

We are all aware that there are stereotypes of men and women in the American culture. From childhood we have consistently heard that men are —or should be—brave, strong, logical, and competitive, while women are— or should be—kind, gentle, nurturant, and supportive. We may be less aware of why we have these particular stereotypes for each sex. It is the purpose of this chapter to show that the stereotypes of male and female behavior, which have developed through a blend of the cross-cultural tradition influencing us and our country's own unique heritage, are maintained through our various formal and informal institutions. We will see that one of the reasons that the stereotypes persist is that our cultural institutions, such as art, popular music, and literature, bombard our eyes and ears with the traditional beliefs about the characteristics and behavior of women.

We want to examine the fact that the stereotypic traits prescribed for men are those associated with positive regard and success in our culture, while those for women may be psychologically damaging and will not allow them the same chances for achievement and success. We will look at how the stereotypes for women are similar to those of minority groups and how the influence of these feminine stereotypes is socially dysfunctional and aids discrimination. We will see that women, themselves, accept these stereotypes and continue to act in ways that perpetuate them.

Finally we will suggest some methods for combating these all-pervasive beliefs. We will show how women's growing sense of identity and unity, combined with their growing participation in society, are powerful forces leading toward change. With this background, let us look at the American value system and the stereotypes of men and women that have emerged from it.

Our culture is to an extreme degree oriented to change and to the future. Its value system and the prescriptions for success emphasize practicality, achievement, individualism, and self-sufficiency. The ideal man is one who succeeds on his own merit, preferably by doing something very practical, and his success is measured in riches ("as good as gold"). According to the democratic ideal, any man can achieve this success by hard effort, no matter what his background, and we have phrases to demonstrate this: "from rags to riches," "from the log cabin to the White House," "he pulled himself up by his own boot straps." As success is measured in practical and material terms, the person who is sensitive, who is contemplative, who nurtures or cares for others, does not have a rewarding or rewarded place in our society.

The French writer de Tocqueville visited our country in 1831 and described American men in terms of the prevailing value system. He pointed out, however, that these values did not apply to women. Although the cultural values were supposed to apply to everyone, in reality women were expected to pursue very different paths. Rather than being ambitious and competitive, they were supposed to be cooperative and supportive. Strength, individualism, and self-sufficiency were not particularly valued in women, except on the frontier and in rural environments. The urban and genteel woman was supposed to be rather delicate; she probably fainted easily and was dependent on her husband and family. She was supposed to be oriented toward people rather than things, and her prime concerns in life were her husband and her children. She was also supposed to be sensitive and nurturant and to uphold the religious and moral tenets of society. De Tocqueville noted that while women did not have a great deal of freedom in any realm of life at this time, they were particularly held in bondage by marriage with its domestic duties and child care. He pointed out, however, that women's roles were valued and women were not considered by the culture to be inherently inferior as were slaves.[1]

The traits associated with males then and now are those associated with success in the American culture. Conversely, the traits expected of the American female in both the past and present are those that frequently contradict the traits needed for success. An American female is supposed to achieve her success not from "doing" (achieving and being successful at everything from a job to sexual relations) but by "being," in particular by bearing children and raising them. She can simply exist and maintain the life-support system. While to achieve and move forward the impatient male pushes onward with practical and logical scientific advance, the woman is supposed to be the cultural guardian of rather stagnant morality, ethics, and tradition. While he is concerned with the economic progress of that culture, she is to be the patron of the arts and smooth away the rough edges of a developing culture. Ironically, her contemporary role of being the support for moral, religious, and cultural tradition puts her in the position of supporting the very institutions that are most likely to keep her in her place. She is expected to teach her children that Eve sprang from Adam's rib and that the Apostle Paul stated that "women should bow in all submission before their husbands."[2] Since literature and art have also been largely dominated by men and reflect negative stereotypes of women, she may work hard to raise money for art museums or libraries where there will be paintings and books that show her as an evil temptress, a shrew-mother, vain and foolish, and the like.

She is also the one to care for people and keep social relationships active, while the male is freed to achieve economic and political goals. Therefore she teaches the children, is a social worker to the poor, and nurses the soldiers in time of war. Jessie Bernard likens the American woman's role to that of an underdeveloped nation. A woman funnels natural resources—that is, emotional support and supportive services such as cooking, housecleaning, and child care—to the developed nation, that is, the male, who is concerned with economic achievement. In return she gets some degree of economic support and protection, much as an underdeveloped nation might get, but she does not have an equal voice in decision making and, contrary to de Tocqueville's impression, is probably viewed as somewhat inferior.[3]

Thus we see that the American woman is not expected to develop or utilize the same traits as men in the culture. She is restricted to a shadow set of values which, if followed, will not gain her success in terms of the dominant culture values. The person who is submissive and dependent and puts loyalty to the group above self-interest is unlikely to have success in terms of individual achievement.

Some of the nonfunctional traits that are part of the American stereotype of proper female behavior are uniquely North American in origin, but others originated in institutions we share with other cultures. As we have seen, institutions have developed in many cultures that have exalted certain male traits and activities while downplaying those of females. Some of this institutional development arose from the fear of women's childbearing capacity and other sexual functions. Valuing of such male qualities as strength and aggressiveness probably also came about because males dominated the public economic sphere, while women did not participate fully in society and were occupied with childbearing and childrearing at home. Cultures with economies based largely on the use of brute physical force or on the strength and aggressiveness needed in military activities especially have valued male traits above female ones.[4]

As men in the public sphere dominated the sources of knowledge and also the developing value systems, it was no coincidence that their work reaffirmed the importance of male characteristics and dominance. Thus scientists portrayed women as naturally less intelligent, and more emotionally unstable, than men. In like fashion, the religious value system came to deemphasize the sexual, fertile qualities of women that had once been valued.

Fertility goddesses gave way to male deities, and women were assigned lower status at the same time that their frightening sexual nature was diluted with cautions to be chaste and pure, although maternal like the Madonna.[5]

Thus many of the traits ascribed to women were outgrowths of a long western cultural tradition and not just the products of the North American heritage. However, the heritage of glorifying such male traits as strength, dominance, and competitiveness was affirmed and strengthened in the United States. As indicated in our discussion of the role of American women, women's qualities and activities were primarily seen to form a supportive system that allowed the dominant males to channel their energy and creativity into a flourishing economic culture. Women were to take care of the daily necessities—the raising of children, the cleaning of houses and clothes, the preparation of food, and the maintenance of social life—while men were freed to write the symphonies, paint the pictures, and run the country.

SOCIETY'S ACCEPTANCE OF LIMITING, DYSFUNCTIONAL TRAITS

Treatment of Women as a "Minority" Group

How has society (and particularly women in the society) been persuaded to accept a role for women defined by limiting and dysfunctional traits and behavior? For women to accept the shadow set of values while men enjoy the sunshine of reward for traits that lead to success, society has had to convince its members that this separate-but-not-equal status is right and proper. To do so, it has used much the same rationale used for other discriminated-against groups. One excuse for keeping women in a submissive or dependent status is that they possess the same traits as such minority groups. Thus women are often said to be biologically inferior, weaker, less intelligent, as well as fearful and frivolous. They supposedly are not smart enough to handle money well or be good drivers, and they are too emotional to hold positions of decision-making power. Helen Hacker has made the point that not only are women seen and treated as a minority group, but they actually have caste status (a status inherited by reason of birth which one is not supposed to change) rather than class status (one that allows the individual possessed of sufficient ability to move upward without discrimination). This caste status is further strengthened by identifiable physical attributes similar to the identifiable skin color of Blacks, which make the target of prejudice easy to identify and discriminate against.

In the economic area, Hacker continues, the treatment of women is similar to that of minority groups. They are confined to monotonous work under the supervision of men and are treated unequally in regard to pay, promotion, and responsibility. Women's colleges are frequently inferior to men's (at least in financial resources), and in coeducational schools women have tradition-ally been restricted from participating in many sports and other activities. Women have less freedom in the social and sexual spheres, and as citizens, they may even be barred from jury service or public office.[6]

Restrictions Related to Women's Sexual "Nature"

Women are also restricted, as they have been historically, by reference to their sexuality. We have seen that in many countries and periods women's sexuality has been viewed in ambivalent ways. They are either considered the good girl (Madonna) or the bad girl (Eve). In our society the stereotypes of both the good girl and the bad girl are used to restrict women. Usually the ideals of behavior are separated. Sometimes, however, they are combined, and American women are asked to walk an impossible tightrope between the two kinds of behavior. If they fall off either side of the tightrope, they lose.

If young girls are to be considered sexual and feminine, they must develop much like a Barbie doll: slim, but big-breasted, sensual; a sex object who adorns herself. This image of the idealized playgirl is difficult to achieve physically, and furthermore, such a girl is frowned upon because she is vain, frivolous, and not really a "nice" girl. Admittedly, sometimes such a playgirl may be tender hearted and have good, nurturing qualities (such as those of the good-hearted prostitute in the movie *Never on Sunday*). However, men usually feel that the playgirl "gets what she asks for" and can be sexually used without much guilt felt on the part of the user. Such a girl is obviously not to be married.

The other half of the sexual myth is the good girl who is moral, pure, chaste, modest, and without much sexual desire. As Victorian books dealing with values phrased it, "Ladies don't move," referring of course to the passive sexual nature of the nice girl.[7] This kind of woman makes a safe and non-threatening wife and a respectable mother for a man's children. He can reassure himself about his masculinity in believing that "he has taught her all she knows," and can happily chase after playgirls knowing that his wife remains faithful at home. Thus a woman is put in a double bind about her sexuality. She is supposed to be attractive and sexy enough to attract and hold a man, but she must be careful to sit with her legs together, not to lean over when wearing a garment with a low neckline, and always to "act like a lady." If she indulges her sexual feelings she is seen as promiscuous (why is this word applied only to women?); if she does not indulge them, she is labeled as frigid. Her own feelings and identity are not really supposed to matter; her image in society is what is important.

Greer Litton Fox has pointed out that the prescription to be a nice girl is the overriding one in our society. The girl who is nice is rewarded with the protection of men and the respectability of marriage. The girl who lapses from nice behavior forfeits these rights and "deserves what she gets." Because there are few external restraints on behavior (such as chaperons) and ladylike behavior is something a girl must produce herself, there is a tremendous emphasis on teaching the value of such behavior. The preoccupation with being a lady is increased, because such a state can never be totally achieved. One must work at being a lady for a lifetime, and any serious lapse from appropriate behavior can disqualify a woman from the rewards of being a nice girl. Thus being nice serves (as do seclusion and chaperonage in other cultures) to limit women's sexuality. It also limits their freedom of movement and access to information and power. Nice girls don't go out at night, do "that" kind of work, travel alone, and the like.[8]

Even in the era of the "sexual revolution" many of these taboos apply. The little license that is allowed is quickly revoked when a women gets married. The girl who ran around in bikinis and braless before marriage may find that her husband has strong ideas about her wearing bras and lengthening her skirts. She must be even more modest if she has become a mother. Jessie Bernard refers to the cultural belief that women should mute or quiet their sexuality after marriage. She points out that this seemingly innocent cultural demand may really be a traumatic change for some women. In proving that they are nice enough to be a wife and mother, they may lose a potent source of their self-esteem and affirmation of their femininity—the approval and attention of men.[9]

Bernard also points out that other changes produced by marriage, which show a woman's linkage with a man, not only define her as sexually ineligible but also make her more dependent in other ways. She loses her name when she marries and becomes Mrs. John Doe; in a sense, she loses a portion of her identity. She may also find that people believe she has lost her ability to think rationally. The political science major may find that others ask her husband's opinion on politics but not hers. She is not expected to know how to handle the family money or take care of the family car, although she may have done both well, before marriage. We can see here that the *femme couverte,* or "woman covered" (smothered, perhaps), by the marriage role, persists today. Woman may lose a great deal of their feeling of identity when they marry.

In addition, the cultural ideal of the married woman's role as stay-at-home housekeeper and child raiser is harmful to women. The isolating, repetitive nature of the housekeeping role may impair a woman's mental health and seriously affect her belief in herself and her ability to achieve.[10] The culture says that the real mother stays home, takes care of her children, and is nurturing, comforting, affectionate, tender, and supportive. She is supposed to provide these qualities, but there is little cultural prescription that she is to receive them in return from either husband or children. There are also an unbelievable number of things at which the housewife is supposed to excel. Not only should she be a good housekeeper, cook, seamstress, gardener, interior decorator, and mother, but she should also be a companion, skilled entertainer, and sexy bedmate. Her own interests and achievements are to be secondary to all of the above. Even if she indulges herself in interests or a job outside the home, she should do well at her mothering and housekeeping tasks. While on the surface it looks as though things have changed and men are doing some of the housework and child care when women work, the man's help can be withdrawn at any time. House and children are still the woman's responsibility. Visitors to a messy house are not likely to say, "John certainly is a messy housekeeper." No matter how the couple has divided their household chores, the final responsibility and blame falls on Mary. In actuality, only about 20 percent of husbands even help with the housework, and this includes the husbands of working wives.[11]

Thus, single or married, the woman finds herself pulled in at least two directions. On the one hand, she is applauded for living under the standards of the female stereotype, which value qualities that suit her well for her role as wife and mother. On the other hand, it is these same qualities that make it difficult for her to achieve in terms of general cultural definitions of success. When excelling by "feminine standards," she is usually not taken seriously in any way (see the section on feminine use of language in Chapter 5) and is often belittled in unfair and untrue terms with words like "illogical," "vain," and "overemotional." If a woman does exhibit male qualities, and even achieves success by using them, she is similarly shunned: "She is a hard, competitive, castrating bitch." Figure 4.1, an excerpt from "How to Tell a Businessman from a Businesswoman," shows the differential perception of men's and women's characteristics in a situation defined as "male."

Thus for American women this shadow set of feminine values is opposed to the dominant cultural values. The alternate values, traits, and behavior considered appropriate for women do keep them from being failures if they cannot participate in society and achieve in the occupational sphere. How-

A businessman is aggressive; a businesswoman is pushy.

A businessman is good on details; she's picky.

He loses temper because he's so involved in his job; she's bitchy.

When he's depressed (or hung over), everyone tiptoes past his office; she's moody, so it must be her time of the month.

He follows through; she doesn't know when to quit.

He's confident; she's conceited.

He stands firm; she's hard.

His judgments are her prejudices.

He is a man of the world; she's been around

He drinks because of the excessive job pressure; she's a lush.

He isn't afraid to say what he thinks; she's power mad.

He's close-mouthed; she's secretive.

He climbed the ladder of success; she slept her way to the top.

He's a stern taskmaster; she's hard to work for.

Figure 4.1.   How To Tell a Businessman from a Businesswoman

ever, all children learn the dominant value system of the culture. One wonders whether women can easily live with the ambiguity of finding it extremely difficult to achieve cultural success if they are feminine and difficult to be feminine if they use the traits needed for cultural success. As more and more women wish to earn their own living or must compete in the male economic and political spheres, this ambiguity and double bind will certainly become even more pronounced.

PERSISTENCE OF THE STEREOTYPES

As we have pointed out, definitions of the female role, and the insistence that women conform to part or all of the feminine stereotype, are constantly being drummed into our eyes and ears. We have seen that the historical, religious, and literary traditions developed and perpetuated feminine stereotypes and still teach them. The stereotypes have also been developed and refined in the popular media and are reinforced by continued presentation.

The Sound of Music: Sexist

Sigmund Spaeth, America's foremost authority on popular music, states that "the popular song has become a revealing index to American life in general. It sums up the ethics, habits, slang, and intimate character of a generation and will tell as much to future students of current civilization as any histories, biographies, or newspapers of the times."[12] One study of over two thousand popular songs found that the vast majority of them (90 percent) were written by men and expressed the male viewpoint about love, sex, and marriage. Many of these popular songs reflect the Eve-Madona image of women.

In the 1880–1910 period, songs that glorified the home and motherhood comprised at least 50 percent of the song titles ("Home Sweet Home," "My Mama Lives in the Sky," "My Mother's Kiss"). Some of the songs warned of the evil that may be expected if the young girl strays from the straight and narrow path. In "The Picture That Is Turned to the Wall" (1891) a mother's heart is "half-broken" and a father is "unforgiving" after a daughter runs away.

By the early 1900s songs such as "You Are Love" and "All the Things You Are" romanticized the idealized qualities of women. "Paper Doll" is another song of this period; although written in 1915, it became popular in the 1940s and 1950s. The lyrics end with the statement: "I'd rather have a Paper Doll I can call my own, than to have a fickle-minded real live girl." In reality, all of these songs portray women as a paper doll. The role stereotypes portrayed for females of the 1940s and 1950s are specifically spelled out in Rodgers and Hammerstein's hit from *Flower Drum Song,* "I Enjoy Being a Girl." This girl is strictly "a female female, with [her] eyelashes all in curl," and "in the arms of a brave and free man" she enjoys being a girl. Another hit by Rodgers and Hammerstein, "A Fellow Needs a Girl," points out the nurturing, supportive function of the female: "A fellow needs a girl to sit by his side at the end of a lonely day," and to hold his hand, comfort him, and support him. We learn from musical comedies of the period that the girl that one marries would "have to be as pink and as sweet as a nursery" (1948) and that "you can't get a man with a gun."

Many of these same themes continued into the 1950s and early 1960s. "Happy to Keep His Dinner Warm," by Frank Loesser, is meant as a satire but could certainly be taken seriously by many as an example of the sacrifices women should make. "One Hundred Easy Ways" (to lose a man), by Betty Comden and Adolf Green (1958), also points out that a woman who is intelligent and capable is not going to keep a man.

In the 1960s and 1970s men seemed to feel the threat of women's increasingly developing their own identities, and more songs dealt with clipping a woman's wings and tying her down. In "Wives and Lovers" (1963) Burt Bacharach and Hal David caution: "Don't you think because there is a ring on your finger you needn't try anymore." Other songs admonish a woman to "stop foolin' around." In a song called the "Wild One" Phil Ochs implies that a woman is threatening; thus he will marry the girl, then "tie her all in leather and then I'm going to whip her."[13] Thus there is an expression of the man's desire to marry but keep the woman forcefully in her place.

Sociologists point to the fact that the image presented in these popular songs is not ignored. S. E. Hayakawa says that popular song is "often memorized and sung most in adolescence—when awareness of the opposite sex is awakening—and contributes to a false image and helps prevent a realistic mature view of woman from being attainable in adulthood."[14] David Reisman adds that these images are ones to which girls are particularly susceptible as they are a subordinate group with few outlets.[15]

Women in Art

Another area in which the stereotypes of women get reinforcement is the realm of art. In art we again see women as Madonna, Eve, and also Venus, the combination of innocence and seductiveness. The Madonna image exemplifies the combined virtues of women: pure, but a mother; also kind, submissive, humble, and chaste. Eve again is the prototype for the sinful woman: causing sin in man as well as in herself. However, she represents a weak woman, unable to resist temptation. While originally the serpent was portrayed as female and the source of evil, the source of evil came to be transferred directly to Eve in later paintings. Gradually Eve becomes portrayed as the temptress, the Venus who is sexually seductive. In the many portrayals of Venus (Bellini's, Titian's, and Rubens') the vanity of woman is emphasized: She has elaborately curled hair, is bejeweled and often is looking into a mirror. With Rubens the nude becomes totally sensual, as the "flaunted poses of the naked bodies" were all used to stress the woman's new role as a sex object. Women are also portrayed in the nude as figures to be contemplated or raped, or as cuddly toys. Frequently they are raped by satyrs, centaurs, or other beast-men, as in Rubens' *The Last Judgment*. Renoir's nudes are also fat and sensual. Only Degas, Rodin, and Toulouse-Lautrec show women as more individualized.[16]

Even in the twentieth century the abstract works of Picasso degrade women. "Distortions are frequently used with erotic expression in mind and always at the female's expense; her breasts become balloons, her thighs, belly, buttocks, and vaginal slit all swell outward to the spectator, while her head disappears into a tiny, indistinguishable speck."[17] In modern pop art the woman is portrayed again as big breasted and wearing stockings, high heels, and heavy makeup. One particularly apt characterization may be seen in Richard Lindner's portrait of gangsters and cops. The women (molls) are elaborate corsets with holes for breasts, lipstick grins, and targets or "hit" signs in the groin.[18] All the women are without identity—stereotyped, grotesque variations of the female body. Thus women have not "come a long way, baby." They are still portrayed as babies, as mindless bodies interested only in beautifying themselves and interesting only as sex objects.

Women in Popular Literature: Homemaker and Hussy

Most of the contemporary popular books and magazines also emphasize stereotypical roles for women. We can clearly see the Madonna-Eve dichotomy when we look at the selection of magazines aimed at women. *Good Housekeeping, Redbook, House Beautiful, Family Circle,* and others of this genre aim at the woman who is home with children and family. They tell her how to cook nutritiously for her children, how to redecorate the family room, how to sew and garden. On the other hand, *Playboy, Penthouse,* and even *Playgirl* (the women's version of *Playboy*) point up the sexual, frivolous nature of women. The playmate of the month, with unbelievably huge breasts and in the buff, stares coyly at you from the centerfold, and the cartoons all emphasize the sex-object nature of women. They remind us that women are primarily for the enjoyment of men and that there are girls out there that aren't "really nice." The lure of being admired is continually dangled before the girl who is planning to be the "everyday housewife."

There is a group of magazines in between these two extremes that profess to cater to the liberated woman who is working and not at home full time with her family. The epitome of these is *Cosmopolitan* with its Cosmo-girl image. Unfortunately, this same woman, who is supposed to have gained her freedom in the world of work, spends a great deal of time prettying herself for men and worrying about how to dress so that *he* will think she is beautiful. A few of the more recent arrivals on the newsstand, such as *Working Woman,* have really shifted the emphasis from ways of appealing to men to the problems of women. However, even these magazines tend to stress the needs of the single working woman rather than those of the married career woman who is trying to combine two roles.

Ms. seems to be about the one magazine where the emphasis is on the liberated woman who can enjoy singlehood and a career, or combine work and family. A recent article on how women athletes have more comfortable pregnancies is a prime example. This publication has also been particularly good about avoiding the learn-it-to-appeal-to-men approach, and the section entitled "No Comment" should be noted for pointing out examples of rampant sexism.

In spite of the more liberated tone of the last-mentioned publications, the advertising in most of the women's magazines portrays women in the stereotypic images of sex object or housewife and mother. In either case, the women are defined by the men in their lives. They adorn the seats of big cars that their men buy; they are advised to purchase cosmetics that will make them young and beautiful for men; or they are advised to buy products (such as detergents) so they can better serve the men in their lives. While a few token women with briefcases are shown in advertisements—usually standing near male engineers or other male experts—on the whole the role of women as creative members of society and the work force has been ignored. There are a few hopeful signs of change, however. One major airline now devotes a substantial percentage of its publicity budget to advertisements appealing to traveling businesswomen, and investment companies and others have recognized the lucrative possibilities in appealing to the working female.

The Total Woman: Liberated or Prisoner

The proper role for women is also defined and debated in the popular do-it-yourself books for women who wish to be appealing to men. Some of the older works of this genre such as *The Sensuous Woman,* describe the Eve image, telling women to enjoy their sexuality but urging them to use it as a ploy to get a man.[19] Recently, a number of books have appeared that represent a backlash to women's liberation themes and preach domesticity as the only appropriate role for a woman. Maribel Morgan's *The Total Woman* sold six million copies and is the most publicized of these books, but there are many more, among them *Fascinating Womanhood, Be a Woman, The Female Woman.*[20] *The Total Woman* and *Fascinating Womanhood* are also the basis for a string of franchised training sessions in which women are taught the appropriate ways to please their husbands.

These books attempt to combine the nice-girl–housewife (maternal-Madonna) role with a bit of spice from errant Eve. They jazz up the role of wife to include an interest in sex, but with the husband only. (It's as good for you as cottage cheese," says Maribel Morgan.)[21] The wife should also know enough about subjects that interest the man so that she can be a good conversational partner. One of the most important points made by these books, however, is the total segregation of male and female roles. Men should be the providers, protectors, and ultimate authorities in the household; women must never work outside the home and must be submissive, support-ive, and nurturant within it. The woman controls the household, hides her feelings, and never bothers "her wonderful man" with her problems. The burden of total acceptance and adaptation is on the wife, with the additional charge that it is her failure if the husband does not succeed or if the marriage is unexciting. Biblical quotations and threats about losing one's man are used as powerful prods to accept this way of life. And while these books talk about communication within a marriage, they advise that the way to achieve a woman's ends is by manipulation. There is not the liberation of honesty and equality, nor is the ideal wife allowed to work outside the home. Thus these books spell out a slightly more liberated role for women within the confines of marriage, but women are still imprisoned in their domestic cocoon.[22]

We do not want to leave the impression that the only popular literature available to women pushes the traditional housewife role. We have stressed these books only because they so dramatically illustrate the persistence of the traditional stereotype. However, there are now increasing numbers of popular books directed to women that reflect more feminist views and challenge the stereotypes. Many of these have been written for single and divorced women or others who want to find meaning in their lives, for example, *Woman Alone, for Better, for Worse.* There are others, however, that deal with the means to liberation such as *How To Become an Assertive Woman,* and *Games Mother Never Taught You.* The more radical feminist literature, as typified by *Sexual Politics* and *Sisterhood Is Powerful,* and the new wave of books dealing with sex roles, are also extremely helpful in developing awareness of, and combating, worn-out modes of behavior.[23]

AGREEMENT ON THE STEREOTYPES

It is one thing to propose that stereotypes of male and female behavior exist and another to show that they are agreed upon and accepted by the average person as appropriate for males and females. There are many recent studies that lead us to believe, however, that the stereotypes described are indeed those held to be true by most of American society. According to one study done in 1972 with college males and females, "a strong consensus about the differing characteristics of men and women exists across groups which differ in sex, age, religion, marital status and educational level. . . . These stereo-types are uncritically accepted and incorporated by college students." Fur-thermore, the study reports that the stereotypic characteristics ascribed to men (competence, rationality, assertion) are seen as healthy and desirable, while women are perceived in negative terms, as less competent, less independent, less objective, and less logical.[24] When she developed her androgyny scale, Bem also found that both male and female judges agreed on adjectives used to describe American men and women.[25] In still another study Williams and Bennet gave a list of adjectives to fifty male and fifty female college students. They got 75 percent agreement between both sexes on a list of thirty-three adjectives (see Table 4.1). Both sexes agreed that the achievement-oriented characteristics—specifically adjectives suggesting dominance,

TABLE 4.1.

Adjectives Associated with Men	Adjectives Associated with Women
Adventurous	Affected
Aggressive	Affectionate
Ambitious	Appreciative
Assertive	Attractive
Autocratic	Charming
Boastful	Complaining
Coarse	Dependent
Confident	Dreamy
Courageous	Emotional
Cruel	Excitable
Daring	Feminine
Disorderly	Fickle
Dominant	Flirtatious
Enterprising	Frivolous
Forceful	Fussy
Handsome	Gentle
Independent	High-strung
Jolly	Meek
Logical	Mild
Loud	Nagging
Masculine	Prudish
Rational	Rattlebrained
Realistic	Sensitive
Robust	Sentimental
Self-confident	Soft-hearted
Severe	Sophisticated
Stable	Submissive
Steady	Talkative
Stern	Weak
Strong	Whiny
Tough	
Unemotional	
Unexcitable	

SOURCE: Williams and Bennett, "The Definition of Sex Stereotypes via the Adjective Check List."

endurance, aggression, autonomy, and desire for order—fit the stereotype of males; whereas men were judged low on such qualities as succorance, abasement, and nurturance. Women were seen as higher on the nurturing qualities of succor and deference, as well as self-control and personal adjustment.[26]

In a recent study Urberg and Labouvie-Vief showed that belief in the qualities of stereotypes continues into adulthood and "socially desirable" qualities are clung to with even more fervor as one gets older.[27] We thus see that there is strong agreement about the correct traits and behavior for males and females among varying age-groups ranging from those of college age, to older professionals. People do not seem to get more flexible with age, nor are they considerably more liberal when they are young. While not all of the respondents to the studies believed that men and women *should* act according to the stereotypes, most believed that they *do.*

There also seems to be evidence that even women believe in the negative stereotypes of themselves. As a minority group comes to accept the negative beliefs of the majority about themselves, so women in a similar fashion believe that in contrast with men they are not as likely to succeed, are less logical, are not good at mathematics, and the like. Goldberg found that both women and men were more likely to devalue an article when they thought it was authored by a woman than when they thought the same article was authored by a man.[28] Much has also been written about the "Queen Bee syndrome" in which women who have achieved high positions do not help others up the success ladder but discriminate against their own sex.[29] Perhaps there is hope, however. In one recent study Soto and Cole found no prejudice among either men or women toward job applicants of either sex. The judges ranked applicants solely according to qualifications. The authors believe these results reflect both the changing consciousness about equal rights and the time elapsed since the Goldberg studies in 1968.[30] The results may also reflect the fact that the sample of judges consisted of men and women in high school and college.

INFLUENCES OF THE STEREOTYPES

Socially Dysfunctional

What is the influence of these stereotypes in general, and what is their influence on the self-concept of women in particular? Tavris succinctly summarizes three ways in which they are limiting. First, stereotypes are socially dysfunctional.[31] The role of the contemporary woman does not mesh with the stereotypical traits of the ideal female. Almost 50 percent of American mothers now work and certainly need the stereotypic male traits of assertiveness and competitiveness. They will find the female stereotypic traits of submissiveness and abasement to be harmful to their careers. As women live longer and have fewer children, the number of working women is likely to increase, and traits of nurturance and succor will no longer be sufficient for their needs.[32]

Legitimize Discrimination

Secondly, social stereotypes make discrimination against a group seem legitimate. If women "can't do analytic tasks" or are "too emotional to make good bosses," then someone has a reason to pay them lower salaries or deny them promotion. The erroneous beliefs that women employees are both absent more than men and more likely to quit their jobs are still prevalent and are used as reasons for not hiring or training women.

Psychologically Stifling

Thirdly, stereotypes are psychologically stifling. As Tavris states: "They brand a whole group of people with the same label, admitting no individual differences, and they linger on even when they have become inaccurate."[33]

This influence of the stereotypic role can be seen in the mental health statistics for housewives. Married women report more anxiety, depression, neurosis, and psychosis than single women or married men do. Apparently much of the problem is due to the housewife role that is prescribed for these women. Women who work outside the home and combat the stereotypic belief that the good mother must be at home twenty-four hours a day do not suffer as severely from mental health problems as do their housewife sisters.[34] However, they may still have to deal with a lingering guilt that tempts them to be supermom in all areas. Chapter 7 examines this role conflict in a dual-career family in more detail.

Goffman's work on body language and Hacker's description of women's behavior also show that negative feelings about oneself come from accepting the feminine stereotype. This identification of self as not valued and some-how unworthy may result in behavior similar to that of a discriminated-against minority group. Goffman points out that women are more likely to smile (a gesture of submission, wanting to be liked), tilt their heads, lower their eyes, cover their mouths when speaking, and make other gestures that are similar to those of a minority group.[35] Thus women are displaying much of the same deference to, and need for, approval of the dominant group as have minority-group members. While some of this deference may be used to manipulate the majority group, it is still an attempt to survive when a group does not have direct access to power.

Hacker also points out that women express much of the self-hatred displayed by other minority groups. They outdo men in their negative views of their own sex. She states; "They express themselves as disliking other women, as preferring to work under men, and as finding exclusively female gatherings repugnant. And more than one-fourth of women wish they had been born a member of the opposite sex."[36] Unfortunately, as Hacker points out, women have not had until recently any sense of identity with their own group that would help them to overcome these negative feelings. Their personality development largely results from interaction with both sexes, and they do not get a sense of their own worth and identity from interaction with only the in-group, as might Jews and blacks.[37] Women's growing consciousness of themselves as a unique group whose members value mutual support, and interact with one another, is too recent in the American experience to have yet had an effect.

PERPETUATION OF FEMININE BEHAVIOR BY THE STEREOTYPES

Hacker's analysis is an insightful look at the discrimination against women and points out that women are still treated in ways that we would not allow for other minority groups. Slurs about women and sexist jokes are still allowed and considered funny, whereas similar slurs about minorities or racist jokes would be considered in extremely bad taste or as "fighting words." In addition, the female self-hatred and the adoption of behaviors smacking of inferiority and deference that she describes are damaging in still another way: They may perpetuate childlike behavior and lack of achievement in such a way as to make the stereotypes come true. As Broverman states:

> To the extent that these results [of her study] reflect societal standards of sex-role behavior, women are clearly put in a double bind because of the fact that different standards exist for women than adults. If women adopt the behavior specified as desirable for adults, they risk censure for their failure to be appropriately feminine; but if they adopt behaviors that are designated as feminine, they are necessarily deficient with respect to general standards for adult behavior.[38]

Thus, in this acceptance of the stereotype for femininity, there is a self-fulfilling prophecy which makes it likely that negative and self-defeating behaviors will occur in the lives of most women. Women are extremely dependent on the approval of others, for it is by this approval rather than by their objective achievements that they identify themselves and define their femininity or success.

This need for approval is a continuing theme in the lives of women. It is especially important for the young girl who cannot define her femininity in terms of childbearing and child raising or in terms of household tasks. Thus, for her, to be feminine is to be pretty and popular. She wastes time that she might spend on sports, career training, or other interests in shopping for clothes, curling her hair, and applying makeup. The really sad result is that she must get her identity from others, not from her own achievements. No matter what she does or how she looks, unless others approve, it is not sufficient. The need for approval carries over into the wife and mother years and shows itself in the almost frantic concern of many women with spotless houses, gourmet cooking, and being supermom. The need for approval of the physical self does not diminish at the same time. American women have an inordinate desire to remain young and beautiful. The older housewife is probably dieting or running to an exercise club and is more and more likely to have cosmetic surgery such as facelifting. One recent magazine article told the story of a forty-three-year-old housewife with three children who had breast augmentation surgery because she had always felt inferior on account of her flat chest.[39]

With identity found only in the approval of others and in roles associated with others (as Jim's wife, Betty's mom), it is no wonder that many women lack faith in their own ability to succeed. As we will see in the next chapter, women of high-school age and older are likely to underestimate their ability to achieve in even simple tasks, while men have no such negative ideas about their own achievement.[40] Some of this lack of faith in their own ability may be due to women's fear of the negative reactions of others if they do succeed (see Chapter 6), but a great part may actually come from early training which causes women to feel they are not capable.

The time taken up with proving her femininity, and the lack of faith in her abilities, are aggravated by the societal expectation that a woman will sacrifice her own achievement for the good of her family. It is commonly expected that a woman will give up her career and stay home with preschool children, and will also sacrifice her own career and interests to those of her husband if relocation is necessary. Women fall into the "compassion trap" and neglect their own development for that of their family. It is difficult for them to catch up when they later start trying to develop their own interests. They probably can never devote undivided attention to their careers as they are too busy being support systems for their husband and children. Even women who go so far as to divorce, and thus must support themselves, retain the care of their children in 90 percent of all cases.[41]

Part of the definition of femininity also holds that it is the woman who is the guardian of a couple's social life: arranging entertainment, writing Christmas cards, thank-you notes, and the like. The woman must also be "nice" and sociable, even when it means the invasion of her personal time. In an article appropriately entitled "The Compassion Trap," Margaret Adams describes a weekend she spent with a family in which both husband and wife were scientific writers. All three adults decided to reserve Saturday afternoon for their own writing and turned down all social engagements for the day. However, unexpected guests dropped in and "of necessity, the two female writers abandoned the 'scribbling' and reverted to their normal expected roles of dispensing tea, entertainment and genial hospitality."[42] Although the woman attempted to hint that they were busy, the guests did not leave—primarily because they saw the wife as housewife and mother, not as a scientific writer. However, the third writer, the husband, was allowed to remain in his study, with tea taken in to him and apologies for his absence relayed to the guests. The women could have insisted that they were busy and refused to welcome anyone, but the compassion for the plight of the guest (and some others in the household visited) kept them from doing so.[43] It is also interesting that it was considered their duty to be the entertainers, while it was perfectly appropriate for the man of the household to get on with the important business of his career.

The feminine social role is made more difficult by the fact that although women were traditionally able to manage some of their roles through reciprocal assistance from other females, this is seldom possible given the way the society is now constructed. The unity women found in less developed societies and in extended families is only occasionally reconstructed in contemporary American society with communal living arrangements. This isolation is not only a psychological problem; for if wives have the sole responsibility for household maintenance and child care, it becomes extremely difficult for them to give up this job unless alternatives are found. Unfortunately, women tend to develop rigid ideas about the role society asks of them, and they may not perceive alternative directions for themselves, or demand that others share their burden.

WAYS OF COMBATING STEREOTYPES

Support Groups

It is difficult for women to combat the stereotypes about their nature and behavior because these stereotypes are so all-pervasive in the culture. As we have seen, women themselves at least partly believe them. The women's movement and the literature it generates have been extremely useful in getting women to question the traditional role definitions and to think about what they would really like. Women's support groups or other types of consciousness-raising activities are also valuable. In a culture where women's role is made palatable by such niceties as having doors opened for them and their chairs pulled out, it is important to assert what is really important. Along with the consciousness-raising groups, assertiveness training sessions are frequently of great help in changing stereotyped behavior. Women learn how to be assertive and feel good about standing up for themselves without being aggressive. They also get reinforcement for the fact that they are unique individuals with value and human rights, and they develop a true sense of their own identity. In addition, women gain an awareness of their unity—an understanding that theirs is a group and not an individual problem. As women continue to seek support from one another and organize to gain further participation in society, stereotypes are likely to be modified extensively.

Experience

Another avenue for combating the stereotypes is that of experience. In *Woman Alone* (mentioned earlier) the author, Patricia O'Brian, leaves her husband with the children and tries living alone for a period of time to develop her own identity and feelings. More and more women have been forced to adopt a similar position when they find themselves alone after a divorce or when a spouse dies. While the adjustment is frequently difficult, many of these women derive a new strength and pride from their newly found identity and their ability to cope on their own. If they can free themselves from the got-to-have-a-man-around syndrome, they often find this way of life extremely liberating and satisfying. Delayed marriages also mean that many women have had a chance to develop their identity and get started on the road to a fulfilling career. More and more have found the single life a rewarding experience they wish to continue. Those who do marry later frequently enter marriage with altered expectations about roles. As more and more married women and mothers also join the labor force (as do 50 percent of all mothers at the present time), they are exposed to the pleasures that may come with individual achievement. In addition, they realize that they do not have the time, nor do they make the effort, to maintain the stereotypical female role. Participation in society and a growing sense of identity are reciprocally reinforcing. Small beginning steps toward the development of individuality may lead to a new perception and a new confidence in questioning the stereotype.

Questioning and Changing the Sources of Sexism

In addition, it is extremely important for all women to question the institutional sources of stereotypes. They must recognize that they and their children are learning from historical, religious, and literary sources. They must recognize the important and subtle source of the stereotypes that are found in the popular media: art and music, popular literature, television (see Chapter 5), movies, and the like. They must learn to recognize the subtle and not-so-subtle forms of discrimination in the working world that hold women back from their true achievement (the myths that women workers quit, and are sick, more often than men, the "locker-room syndrome" of shutting women out, and the like). They must also recognize the political discrimination against women in decision-making, general laws (credit laws, for example), and laws dealing with such things as women's control of their own bodies (sex education and abortion laws). When the source of the stereotype or the injustice is recognized, it must be combated and all women must work for change. Combat may be as quiet and personal as sitting through a TV show and the attendant commercials with a child and pointing out the wrong ideas about women that are presented. It may be as public and volatile as getting out and organizing people to write their legislators to vote in favor of the Equal Rights Amendment. In all cases, such combat stimulates the questioning process and helps women perceive new options.

Women have gained a new sense of individual identity today, and they are participating more actively in society. If they can expand these gains while achieving a true sense of solidarity as a group, they can combat the stereotypes and open up new possibilities for their own behavior and new directions for their lives.

NOTES

1. Alexis de Tocqueville, *Democracy in America,* 2 vols. (New York: 1953).

2. I Cor 14:34–35

3. Jessie Bernard, *Women in the Public Interest* (Chicago: Aldine-Atherton, 1971).

4. Roy G. D'Andrade, "Sex Differences and Cultural Institutions," in *The Development of Sex Differences,* ed. Eleanor Maccoby (Stanford: Stanford University Press, 1966), pp. 173–204.

5. Vern L. Bullough, *The Subordinate Sex* (Baltimore: Penguin, 1973).

6. Helen Hacker, "Women as a Minority Group," *Social Forces* 30 (1951): 60–69.

7. William H. Chafe, *The American Woman: Her Changing Social, Economic, and Political Role, 1920–1970.* (New York: Oxford University Press, 1972).

8. Greer Litton Fox, "Nice Girl: Social Control of Women through a Value Construct," *Signs* 2, no. 4 (Summer 1977): 805–817.

9. Jessie Bernard, *The Future of Marriage* (New York: Bantam, 1972).

10. Ibid.

11. Ibid.; see also Joan Vanek, "Housewives as Workers," in *Women Working,* ed. Ann Stromberg and Shirley Harkness (Palo Alto, Calif.: Mayfield, 1978).

12. Kay F. Reinartz, "The Paper Doll: Image of American Women in Popular Songs," in *The Feminist Perspective,* ed. Jo Freeman (Palo Alto, Calif.: Mayfield, 1975), p. 294.

13. Ibid., pp. 293–308.

14. Ibid., p. 307.

15. Ibid., p. 306.

16. Lyvia Morgan Brown, "Sexism in Western Art," in Freeman, *Women: The Feminist Perspective,* pp. 309–332.

17. Ibid., p. 319.

18. Ibid., pp. 309–332.

19. "J," *The Sensuous Woman* (New York: Lyle Stuart, 1970).

20. Maribel Morgan, *The Total Woman* (New York: Simon & Shuster, 1973); Helen B. Andelin, *Fascinating Womanhood* (New York: Bantam, 1965); Oleda Baker, *Be a Woman* (New York: Ballantine, 1975); Adrianna Stassinopoulous, *The Female Woman* (New York: Dell, 1973).

21. *Total Woman,* p. 141.

22. Marie Richmond-Abbott and Nadean Bishop, "The New Old-Fashioned Womanhood," *Human Behavior* (April 1977), pp. 64–69.

23. Patricia O'Brian, *Woman Alone* (New York: Quadrangle, 1973); Betty L. Harragan, *Games*

Mother Never Taught You, (New York: Warren Books, 1978); Jennifer Fleming and Carolyn Washburn, *For Better, for Worse: A Feminist Handbook on Marriage and Other Options* (New York: Scribner, 1977); Bryna Taubman, *How to Become an Assertive Woman* (New York: Pocket Books, 1976); Kate Millet, *Sexual Politics* (New York: Doubleday, 1970); Robin Morgan, ed., *Sisterhood Is Powerful* (New York: Random House, 1970).

24. Inge K. Broverman et al., "Sex-Role Stereotypes: A Current Appraisal," *Journal of Social Issues* 28, no. 2 (1972): 59–78.

25. Sandra Bem, "The Measure of Psychological Androgyny," *Journal of Consulting and Clinical Psychology* (1974), p. 42.

26. John E. Williams and Susan M. Bennet, "The Definition of Sex Stereotypes via the Adjective Check List," *Sex Roles* 1, no. 4 (1975): 327–337.

27. Kathryn A. Urberg and Gisela Debouvie Vief, "Conceptualizations of Sex Roles: A Life Developmental Study," *Developmental Psychology* 12, no. 1 (1976): 15–23.

28. Philip Goldberg, "Are Women Prejudiced Against Women?" *Transaction* 5, no. 5 (1968): 28–30.

29. Graham Staines, Carol Tavris, and Toby Epstein, "The Queen Bee Syndrome," *Psychology Today* (January 1974), pp. 55–60.

30. Debbie Halon Soto and Claudia Cole, "Prejudice Against Women: A New Perspective," *Sex Roles* 1, no. 4 (1975): 385–394.

31. Carol Tavris and Carol Offrer, *The Longest War* (New York: Harcourt Brace Jovanovich, 1977).

32. Roxanne VanDusen and Eleanor Sheldon, "The Changing Status of American Women," *American Psychologist* (February 1976), pp. 106–115.

33. Tavris and Offrer, *The Longest War.*

34. Walter Cove and Jeannette Tudor, "Adult Sex Roles and Mental Illness," *American Journal of Sociology* 78, no. 2 (1973): 812–832; Jessie Bernard, *Women, Wives and Mothers* (Chicago: Aldine, 1975).

35. Irving Goffman, *Interaction Ritual* (New York: Doubleday, Anchor Books, 1967).

36. Hacker, "Women as a Minority Group," p. 64.

37. Ibid.

38. Broverman et al., "Sex Role Stereotypes," p. 75.

39. *Family Circle Magazine,* March 1976.

40. Eleanor Maccoby and Helen Jacklin, *The Psychology of Sex Differences* (Stanford: Stanford University Press, 1974), pp. 134–162.

41. E. Mavis Hetherington, Martha Cox, and Roger Cox, "The Development of Children in Mother-Headed Families" (Paper presented at the conference on Families in Contemporary America, George Washington University, June 11, 1977; Census Bureau, Current Population Report, series P-20, 1975, cited).

42. Margaret Adams, "The Compassion Trap," in *Women in Sexist Society,* ed. Vivian Gornick and Barbara K. Moran (New York: Basic Books, 1971), p. 574.

43. Ibid., pp. 555–575.

REVIEW QUESTIONS

1. Describe the dominant set of cultural values prescribed for gaining success in American society. What is the shadow set of values for women?
2. How have women been restricted by having their sexuality defined in both positive and negative ways?
3. Why does Helen Hacker say that the behavior of women is like that of a minority group?

4. In what three ways are the stereotypes for either men or women described as harmful?
5. What types of images of women have been presented in popular songs over the past fifty years or so? How have these images changed recently? Do the images presented in these popular songs have any real impact on young people?
6. Describe the development of the Eve and Madonna images in art depicting women. How has modern art fused these images?
7. How do books of the popular Total Woman genre reconcile the image of the woman as a housewife and mother with the need for men to have a sexual playmate?
8. What three means can you suggest for combating sexual stereotypes as they are now presented in our society?

CLASSROOM EXERCISES

1. List ten qualities that are important to your definition of self. These should be qualities you would be likely to include when telling someone about yourself. Which of these are "male" and which are "female"? Do you feel comfortable with the mixture in yourself? Are there things you would like to change?
2. Under the headings "What men are" and "What women are" list the qualities that you think the culture believes appropriate for men and women. Then add qualifications to the lists according to what *you* believe about the qualities listed. How much do your beliefs differ from those in the general culture? How much are they the same?
3. Using the list of what you *believe* that you developed in exercise 2, develop a corresponding list of *behaviors* that you actually do. If you believe that men and women are equally intelligent, for example, do you speak up for yourself at parties or in other places where a man is expressing an opinion contrary to your own? Or do you remain silent so that you will not create any social discord?
4. Using the format "I feel masculine/feminine (as appropriate) when I. . . . . ," list behaviors that you judge to be sex related in your own life. Now review your list. Which of these things are really important to you? Are there any that do not fit with the definition of self you described in exercise 1? Are there any behaviors that do not fit with what you believe about men and women's roles as you described them in exercise 2? Are there any things you would change?
5. List five areas of your life (for example, work, sports) where you think you have control over what you do and the speed at which you grow or move toward a goal. List five areas of your life in which you do *not* feel you have this control and who or what is holding you back in those areas.
6. What things are you waiting for before you move forward in your life? ("I am waiting until I finish college, meet someone to marry, lose weight, before I. . . .")
7. In what ways could you take more control over your own life and change the cultural pressures that are holding you back? (You may want to refer to the two books on assertiveness listed in the bibliography for suggestions on this exercise.)

SELECTED READINGS

Bem, Sandra. "Beyond Androgyny: Some Presumptuous Prescriptions for a Liberated Sexual Identity." Keynote address for American Psychological Association–National Institute of Mental Health Conference on the Research Needs of Women, Madison, Wisconsin, May 31, 1975.

Contains a good description of the concept of androgyny and an analysis of why androgynous roles are more productive human roles. Also describes the Bem Sex Role Inventory which measures androgyny, and discusses the results of some recent research.

Bernard, Jessie. *The Future of Marriage.* New York: Bantam, 1972.

An excellent analysis of the "his" and "her" roles in marriage. The constricting nature of the stereotypic domestic role for women and the effects on their mental health are well documented.

Bullough, Vern L. *The Subordinate Sex: A History of Attitudes toward Women.* Baltimore: Penguin, 1974.

This book does not attempt to be an exhaustive study of the status of women but is quite literally a history of the attitudes toward women from ancient times, through Rome, the Byzantium, and Christianity, and into urban culture. The author also includes sections on women in Oriental cultures and under Islam. The book is particularly notable for its use of literary documents to establish the attitude toward women in any particular time. Author cites sources that, although fairly well known in the historical literature, one would think unlikely to deal with women.

Broverman, I. K., et al. "Sex Role Stereotypes: A Current Appraisal." *Journal of Social Issues* 28, no. 2 (1972): 59–78.

Although a little out of date, this is one of the classic articles dealing with how Americans view sex-role stereotypes.

Chafe, William H. *The American Woman: Her Changing Social, Economic, and Political Role, 1920–1970.* New York: Oxford University Press, 1972.

A look at the historical changes that have affected American women, particularly from 1920 to 1960. This is good, documented history, particularly good on women after World War II. Fairly easy reading.

D'Andrade, Roy G. "Sex Differences and Cultural Institutions." In *The Development of Sex Differences,* edited by Eleanor Maccoby. Stanford: Stanford University Press, 1966.

Another look at sex roles historically and cross-culturally, which enables us to gain a perspective on the roles that American women are now asked to play. There is a very good analysis of the forces that have relegated women to a secondary status across cultures.

deReincourt, Amaury, *Sex and Power in History.* New York: McKay, 1974.

An extremely comprehensive treatment of the status of women throughout history. It is more a reference book than one for reading or for the student.

Filene, Peter Gabriel. *Him/Her Self: Sex Roles in Modern America.* New York: Harcourt Brace Jovanovich, 1974.

A good overview of the roles of men and women in American history from 1890 to the present. While it is scholarly and extremely well referenced, it is also readable.

Fox, Greer Litton. "Nice Girl: Social Control of Women through a Value Construct." *Signs* 2, no. 4 (Summer 1977): 805–817.

An illuminating analysis of the subtle cultural pressures restricting women—and particularly their sexuality—so that they will be "nice" girls. Points out the rewards promised the nice girl and the negative sanctions applied to those who fall from grace, in particular the sanction of not being "good enough" for a man. The fact that the nice-girl status can never be totally achieved and must be perpetually earned makes it a focus of socialization pressure in our culture.

Freeman, Jo, ed. *Women: A Feminist Perspective.* Palo Alto, Calif.: Mayfield, 1975.

An excellent reader with some fine articles on socialization, sex-role stereotypes, and the structural discrimination that women suffer in the economic and political spheres. Several articles are particularly pertinent for a look at American sex-role stereotypes: Lenore Weitzman's "Sex-Role Socialization," Jo Freeman's "How to Discriminate Against Women Without Really Trying," Kimberly Snow's "Women in the American Novel," Kay Reinartz's "The Paper Doll: Images of American Women in Popular Songs," Lyvia Brown's "Sexism in Western Art," and Helen Hacker's "Women as a Minority Group."

Gambrill, Eileen, and Cheryl Richey. *It's Up to You: Developing Assertive Social Skills.* Milbrae, Calif.: Les Femmes Press, 1976.

A guide for using behavioral modification techniques to develop skills leading to more assertive behavior. It is extremely specific, clearly written, and intended for individual or group use.

Gump, Janice Porter. "Sex-Role Attitudes and Psychological Well-Being," *Journal of Social Issues* 28, no. 72 (1972): 79–92.

An examination of research differentiating the happiness and self-esteem of women holding traditional and more liberated sex-role ideologies.

Huber, Joan. *Changing Women in a Changing Society.* Chicago: University of Chicago Press, 1973. (Also appeared as volume 78, number 4 of the *American Journal of Sociology.*)

A collection of some of the classic articles pertaining to the roles of women in contemporary American society. It does not bear directly on sex stereotypes but is a fertile ground for ideas in this area.

Oakley, Ann. *Sex, Gender and Society.* New York: Harper & Row, 1972.

Basically an attempt to answer the question of whether the difference between the sexes lies in gender or culture, and what the implications of the answer might be. There is a thorough description of sex-role socialization in several cultures which gives us a good perspective for examining the sex-role stereotypes of American women.

Taubman, Bryna. *How to Become an Assertive Woman.* New York: Pocket Books, 1976.

One of the more clear and concise books dealing with assertiveness. The book is full of clear examples of situations where assertiveness could be used. It does not have the failing of the moralistic tone common to many others of this genre.

CHAPTER 5

Early Socialization of the American Female

Marie Richmond-Abbott

THE OLD HEREDITY VERSUS ENVIRONMENT ARGUMENT

In a discussion of the status of women in any culture it is important to spell out clearly what we know about the inherited characteristics of men and women and what the culture itself may contribute to their traits and behavior. As we have seen, common assumptions about the nature of men state that men are aggressive, dominant, and competitive, and have a high sex drive. Similar assumptions about the nature of women state that they are dependent, passive, nurturant, interested in people more than things, and naturally maternal. The average person does not usually stop to wonder if these supposed characteristics of men and women are physically inherited, come from cultural training alone, or arise from a combination of physical beginnings and cultural reinforcement of these tendencies. Recently, many scientists have studied the physical and behavioral differences between men and women. Two psychologists, Maccoby and Jacklin, have made a massive effort to compile thousands of these studies into a comprehensive reference book, and their effort has spurred others to do even more detailed research.[1] This new information has led us to discard some of the old myths regarding the differences between the sexes, and to reaffirm others.

In this chapter we shall first try to see what these scientific studies tell us about the characteristics of men and women that are determined by physically inherited factors. We shall look at the role played by chromosomes and hormones in determining such diverse physical characteristics as body size and the ability to handle concepts about three-dimensional space. We shall also see how some physical factors, like hormones, may interact with cultural training to produce different behaviors or moods in many men and women, such as aggression or "premenstrual tension."

Then we shall take a close look at how this cultural training itself begins to shape sex-role behavior in three primary areas: parental expectations, cultural areas such as language and the mass media, and cultural institutions such as schools. We shall examine some theories about how children learn sex-role behavior and how it is reinforced in each of the three areas. We shall also look specifically at each area to see how extensively influences (like parental training, games children play, and television) push each sex to conform to stereotypes of behavior. We shall see that sometimes the culture's message about appropriate sex-role behavior is very subtle; but sometimes it is very clear, and rewards and punishments for inappropriate behavior are painfully obvious. We shall end the chapter by looking at the results of all these messages: learned differences in behavior between males and females.

Let us now look at the years from birth to early adolescence to see what factors are shaping boys and girls so that they behave differently then and in later life.

OUR PHYSICAL INHERITANCE

Gender

Gender is the combination of physical characteristics that determine the sex of the newborn infant. It consists of chromosomes, hormones, internal gonads, external genitalia, and (later) psychosexual identity. When an embryo is conceived in the form of a fertilized egg cell, the ovum and the sperm each contribute twenty-three chromosomes which align in twenty-three pairs in the fertilized egg. One of these pairs is the chromosomes that determine the sex of the fetus. The ovum always contributes an X chromosome, and the sperm contributes either an X or a Y chromosome. If there are two X chromosomes, the fetus becomes a female; if there are X and Y chromosomes, the fetus becomes a male.

Although we are used to thinking of gender as something that can be easily determined by looking at the chromosomes that are present, knowledge of a person's sex is not always a straightforward matter. We have all heard of the Olympic Games athletes who have had to undergo a cheek smear test where their chromosomes were examined to see if they were male or female. Sometimes nature makes a mistake, however, and in the process of fertilization some of the genetic material may be duplicated or lost. While the embryo cannot survive with only the smaller Y chromosome, it can survive with only one X chromosome. This condition is called Turner's Syndrome (XO); the embryo has external female genitalia, but internal gonads (ovaries, uterus) are vestigial or missing entirely. In another abnormality known as Klinefelter's Syndrome (XXY or even XXXY), the Y chromosome exists, and the fetus becomes partly male; but the influence of more than one X chromosome may overwhelm the Y chromosome and make male external genitalia difficult to distinguish, and male internal gonads may be absent.[2] In both cases the child is probably thought a female and raised as a girl, even though the child is in one case chromosomally female (XO) and in the other chromosomally male (XXY). Thus we can see that in some cases there can be a conflict between the various parts of gender such as chromosomes, gonads, and genitalia. The chromosomes, nevertheless, have a direct linkage to some of the traits possessed by the sexes.

Certain characteristics such as hemophilia, color blindness, and ability to handle concepts about three-dimensional spaces seem to result from recessive genes carried on particular X chromosomes, the carriers of recessive traits. These traits do not show up in females with a normal X chromosome (or two normal ones), as an X chromosome with no recessive traits is dominant and cancels out the recessive characteristics on the other chromosome. The traits will show up in men, however, as the Y chromosome does not have this canceling effect, and they will show up in women with two "recessive" X chromosomes. Thus, in the possible combination of chromosomes that can result, approximately 50 percent of men and 25 percent of women will have such recessive characteristics as spatial ability.[3]

The chromosomes determine the sex of the fetus largely through their ability to form the testes or ovaries that produce the sex hormones. The sex hormones for men are the androgens (primarily testosterone) and for women are estrogen and progesterone, although each sex possesses some of each. Nature's first choice is to make a female, and the fetus will differentiate as a female unless the Y chromosome and a sufficient amount of androgen are present. Apparently, the female hormones themselves are not needed; the mere absence of the male hormone is sufficient to produce a female. During the second six weeks of fetal development, while the testes or ovaries are secreting the appropriate sex hormone, the rest of the internal gonads and the external genitalia are formed. Sometimes the effect of the proper sex hormones in the fetus will be canceled out by other hormones or factors. Occasionally androgens (the male hormones) are given to a pregnant woman as treatment for other physical problems. When this happens, and the fetus being carried is female, the child will often turn out to have some masculine characteristics: for example, developing a boyish build with slender hips and small breasts or, as a child, displaying more tomboyish behavior and a lack of interest in doll play. Conversely, a male fetus whose mother has an element in her blood that cancels out the effect of androgens will have female external genitalia, as androgens must be present for complete male development.

There are two particularly interesting aspects of these hormonal effects. There seems to be a critical period early in pregnancy when the hormones must exercise their influence. A female fetus, for example, that is exposed to androgens after this critical period does not suffer from their effects. The other interesting aspect of the hormones is that their effect may be long-lived, perhaps through the effect of imprinting on the part of the brain known as the hypothalamus. Thus the female fetus exposed to androgens at a critical time not only develops a more tomboyish build but also appears to have more "masculine" behavior at a later stage in her development.[4] Abnormalities such as those discussed in this section are rare, but we can see that gender is not necessarily an either/or matter. The picture of distinct genders with specific traits and behaviors stemming from their physical makeup is further muddied by new evidence that androgens may undergo transformation into estrogens at the cellular level in the brain and that some female hormones may be present when their production sources (the ovaries) have been removed.[5]

Other Male and Female Physical Differences: Real and Imagined

The chromosomes and their related sex hormones determine other physical differences in male and female infants and activate certain behavior characteristics. One of the specific effects of the male hormones is to facilitate the synthesis of proteins from amino acids, helping muscle and bone development. At birth males exceed females by 5 percent in weight and nearly 2 percent in height.[6] Boys also have a consistently higher basal metabolism after the age of two years, which is particularly accounted for by this greater muscle and bone mass. They develop proportionately larger hearts and lungs and have a lower resting heart rate.[7] Unfortunately, the androgens, which aid in the physical development of males, also increase formation of cholesterol and free fatty acids in the blood and may later predispose males to heart attacks. By contrast, the estrogens produced by the young girl help to reduce serum cholesterol, although they later encourage tissue deposits, particularly in characteristically "feminine" locations, such as the hips.

In spite of their greater bone and muscle mass, however, the male's development lags nearly two years behind the female's. Bone ossification is completed 8–27 months later than for females, and physiological maturity is usually achieved about 2½ years later. In early infancy boys show greater speed and coordination of gross body movements, that is, of large muscles. Girls show more manual dexterity and use of fine muscles. It has been thought that boys showed greater activity levels, but this finding varies with age and experimental conditions. There is no sex difference in activity level during the first year of life. After that, findings vary; but when a difference is found it is that boys are more active.[8]

The Senses

It has been believed for many years that boy and girl babies differed in the way they used the senses of sight, hearing, smell, taste, and touch. Some differences have been confirmed by recent studies, but other beliefs are shown to be largely unfounded. It was originally believed that females responded more readily to auditory stimulation, but this is not supported by recent studies. Newborns of both sexes are very similar in the speed and duration of their responses to a variety of auditory cues. Although girls respond slightly more when some measures are used, they do so only for a very limited age span.[9] We are not sure how these unfounded beliefs about the hearing of infants ever developed originally. Perhaps because girl babies are more likely to use the small muscles around the mouth, parents felt girl babies were "smiling" or responding to sounds.

In the area of vision Maccoby and Jacklin also report that most studies show no differences between the two sexes in infancy, although in adulthood there is some indication that men have better spatial and depth perception. The sexes also seem to be similar in interest in, and utilization of, information that comes to them through the visual and auditory senses.[10]

In a similar fashion, boy and girl babies do not seem to vary in their sensitivity to touch. Both sexes quiet equally well when soothed with a blanket or soft fabric, and neither sex shows any stable difference on touch sensitivity when meters measure their skin responses. However, girls seem to be more sensitive to odors. There is some evidence that changes in estrogen levels are associated with this sensitivity. The idea is given more credibility by evidence that animal sensitivity to odors is linked to sexual behavior and sex hormones. There is also some slight evidence that girl and boy babies experience tastes differently. Girl babies will increase their sucking rate for sweet solutions, whereas boy babies will not.[11]

Learning and Cognitive Abilities

It has been believed for years that there are distinct differences in the way men and women use their minds and in their ability to do tasks or learn things. How many of us have heard that "girls can't do math very well" and "girls aren't logical—or creative—in their thinking"? In examining these beliefs, however, we have found that most of the presumed differences between the abilities of boys and girls, or men and women, have been found to be nonexistent or only minimal in nature. For example, Maccoby and Jacklin surveyed more than a hundred recent studies and found almost no difference between male and female infants in verbal ability. Apparently, verbal ability is about the same in the sexes from ages three to ten, although when a difference is found in skills, it is usually in favor of girls. Maccoby and Jacklin believe that a girl's verbal abilities (reading, writing, and speaking) may mature somewhat more rapidly. At around age eleven girls move ahead of boys and lead in verbal skills through high school and afterward as well. They score higher on both simple verbal tasks and higher level tests such as creative writing.[12]

Mathematical Ability

The two sexes are also similar in their early learning of mathematical concepts, but beginning at about age thirteen, boys increase their mathematical skills faster than girls do. This does not seem to be just because boys take more math courses, although we need to know more about this subject to be sure.[13] Some scientists believe that girls fall behind in mathematics because they are not expected to do well, and they become anxious about the whole process. In addition, they are stigmatized when they do well in this "masculine" area. As we shall see, mathematics books are almost always geared to the male student, making it even more difficult for the girl in this area.[14] They reflect the cultural beliefs and jokes that women overdraw their bank accounts, cannot add up bills, buy only hair ribbons, and the like.

Visual-Spatial and Analytic Performance

The sexes do not differ on visual-spatial tasks in childhood, but males excel after the beginning of adolescence. This spatial ability has often been thought to be linked with "field independence" and also with a cluster of abilities called "analytic." Supposedly, a field-independent person can focus on a particular problem and ignore extra elements; in addition, the person is thought to be better in breaking a "mental set" (finding a new solution to problems). As we have seen, it is extremely likely that the ability to perceive in specific spatial ways is a genetically carried aptitude. There is also the possibility of hormonal effects on spatial abilities. Males with highly "masculine" characteristics of body or personality tend to have low spatial scores, while females with masculine characteristics have high spatial scores.[15] Maccoby and Jacklin discovered in their review of the relevant studies, however, that while men were better at seeing a problem without other distractions, there was no greater tendency for them to do better on analytic tasks.[16]

Girls: Less Logical Than Boys?

Although we are always hearing that females are not logical, neither sex seems to have an advantage in terms of concept mastery and reasoning (being logical). Only in tests directly using mathematical processes do men seem to have any edge in reasoning. In creativity tests measuring the "ability to produce unique and novel ideas," girls seem to show a slight superiority to boys from about age seven on, but this may be because of verbal fluency.[17]

In summary, until the beginning of adolescence boys and girls tend to display very similar abilities in the verbal, mathematical, and spatial areas. With the onset of puberty, girls move slightly ahead in some areas and boys in others. With the exception of spatial ability, it is difficult to propose a physical reason for an advantage in either sex. In many cases where there is a difference, it may be due to what society expects and rewards—as in the cases of boys doing well at math and girls doing well at verbal tasks.

Moods and Behaviors

When we turn to the areas of mood and behavior to see if there are inherited physical differences between males and females, we find more evidence for physical reasons for differences in behavior. Frequently, the physical activators of behavior and mood are thought to be hormones. Of course, it is still difficult to know to what extent behavior or mood depends on physical causes and to what extent either is learned because society rewards its expression in a particular sex.

One good example of a behavior in which it is difficult to differentiate physical from social causation is aggression. Maccoby and Jacklin point out that it is difficult even to define aggression. Boys tend to engage in more physically active behavior at older ages and thus are more likely to be defined as aggressive. Males are also more likely to act in ways defined as aggressive in a variety of cultures and in a variety of conditions: physical aggression, verbal aggression, aggression in play and in fantasy.[18] Maccoby and Jacklin thus believe that aggression has a biological basis because in almost all human societies this aggressiveness is found early in life when there is no direct evidence that socialization pressures have been brought to bear.[19] Similar differences are found in subhuman primates such as monkeys.

Aggression seems to be related to levels of sex hormones, and the level of aggressiveness can be changed by administration of these hormones. Receiving male hormones increases aggressive behavior in animals and humans. Excessive doses of estrogens will have the same effect in female rats but not in males.[20] In some cases of aggression there seems to be confusion of cause and effect. It is not only that androgens increase aggressive behavior; in animal experiments aggressive behavior stimulated high levels of androgens where none existed before. Dominance behavior is also related to high levels of male hormones, and dominant males tend to have higher levels of androgens.

Some aspects of dominance behavior and the related characteristic of competition appear to be learned, however, and will be discussed in the section on learned sex-role behavior.

In any examination of behavior we must be very careful not to credit hormones with causing a specific behavior when, indeed, some other elements are functioning. We can see the dangers by examining the case of another chromosomal abnormality where a fetus has an extra Y chromosome (XYY). It was thought that the extra Y chromosome caused unusually high levels of aggressive behavior in males possessing it, because there were many males with extra Y chromosomes in prison—far more than their percentage in the population as a whole. It was discovered, however, that these men were not convicted of crimes that were any more aggressive in nature than those committed by other prison inmates. At the same time, it was noticed that these men were extremely tall and had lower than usual intelligence. It was finally hypothesized that such men were more frequently found in prison because with their rather low intelligence, they were arrested more often than were men with normal chromosomes who committed similar crimes.[22] Thus we see that we must be extremely careful about jumping to conclusions about either behavior based on chromosomal inheritance or the other parts of gender.

The sex hormones have also long been believed to be associated with changing moods in women. Many women note increased irritability, anxiety, depression, and paranoia in the days right before their menstrual periods when estrogen and progesterone levels are low. By contrast, they report feelings of well-being at mid-cycle when estrogen levels are high. Unfortunately, it is very difficult to differentiate physical symptoms from culturally learned feelings about the menstrual cycle, as we shall see in Chapter 6. In addition, it is difficult to know whether the hormones act directly on mood or perhaps indirectly through the medium of fluid retention and pressure on sensitive nerves.[23] Some contradictory findings also confuse us: Women taking the pill and having stable hormone levels may experience mood cycles, and during the period of high-estrogen levels in early pregnancy many women experience symptoms similar to the premenstrual "blues," when estrogen is low. However, the evidence overall certainly points to some effect of the fluctuating levels of sex hormones on mood and behavior.

This evidence is strengthened by new findings that show that men have cycles of testosterone levels that are associated to some degree with levels of aggression and hostility.[24] Obviously, for both sexes, these hormone cycles do not act alone to influence mood. Many other physical, psychological, and environmental factors are important, such as an individual's own time cycle (the "morning" versus the "afternoon" person).

As we have seen, the whole question of hormone effect is further complicated by the new evidence that hormones can be transformed in the body. Thus we are not always sure which hormone, or how much of it, is operating. We must be very careful in saying that certain behavior is caused by levels of a particular hormone. Even when some behavior changes seem to result from hormones, they are usually not extreme and vary greatly from individual to individual. Not all males are aggressive in the presence of an androgen, and not all females are passive or moody in the absence of estrogen.

Thus our physical inheritance can be seen in the action and interaction of chromosomes and hormones. Let us now look at another part of gender which we believe to be learned. We shall then examine other learned sex-role behavior.

Psychosexual Identity: A Learned Part of Gender

As you might imagine, the major difference between males and females is in their belief that they are, indeed, male or female. This belief about one's sex is called psychosexual identity. Although there has been some research examining the question of whether or not sexual identity is imprinted during the critical period of hormonal development, it is believed at the present time that psychosexual identity is overwhelmingly a learned belief: It is a matter of the sex assigned the child and how she or he is raised. This can be demonstrated most clearly when there are possible contradictions between gender and the sex a child *thinks* he or she is. As we have seen, chromosomes and hormones possessed by a child may be of a different gender from that of the external genitals, and children may be reared as one sex when they are "officially" of the other gender. In addition, sometimes parents with psychological quirks of their own may even deliberately raise a child as one of the wrong, or opposite gender. In all of these possible contradictions the sex of rearing almost always seems to win. Even in the dramatic instance where external genital appearance contradicts the sex of rearing, Money discovered that twenty-three out of twenty-five patients believed themselves to be the sex in which they were reared.[25]

The result of one medical accident points this up even more clearly. The parents of seven-month-old twin boys took their infant sons to be circumcised by means of electrocautery. By a tragic mistake the current used on one of the boys was too strong. His penis was severely burned, and later the tissue sloughed off. A plastic surgeon recommended that the child be sex-reassigned as a girl, and the parents made the decision to raise the twin in this way. They started the sex change at seventeen months with a change of name, new clothing, and a new "feminine" hairdo. Of course, in time, the child would have the necessary sex-reassignment surgery and hormone-replacement therapy. The mother dressed her new "daughter" in dresses and hair ribbons, gave her dolls and other feminine toys to play with, and treated her completely as a girl from that time on. By the age of five the little girl was helping her mother with household tasks, exhibiting motherly behavior toward her twin brother, and had asked for a dollhouse and doll carriage for Christmas. She had only a few tomboyish traits such as a high activity level and a lot of dominance behavior.[26]

Hampson, who is one of the authorities on gender identity, believes that although there may be some imprinting of sexual identity during critical periods of fetal development, "psychologic sex or gender role appears to be learned . . . we can [postulate] a concept of psycho-sexual neutrality in humans at birth."[27] Thus we see that while there are certain physical predispositions in men and women which may influence them to act in certain ways, their sexual identity is probably *not* determined by inherited characteristics.

SEX-ROLE BEHAVIOR

Besides the difference we have already discussed, there are many other beliefs about the behavior of males and females. We have been told that males are logical and females are emotional or that males are competitive and females are sociable, for example. These differences cannot be explained by physical inheritance, but they can often be understood by looking at learned behavior for each sex or what we call sex-role behavior.

Sex roles are defined as a cluster of socially or culturally defined expectations that individuals of a certain sex are expected to fulfill in given situations. These expectations vary by time and by culture and may be explicitly stated or very subtly implied by the society. Many social scientists believe that physical leanings toward a certain type of behavior can be largely overcome by different cultural expectations and training. The majority of studies seem to agree that even when individuals have different needs, the training received seems to push almost all of them into the mold of the cultures. Remember the three cultures that Margaret Mead describes in *Sex and Temperament?* In each one the sexes take very different cultural roles. We saw that in the Arapesh culture both sexes are passive and maternal and care for children in nurturing ways; in the Mundugumor culture both sexes are aggressive and competitive; and in the Tchambuli culture men giggle and are very emotional, while women are the economic providers and take sexual initiative.[28]

Theories of Learning Sex Roles

Many psychologists and sociologists have tried to describe the ways in which children learn their psychosexual identity and appropriate sex-role behavior. These theories are simply a structure or patterning that describes what *may* happen in *many* children's lives. They help us see common elements in how parents and the culture teach sex roles or how children develop them naturally. Some of the theories put more emphasis on the inherited, physical nature of sex-role differences, and others stress the social role of learning.

According to the *social-learning theory,* children learn appropriate sex-role behavior through observation and imitation, particularly of the parent of the same sex. Sometimes this behavior is rewarded by the parent, and sometimes the child just feels good about acting like the parent of the same sex. Children particularly learn from nurturing, powerful models. They will imitate behavior, however, even when such behavior is harmful to themselves (children who are beaten often become child-beaters in adult life). The child may "try on" or imitate the behavior of both sexes, but usually he or she is more likely to act like those of the same sex. This theory states that learning appropriate sex-role behavior is gradual and continues throughout life.[29]

Freudian theory takes a slightly different approach to the acquisition of sex-role identity and behavior. We shall examine Freud's theories, and how they affect women, in more detail in Chapter 6, but a brief summary here will show how his theory compares with the others. Freud believed in the importance of both parents being present to enable the child to have same-sex and cross-sex models to imitate. However, he believed that psychological development is not gradual and continuous but is a sequence of stages based on physical growth. The child's sexual identity is established during an oëdipal or phallic stage that occurs between the ages of three and six. He believed that sex-role identity develops differently for each sex during this phase. For boys, the way to gain sex-role identity is to shift identification from mother to the father while retaining the mother (or women in general) as the love object. For girls, the problem is to shift the choice of love object from the mother to the father while identifying with the mother.[30] Freud believed the basic patterning of sexual attitudes and behavior is instinctive and natural but varies somewhat from culture to culture.[31]

A third way of looking at the acquisition of sex-role identity and sex-role behavior is the *cognitive-developmental perspective* of Kohlberg. According to this theory, the child's development is not just a natural progression of physical stages nor just a pattern of imitation with reward and punishment. Kohlberg believed that sex-role attitudes are patterned by "cognitive development." They are rooted in the child's mental ability to handle ideas such as those about the bodies of himself or herself and others and their relationship to other physical objects. According to this approach, children learn by observation and imitation of parents, and also by experience and maturation. Sex-role development begins when the child is first labeled "boy" or "girl." After children learn which label to apply to themselves, they gradually learn to apply the proper labels to other people, usually using such external cues as clothing or hair length. However, they do not yet have the concept that sex is a fixed and unchanging thing. A young child may say to his or her mother, "When you get big, you can be a man like Daddy." By the age of five or six, children's beliefs about their gender identity are firmly established, and they want to behave in ways that are consistent with these labels.[32]

At this age children value anything associated with or like the self, including gender identity. When parents asked a boy why he liked a boy babysitter better, he stated; "Because he's a boy himself, of course."[33] Both sexes prefer their own sex when asked—but girls less so than boys (about 50 percent of girls questioned prefer the female role at ages 3½ to 5½, as compared with 80 percent of boys). Apparently, adult female stereotypes are positive enough to make femininity attractive to some young girls, although they see adult females as less powerful and competent than males. Thus a child wants to behave like his or her appropriate sex. If a child were to think in these terms, he might say something like: "I am a boy, therefore I want to do boy things, therefore the opportunity to do boy things is rewarding."[34] Motivation to do the right things comes from the desire to act in a way consistent with one's gender. It is not a matter of only external rewards. There is a direct application of cultural norms learned from parents and the subtle expectation and teaching of the culture.

One may believe in any one of these theories of the development of sex-role identity and behavior. It seems likely that all of the theories are partly true, but that none offers the total picture. Freudian theory has many followers and may tell us something about the child's formation of sexual identity. In many circumstances, however, it cannot account for a child's learning of a range of sex-appropriate behavior without going through the necessary stages or without models, and it has many negative implications for women. Social learning theory shows us the importance of imitation and rewards for behavior but does not tell us why children will learn appropriate behavior at different times, when models are not present, or when such behavior is not rewarded. Cognitive-developmental theory is probably the most comprehensive theory of the three. It helps us see that learning sex-role identity and behavior is a matter of a child's passing through physical and mental stages of growth, as well as having models and receiving rewards for appropriate behavior. All three theories show us the complex interaction of the child's development with the actions of the parents and the rules and expectations of the culture.

REINFORCERS OF SEX-ROLE BEHAVIOR

Although all of the preceding theories are helpful in explaining the way in which children internalize beliefs about sex roles, it is also useful for us to look specifically at ways in which sex-role behavior is encouraged. For convenience, we can divide these means of encouragement into three categories: parental expectations and actions; cultural reinforcers such as language, clothing, and media; and cultural institutions such as the schools.

Parental Expectations and Actions

Parents may reinforce sex-role behavior either in subtle and perhaps unconscious communication of their expectations or in direct attempts to teach by reward and punishment. For example, a parent may treat a boy or girl differently because boys or girls really do stimulate their parents differently. Here we may see an interaction of the physical nature of the child and the parents' ideas of how to respond to it. We have seen that parents may actually respond to different kinds of stimulation from boy and girl babies. A parent who talks more to a female infant who is mouthing and seems to be "smiling" is responding to a physical difference. Boy babies sleep fewer hours than girl infants and are likely to be more irritable. Thus they may be picked up and held more often than girl babies.

Parents may also treat their child in a way consistent with what they *think* a child of that sex is probably like. Parents appear to have differential expectations of the nature of boys and girls from birth onward. In one study of thirty pairs of new parents, fifteen with newborn sons and fifteen with newborn daughters, daughters were significantly more likely than sons to be described as little, cute, or pretty. Interestingly enough, fathers were more likely to describe traits according to the sex of the child than were mothers.[35] Boys were described as being more likely to be rough at play, noisy, physically active, defiant, competitive, adventuresome, and mechanical. Girls were described as likely to be helpful, neat and clean, quiet and reserved, sensitive to the feelings of others, well-mannered, fearful, and emotional.

In personal interaction parents were likely to treat their male and female children in ways consistent with how they viewed that sex. Fathers returning home from work were more likely to tickle their little girls under the chin or bounce them gently on their knees, while they would often toss boy infants rather roughly in the air and speak to them in louder, rougher tones.[36] It has also been shown that mothers put up with more angry behavior from male children and even humorously, but symbolically, give in to their unreasonable demands, while they would not do the same for girls.[37] However, fathers reacted in a reverse fashion and put up with more aggressive behavior from girls.

Another type of indirect parental influence is, of course, the types of things the child sees the parent doing. Children learn from observation and imitation. A child is quick to notice that Mother moves over and lets Dad drive the car when she picks him up at work. Perhaps the child may notice that Mom always does the cooking. Nothing may be said directly, but a child picks up many important messages about sex roles in this way.

A parent may also directly attempt to teach a child appropriate behaviors. A father is more likely to practice throwing a football with his male child than with his female child, and a mother is more likely to teach her daughter to sew than she is to teach her son. The parent may also reward or punish unsolicited behavior on the part of the child. A preschool male who cries when he gets hurt is more likely to be told "you shouldn't cry" or "big boys don't cry," while a girl will probably be allowed her tears. The boy is also more likely to face prohibitions on wearing women's clothes or playing with girls' toys such as dolls than a girl is likely to be forbidden to wear boys' clothing or to play with boys' toys.[38] Conversely, fathers encourage feminine behavior in their girls. Over half the fathers of two- or three-year-old children described their daughters as being cuddly, flirting, and soft and encouraged that behavior.[39] Ironically, parents who behave differently with their boys and girls often believe that both sexes *should* behave in the same way. They believe that boys and girls should both be competitive and both sexes should help around the house, for example. In one study parents said that they wished their children of both sexes would have the same skills (such as confidence, ability at sports, and the like), but they assigned chores to their children according to their sex and gave them sex-typed toys.[40] Parents, thus, simply did not seem to act upon their own value systems.

Some research suggests that especially in the area of independence training parents treat their male and female children differently. Early studies of infants seemed to suggest that male infants were more exploratory and independent. Goldberg and Lewis, in a 1969 study, showed that when infants were left in a room with their mothers, boys moved farther away from their mothers than girls did. Boys were also less likely to return to the mothers for reassurance and more likely to try actively to get around a barrier placed between them and their mothers. This study and others like it seemed to imply that boys were more independent—perhaps because of differences in the way they were treated at home, Goldberg and Lewis speculated.[41] More recent studies, however, are not consistent in their findings about the independence training or behavior of little boys and girls. Some show a difference and some do not. The sexes are allowed equal range of movement, checked on as often, and expected to do the same types of things to help themselves. Mothers and fathers tend to use firmer enforcement with boys, however,[42] and at about age seven girls begin to receive more "chaperonage," such as being met at school and escorted home. It is this last area that seems to be an important clue in how boys and girls may develop different ideas about independence; at this early age females are more restricted and cannot participate fully in society.

Even if direct teaching of independence does not differ between the sexes, children can pick up other behavior clues. A boy may be allowed to take an early morning paper route or be out after dark, where a girl will be forbidden these activities. While the reasons for the prohibition may be concern for the safety of the girl—related to sexual abuse or physical strength—the message that boys have more independence is clear. This is an area, too, where a child may see very different behaviors modeled by his father and by his mother. His father may readily pack and go off on a trip alone, whereas his mother may hesitate to do the same thing.

In young girls, this kind of timidity, which is the opposite of independence, does not seem to be linked to actual fearfulness, however. Girls act in the same ways as boys do, although they may report more fears.[43] For example, girls may report that they are afraid of snakes, but given an opportunity, will pick up a snake as readily as a boy will.

The fact that parental actions do have an effect in shaping sex-role behavior should be evident to us just from observation, but research reinforces our beliefs. Minuchen showed in one study that the children from more conventional homes showed more unequivocal commitment to their own sex-role stereotype and more sex-typed play and other behavior.[44] We should note, too, that the childrearing practices for girls are often contradictory to those that lead to achievement. Little girls who are taught to be appropriately "feminine" pay a high price in terms of possible achievement and success orientation. Maccoby and Jacklin point out, for example, that among six-year-old children, those who are likely to increase their IQs are competitive, self-assertive, independent, and dominant in action with other children. Those who are passive and dependent are likely to have declining IQs as the years pass.[45]

Parental Expectations of Working-Class and Black Families   Parental expectations of boy and girl children also differ somewhat by social class and by race. Although the schools and the media may largely reflect white, middle-class stereotypes, the values taught in the home may differ. The working-class parent is even more likely to stress the traditional role for women by modeling and teaching. The child in these families is likely to see a father who, at least on the surface, is dominant in decision making. The mother may work outside the home; but this work is seen as an extension of her helpmate role, and she is still expected to do all the housework. The child may well see the parents doing very separate types of household chores and other activities and may see little communication between them.[46]

There is also some indication that working-class parents stress different values in raising their children. In 1959 Kohn did a study of twenty-two working-class and middle-class parents. He asked them all what characteristics they would value in a fifth-grade child. The middle-class parents stressed things like happiness and curiosity, while the working-class parents stressed neatness, cleanliness, and ability to defend oneself, for both boys and girls. While both middle-class and working-class parents wanted their girls to be popular and obedient, this was particularly stressed by working-class parents.[47] Working-class parents were also less likely to encourage their girls to go to college.[48]

Weitzman speculates that the working-class girl may be pushed to pursue a traditional role for another subtle, but important, reason: If she were to do well in a career, she might outshine males in the family.[49]

By contrast, the role model for the young girl in a Black family is a strong one. The mother in the Black family is likely to be working outside the home and to have more say in decision making within it. The young Black girl is likely to see female relatives and their children who are coping alone without feeling the need for a particular man to take care of them. Young girls frequently learn at an early age that marriage may be problematic or difficult and that they will have to take care of themselves as adults and should plan on working. For this reason, young girls are encouraged early to do well in school and to make plans for the future. Thus independence, self-reliance, and assertiveness are valued and encouraged in the young Black girl much more so than in her White counterpart. As we shall see, this differential self-esteem and emphasis on achievement for females in Black families leads to a higher proportion of Black females achieving professional success compared to Black men than of White women achieving such success when compared to White men.[50]

Parental expectations and training are only one factor influencing the young child, however. Let us look at some of the other cultural influences on a child's learning of sex-role behavior.

Cultural Influences on Learning Sex-Role Behavior

Language.   Language is a subtle socializer for children. They soon learn that certain adjectives are applied almost entirely to one sex or another, or with implications that they include only one sex. "Bitchy" and "catty," for example, are terms almost entirely applied to women while "tough," "successful," and other positive adjectives have masculine implications. In certain cases (as in "tough"), these terms may have a negative implication when applied to women. Women also soon learn that frequently they are part of man (wo*man*), and many important things are referred to only in male terms. Women are included in the term mankind—often shortened to "man"—but does a young girl feel included in such phrases as "one small step for man, one giant leap for mankind?"

Important and exciting jobs are referred to by masculine terms such as police*man* and fire*man.* One realizes how unnecessary such designations are when we think of how quickly we have become used to such words as policewoman or chairperson. Certain titles and occupations are also masculine in their gender. One gets a Bachelor or Master of Arts from college, not a spinster or Mistress of Arts degree. Doctors, dentists, and other similar professionals, including college professors, are referred to as "he"; while nurses, dental technicians, and elementary school teachers are referred to as "she."

The words used to refer to women have, in themselves, often acquired a certain negative meaning. Women of all ages and kinds are called "girls," a term that implies immaturity and frivolity. One hears about the "girls" at the office engaging in "girl talk," but one does not hear that the male colleagues engage in "boy talk." The term "lady" is frequently used in a rather rude fashion ("Hey, lady"), and it may imply immaturity, frivolity, or promiscuity (as in "ladies of the night"). The equivalent term for men, "gentlemen," does not have such implications. "Mistress" has a sexual meaning connoting the power of a man over the woman; while "master" implies the power of a man over the world ("master of his trade"). Women are also defined in terms of their sexual desirability to men, and men, in terms of their ability to dominate women sexually. Thus a woman may be a "dog," "broad," "nice piece," "chick"; while men are "dudes," "studs," "jocks," "hunks." There are over a thousand words and phrases that denigrate women sexually, but nowhere near this number exist for men.[51]

Other words have derogatory implications for women, although we may not be totally aware of them: The weak man is called a "sissy" (a diminutive of "sister"), and a person with whom one is extremely angry is often referred to as a "son-of-a-bitch," implying the promiscuity of his mother.[52] Words referring to men and women and their marital status also have different meanings. The noun "bachelor" is often preceded by the adjectives "gay" or "eligible," whereas the noun "spinster" implies old and nonsexual. Women are also defined in terms of their relationship to particular men (Miss, Mrs.), whereas men are not defined in this way.

The words that women learn to use frequently also imply a certain sense of silliness or weakness. A book review that describes a book as "pleasant" or "darling" will hardly have the same influence as one that speaks of that book as "clever" or "stimulating." Walum points out that women's vocabulary tends to make ideas seem trivial. As an example, she cites the difference in impact between the phrases "Oh, my—such a lovely idea!" and "Damn, yes—that's a tremendous idea!"[53] It is easy to guess which sex said each of the phrases. Thus the language women use teaches them to appear indecisive and constrained and prevents them from being taken seriously. Their speech patterns keep feminine stereotypes alive.

Children also learn early that the patterns of language usage are different for men and women. There is an ingrained assumption that women talk more than men, but this is not true. Women talk much less than men in mixed conversations and are interrupted more by men. In one observation 96 percent of the interruptions and 100 percent of the overlaps in conversations were made by male speakers.[54] Such interruptions and contradictions are all privileges of the superior. Women bear out their own acceptance of this inferior status by a greater tendency to hesitate, apologize, and disparage their own statements.

Incidentally, Goffman points out that this same sense of inferiority is transmitted by women in their body language. Women smile much more than men—a sign of submission. When confronted with a stare, a woman will avert her eyes and drop her eyelids. When talking, she will tilt her head—the beginning of a submissive gesture.[55] In terms of space, women's territory, personal space, and posture are restricted. Women are supposed to be compact not sprawled out. Their space is more invadable—especially by children, but also by men. When persons touch, it symbolizes status.[56] Usually those of higher status touch those of lower status: The physician touches the orderly; the teacher, the pupil. Men are more likely to initiate touch with women, and women are likely to cuddle, a submissive response to the touch.[57]

Toys. Up to the age of about two years, children of both sexes play with many of the same toys: stuffed animals, pull toys, blocks, and the like. After about two years of age, the toys become much more differentiated. Boys are far more likely to get mobile toys, such as trucks and engines; girls get more dolls and passive toys, such as dish sets, dress-up jewelry, and clothes. They may also get toys associated with housekeeping such as irons, little sweepers, and easy-bake ovens. A little later, they are likely to get doll houses where they can move the furniture and play house. Many of the housekeeping toys are a realistic representation of the things that girls are likely to do later in life (bake, sew, iron, sweep) and the dolls played with may even be ones that can be fed, diapered, and bathed as real babies could be.[58]

Few of these dolls, however, have any sexual anatomy. Only recently has a little boy doll with appropriate anatomy been developed by Mattel. The Barbie doll and her counterparts are for slightly older girls, and show how a little girl is taught the physical ideal of what she should be as a woman. The Barbie doll, with its unrealistic big breasts and long slender legs, is made to be dressed up in a variety of elaborate outfits. It is not soft enough to be cuddled, and it does not come with really mobile accessories as do the more unisex early childhood toys. Perhaps the ultimate in expressing the idea of becoming a grown-up sexual object is Barbie's little sister, Skipper. In one version of the Skipper doll, a child can rotate Skipper's arm and she will grow breasts and develop a thinner waist—truly a model of how to become a desirable sex object in a hurry.

Even at early ages, boys are likely to get toys that are more connected with exciting occupations: fire engines, planes, and the like. However, they learn, perhaps unrealistically, that the world of men is a world of excitement and toughness. It is seldom that a little boy would get a toy briefcase and a bunch of papers to shuffle in an imitation of a father's likely role. Boys are also more likely than girls to get sports equipment from an early age onward. Bats, balls, basketballs, footballs, hockey sticks, and all such accessory items are not only given boys, but boys are encouraged to use them actively. Although the parents in one study said that a baseball glove and similar items would be appropriate toys for either sex, they gave their children toys stereotyped for their particular sex.[59] Boys seldom get dolls to play with after they are two or three years old. Dolls and stuffed animals become sissy or babyish for a boy (yet a girl may keep her stuffed animals on her bed through the college years). Toy catalogs do show about 68 male dolls (as opposed to the 356 female dolls),[60] but these are male dolls that are justified in terms of military activity or occupations. Thus the little boy is given his choice of a GI Joe with a kung-fu grip (it can chop a board in two on the pressing of a button) or an Action Jackson in a basketball uniform. Clothes for the male dolls include such things as scuba outfits and mountain-climbing equipment, and the accessory equipment may include a special rescue rig or a spaceship.

There is little research on which toys children do receive or play with. One study by two Yale sociologists surveyed forty-two boys and forty-two girls. The subjects reported receiving an almost identical number of gift items; however, 73 percent of the boys' gifts were toys and only 57 percent of the girls' gifts were toys.[61] Later, advertising plays a large role in stimulating people to buy different toys for each of the sexes. Boys get more expensive toys and toys they can manipulate more, such as microscopes, chemistry sets, and model planes, which stimulate their imagination. Even similar items for boys and girls, such as doctor and nurse kits, can actually be very different. Goodman and Lever report that a doctor kit marketed for boys had "stethoscope with amplifying diaphragm . . . miniature microscope . . . blood pressure tester . . . prescription blank, and more," while the nurse kit came equipped with "nurse apron, cap, plastic silverware, plate, sick tray and play food."[62]

Even in unisex equipment, such as bicycles, boys' equipment is more expensive and intricate. They also get equipment that is different in kind. Thus a boy will get hockey skates and a girl will get figure skates—and the subtle message is not lost: Boys skate fast and play rough games, whereas girls do graceful figure eights. As boys and girls get older, the presents given them tend to converge somewhat, and both sexes get clothes, records, books, and similar items.

One interesting sidelight is that toy salespersons may be the determining factor in what type of toys are chosen. In a recent study of what types of choices such salespersons would recommend, it was discovered that they recommended sex-stereotyped toys over half the time, and they were more likely to recommend sex-stereotyped toys for boys in particular.[63]

Games.   The sex-role messages implied in girls' and boys' toys may be further emphasized in the games that males and females play. Girls tend to play more individual games and those requiring only two or three playmates, such as jump rope, jacks, baton twirling, and skating. Their play is also more realistic than that of boys, which is not surprising given the type of toys they receive: play stoves, irons, and sweepers. The sports that they play—skating, horseback riding, and swimming—usually put more emphasis upon the individual, and neither cooperation nor competition of a team nature is usual. It has been typical for girls to actually be barred from participation in sports such as Little League baseball. If teams for girls are allowed, they are frequently differentiated in kind and nature, as in slow-pitch softball teams for girls.[64] Girls are also more likely to join groups such as the Girl Scouts in the course of their play.

Boys not only play in larger groups but are more likely to engage in both individual and team competition. The boy who learns skateboarding must either equal or surpass his neighborhood playmates in the number of daring feats performed. If he plays baseball, shoots baskets, or plays hockey, then he must do it well so that he will be chosen for the neighborhood and school teams. Many of the boys' team sports are quite complex and require learning rules, strategy, and cooperation, as well as competition. Boys also learn early that they must be tough and willing to play in spite of injury or difficult conditions. In their early years boys show more fantasy play than girls. They are more likely to play cops and robbers, cowboys and Indians, and occupation-related and other games (with the exception of war games) that they are not likely to engage in as adults.[65] When boys do affiliative activities, these are often connected with at least subtle competition. The boy scout works to become an eagle scout; many boys' clubs or fraternities emphasize team sports.

Clothing.   Clothes are not so much the inhibiting factor for girls that they were (unless you consider that girls frequently receive clothes, instead of toys, as gifts). The sexes now seem uniformly to wear jeans, shirts, and sneakers in preschool and elementary school. For dress and occasionally at other times, however, little girls are supposed to look stereotypically feminine. The difficulty of being active in a skirt and slick-soled shoes, combined with still prevalent injunctions to "not let your panties show," make any real movement doubtful. Even the more unisex girls' clothes may have some disadvantages: Pants for girls have traditionally had few or no useful pockets, thus making it necessary for even young girls to awkwardly carry change, comb, and Kleenex in their hands or in a purse. In late elementary school clothes for girls become increasingly less functional. Platform shoes for women have been the style in the 1970s, leading to sprained ankles, inhibited movements, and just plain difficulty in walking. The preteen adopts these styles, as well as the hose and high heels worn by older girls and women for dressier occasions. These kinds of clothes are obviously uncomfortable, unhealthful, and inhibit active motion, yet girls and women who do not wear them on "appropriate" occasions may well be reproved. It is in late elementary school, too, that a girl starts spending more time and money on her appearance. Girls of ten or eleven frequently have their ears pierced and start acquiring earrings and other kinds of jewelry. They spend time curling their hair—and later perhaps bleaching it—and applying makeup. They may worry about the length of their fingernails and may keep away from certain activities so their nails can stay long and polished. Most girls and women spend a great deal of time and money attempting to improve their appearance, and their interest in, and ability to engage in, more active pastimes may be limited by this fact.

The Media: An Important Influence.   One of the other important influences on young children today is television. It is estimated that between kindergarten and sixth grade children watch from ten to twenty-five hours of television a week. Frequently television viewing begins at about three years of age and remains high until about twelve years, with a decline in the teenage years. Upon marriage, television viewing increases again. Children spend more time watching television than they do reading books or comic books, listening to the radio, or going to the movies. The types of things they watch vary from early childhood shows, such as "Captain Kangaroo" and "Sesame Street," to later interests such as detective shows, family-style programs (like "The Brady Bunch" or "The Waltons"), and certain movies. Of course, they probably see 100–250 commercials during their hours of television watching each week. The average television is turned on six hours and eighteen minutes a day. By the time an American child is sixteen, he or she has spent approximately fifteen thousand hours in front of a television set—four thousand more than in the classroom. What exactly do young boys and girls learn about sex roles as they watch their sets?

Even with recent attempts at improvement, television shows are overwhelmingly stereotyped in their presentation of male and female roles. Recent studies by Women on Words and Images rank sixteen of the top-rated programs of the 1973 and 1974 viewing season in terms of the number and occupation of female and male characters and their positive and negative behaviors. According to these studies, there is no question that many of the shows watched by children are violent and present a distorted view of family life and the roles of men and women. It was found that about 75 percent of the roles in prime-time and Saturday-morning programs portrayed middle-class American males who were unmarried and without responsibility. The men were shown as active and tough, whereas women were shown as lacking in social power and influence. They were objects of victimization by men, and sexual objects or mates in marriage rather than responsible individuals acting on their own.[66] Even in the "educational" shows women were often shown in negative ways. The female puppets on "Sesame Street," for example, often portrayed strident, mothering types.[67] Recently some attempts have been made to improve the situation. However, more recent prime-time shows that attempt to show women in action roles ("Charlie's Angels" or "Police-woman") frequently end up showing them subservient to a man or rescued by one.

The research found that in the shows surveyed children saw nearly six times as many men as women, and women were overwhelmingly shown in wife and mother roles. Only about 25 percent of the married women worked and even less frequently did they contribute significantly to the family's support. If unmarried, working women were almost always seen in traditional female occupations. Male behavior was usually identified as independent, logical, worldly, skilled in business, self-confident, and showing leadership. Women seldom showed these behaviors, except in situation comedies, and they were twice as likely as men to show bungling behavior. "The prime-time message is that there are more men around, and that they are dominant, authoritative and competent."[68] Women get the message that their roles and their participation in society will be limited.

Another study showed that out of 2,750 commercials, 90 percent used a male narrator, although over 50 percent of the products advertised were used in the home. Women's professional status was virtually ignored in commercials, and if a woman was shown working outside the home, she was, as usual, in a traditional women's occupation. Most often, women were shown as sex objects using domestic products in the home while being instructed in their use by men.[69]

The fact that these images do affect children's views is reflected in research results showing that children who watched the most television had strong traditional sex-role development (even when compared within each social class). This relationship of television viewing to believing in traditional sex roles holds equally true for boys and girls and does not change with increasing age.[70] The influence of television has become so widespread that even the courts are willing to blame it for children's behavior. In a 1977 murder trial in Miami the young criminal's defense was that he had been so indoctrinated by the violence of one television show ("Kojak") that he was driven to kill.[71]

Books: Another Important Influence.   Books are probably as important a socializer of children's beliefs as television. The time spent reading may not equal the time spent watching, but children and parents sometimes do not have a choice about what is read. Children can only escape a required schoolbook by refusing to open it (with the imagined consequences of that action). In addition, any message presented by schoolbooks carries the stamp of authority's approval.

Both preschool and elementary school books have been shown to have extensive sex stereotyping. Boys far outnumber girls in titles and as central characters for stories in most books. Even the animated characters and the educational books (like Dr. Seuss) reflect a difference in the presentation of males and females. The inanimate objects that are personified as achievement oriented (Toot the Tugboat) are invariably male. Male animals are exciting lions or tigers, and female animals are often sloths, badgers, and geese.[72]

Girls are not only ignored but shown in an unflattering light when they are included. Boys explore, create, try new things, and are skillful at what they do; they form friendships; they are independent and aggressive. Girls usually engage in passive play or household chores; they admire boys who are doing things. They are portrayed as fearful, clumsy, and unable to make friends. In mathematics books they are shown earning lower salaries, being confused by complicated problems, and using math always for typically female tasks such as grocery shopping.[73] Girls as a group are also degraded with such descriptives as "silly," "boring," and "vain." Sometimes their status is explicitly pointed out. One oft-quoted phrase from an elementary school reader advises girls to "accept the fact that this is a man's world and learn to play the game gracefully."[74] Girls thus get a special and not always pleasant picture of their separate identity.

Adult women fare little better. Mothers are shown in typical housewife roles: cooking, cleaning, helping children, and the like. They are seldom doing anything fun with children or adults and are frequently scolding or harassing. The 46 percent of adult women in the labor force are practically ignored.[75] A survey of schoolbooks in the Michigan school system found that men were portrayed in 213 different occupations, but women were portrayed in only 39. Only 7 of these 39 occupations were mentioned in more than one book. As you might guess, the women were nurses, librarians, teachers in elementary school, seamstresses, secretaries, and mothers. Incredibly, pronouns of the female gender were totally absent from the first two readers surveyed in Michigan, the excuse being that the word "she" does not appear high enough on word lists. Therefore, if "he" and "it" are talked about more in print, they must continue to be talked about first—and so the cycle of discrimination continues.[76]

It is easy to learn the lesson that women are not important and that they have dull, routine lives and jobs. Males are not only talked about first but are shown in numerous stimulating occupations. In a popular preschool book entitled *I'm Glad I'm a Boy, I'm Glad I'm a Girl* we read the following: "Boys are football players, girls are cheerleaders; Boys are doctors, girls are nurses; Boys are policemen, girls are metermaids; Boys are pilots, girls are [you guessed it] stewardesses."[77] Fathers are also the good guys: They play with children and show them how to do exciting things. Unfortunately, in the portrayal of family life, the fathers also make decisions in the family, and the mothers do the housework—alone. The books portray families unrealistically in still another way as well. The families shown are overwhelmingly white and middle class, and both parents are present in the home. Although one in six children now grows up in a single-parent family, this fact is totally ignored.[78]

Attempts to change the stereotypes often fail and may even produce more sexism. In one book, *Mommies at Work,* the final sentence reads; "all Mommies loving the best of all to be your own Mommy and coming home to you."[79] Would this have been said in a book about working Daddies? In another children's book which attempts to deal with sexism, *The Snake in the Carpool,* a little girl calmly adopts a snake as a pet but in the end loses it and must be shown by a boy how to house and feed it.[80]

Institutional Reinforcers of Sex Roles: Preschool and Elementary School

The general classroom environment may also enhance the girl's feeling that she is different and perhaps not quite equal. In preschool little boys and girls line up separately, usually use different bathrooms, and may be separated by sex in spelling teams and other activities. The boys' groups may be chosen to carry chairs or wash blackboards and the girls' groups, to pass out cookies. The general classroom atmosphere may also reinforce traditional roles by showing charts and pictures depicting mothers doing the wash on Monday; ironing on Tuesday.

Research on teacher-student relations has shown that teachers also tend to confirm traditional sex-role behavior by reacting differently to boys and girls. In one large study involving twenty-one fourth- and sixth-grade classes (thirteen taught by males and eight by female teachers), it was found that teachers disapproved of boys more. Many have pointed out that the usual reason for this disapproval is that boys disrupt the atmosphere of an elementary school classroom where the qualities of neatness, conformity, and obedience are stressed. They have warned that because of this disapproval and the push toward conformity, "schools are emasculating our boys." They need not have been troubled. The large study showed that while teachers disapproved of boys more, they also listened to them more, gave them more instruction, and approved of them more.[81] Other research has shown that teachers taught the boys more mathematics, gave them more explicit directions, and gave them more opportunity to try new experiences.[82] Female teachers were also shown to encourage aggression in boys, although they rewarded dependency in both sexes.[83]

The studies in this area all agree that teachers see girls as less creative than boys, give less attention to girls, and reward girls for conformity.[84] Remember that the qualities needed for increased IQ and achievement orientation are not conformity and dependency but assertiveness and independence! Maccoby and Jacklin summarize the generally different treatment of the sexes when they say "adults respond as if they find boys more interesting and attention-provoking than girls."[85] These are powerful data, as teacher expectations often become self-fulfilling prophecies.[86] The teachers may be opposed in theory to what they are doing, but they are often unaware of their own behavior.[87]

The conformity and docility asked for in the elementary-school classroom affect both sexes. However, the negative concepts of females presented and the reinforcement of traditional sex-role behavior in teacher-student relationships particularly affect young women.[88] Girls seem to accept the stereotypes of their abilities, often unnecessarily. Their opinions of themselves become lower as they progress through school, whereas the self-evaluation of boys becomes higher.[89] Girls give lower estimates of their chances for success in many areas, even when their past performance has been superior. They are also less likely to try creative solutions to problems, they avoid mathematics classes, and they are less willing to risk failure.[90] Motivation in the elementary years is extremely important. Although adolescence puts new pressures on girls (as we shall see in Chapter 6), it does not create entirely new patterns. Motivation for females in the adolescent and college years is correlated with motivation during the elementary years.[91]

Girls also seem to narrow down their career choices in accordance with the presented stereotypes. By the ninth grade only 3 percent of the girls, as compared with 25 percent of the boys, are considering careers in science or engineering.[92] In later years this trend continues. In a longitudinal study begun in 1920 Terman and Oden have shown that 61 percent of women who tested as "highly gifted" while young ended up being full-time homemakers, rather than achieving prominence in professional and managerial occupations; yet 86 percent of the "gifted" men achieved such success.[93] Although this study does not reflect the recent increases in the numbers of women entering the labor force, statistics continue to show that women do not achieve the career success that would be predicted on the basis of their IQ and education.

Thus we begin to see that the school environment is often an unhealthy one in which girls begin to believe that they are less important, less intelligent, and less able than boys. In combination with the messages sent by other socializers such as language, books, television, and general cultural norms, the school atmosphere has a powerful effect. Little girls indeed learn that "it is a man's world and they had better learn to play the game." They lower their aspirations and chances for success or even active participation in society accordingly.[94]

In our observation of the various parental, cultural, and institutional socializers and reinforcers of sex-role behavior, we have seen that there are distinct differences in the ways that males and females are treated and in the ultimate type of behavior that is expected for each sex. Let us look a little further now at some of the research about the differences between males and females. With what we know, we may be able to judge better whether these differences are inherited or learned. We may even discover in some instances that believed differences or stereotypes really do not exist at all.

What were some of the differences believed to exist between men and women, or boys and girls? Parents, we learned, tend to describe their boys as independent, rough, and competitive, and their girls as gentle, sociable, thoughtful, and the like. Let us see how much these descriptions may really apply to each sex and how much the traits described are inherited and how much they may be learned.

STEREOTYPIC BEHAVIOR: THE RESULTS OF LEARNING

Competition and Dominance

We discovered, when talking about the effects of hormones, that there may be a tendency for boys to be slightly more aggressive than girls because of higher levels of testosterone. Does this tendency toward more aggressive behavior in males carry over into their being more competitive than females and exercising more general dominance than females? If so, how much of the aggression, dominance, and competition is learned and reinforced by childhood patterns of play, games, and the like?

Maccoby and Jacklin point out that dominance or competition is not necessarily the same thing as aggressiveness. In the case of dominance, for example, aggressive behavior may result in dominance, but efforts to control or manipulate the behavior of another person may not depend on being tough at all. In addition, other elements may enter into dominance, such as the ability to do something well. It does seem that among younger children, boys seem to dominate girls (although they usually play in sex-segregated groups), but these other factors must be considered.[95]

There is mixed evidence on the question of whether or not boys are more competitive than girls. Boys seem to need some stimulus to compete but, when aroused, seem to sustain a competitive level that is higher than that of girls. Girls seem to care less about competition as such, but it is interesting to note that if they do compete, they will try harder when their opponent is a boy.[96]

It is difficult to explain why girls seem to care less about competition than boys do. It has been suggested that competition is tied up with achievement motivation and an orientation to people rather than things. According to this belief, girls need more approval from others, and their lower level of competition reflects their fear of disrupting social situations. However, actual studies show that girls are no more affected than boys by social approval or by information about the correctness of their response.[97] We are therefore left with little to explain the more competitive nature of boys, except that it may be a factor which is expected of them and encouraged by society. Thus boys are probably placed in more competitive situations than girls are and may learn to expect this as part of their daily life—or their self-image. On the contrary, girls are not expected to be competitive and are seldom rewarded for being so. The fact that girls can certainly learn to be competitive when the rewards are sufficient is shown by the recent success of women athletes in all areas.

Some scientists believe that boys are both more competitive and more cooperative as they must learn the rules of game when they play in large groups and in team sports. This training may be used later in life when men learn to play the "team game" in corporation settings, although competing for individual success at the same time. By contrast, girls usually play in groups of two or three as youngsters, and their play cannot be characterized as either particularly competitive or cooperative.[98] The unity and team spirit that boys develop are not typical of girls' activities, nor do women have the training in cooperation that enables them to establish a group unity easily in later life. It has been pointed out by many that this makes it difficult for women to succeed in the typical corporation setting. Girls are also not trained in competition. In the adolescent years girls may compete for popularity and the attention of men, but they do so covertly.

Self-Esteem, Competition, and Success

It is believed by some that general self-esteem or achievement motivation may account for differences in dominance or competitiveness. However, younger girls seem to have self-esteem and a general self-concept that is as good as that of boys, and they want success in a similar fashion. Only as men and women reach adolescence do we see that females are less likely than males to predict success on specific tasks in spite of past performance. Women are also more likely to underrate their sex in general. They rate stereotypic "masculine" qualities such as strength and assertiveness higher than they do "feminine" qualities such as gentleness and sociability. Both men and women think that work done by women is not as good as the same work done by men.[99] Thus, although women may have a generally good self-concept, they may not feel positively about their abilities and characteristics as compared with those of men or when they are working in a masculine area. We shall examine some of the reasons for this self-doubt or "fear of success" in the next chapter.

Sociability

Are girls indeed more sociable and interested in relationships with others? There seems to be no evidence for any inherited or instinctive degree of sociability in females. Earlier studies seemed to show that infant girls preferred toys representing faces and people-toys over other objects, but new information shows little difference between boys and girls in toy preference. Other evidence for early sociability is likewise lacking. Girls play in smaller groups than boys, and they are not any more accepting of strangers who come into their group.[100]

Maccoby and Jacklin also did not find that the majority of studies showed girls as being more sensitive to social cues than boys. In one study, for example, when given a series of pictures and asked to tell what the central character was feeling, girls were better at identifying the feelings of female characters, and boys, of male characters.[101] Maccoby and Jacklin discovered, however, that girls and women were more interested in social activities than males were and that girls developed an earlier interest in the opposite sex. Females also showed more interest in "gentle" types of interaction with others than in aggressive behavior. [102]

It is also interesting that in her androgyny studies on college-age women Bem found that women who accepted beliefs concerning traditional female roles were more likely to be able to decode feelings in others.[103] Perhaps because of the social stereotypes that women are empathetic and more social, traditional women believe that knowledge of, and sympathy for, the feelings of others are what they "ought" to have and thus are more tuned in to obtaining. At the same time, females are probably more rewarded than males for general empathetic behavior.

Girls also seem to learn to suppress their negative emotions more than boys do—so that they may *seem* "nicer" and "more sociable." That boys show more anger than girls after eighteen months of age is due not to the fact that they are getting angry more frequently but that girls are decreasing the number and intensity of their outbursts.[104] Some have thought that girls are simply more likely to express anger in words, whereas boys continue to do so in less verbal ways such as crying. However, boys seem to be equally able to use words if they want to be aggressive, so they should be able to use them to show anger as well. We can only speculate that boys may be allowed more freedom to express anger and frustration because parents believe this to be evidence of their spirit, strength, and boyishness. Thus we see that there may be subtle factors in early socialization that encourage boys to express direct, positive, perhaps aggressive emotions, while girls are taught to suppress these feelings and to react in nice, kind, sociable ways.

Nurturance

What about nurturance? Is the ability to nurture and care for young infants also something that females learn, or is this one of the areas where inheritance and instinct plays a dominant role? With the recent changes in sex roles and the controversy about whether or not men are able to care for children as well as women do, it is particularly important to examine this behavior.

The majority of research shows that there is no evidence for a mothering or maternal *instinct* in human beings, although hormones may play some role in stimulating maternal behavior, as may critical periods of interaction with a newborn. In experiments with rats Rosenblat showed that plasma from a new mother stimulated maternal behavior in other virgin female rats. This was especially pronounced when the virgin rats were exposed to litters of babies.[105] Recent studies with human infants and their mothers also seem to show that mother-child bonds are the strongest when the mother can hold the child and care for it immediately after birth.[106] The belief that the response to infants is in the learned rather than the instinctive category, however, is based on the fact that all mothers do not exhibit this maternal behavior, even when in constant contact with their infants after birth. It has been common for mothers throughout history to kill their unwanted babies, and child-abuse cases where mothers beat their children are frequent and coming more to the public's attention today.

It is also believed that nurturing is learned because male animals may exhibit this behavior. Although male rats are often initially cannibalistic, they usually improve their nurturing behavior if given successive litters of baby rats to care for.[107] When allowed close contact with newborn infants after birth, men seem to establish the same bonds with them as females do. In fact, often many men seem to exhibit the same nurturing feelings as women when allowed to do so without public disapproval. In one experiment men who did not define themselves as "macho" or supermasculine were equally as willing as women to play with a small kitten or baby. In fact, some of the more androgynous or feminine men were *more* likely to play with the baby than were *women* who had "stereotypically feminine" scores.[108]

Thus we can see that nurturing behavior may be partly stimulated by hormones but is probably largely a learned behavior in human beings. Such behavior is not often found in very young children of either sex, and when it does occur, it does not differ by sex. In one cross-cultural study which compared children in Kenya, India, Okinawa, the Philippines, and Mexico, there was no difference in nurturing behavior among three- to six-year-olds. In seven- to eleven-year-olds, however, the girls offered more help to younger children and gave them more emotional support.[109] This additional nurturing by females seems to be a result of society's encouragement of nurturance as a feminine quality. In one American study women saw nurturance as a desirable feminine trait and mentioned it as a strong point in their personalities;[110] by contrast, males are often taught to define nurturing behavior as unmasculine.

From this short look at some of the behaviors believed to be associated with each sex, we can see that many of the behaviors that are supposed to be inherited and "natural" for a particular sex are actually learned. We see that in some cases there may be a "leaning" toward a sex-role behavior that is largely physical but is reinforced by society (such as higher levels of aggression in boys); in other cases there may be a physical predisposition that is not directly reinforced but comes to be expected (such as spatial ability in boys). In still other instances the culture's definition of sex-role behavior may be largely responsible for a person of a given sex acquiring a trait and maintaining it (such as empathetic behavior in women).

In all cases the part played by the socializing agents—that is, parents, cultural reinforcers, and social institutions—is extremely important in shaping behavior. Consciously or unconsciously, the society tends to pass on and reinforce its traditional beliefs about sex-role behavior. Parents still expect little boys to be noisier than girls; and books tell little boys they must be strong and not cry, while they tell little girls they are good at taking care of babies. As the message is repeated in a hundred different ways, it has its effect: Boys do become strong and assertive, and girls do become nurturant. What we must recognize is that these qualities are not necessarily inherited but are learned by cultural training. Without this training there might be little or no difference between the sexes.

WOMEN'S SOCIALIZATION: DIFFERENT AND UNEQUAL

In summary, we see that men and women differ in appearance and behavior for many reasons. We have seen that many physical characteristics, some abilities (spatial), and even some mood behaviors are largely a matter of inherent physical factors. On the other hand, a child's belief in what sex he or she is, and what behaviors to follow for that sex, is almost entirely a matter of cultural training. We have seen that there are subtle influences that operate early in childhood on the learning of this behavior— such as parental expectations and the role of language. In addition, we have seen that there are other, not so subtle, forces at work that push the young boy or girl toward stereotypical sex-role behavior. Toys and games, television and books, school environment, and interaction with peers and teachers are all powerful forces reinforcing sex stereotypes. It is clear that this sexism is all-pervasive and that it is almost impossible for a child to avoid its influence.

At best, such powerful persuasion to follow certain sex-role behavior is a factor that limits choices and constricts creative possibilities. In many cases it is clear that the sexism has extremely negative effects on the achievement potential of women and the personality development of both sexes. Aside from the very few inherited traits and abilities that distinguish men and women from each other, we all have almost unlimited possibilities for behaving in a variety of ways. Instead, traditional sex-role socialization is pushing children into confining and limiting roles. It is important to examine our values and our behavior as we have done above so that we can be aware of the sources of this constricting sexism and try to eliminate its influence.

NOTES

1. Eleanor E. Maccoby and Carol Jacklin, *The Psychology of Sex Differences* (Stanford: Stanford University Press, 1974).

2. John Money and A. Ehrhardt, *Man and Woman/Boy and Girl* (Baltimore: Johns Hopkins University Press, 1972).

3. Maccoby and Jacklin, *Psychology of Sex Differences,* pp. 120–124.

4. Money and Ehrhardt, *Man and Woman.*

5. Alice Rossi, "The Missing Body in Sociology: Closing the Gap." (Presidential Address, Eastern Sociological Society, Philadelphia, April 6, 1974).

6. John F. Traverse, *The Growing Child* (New York: Wiley, 1977).

7. Maccoby and Jacklin, *Psychology of Sex Differences,* pp. 176–177.

8. Anne Anastasi, *Differential Psychology,* 3rd ed. (New York: Macmillan, 1958).

9. Maccoby and Jacklin, *Psychology of Sex Differences,* pp. 24–46.

10. Ibid., pp. 27–29.

11. Ibid., pp. 19–20.

12. Ibid., pp. 75–85.

13. Ibid., pp. 86–91.

14. Marsha Federbush, "The Sex Problems of School Math Books," in *And Jill Came Tumbling After*, ed. Judith Stacy, Susan Bereaud, and Joan Daniels (New York: Dell, 1974), pp. 178–184.

15. Maccoby and Jacklin, *Psychology of Sex Differences*, pp. 121–122.

16. Ibid., pp. 91–105.

17. Ibid., p. 108.

18. Ibid., pp. 227–247.

19. Beatrice Whiting, *Six Cultures: Studies of Child-Rearing* (New York: Wiley, 1963).

20. Maccoby and Jacklin, *Psychology of Sex Differences*, pp. 244–247, 255–265.

21. See ibid.

22. *New York Times*, December 21, 1976, sec. 4, p. 7.

23. See Alice Rossi, "The Missing Body in Sociology: Closing the Gap" (Presidential Address, Eastern Sociological Society, Philadelphia, April 6, 1974), Barbara Sommers, "Mood and the Menstrual Cycle" (Paper presented at the American Psychological Association Convention, August 1975).

24. Estelle Ramey, "Men's Cycles, They Have Them Too, You Know," xeroxed.

25. Money and Ehrhardt, *Man and Woman*.

26. Ibid., p. 123.

27. Bernard Rosenberg and Brian Sutton-Smith, *Sex and Identity* (New York: Holt, Rinehart and Winston, 1972).

28. Margaret Mead, *Sex and Temperament* (New York: Dell, 1963).

29. Walter Mischel, "A Social-Learning View of Sex Differences in Behavior," in *Development of Sex Differences*, Maccoby, pp. 56–81.

30. Calvin S. Hall, *A Primer of Freudian Psychology* (New York: World Publishing, 1954).

31. C. S. Ford and F. Beach, *Patterns of Sexual Behavior* (New York: Harper & Brothers, 1951).

32. Lawrence Kohlberg, "A Cognitive-Developmental Analysis of Children's Sex-Role Concepts and Attitudes," in *Development of Sex Differences*, Maccoby, pp. 82–166.

33. Ibid., p. 113.

34. Ibid., p. 111.

35. Jerry Z. Rubin, Frank J. Provenzano, and Zella Zuria, "The Eye of the Beholder: Parents' Views on Sex of Newborns," *American Journal of Ortho-Psychiatry* 44, no. 4 (July 1974), pp. 512–519.

36. Maccoby and Jacklin, *Psychology of Sex Differences*, p. 309.

37. Ibid., p. 325.

38. Ibid., p. 328.

39. Ibid., p. 329.

40. Marie Richmond-Abbott, "Sex-Role Attitudes and Behavior in Single-Parent Families," in preparation.

41. S. Goldberg and M. Lewis, "Play Behavior in the Year-Old Infant: Early Sex Differences," *Child Development* 40 (1969): 21–31.

42. Maccoby and Jacklin, *Psychology of Sex Differences*, p. 319.

43. Eleanor E. Maccoby, "Women's Intellect," in *The Potential of Women*, ed. Seymour Farber and Roger Wilson (New York: McGraw-Hill, 1963).

44. Patricia Minuchen, "Sex-Role Concepts and Sex Typing in Childhood as a Function of School and Home Environments," in *Beyond Sex-Role Stereotypes: Reading toward a Psychology of Androgyny*, ed. A. Kaplan and J. Bean (Toronto: Little, Brown, 1976), pp. 206–223.

45. Maccoby and Jacklin, *Psychology of Sex Differences*, p. 319.

46. Mirra Komarovsky, *Blue-Collar Marriage* (New York: Random House, 1962).

47. Melvin Kohn, "Social Class and Parent-Child Relationships: An Interpretation," *American Journal of Sociology*, 74, no. 4 (1968) pp. 471–480.

48. David Aberle and Kasper Naegele, "Middle-Class Fathers' Occupational Role and Attitudes toward Children," in *The Family*, ed. N. Bell and E. Vogel (New York; Free Press, 1968).

49. Lenore J. Weitzman, "Sex-Role Socialization," in *Women*, ed. Jo Freeman (Palo Alto, Calif.: Mayfield, 1975), p. 121.

50. Joyce Ladner, *Tomorrow's Tomorrow: The Black Woman* (New York: Doubleday, 1971).

51. Laurel Walum, *The Dynamics of Sex and Gender: A Sociological Perspective* (Chicago: Rand McNally, 1977), p. 18.

52. Ibid., p. 21.

53. Ibid., p. 29.

54. Don H. Zimmerman and Candace West, "Sex Roles, Interruptions and Silences in Conversations," in *Language and Sex: Difference and Dominance,* ed. Barrie Thorne and Nancy Henley (Rowley Mall: Newbury House, 1975).

55. Irving Goffman, *Interaction Ritual* (New York: Doubleday, Anchor Books, 1967).

56. Ibid.

57. Walum, *Dynamics of Sex and Gender,* p. 23.

58. *Ms.* "A Report on Children's Toys," in Stacey, Bereaud, and Daniels, *And Jill Came Tumbling After.*

59. Marie Richmond-Abbott, "Some Preliminary Findings about Sex-Role Attitudes and Behavior in Single-Parent Families," in press.

60. *Ms.* "A Report on Children's Toys," p. 123.

61. Ibid., p. 124; Letty Cottin Pogrebin, "Gifts for Children," *Ms.,* December 1974, pp. 63–68, 76–79.

62. Pogrebin, "Gifts for Children."

63. Nancy G. Kutner and Richard M. Levinson, "The Toy Salesperson: A Potential Gatekeeper for Change in Sex-Role Definitions" (Paper presented at the annual meeting of the American Sociological Association, New York, August 1976).

64. Maccoby and Jacklin, *Psychology of Sex Differences,* pp. 250–254; Beverly Fagot and Isabelle Littman, "Stability of Sex Role and Play Interests from Preschool to Elementary School," *Journal of Psychology* 89 (1975): 293–299; Sheila Fling and Martin Manosevitz "Sex Typing in Nursery School Children's Play Interests," *Developmental Psychology* 7, no. 2 (1972), pp. 146–152.

65. Maccoby and Jacklin, *Psychology of Sex Differences,* pp. 210–211, 352.

66. *Channeling Children* (Princeton, N.J.: Women on Words and Images, 1975).

67. Jane Bergman, "Are Little Girls Harmed by Sesame Street?" in Stacy, Bereaud, and Daniels, *And Jill Came Tumbling After,* pp. 110–116.

68. Women on Words and Images, *Channeling Children,* p. 30.

69. Ibid.

70. Freugh and McGhee, *Developmental Psychology* 11, no. 1 (1975): 109.

71. *Detroit Free Press,* October 17, 1977, p. 11-A.

72. See these articles in Stacey, Bereaud, and Daniels, *And Jill Came Tumbling After;* Women on Words and Images, "Look, Jane Look, See Sex Stereotypes," pp. 159–177; and Elizabeth Fisher, "Children's Books: The Second Sex, Junior Division," pp. 116–123. See also Lenore Weitzman, Deborah Eiffler, Elizabeth Hokada, and Catherine Ross, "Sex-Role Socialization in Picture Books for Preschool Children," *American Journal of Sociology* 77, no. 6 (1971): 1125–1148; Florence Howe, "Sexual Stereotypes Start Early," *Saturday Review,* October 16, 1971, pp. 76–83.

73. Federbush, "Sex Problems of Math Books."

74. Inge K. Broverman et al., "Sex-Role Stereotypes and Clinical Judgments of Mental Health," *Journal of Consulting and Clinical Psychology* (1974), p. 34.

75. Women on Words and Images, *Dick and Jane as Victims* (New York: Women on Words and Images, 1974).

76. *Sex Discrimination in an Elementary Reading Program* (Lansing, Mich.: Michigan Women's Commission, 1974).

77. Whitney Darrow, Jr., *I'm Glad I'm a Boy, I'm Glad I'm a Girl* (New York; Simon & Schuster, 1970).

78. See *Sex Discrimination in an Elementary Reading Program.*

79. Eve Merriman, *Mommies at Work,* quoted in Fisher, "Children's Books," p. 120.

80. Miriam Schlein, *The Snake in the Carpool* (London, New York: Abelard-Schuman, 1963).

81. Robert Spaulding, "Achievement, Creativity, and Self-Concept Correlates of Teacher-Pupil Transactions in Elementary School," in *Sexism in School and Society*, Nancy Frazier and Myra Sodker (New York: Harper & Row, 1973), p. 90.

82. Claire Etaugh and Valerie Hughes, "Teachers' Evaluations of Sex-Typed Behaviors in Children," *Developmental Psychology* 11, no. 3 (1975): 394–395.

83. S. Feshbach and N. Feshbach, "The Young Aggressors," *Psychology Today*, 1973, pp. 90–95: Lisa Serbin and Daniel O'Leary, "How Nursery Schools Teach Girls to Shut Up," *Psychology Today*, December 1975; Carol Koffe, "As the Twig is Bent," in Stacey, Bereaud, and Daniels, *And Jill Came Tumbling After*, pp. 91–109.

84. W. Meyer and G. Thompson, "Sex Differences in the Distribution of Teacher Approval and Disapproval among Sixth-Grade Children," *Journal of Educational Psychology* 47 (1956): 385–396; P. S. Sears and D. H. Feldman, "Teacher Interactions with Boys and with Girls," *National Elementary Principal* 46 (1966): 30–35; E. P. Torrance, *Guiding Creative Talent* (Englewood Cliffs, N.J.: Prentice-Hall, 1962).

85. *Psychology of Sex Differences*, p. 70.

86. J. Douglas, *The Home and the School: A Study of Ability and Attainment in the Primary School* (London: MacGibbon and Kee, 1964); Kranz et al., "The Relationships between Teacher Perception of Pupils and Teacher Behavior toward Those Pupils," (Paper delivered at the annual meeting of the American Educational Research Association, 1970); R. Rosenthal and L. Jacobson, *Pygmalion in the Classroom: Teacher Expectation and Pupils' Intellectual Development* (New York: Holt, Rinehart and Winston, 1968); W. Schrank, "The Labeling Effects of Ability Grouping," *Journal of Educational Research* 162 (1968): 51–52.

87. L. Good and J. E. Brophy, *Looking in Classrooms* (New York: Harper & Row, 1973).

88. Lois W. Hoffman, "Early Childhood Experience and Women's Achievement," *Journal of Social Issues*, 28 (1972): 18–23.

89. Maccoby and Jacklin, *Psychology of Sex Differences*, p. 105.

90. Ibid., p. 154.

91. V. C. Crandall and E. S. Battle, "The Antecedents and Adult Correlates of Academic and Intellectual Achievement Effort," in *Minnesota Symposia on Child Psychology*, J. P. Hill, ed. vol. 4 (Minneapolis: University of Minnesota Press, 1970); J. Kagan and H. A. Moss, *Birth to Maturity* (New York: Wiley, 1962).

92. W. R. Looft, "Vocational Aspirations of Second-Grade Girls," *Psychological Reports* 28 (1971): 241–242.

93. L. M. Terman and M. H. Oden, *Genetic Studies of Genius V. The Gifted Child at Mid-Life: Thirty-Five-Year Follow-up of the Superior Child* (Stanford: Stanford University Press, 1959); Torrance, *Guiding Creative Talent*.

94. Janice P. Gump, "Sex-Role Attitudes and Psychological Well-Being," *Journal of Social Issues* 28, no. 72 (1972): 79–92.

95. Maccoby and Jacklin, *Psychology of Sex Differences*, pp. 250–265.

96. Ibid., pp. 247–254.

97. Ibid., p. 147.

98. Ibid., p. 257.

99. Ibid., pp. 151–154.

100. Ibid., pp. 203–214.

101. Ibid., P. 213.

102. Ibid., pp. 211, 229.

103. Sandra Bem, "Beyond Androgyny: Some Presumptuous Prescriptions for a Liberated Sexual Identity" (Keynote address for American Psychological Association–National Institute of Mental Health Conference on the Research Needs of Women, Madison, Wisconsin, May 31, 1975).

104. Maccoby and Jacklin, *Psychology of Sex Differences*, p. 180.

105. Ibid., pp. 214–221.

106. Carol Tavris and Carol Offrer, *The Longest War* (New York: Harcourt, Brace or Janovich, 1977), p. 126.

107. Maccoby and Jacklin, *Psychology of Sex Differences*, p. 216.

108. Sandra Bem, "Probing the Promise of Androgyny," in Kaplan and Bean, *Beyond Sex-Role Stereotypes*, pp. 47–63.

109. Whiting, *Six Cultures.*

110. Gerald Gurin, Joseph Veroff, and Sheila Feld, *Americans View Their Mental Health* (New York: Basic Books, 1960).

REVIEW QUESTIONS

1. Define gender and sex role. Describe the component parts of gender, including types of chromosomal or hormonal abnormalities.
2. Describe the physical differences between infant boys and girls. Be sure to include any physical hormonal differences.
3. Discuss the influence of parental expectations and modeling on the early socialization of children. In what ways can infant boys and girls stimulate their parents to react differently?
4. Discuss the influence of toys and games on children's early socialization into sex-role behavior. Be very specific and discuss the nature of the toys and games as well as their later influence.
5. Discuss the influence of books and television on children's sex-role socialization. Be very specific as you discuss the stereotypes presented in the media. Discuss ways in which these stereotypes could be changed.
6. How is language (both verbal language and body language) a subtle socializer of children's sex-role behavior?
7. Discuss briefly the three schools of sex-role development theory (Freudian, social learning, and cognitive developmental). Point out the major ways in which the schools differ from one another.

CLASSROOM EXERCISES

1. Imagine a scene in a hospital waiting room with two sets of grandparents talking about the baby that is soon to be born. What are they likely to say about the baby's characteristics and role in life if the baby is a boy? And if the baby is a girl?
2. One of the important early socializers is language. Imagine that you are a man and speak only as a man would speak as you discuss a movie that you have recently seen. Now imagine that you are a woman and discuss the movie as a woman would discuss it.
3. Another important difference between the sexes is their use of space and body language. Imagine that you are a man having a casual conversation with a woman employee. Without depending on language, use space and body language to show your masculinity and your relationship to this woman.

4. Make a list of the types of toys you would buy a five-year-old boy. Make the same list for a five-year-old girl. Discuss why you would buy the types of toys you have chosen.

5. Make a list of what you would try to teach (either directly or by setting a good example) your girl child. Would you try to teach any different behaviors to your boy child? If so, why?

6. Gather a group of children's preschool and elementary-school readers and analyze the books for:
   a. numbers of boys and girls who are the central characters in the stories
   b. number of times boys and girls (and men and women too) are shown in illustrations
   c. what the girls (and women) are doing in the stories; what occupations they have
   d. what the boys (and men) are doing in the stories; what occupations they have
   e. what characteristics (fearfulness, etc.) the boys and girls are shown as having
   f. what it takes for a character to succeed in the type of story you are analyzing and whether this behavior is most likely to be displayed by a man or a woman
   g. who has the power and who makes the decisions in the stories
   h. how family roles and tasks are shown
   i. any derogatory comments about either boys or girls

7. Using items a to i in exercise 6, do the same type of analysis for one prime-time and one Saturday-morning television program. Be sure to analyze the commercials as well.

8. Complete each of the following, listing as many behaviors as you can:
   a. Since I am a woman (man):
   I am required to ——— I am allowed to ——— I am forbidden to ———
   b. If I were a woman (man):
   I could ——— I would ——— I would not ———

SELECTED READINGS

A Feminist Look at Children's Books.

A critical review of some of the highly regarded fiction for children taken from such lists as Notable Children's Books of 1969, the Newberry Medal award winners of the "best book of the year," and the like. The publishers also print a bibliography of recommended nonsexist books, entitled *Little Miss Muffet Fights Back.* (Both reviews also appear in the March 1971 issue of *School Library Journal.*)

Gornick, Vivian, and Barbara K. Moran, ed. *Women in Sexist Society.* New York: Basic Books, 1971.

A useful reader including a wide variety of articles from several disciplines. There are some classic pieces dealing with the cultural factors that influence the socialization of women: Naomi Weisstein's "Psychology Constructs the Female," Judith Bardwick and Elizabeth Douvan's "Ambivalence: The Socialization of Women," Nancy Chodorow's "Being and Doing: A Cross-Cultural Examination of the Socialization of Males and Females," and Margaret Adams's "The Compassion Trap." The level of the articles is uneven, but this is a good reader to be used with an integrating text and perhaps other supplementary material.

Maccoby, Eleanor E., ed. *The Development of Sex Differences.* Stanford: Stanford University Press, 1966.

Although this book is twelve years old, it contains one of the most thorough annotated bibliographies in the area of the development of sex differences until the publication of Maccoby and Jacklin's more recent book in 1974. As none of the sources described in this book are included in the 1974 one, however, it is important for the informed scholar to have both books. In addition, the book includes important chapters by Mischel and Kohlberg on the theories of learning sex-role identity and an excellent chapter by D'Andrade on the reasons for men's and women's different status cross-culturally.

Maccoby, Eleanor E., and Carol Jacklin. *The Psychology of Sex Differences.* Stanford: Stanford University Press, 1974.

The source book for information about research findings in the areas of perception, cognition, self-concept, aggression, socialization hormonal levels, and genetic factors. It reviews the results of thousands of different studies in these areas and summarizes their findings. In some cases the authors have reanalyzed the data themselves to be sure of the accuracy of their presentation. In addition, it presents an annotated bibliography of over 1,400 research studies published since 1965 or not included in the original bibliography of Maccoby's earlier work, *The Development of Sex Differences.*

Money, John, and A. Ehrhardt. *Man and Woman/Boy and Girl.* Baltimore: Johns Hopkins University Press, 1972.

A detailed and informative description of the component parts of gender, the development of gender from conception onward. The book has extensive descriptions about gender abnormalities and information about such things as transsexuality. The biological emphasis is kept in perspective, however; the authors also discuss the importance of the sex of assignment and rearing.

School Psychology Digest, February 1973.

This issue of the journal is devoted to the problems of constricting stereotypes for both sexes which are created in school, the various kinds of media, and the culture in general. It includes excellent articles about teacher interaction with students, as well as articles by Sandra Bem and others dealing with why sex stereotyping is harmful, and how more androgynous roles would be liberating.

Stacey, Judith, Susan Bereaud, and Joan Daniels. eds. *And Jill Came Tumbling After: Sexism in American Education.* New York: Dell, 1974.

An excellent collection of articles from a variety of sources describing the early socialization of children by sex-stereotyped games, toys, books, and nursery and elementary schools (including the classic article by Ruth Hartley, "Sex-Role Pressures and the Socialization of the Male Child"). Other selections discuss books and counseling for women in high school and college, views about women in the teaching profession, and feminist views about the need and possibilities for truly equal education for women.

Walum, Laurel Richardson. *The Dynamics of Sex and Gender.* New York: Rand McNally, 1975.

A simplified sociological treatment of the learning of gender identity and early sex-role socialization. Its strengths are the extensive chapter dealing with the role of language in learning sex-role norms, and the overview of socialization in the early years. Material on adolescent roles and women's roles in the family is a bit thin, but there are good chapters on institutional discrimination against women.

Women on Words and Images. *Channeling Children: Sex Stereotyping on Prime Time T. V.* Princeton, N.J.: Women on Words and Images, 1975.

A description of the findings of research that analyzed the roles of men and women on prime-time and Saturday-morning television shows in the 1973 and 1974 viewing seasons. General findings for all the shows are presented, as well as a description of the stereotypes portrayed in each of the programs surveyed.

Women on Words and Images. *Dick and Jane as Victims: Sex Stereotyping in Children's Readers.* Princeton, N.J.: Women on Words and Images, 1974.

An analysis of 134 books from 14 widely used series of elementary-school readers. Documents and discusses sex-role stereotypes in the books in general, with lists and examples of the stereotyping in particular books.

CHAPTER 6

The Psychology of Female Adolescence: Identity and Conflict

Barbara Brackney

Investigation of the adolescent, or teenage, years is a fairly recent event in psychology. One of the first careful studies of this phase of life was made by Erik Erikson who defined adolescence as a time between childhood and adulthood when the young person acquires a sense of *personal identity*. These years, according to Erikson, are characterized by an identity crisis in which the adolescent must bring together and use the skills learned during childhood, develop a sense of being a unique individual, and become integrated into the community of adults. The formation of an identity is a difficult task because "the young person, in order to experience wholeness, must feel a progressive continuity between that which he has come to be during the long years of childhood, and that which he promises to become in the anticipated future."[1]

In the adolescent's attempt to form a stable and adaptive identity, he or she is influenced greatly by society's definitions of adulthood—the possible roles, responsibilities, and rewards of adult status. What about the female adolescent? In her search for an identity, how is the adult role defined for her? Unfortunately, the message she receives from society is distorted by many negative stereotypes about women. These stereotypes portray women as weak, ruled by emotions, and not very intelligent.

One of the most important goals of psychology is the scientific study of human personalities. Yet even psychologists have been guilty of describing women in terms of stereotypes, making false assumptions about the nature of the female personality. To illustrate, Sigmund Freud has been one of the most influential figures in psychology, yet his description of feminine development is often degrading. He believed that, along with *penis envy,* the female personality was characterized by *passivity* (lack of an active approach to life), *masochism* (satisfaction from painful experiences), and *narcissism* (an excessive concern with the self).[2] The mistake Freud made was a serious one: He assumed that these personality traits were due to biological factors. He neglected to see that women may envy the male role, the male's freedom to choose among a wide variety of opportunities and to become a respected member of society. Freud failed to understand that passivity, masochism, and narcissism may be characteristic of any individual who has been denied a valued role in society.

A psychological theory that is somewhat less biased is the cognitive-developmental model of Kohlberg, also discussed in the last chapter. According to this theory, all children want to value their particular sex to feel good about themselves. Young girls, therefore, grow up believing that being female is "good" and that the female role is a desirable one.[3] Our society obviously has high regard for the male role, but the female role is a relatively devalued one. This points to a painful dilemma for the adolescent girl in her quest for an identity: She needs to value being female, but her role is not valued.

Any investigation of female adolescence must deal with stereotypes at two levels. First, the negative stereotypes about women that have become a part of psychological theory must be questioned closely and discarded or modified if not based on fact. Fortunately, the women's movement has served to increase awareness among psychologists of the presence of false assumptions, and the lack of objective knowledge, about issues pertaining to women. This new sensitivity can be seen in the recent research by psychologists (mostly women) on female sexuality, achievement motivation, and self-concept which will be discussed in this chapter. Second, psychology must explore the interaction between cultural stereotypes and female identity. When young women are told by adults and by the media that they are "naturally" dependent and lacking in ambition, self-confidence, and rationality, psychologists must discover the effects this information has on personality development. Since one great aim of psychology is to promote emotional health, it is especially important to understand the damaging possibilities of such stereotypes.

With these thoughts in mind, the issues of female adolescence may be studied in terms of identity formation. There are four basic aspects to personal identity: (1) *biological aspects,* such as menstruation and sexuality; (2) *intellectual aspects,* such as academic abilities and skills; (3) *psychological aspects,* such as self-concept and self-esteem; and (4) *social aspects,* such as relationships with friends and family. Each of these aspects is critical to the final identity "solution" reached by the young woman as she leaves adolescence to enter the adult world.

BIOLOGICAL ASPECTS OF IDENTITY

Feelings about one's body and its functions are an important part of personal identity. During adolescence the girl reaches biological maturity. She begins to menstruate and must deal with new sexual feelings. Both of these biological events, menstruation and sexuality, are mixed with psychological experiences which, in turn, will affect her unique adult identity.

Menstruation

The transition from sexually immature child to sexually mature adult is a developmental phase, called *puberty,* during which enormous changes in the appearance and functioning of the body occur. At the beginning of this phase there is a rapid spurt of growth, the appearance of secondary sexual characteristics, such as budding of the breasts and emergence of pubic hair, and the maturation of the sexual-reproductive system. The most dramatic event of puberty, however, is the onset of menstrual bleeding. This event, *menarche,* is a physiological one that marks the beginning of approximately thirty-five years of regular, cyclic fluctuations in the body of the female. Yet menarche has a significance that extends far beyond these physiological changes. The first menstrual period is often symbolic of womanhood and, therefore, is an important psychological event in the life of the female.

Pubertal girls show a wide variation in their reactions to menarche. For some girls, menstruation is greeted with joy and pleasure. For others, it is met with only negative feelings, such as embarrassment and fear. For most girls, however, menarche involves mixed feelings or *ambivalence.* As Bardwick states, girls receive a double message about menstruation: On the one hand, menstruation is an entry into the privileges of womanhood; on the other hand, it is a messy business, with bleeding and often discomfort.[4]

Studies of psychological responses to menstruation have focused on the *premenstrual syndrome,* the "blues" that often occur just before and during menstruation. While psychologists agree that many women experience sharp increases in anxiety, depression, or hostility during this time, there is disagreement concerning the source of these unpleasant emotions. Some psychologists state that the blues are a result of extreme changes in hormone levels and are, therefore, attributable to purely physiological factors. Other psychologists believe that these feelings of distress originate in negative cultural attitudes about menstruation that are learned quickly by young women.

Evidence to support the idea that the blues are a result of hormone changes was provided by Ivey and Bardwick in a study of twenty-six normal college students over two menstrual cycles.[5] The students were asked to tell of past experiences twice at mid-cycle when the hormone *estrogen* is at the highest level and twice during the premenstrual phase when estrogen is at the lowest level of the cycle. These four stories were scored for themes showing the presence of anxiety, such as themes of death, separation, and mutilation. The results were clear: The subjects' stories told during the low-estrogen phase were significantly more anxious than stories told during the high-estrogen phase. For example, one subject related the following positive experience at mid-cycle:

> Well, we just went to Jamaica and it was fantastic. The island is so lush and green and the water is so blue. . . . The place is so fertile and the natives are just so friendly.[6]

The same subject described a much different experience premenstrually:

> I'll tell you about the death of my poor dog. . . . Oh, another memorable event —my grandparents died in a plane crash. That was my first contact with death, and it was very traumatic for me. . . . Then my other grandfather died.[7]

Ivey and Bardwick concluded that increases in anxiety during the premenstrual phase are due to a dramatic decline in estrogen levels.[8]

There are other investigations, however, that look to negative cultural attitudes toward menstruating women and menstrual blood as the source of the "blues". As we have seen, throughout history men have reacted to menstruation with fear, disgust, and wonder, believing that menstrual blood has evil powers, such as the power to sicken cattle and contaminate food. You will remember that to protect themselves, men created elaborate rituals to separate the menstruating woman from contact with men or the food they ate. In our own society we do not segregate the menstruating woman in an isolated menstrual hut, but taboos and negative stereotypes are still evident. Menstruating females are often thought to be emotionally unstable, physically weak, and in need of many hygienic precautions.

Paige provided evidence that menstrual distress is a reaction to such cultural beliefs. She found, for example, that women who adhere to different religious orientations experience different levels of premenstrual and menstrual anxiety: Orthodox Jewish women and devout Catholic women tend to undergo higher levels of anxiety than do Protestant women. According to Paige, all women have essentially similar hormonal variations accompanying the menstrual cycle, but these religious orientations traditionally have espoused differing views of the menstruating woman. When the attitudes are negative, such as the Orthodox Jewish belief that the menstruating woman should abstain from sexual relations until she has been "cleansed" in a ritual bath, the woman responds with increased menstrual distress.[9]

It is likely that both factors—hormone changes and learned negative attitudes—operate together to produce the psychological discomfort often associated with menstruation. The fact remains that menstruation is frequently marked by ambivalent feelings in the young woman.

Sexuality

One of the more perplexing issues of adolescence—for teenagers and researchers alike—is the difference between male and female sexuality. For the boy, the ability to achieve *orgasm* (ejaculation) coincides with reproductive maturity. This is rarely true for girls. The arrival of menarche does not mean necessarily that the girl has attained sexual maturity. Typically, there is a lag of several years before the biologically mature girl is capable of experiencing orgasm, or sexual "climax." Moreover, the frequency of sexual expression, such as masturbation, petting, and sexual intercourse, for girls is much lower than for boys, and sexual expression itself occurs at a higher average age in females. This sex difference holds true even in the realm of fantasy, with female adolescents reporting fewer sexual dreams than males.[10] Psychological research has shown that the low frequency of female sexual expression is a characteristic of the adolescent period. Tooley requested high-school, college, and adult females to tell stories to the Thematic Apperception Test, a series of standard drawings. When these stories were analyzed for sexual content, it was found that the youngest group, the high-school girls, tended to avoid telling stories with explicit sexual themes to a much greater extent than the two older groups.[11] In fact, girls' stories actually show a decrease in the number of sexual themes with the onset of puberty, unlike the increased incidence of such themes in the stories of males who have reached puberty.[12]

While psychologists agree that important differences exist in the development of sexuality for boys and girls, they do not agree about the sources of these differences. Some psychologists believe that the girl's sexual drive is simply less intense than the boy's. For the male, sexual urges are located in his penis, an organ that is highly visible and is the source of pleasurable sensations since early childhood. The girl's sexual sensations, on the other hand, are not associated with such a visible organ.[13] According to this view, the male develops an early genital focus, while the female pattern is general body sensuality. She values the sexual aspects of other areas of her body, for example, breasts and curved hips, but usually does not experience specific sexual feelings in her genitals until adulthood.[14]

That girls' sexual interest is not focused on their genitals may be due in part to certain negative ideas about the vagina. Despite careful reassurance from adult women, menstrual bleeding from the vagina is often associated with wounds and injuries, leading to anxiety. Even among mature, healthy women the most frequently found attitude about menstrual periods may be a neutral one.[15] Also, because of the nature of most sex education, the genitals are frequently linked to maternity. Because the adolescent girl fears pregnancy, this anxiety may generalize to the genitals.

Other psychologists think that the dating system in our society reinforces a lack of genital focus and an emphasis on whole body "sexiness" among adolescent females. From a very early age, the girl has received messages from the media and other people that she will have both popularity and love if she maintains an attractive physical appearance.[16] As we saw in the discussion of stereotypes, the girl, desiring attention from boys as a measure of her social value, often spends endless hours polishing and grooming the external parts of herself to assure social success. The girl receives another message as well: She must be sexually attractive but she must not behave sexually. To be popular with her peers, she knows that she must attract boyfriends by appearing "sexy," but she also knows that she may quickly lose popularity if she enthusiastically engages in sexual intercourse. The dating system, therefore, encourages her to become a sexual tease: "This ambivalence is epitomized in the girl's response to her boyfriend's sexual demands—if she refuses him, she risks losing him, resulting in a psychological blow, but if she yields to him, she may also lose his respect and her own self-esteem."[17]

During the early part of the century, the sexual double standard was in full force: The girl was expected to remain a virgin until marriage, to "save" herself for her husband, while realizing that he probably would not do the same. Is the double standard still strong in our society or are attitudes becoming more permissive? There are people who believe that premarital sex is permissible if a strong bond of affection and commitment exists between two young people. Others, particularly among the strongly religious, consider intercourse prior to marriage an act that should be condemned for any reason. Social attitudes about virginity, therefore, are not uniform among all groups of Americans and may be in a state of transition.

Psychologists know that attitudes and actual behaviors are not necessarily the same. Are young women tending to remain virgins in accordance with traditional values, or is virginity on the decline in the face of a sexual revolution? The data from recent studies of premarital sexual activity among young, unmarried women show that a virgin bride is becoming increasingly rare. One national study found that 81 percent of married women between the ages of eighteen and twenty-four reported having had premarital sex.[18] Similarly, in a recent survey of 100,000 readers of *Redbook* magazine, nine out of ten wives under age twenty-five had experienced premarital intercourse.[19] Although males are more likely than females to have sex before marriage, this double standard of behavior may disappear in the next few years if present trends continue.

Even though the number of young women engaging in premarital sex has increased dramatically in the last two decades, strong differences between males and females remain. Unlike the young man, the young woman typically has her first experience with sexual intercourse in the context of a serious, monogamous relationship and tends to have fewer sexual partners than the male.[20] An interesting conclusion may be drawn: Although the frequency of premarital sexual experiences has risen, psychological attitudes about these experiences may not have changed. The justification used by young women is love—a long-term, affectionate relationship that may result in marriage is often the prerequisite for sex.

How can we reconcile the frequency of premarital intercourse with the previously mentioned low level of interest in genital sex among adolescent girls? An answer to this apparent contradiction may come from Bardwick's study of the motivation for intercourse among 150 young college women.[21] When asked why they made love, very few subjects said they were motivated by their own sexual desires, and few subjects reported ever having experienced orgasm. Instead, it seems that their motivation was mostly psychological: They wanted a feeling of closeness and love with their partners. Sex was seen as a technique for communicating love and for preventing a breakup of the relationship:

I guess because I love him.

I don't know. I think it's really necessary as a symbol of involvement.

Well, a great strain not to. I was fairly reluctant for a while, but then I realized it had become a big thing in the relationship and it would disintegrate the relationship. . . . I wanted to also.

Mostly to see my boyfriend's enjoyment.

Since we're getting married, it's not wrong.

I gave in to Sidney because I was so lonely.[22]

Bardwick stresses the possible emotional hazards for young women in these experiences. These subjects felt very vulnerable because they were afraid of being used and then abandoned by their boyfriends. Bardwick also points to a basic injustice: Society encourages restraint of sexuality by defining "good girls," permits premarital intercourse if it happens in a permanent relationship, and glorifies the experience of orgasm. In this way girls often experience disappointment when they discover that sexual pleasure does not automatically appear in a love relationship.

Any discussion of female sexuality would be incomplete without mention of the lesbian, a female who prefers a sexual partner of the same sex. Until recently, this sexual variation was considered to be deviant or abnormal, since it fell outside society's standards for "proper" sexual conduct. Fortunately, old prejudices are being replaced gradually by more realistic, tolerant attitudes. To illustrate, the American Psychiatric Association formally removed homosexuality from its list of mental disorders in 1973; and despite the opposition of conservative voices in the United States, there is a general move toward decriminalization of homosexual acts between consenting adults, with the further goals of eliminating discriminatory practices directed against homosexuals in the areas of employment and housing. Currently the consensus among psychologists is that lesbian sexual behavior is in no way evidence of either sexual or emotional disturbance, and that the only psychological difference between the lesbian and her heterosexual peer is simply in the choice of love object.[23]

The risk implicit in any discussion of lesbianism is that of perpetuating or creating stereotypes. First, it is important to realize that homosexual desires and experiences are not at all rare for females. For example, it is estimated that about 10 percent of adolescent girls have had one or more homosexual experiences, and that by age thirty, approximately 25 percent of all women acknowledge that they have experienced erotic feelings toward other females, even if these feelings were not acted upon.[24] Second, homosexuality and heterosexuality are best conceptualized as a continuum. Just as there are women who are exclusively heterosexual and women who are exclusively lesbian, there are also females who engage in both forms of sexual behavior in varying proportions depending on their situation and preferences at a given moment. Given this wide range of sexual behavior and the fact that arbitrary distinctions between heterosexuality and lesbianism tend to be artificial, the question of personality traits that are characteristic of the lesbian female seems to be a meaningless one.

With the risk of stereotyping firmly in mind, one may wonder about what factors are significant in the life histories and current behaviors of women who have chosen an exclusively lesbian life-style. In contrast with less recent psychological literature that studied lesbians who came to the attention of mental health professionals for difficulties that may have been unrelated to their sexual preferences, Wolff interviewed a normal population of lesbian women and concluded that the most striking characteristics of lesbian relationships were emotionality and romanticism. There was often an emotional commitment to the partner that is rarely seen in heterosexual relationships.[25] Contrary to popular stereotypes, there is little evidence to support the notion that one partner assumes a masculine, or "butch," role while the other partner is the *"femme."* There is also no evidence that lesbian females are characterized by certain differences in appearance or behavior from the heterosexual woman. To best understand lesbianism, it is important to remember that these women have made a strong feminine identification and do not wish to be men.

There have been many explanations of the sources of lesbianism, the majority of which, again, were colored by the negative attitudes of the authors. Wolff, on the other hand, emphasized the deep, intense attachment all young girls have for their mothers. At the same time, she hypothesized, the girl soon becomes aware that her mother values males (e.g., husband, son) much more than females. This realization leads the girl to become uncertain about her own value and the security of love from the mother. Rather than identifying with the mother by seeking love from the "valued" males, a heterosexual resolution of the conflict, the lesbian does not turn to males as a substitute for the mother but continues, instead, to strive to become worthy of her mother's love through substitute females.[26]

While Wolff's theory seems to merit further investigation, it must be emphasized that these ideas remain speculative and that generalizations about the sources of lesbian behavior ignore important individual differences among many women.

INTELLECTUAL ASPECTS OF IDENTITY

One familiar stereotype is that man is the hunter and woman is the nest-builder. The operation of this stereotype is reflected by the segregation of men into the breadwinner role and women into the wife/mother role. The persistence of this rigid distinction is often justified by pointing to the relative lack of prestigious and creative achievement on the part of women when compared with men. Even very current statistics reveal a gloomy picture of women's accomplishments. Despite anti-sex-discrimination legislation, there has been no significant increase in the number of women entering the professions since World War II. How can we explain women's poor record of achievement? Are women less intelligent than men? Or is it possible that women are simply not motivated to achieve? Psychologists have attempted to answer these questions through research on sex differences in intelligence and achievement motivation.

Intelligence

Quite simply, there is no evidence that males are more intelligent than females. As we saw earlier, males tend to score somewhat higher on mathematical tasks and females tend to perform better on verbal tasks; however, there are no consistent differences in general intelligence (IQ) between males and females.[27] Yet there is an interesting sex difference in the development of intelligence as measured by standard IQ tests: Girls tend to score higher on IQ tests until the high-school years, but by adulthood men tend to score higher than women. Moreover, it has been found that girls who are under-achievers in high school usually begin to show a drop in achievement levels at puberty.[28] How can we explain the decline in both IQ and school achievement often occurring for females during adolescence? The answer to this question can be found in the cultural belief that achievement and femininity are mutually exclusive goals.

Achievement Motivation and Performance

By the time a girl enters adolescence, she has internalized the values of competence and mastery as indications of self-worth, just as boys have done. Achievement in school and preparation for a future career are desirable because accomplishment itself is pleasurable, as is the reward of approval received from parents and teachers. Yet during adolescence the female is subjected to pressure, both social and psychological, to conform to an adult feminine image. The adolescent girl, then, is faced with a serious dilemma: The feminine image ("fun" date, wife, mother) conflicts with the values of achievement and intellectual competence. If she continues to strive for achievement, she may risk being viewed as unfeminine—as too aggressive, too competitive. If she strives for femininity, she may have to give up her goals of academic or vocational success. Frequently this conflict is resolved in favor of assuming the adult female role according to norms of our society. She abandons her early desire for successful accomplishment to enhance her attractiveness to potential dates and her popularity with peers. This particular resolution is reinforced by high-school counselors and "tracking" systems that encourage the pursuit of "feminine" studies, such as secretarial skills or home economics courses, while discouraging more ambitious academic preparation.[29] There is a "flight into femininity."[30]

While experimenters can easily increase males' need for achievement by emphasizing the relationship between intelligence and leadership and performance on the achievement motivation measures, women do not respond to these conditions with a greater need to achieve.[31] Psychologists remained puzzled about female achievement behavior (and often resolved their confusion by ignoring female behavior that did not correspond to theory) until 1968 when Horner discovered another motive related to achievement, the fear of success.

Given present cultural conditions, Horner hypothesized that the goal of femininity will inevitably conflict with the goal of successful achievement. Faced with this conflict, the young woman often chooses the feminine option because she anticipates and fears certain negative consequences following successful behavior, such as social rejection, loneliness, and not being a "normal" woman. Because women expect these negative consequences, she concluded, they fear and avoid success.

Horner measured the motive to avoid success by presenting male and female college students with the statement: "At the end of the first-term finals, Anne [for female respondents]/John [for male respondents] finds herself/himself at the top of the medical school class." The students were then asked to write stories about the Anne or John character. Horner analyzed the stories by looking for themes reflecting the fear of success, such as fear of social isolation, doubts about femininity or masculinity, and guilt. The following excerpts are examples of fear-of-success themes found in the females' stories:

> No one will marry her. She has lots of friends but no dates.

> Unfortunately, Anne suddenly no longer feels so certain that she really wants to be a doctor. She wonders if perhaps she isn't normal.

> Anne is a code name for a nonexistent person created by a group of med students.

> She starts proclaiming her surprise and joy. Her fellow classmates are so disgusted with her behavior that they jump on her body and beat her. She is maimed for life.[32]

The results of the story analyses were astonishing: While only 9 percent of the male students' stories (in response to the John cue) showed evidence of fear of success, 65 percent of the female students' stories (told to the Anne cue) revealed this fear.[33]

While some psychologists quickly agreed that most women fear and avoid success, others were not so easily persuaded and wondered if using a story character of the same sex as the subject clouded the issue. For example, would stories written by women using the John cue continue to show high levels of fear of success? The method used by Horner made it impossible to determine whether the different levels of fear of success resulted from the sex of the story character, the sex of the subject, or the situation, i.e., medical school. It may have been, for instance, that the females' fear-of-success responses reflected only their anxiety about competing in the male-dominated field of medicine, rather than anxiety about success in general.

Monahan, Kuhn, and Shauer suggested that fear of success may be anxiety about sex-inappropriate success as defined in our culture. They used Horner's method with one modification: Both male and female subjects wrote stories about both Anne and John. When these subjects wrote about the same-sex character, i.e., when females wrote about Anne, Horner's original results were replicated. However, when the subjects wrote stories about the character of the opposite sex, i.e., when males wrote about Anne, *both* the male and female subjects displayed a higher fear of success in relation to Anne than to John. It seemed possible that the sex of the story character was the critical variable and that fear of success was actually a fear of deviation from sex-role standards.[34]

What if there were a change in sex-role standards so that Anne's success would not be perceived as deviant? Would the fear-of-success imagery decrease? To explore these questions, Cherry and Deaux modified the method once again. In addition to the cues of Anne and John in medical school, subjects were asked to write stories about Anne and John in nursing school, in a traditionally feminine vocation. The investigators found that male subjects showed much more fear-of-success imagery in response to John's success in nursing school than in medical school, while the reverse was true of the female subjects.[35]

From studies such as these, psychologists now conclude that fear of success simply reflects realistic expectations of negative consequences when *any* person deviates from cultural norms for sex-appropriate behavior, and successful achievement behavior traditionally has been deviant behavior for females in most academic and vocational areas. Despite a fresh climate for change, many young women may actively withdraw from competition and preparation for high status "male" professions because they realistically expect that such success involves great personal cost—not because they lack intellectual ability or a desire to achieve. We now know that increased career opportunities are necessary but not sufficient conditions to encourage young women to fully utilize their abilities. The adolescent female also needs to see mature women clearly demonstrating that achievement is legitimate, not deviant, behavior that is approved and applauded in our society.

Despite strong cultural pressures on the young female to avoid entry into competitive, achievement-demanding professions, there have always been women who have chosen this "deviant" course, deriving much pleasure and satisfaction from the actualization of their high achievement aspirations. An important question confronting psychologists, therefore, concerns the personality differences between capable young women who maintain a strong desire to achieve and those who, although equally capable, withdraw from the competitive arena.

Tangri's study of the personal determinants of non-sex-typical career choices among college women was a significant attempt to explore this question. Using two hundred women seniors from the University of Michigan as subjects, Tangri was interested in the family backgrounds and personality factors that differentiated between "role innovators," women entering male-dominated occupational fields (fewer than 30 percent women), and "traditionals," subjects educating themselves for careers in which the proportion of women is at least 50 percent. With respect to family background, Tangri found that the most powerful predictor of a young female's role innovation was the innovativeness of her mother's own occupation and whether the mother was sufficiently invested in her own career aspirations to continue her vocational pursuits.[36] These findings agree with other psychological research in this area: Having a career-oriented, working mother tends to increase the likelihood that the daughter will have both similar high occupational goals and "masculine" professional aspirations.

While some investigators have speculated that the young female who enters a male-dominated field has done so because of an early identification with her father, the results of Tangri's study dispute such conclusions. Role innovators did not show evidence of a greater identification with their fathers; instead they felt closer to, and agreed more on values with, their mothers as compared with their fathers. They utilized their mothers as role models, while also maintaining relatively autonomous relationships with both parents.[37]

Autonomous, independent relationships with parents, particularly with the mother, seem to be one of the most significant correlates of achievement behavior in young women. Encouragement of such autonomy, however, is not a common practice in the rearing of daughters as compared with sons. As summarized by Hoffman, the girl typically receives fewer rewards for independent behaviors, more parental protectiveness, and less pressure to establish an identity that is separate and distinct from the mother. The results of such rearing patterns are potentially detrimental to the development of high achievement aspirations, since the daughter is less likely than the son to acquire skills to master her environment. Rather than approaching novel situations with confidence and self-sufficiency, the young woman reared in the traditional style continues to rely heavily on others for the solution of problems and is most concerned with maintaining dependent, affectionate ties with adults. When achievement behavior is displayed, the desire to please others tends to be the motivational force; and if her aspirations or goals come into conflict with the stronger need to receive supplies of affection and approval, the traditionally reared girl often experiences anxiety that is powerful enough to propel her away from further achievement-oriented behaviors.[38]

What personality traits are associated with Tangri's role innovators? Despite their choice of a "masculine" field of endeavor, these young women did not reject the female roles of wife and mother, although they did expect to marry later and have fewer children than their traditional peers. In comparison with the traditional subjects who were preparing themselves for "feminine" occupations, role innovators were "more autonomous, individualistic, and motivated by internally imposed demands to perform to capacity."[39] One may speculate easily that these personality traits are closely linked to the above-mentioned relationships with parents.

The results of the above studies also pertain to the development of creativity in young women. Even though girls past the age of seven score higher on tests of verbal creativity than boys and equivalently on tests of nonverbal creativity, it is well known that women are grossly underrepresented in the creative-artistic professions.[40] Yet there are women who do fulfill their creative potential in a productive, self-satisfying fashion. Are there personality characteristics typical of this small group of women?

Helson studied creative women mathematicians and found that they shared the following personality traits: independence, rejection of outside influences, introversion, flexibility, and a strong self-centeredness.[41] These traits, again, are obviously in opposition to the stereotyped feminine personality. Are there unique aspects in the life histories of these women that would account for their ability to resist conforming to the traditional pattern? Anastasi and Shaefer explored autobiographies written by creative high-school girls and discovered that not only had they been intensely interested in creative endeavors throughout childhood, but also, and very importantly, they had received consistent recognition and approval for their efforts from parents and teachers alike.[42]

The most succinct generalization that may be made is that the creative individual of either sex has an ability to think along original lines, to be inventive, and to see reality in a special way. As Bardwick notes:

> But the stereotyped male, like the stereotyped female, is not creative. While independence and autonomy are perceived as masculine characteristics, a high degree of sensitivity is feminine. Many studies now conclude that the really creative individual combines "masculine" and "feminine" personality qualities. . . . The creative person resists pressure to be limited and conform to the sex role stereotype.[43]

What are the personal consequences of choosing to work in a professional capacity, regardless of the sex-typing of that particular career, versus investing exclusively in the traditional homemaker role? Birnbaum compared the level of satisfaction and self-esteem of three groups of women: the homemaker, the married professional, and the single professional. She found that "working professional women, whether married or single . . . hold themselves in higher regard than equally gifted non-employed women."[44] Based on these findings, Birnbaum made the cogent argument that we cannot afford to continue to rear young girls to seek fulfillment and self-esteem solely within the home. If an intelligent young woman develops no sources of personal gratification other than those contained in the traditional realm of marital and maternal roles, she is prone to lowered self-esteem and profound experiences of loneliness and uncertainty, unlike the professional woman who gains a firm sense of self-worth and identity through her work-derived satisfactions.[45]

The above studies concerning female achievement utilized predominantly white subjects; it is important, therefore, to recognize that the conclusions drawn may be generalized only to this sample. When one turns to an exploration of the achievement motivation and performance characteristics of Black women in the United States, the relevant psychological literature is sparse but informative.

Because of a long history of discrimination and poverty, the role of full-time, middle-class wife and mother has been denied to the majority of Black women. Owing to economic necessity, the Black female frequently had to assume the "masculine" roles of breadwinner and head of household in addition to that of mother/wife. This economic reality, in turn, has led to the evolution of attitudes about female achievement within the Black community that are somewhat different from those among Whites. To illustrate, Entwistle and Greenberger found that Black adolescent males tend to have more positive attitudes toward female employment outside the home than White boys.[46]

The greater social acceptance of female employment among Black people has led to another significant difference between White and Black women: The Black woman is less likely to perceive conflict between achievement aspirations (in the form of commitment to employment) and the traditionally feminine roles of mother and wife than the White female. The greater compatibility of these dual roles is reflected, for example, in Weston and Mednick's research with Black samples in which fear-of-success imagery was considerably lower among Black female college students than among Whites.[47] As further evidence that achievement and femininity are not perceived in mutually exclusive terms among Black women, Harrison notes that "the educational and career aspirations of Black women appear to be influenced by the recognition that their potential earning power may improve their marriage prospects," a perception quite different from that of most White women.[48] In the struggle to resolve the culturally induced conflict between desires for high achievement and traditional feminine goals, therefore, the White female adolescent may well benefit from the example set by her Black counterpart.

PSYCHOLOGICAL ASPECTS OF IDENTITY

One of the traditional frontiers of psychological research has been the study of enduring personality traits. Even though experiences during adulthood may modify these traits, it is believed that the basic structure of a person's personality crystallizes by the end of the adolescent period.

Self-Concept

During adolescence the young woman seeks to define herself as a unique individual with a pattern of personal characteristics that will allow her to function with a minimum of psychological pain and to function well in her relationships with other people. In this search she uses both private introspection and information from others to form a *self-concept*—that is, a stable image of herself. An important aspect of her self-concept, of course, is that of being a woman. When she asks the question, What are women really like? some of the information she receives is stereotypes about women held by the society in which she lives. As mentioned earlier, many of these stereotypes are negative ones: Women are perceived as incompetent, overly emotional, and passive.

As we saw, the study by Broverman et al. discussed in the last chapter illustrates the operation of negative stereotypes. Seventy-nine psychotherapists, both male and female, who were given a sex-role stereotype questionnaire concerning personality characteristics of psychologically healthy adult men and women, concluded that healthy women differ from healthy men by being more submissive, less independent, less adventurous, less competitive, and more emotional.[49] If this is the message the adolescent female receives about "healthy" adult women, it can only have a damaging effect on her self-concept and her feelings of competency and self-worth.

Is there any truth to these stereotypes? As we saw before, Maccoby and Jacklin reviewed all research on sex differences in personality traits and found no evidence to support several stereotypes. For example, there is no reason to believe that females are more social, more suggestible, or less motivated to achieve than males, at least before adolescence. On the other hand, research does support the common observation that males are more aggressive, both verbally and physically, than females. There is insufficient evidence of sex differences on several other personality dimensions. For instance, although females often are more willing to admit to anxious feelings, observations of fearful behaviors usually do not uncover differences between the sexes. When competitiveness is studied, males are often found to be more competitive, but many studies show a strong similarity between the sexes. Further, there is no strong evidence that females are less dominant, more compliant, less active, or more nurturant than males.[50]

Self-Esteem

One important aspect of self-concept is *self-esteem,* the degree of positive or negative attitudes one holds about oneself. A person who has high self-esteem has mostly positive feelings about the self, whereas a person low in self-esteem thinks of the self in mainly negative terms.

Our society has very different expectations of young men and women. Males are expected to develop vocational skills and competence to prepare for the future. Adolescent females, on the other hand, are expected to prepare themselves primarily for marriage and motherhood—to develop interpersonal skills. So males may base their feelings of self-worth on goal achievement, while females' self-esteem may rest on attractiveness, "warmth," and popularity.

Psychological research seems to confirm the notion that there are different sources of self-esteem for male and female adolescents. On the basis of interviews with over three thousand adolescents, Douvan and Adelson found that boys' self-esteem is obtained from evaluation of their work skills, responsibility, and personal achievement. For girls, however, self-esteem is dependent on the acquisition of social skills.[51] When the difference between actual-self and ideal-self descriptions were used as a measure of self-esteem, Carlson discovered that males use an individualistic or personal definition of self, whereas females stress an interpersonal definition based on social skills.[52] Thus it seems that girls obtain self-esteem from social success and acceptance by other people. If this is generally true, then it might be predicted that females' self-esteem will be lower than that of males simply because "feminine" success, such as interpersonal popularity, is viewed as much less valuable in our society than "masculine" success, such as independent mastery of the environment.

This prediction was supported in a study by Rosenkrantz et al. They presented adolescent subjects with 122 items related to sex-role stereotypes; each item ranged along a seven-point scale; for example, "not at all aggressive" through "very aggressive." The investigators asked the subjects to rate each of these traits in terms of desirability. Another group of subjects were then requested to indicate the degree to which each trait characterized men and women. Both the male and female subjects in the second group consistently agreed about which items were typical of men and women. These adolescents perceived that the more valued, desirable traits were possessed by men and that less worth attached to "feminine" characteristics.[53] Connell and Johnson reported similar results with a group of young adolescents. The highly masculine boys were more self-confident than the less masculine boys, and they also displayed more self-esteem than both the highly and the less feminine girls.[54] Finally, the differences between male and female self-esteem appear to increase with age.[55]

As we saw, the effect of lowered self-esteem on females may be seen clearly when both sexes are presented with a task and asked to predict how well they will perform. Investigations have found that men and boys consistently predict that they will perform better than do women and girls. Regardless of the nature of the task or achievement (e.g., arithmetic problems, grade-point average, anagrams, verbal tests), males are more confident of their performance than females, even though both sexes actually do equally well.[56]

It has also been found that females are more likely to deprecate or "put down" their performance than are males. When the subjects of both sexes were asked whether identical successful performances on the part of males and females were "mainly due to luck" or "mainly due to skill," the subjects explained that the males' success was due to skill, while luck accounted for the females' success.[57] In a similar study a group of high-school girls was asked to explain the reason for the success of a particular graduate student. The girls indicated that the male student's success was due to greater ability, while the female student's success was attributed to luck, easy courses, and even cheating on exams. When the graduate student was described as a failure, the high-school girls reversed their explanations. The woman student's failure was explained in terms of lack of ability and hard work, whereas the male's failure may have been due to bad luck, such as being subject to unfair accusations of cheating.[58]

We can conclude that as girls respond to social and psychological pressures to assume the adult female role, they also include traits into their self-concepts that are considered to be inferior to those of males, with a corresponding lowering of feelings of self-worth, competency, and value. As Douvan states: "Moreover, her attention to charm and the winning of affection serves an important defensive function in that it forestalls anxiety about whether she will in fact be chosen in marriage. But, for most women, popularity and social charm will not sustain self-esteem for a lifetime."[59]

While the White female tends to derive self-esteem primarily from her success in interpersonal relationships, the Black female may use a different standard for defining her self-worth. In particular, Wright has found that Black females base their self-esteem on individual action or initiative, a possibly less passive stance than that of White females.[60] Further, the assumption that the historical devaluation of Black people has resulted in lowered levels of self-esteem among Black females is not warranted. Despite the potentially destructive aspect of racism, the Black female does not fall victim to feelings of inadequacy. To illustrate, Ladner interviewed adolescent Black girls in a lower-class housing project and concluded that "there was no evidence of low self-esteem and severely damaged psyches among these young ladies."[61] Instead there was a remarkable degree of pride and psychological strength to continue coping with their often difficult life situations.

SOCIAL ASPECTS OF IDENTITY

Any discussion of female adolescence would be incomplete without a description of a girl's relationships with her friends and family. These two groups of people have an important and lasting effect on her identity as a social person, as well as on all other aspects of identity discussed so far. If these relationships are primarily close and rewarding for the girl, her identity is strengthened and made more positive. If she is alienated or mistreated, the possibility of disturbances in her identity increases.

Friendship

Although information concerning the role of friendships with other girls is sparse, some interesting speculations have been made about the nature of these unique relationships.

In their national survey of girls between the ages of eleven and eighteen, Douvan and Adelson found that same-sex friendships tend to undergo regular changes from early through late adolescence.[62] Between ages eleven and thirteen, the girls formed friendships on the basis of mutually enjoyable activities. The personal qualities of the friends were relatively unimportant and were described in superficial terms. For instance, these girls referred to a good friend as cooperative, fair, neither mean nor selfish. These friendships did not seem to be relationships; instead the girls were simply enthusiastic partners for various activities. In the group of middle and late adolescents this picture changed a great deal. The friendships were characterized by a sharing of experiences, emotional responsiveness, and intimacy. There was much emphasis on the personal qualities of a friend, such as loyalty, the ability to keep confidences secret and give emotional support. Douvan and Adelson concluded that true, intimate friendships among girls do not develop until about age fifteen or mid-adolescence.[63]

Once formed, these same-sex friendships are very significant for the girl. In fact, Douvan suggests that these relationships are of greater importance for the girl than are opposite-sex relationships during the entire adolescent period and are characterized by a maturity that is not observed in boy-boy friendships. While the boy uses his friends within the peer group to break away from his family and establish independence from the home, the girl looks to her "best friend" as someone with whom she can talk and clarify her identity, especially her sexual self.[64]

Dating

Dating during the adolescent years is considered an apprenticeship for mature love in adulthood. For both males and females, dating can be the cause of much strain as well as enjoyment. While the specifically sexual aspects of opposite-sex relationships have been described previously, there are certain social aspects of dating that may cause the adolescent girl a great deal of stress and disillusionment.

Since femininity is defined in terms of interpersonal success rather than individual achievement, the adolescent girl encounters strong social pressure to acquire dates. The high-school boy may be regarded highly by his peers because of athletic skills or academic success, whereas the girl's status among friends is often judged primarily in terms of her popularity with the opposite sex. This pressure is compounded by the social expectations that the most important goal of any young woman is to find a man who will marry her, and that all other goals are secondary ones at best. Dating, then, may easily become the means by which the girl and her peers measure her worth as a person. If these expectations are held by the young woman, her self-esteem may suffer if she does not date, despite other rich personal accomplishments.

To acquire dates, the girl often anxiously tries to mold herself to a ritualized model of a "good date." She attempts to be neither too serious nor too silly and to become a sympathetic listener, and she formulates subtle praise for her partner to ensure an additional date. The problem with such personality molding is that the young woman may become so concerned with the most superficial aspects of herself that she may lose touch with her own inner feelings and may also never learn to experience true emotional intimacy with the opposite sex.

While the female is expected to be quite active in terms of preparing herself to be an attractive date, she is also expected to be passive—to wait for the male to take the initiative as part of the dating ritual. Even when she is attracted to a young man and wishes to develop a friendship with him, the adolescent girl must not seem "pushy" by directly stating these feelings to the boy. Whether she will be able to form a friendship with him or not is often under the control of the male. The female is expected to signal subtly that she is available but usually may not take direct action. This expectation, in turn, may cause the girl to feel that the only way to relate in an opposite-sex relationship is in a disguised, passive fashion with little personal control.

The dating ritual and stereotypes about the sexes can also be the source of disillusionment for the young woman. During her teenage years she frequently receives the stereotyped message that males are strong, capable people who will take care of her, much like her parents have in the past. When she is sought out by a young man, these romantic expectations may bloom in an overidealized way. Instead of viewing her partner in a realistic light, with both positive traits and faults, she reacts to him in terms of stereotypes. All too often it is not until the marriage ceremony is over that she comes to the realization that her partner is not the pillar of strength she had believed him to be. This realization can be an extraordinarily painful one if the young woman has not developed her own resources and strengths.

Finally, the adolescent girl's participation in the dating ritual has an impact on other areas of her identity:

> In sum, the well-socialized American girl learns three clear lessons: one concerning her personality, a second concerning her capability, and a third concerning her future role. With regard to her personality she "knows" that to be truly feminine she will be sweet, expressive, not too intelligent, nurturing, cooperative, pretty and fairly passive. With regard to her capability, she "knows" she will always be less capable and less important than most men. With regard to her future, she "knows" she will be a wife and mother. If she is a successful woman, she will acquire this status soon.[65]

Family

Do most adolescent females rebel against their families, or are these relationships usually free of conflict? Evidence from psychological research indicates that the typical teenage girl not only strongly identifies with the values and beliefs of her parents but also tends to consult them when important decisions are to be made. Even though there may be an increase in disagreements between girls and their parents, the arguments are usually about small matters, and most girls report that their home lives are relatively content and tranquil.[66]

Konopka interviewed a large sample of adolescent girls from all areas of American society to learn about their attitudes toward their families. She found that there were four major categories of attitudes:

1. Most of the girls felt more emotionally involved with their mothers than with any other adult. Even when a girl felt alienated from the world of adults, she often expressed a yearning for a mother. Although most girls held very positive feelings for their mothers, when conflict of dislike was present, it was mixed with feelings of pain, sadness, and regret.

2. The relationships with fathers tended to be more formal or more distant than those with the mothers. The fathers were often the more authoritarian parent, viewed as overly restrictive, not wanting their daughters to grow up.

3. Almost all the girls had in mind an ideal of loving parents who were both friends and protectors. The girls longed for harmony in the family and found conflict between the parents especially disturbing.

4. Next to the parents, the most loved adults were often the grandparents, particularly the grandmother. When the relationships between the girls and their parents became tense, it was helpful to turn to the grandparents for a "cooling off" period.[67]

The girls expressed strong opinions about qualities that they disliked and admired in adults. The qualities that were most admired were the following:

They are generally friendly; they are fun to be with.

They are understanding; they respect us; they listen and care about us; they are helpful to us.

They are older, more experienced and knowledgeable; they tell us things, the rights and the wrongs.[68]

The qualities that were the most frequently disliked in adults were:

They don't respect us; they don't listen or try to understand us; they think that they are too good for us and that they are always right.

They push their ideas and expectations on us and force us to do things; they are too demanding.

They are too strict; they don't trust us to do anything.

They are old-fashioned; they want us to do things the way they used to do them when they were kids.[69]

Finally, it should be mentioned that during their daughters' adolescence parents often strengthen their efforts to direct them toward increased conformity to culturally approved models of femininity. Frequently, viewing adolescence as a last chance to socialize the young female, the parents may focus their concern on her popularity with her peers as an indication of her future "marriageability," to the detriment of other values, such as intellectual and/or creative fulfillment. For traditional parents, their daughter's ability to attract potential marriage partners, rather than her career aspirations, is perceived all too often as a measure of their success in parenting.

IDENTITY SOLUTIONS

When the biological, intellectual, psychological, and social aspects of identity are brought together, a personal identity is formed. The particular identity achieved by a young woman may have elements in common with that of many other females in our society, while still being a highly individual "solution." Some young women, because of unique abilities or circumstance, form an identity that is less usual in our society, adding diversity to the female experience.

One of the most significant aspects of identity is the person's sex-role *identification,* an individual pattern of sex-related personality traits, which range from "masculine" to "feminine" as defined by our society. There is a wide variation in the kinds of sex-role identifications made by adolescent females, but several overlapping patterns have been isolated by Douvan and Adelson.[70] These patterns may be imagined as falling along a continuum, or scale, of "femininity." On the extreme feminine side of the continuum are the "unambivalent feminine" girls who are concerned almost exclusively with issues of popularity, dating, and their future roles of wife and mother. Somewhat further along the scale are the "ambivalent feminine" girls who have a strong desire for traditionally female roles but who are also interested in developing skills and competence for personal achievement beyond such roles. Still further along the continuum are the "achievement-oriented" girls who display an intense investment in future occupational achievement; although they do not reject the possibility of marriage, their dreams revolve around themes of personal success. At the other end of the scale are the "boyish" girls who express a desire to be male, believing that the feminine role is associated with many annoying restrictions on their freedom, and the "antifeminine" girls who are characterized by a strong wish to avoid marriage at all costs and yet have no alternate positive wishes for the future.

With the exception of the antifeminine type who lacks future goals, each of these patterns is considered to be a normal variation of feminine sex-role identification among adolescent females. Douvan and Adelson note that identity solutions are more difficult for the average girl than for the typical boy. When designing his own identity, the boy asks the question, What will I do? and supplies specific answers, such as "I will be a lawyer." For the girl, the answer to this question is a general one, preformed by society: She will be a wife and mother. These are identity goals that cannot be achieved by personal control or competency; instead adult female identity remains unformed until the woman meets the man she will marry.[71] As Douvan points out: "We encourage her to remain tentative in self-outline so that she may adapt more easily to the man she marries and so that she does not develop herself out of any part of the market of potential husbands."[72]

IDENTITY AND CONFLICT: A SUMMARY

At the end of the adolescent period the young woman enters the adult world with a personal identity. While the foundation of her identity is laid down in childhood, the basic structure, which will remain essentially unchanged throughout her adult years, is formed during adolescence. Since a person's identity is the fundamental core of personality, affecting all feelings and behaviors, it is important to understand the very special nature of identity formation among female adolescents in our society.

Although acquiring a personal identity is often a difficult and stormy process for the male, certain conflicts that are experienced only by females further complicate their identity formation. Even though there are differences in degree across individuals, the majority of adolescent girls encounter conflicts within and among the biological, psychological, intellectual, and social aspects of identity. For example, one significant element in identity formation is the anticipation of future roles to be played in adulthood. Yet the range of possible roles has been restricted historically for females. Society has approved only a narrow range of "feminine" occupations and viewed females' entry into the "masculine" professions with skepticism. The typical conflicts encountered by adolescent girls have been suggested throughout this chapter. It may be helpful, nevertheless, to highlight six prominent dilemmas faced by many young women in our society.

First, the beginning of adolescence is marked by menstruation, an event that is greeted with a mixture of positive and negative feelings by most girls. This ambivalence reflects the fact that menstruation is a positive symbol of womanhood, but it is also often a source of unpleasant mood changes and physical discomfort.

Second, the onset of regular menstrual cycles, reproductive maturity, does not necessarily mean that the young adolescent is sexually mature, that is, emotionally ready for sexual excitement in intercourse. Because her genitals may not have been associated with strong sexual feelings during childhood and because her sexuality usually is expressed in an overall body sensuality, the young female may experience conflict when she engages in intercourse at an early age.

Third, there is an unwritten rule in our society that femininity and achievement are contradictory. Many high-school girls are aware of this conflict, choose the "feminine" path of low achievement, and do not prepare themselves adequately for future occupations other than the traditional wife-mother role.

Fourth, the adolescent girl's self-concept may be adversely affected by negative stereotypes about women. Her strong wish is to become an adult woman, but women are often portrayed as illogical, incompetent, and inferior when compared with men. Even when stereotypes are expressed in positive terms, such as women are "naturally" mothers, the possibility of conflict exists, particularly for girls who sense that their personalities are different from a cultural ideal of femininity.

Fifth, a girl's desire for close friendships may be a source of conflict as well as support. Her friends, both male and female, may expect her to conform to standards of feminine behavior, withholding approval and companionship if she deviates from these standards.

Sixth, the family may foster conflict in the adolescent girl, even when acting with the best intentions. They may stress traditional values, for instance, that discourage independent judgment, competition, and exploration of less traditionally feminine avenues of expression. The danger of this protective attitude is that the young woman may never learn that she is capable of handling freedom well and that pleasurable feelings of competence may come from controlling her own personal destiny.

These are only a few examples of the conflicts commonly encountered by female adolescents in our society. Each individual girl faces dilemmas that are different in kind and degree from those experienced by others. For some girls, the conflicts are minimal, and they develop full, productive, and positive identities. For others, the conflicts are so intense that the only possible solutions are either strict conformity to cultural stereotypes or a self-defeating rebellion, resulting in restricted personal growth and identities that are both damaged and devalued. For these young women, we can only hope that our society will evolve in a direction that encourages freedom of choice so that females may choose an identity solution that conforms to their unique experiences and abilities rather than to a narrow set of expectations according to sex.

We can see the beginnings of such evolution among psychologists who have recently become more aware of the many conflicts experienced by young women attempting to form a fulfilling, productive identity. This awareness has led, in turn, to a radical reconceptualization of sex roles and the formulation of an ideal model of the psychologically healthy identity. Rather than relying on the traditional dichotomies between male and female personalities and advocating increased conformity to these restrictive roles, psychologists have reached out to the concept of *androgyny,* defined as an optimal integration of valued and viable personality characteristics formerly assigned on the basis of biological sex. Androgyny, therefore, is conceived as an identity solution that enhances individuality by the expression of both "masculine" and "feminine" traits, thereby eliminating the necessity of being locked into an identity that is defined solely in terms of sex-role expectations.[73] This model recognizes that there is a great deal of diversity within each individual identity, and expression of this diversity is desirable not only for the actualization of the full potential of each person but also for the benefit of society.

The concept of androgyny has important implications for the identity solutions toward which the adolescent female strives. As emphasized in this chapter, one of the most prevalent conflicts experienced by young women is the conflict between the mutually exclusive goals of femininity and achievement. In concrete terms, this dichotomy implies that a young girl may strive either to attain enduring love relationships or to express her intellectual or creative skills and talents seriously in the world of work—but not both. The former is perceived as the goal with the highest priority, as the symbol of successful femininity, whereas the latter is seen often as either an unimportant, temporary goal or an obstacle in the path of becoming a supportive wife and tender mother. The model of androgyny throws a much different light on these issues by noting that some women may prefer serious work to the exclusion of traditional marriage, some may prefer to express themselves primarily in the nurturing and rearing of children, and others may prefer to combine such roles. The point becomes, then, that life choices are made most healthily on the basis of one's identity—one's skills, style of expression, temperament—rather than on the basis of one's gender.[74]

Another significant implication stemming from the concept of androgyny is that the social environment of the adolescent girl, her family, peers, and teachers, should encourage the development of the full spectrum of her identity, rather than exert subtle pressure to conform to the exclusively feminine model. The encouragement of expression of both independent initiative (formerly seen as "masculine") and interpersonal skills (formerly seen as "feminine") may enable the adolescent girl to discover and actualize all the valued aspects of her identity and, one hopes, to steer away from the psychological pitfalls of extreme femininity, such as excessive dependence on the approval of others as a basis for self-esteem.

Finally, the androgynous model of healthy identity formation goes far beyond the individual and implies an equality among all people that has enormous, even startling scope:

> An analysis of sex equality goals may start with the reality of contemporary life, but soon requires an imaginative leap to a new conception of what a future good society should be. With the hybrid model of equality (androgyny) one envisages a future in which family, community, and play are valued on a par with politics and work for both sexes, for all the races, and for all social classes and nations which comprise the human family.[75]

NOTES

1. Erik Erikson, *Identity: Youth and Crisis* (New York: Norton, 1968), p. 87.

2. Sigmund Freud, "The Psychology of Women," in *New Introductory Lectures on Psychoanalysis* (New York: Norton, 1933), pp. 153–185.

3. Lawrence Kohlberg, "A Cognitive-Developmental Analysis of Children's Sex-Role Concepts and Attitudes," in *The Development of Sex Differences,* ed. Eleanor E. Maccoby (Stanford: Stanford University Press, 1966), pp. 56–173.

4. Judith M. Bardwick, *Psychology of Women: A Study of Biocultural Conflict* (New York: Harper & Row, 1971), p. 48.

5. M. E. Ivey and J. M. Bardwick, "Patterns of Affective Fluctuation in the Menstrual Cycle," *Psychosomatic Medicine* 30 (1968): 336–345.

6. J. M. Bardwick, "Psychological Conflict and the Reproductive System," in *Feminine Personality and Conflict,* ed. J. M. Bardwick et al. (Belmont, Calif.: Wadsworth, 1970), p. 24.

7. Ibid.

8. Ivey and Bardwick, "Patterns of Affective Fluctuation," pp. 336–345.

9. Karen Paige, "Women Learn to Sing the Menstrual Blues," *Psychology Today,* September 1973, pp. 41–46.

10. A. C. Kinsey et al., *Sexual Behavior in the Human Female* (Philadelphia: Saunders, 1953), p. 215.

11. Kay Tooley, "Ego Adaptation in Late Adolescence" (Ph.D. diss., University of Michigan, 1966), pp. 123–157.

12. P. M. Symonds, *Adolescent Phantasy* (New York: Columbia University Press, 1949), p. 193.

13. Elizabeth Douvan, "New Sources of Conflict in Females at Adolescence and Early Adulthood," in Bardwick et al., *Feminine Personality and Conflict,* p. 35.

14. See Bardwick, *Psychology of Women,* p. 52; and James L. McCary, *Human Sexuality* (New York: Van Nostrand, 1973), p. 280.

15. Bardwick, *Psychology of Women,* pp. 47–50.

16. McCary, *Human Sexuality,* p. 280.

17. Janet S. Hyde and B. G. Rosenberg, *Half the Human Experience: The Psychology of Women* (Lexington, Mass.: Heath, 1976), p. 158.

18. Morton Hunt, *Sexual Behavior in the 1970's* (Chicago: Playboy Press, 1974), p. 308.

19. Robert J. Levin and Amy Levin, "Sexual Pleasure: The Surprising Preferences of 100,000 Women," *Redbook,* September 1975, pp. 51–58.

20. Hunt, *Sexual Behavior,* pp. 301–340.

21. Bardwick, *Psychology of Women,* pp. 55–56.

22. Ibid., p. 55.

23. D. H. Rosen, *Lesbianism: A Study of Female Homosexuality* (Springfield, Ill.: Charles C Thomas, 1974), p. 65.

24. A. C. Kinsey, et al., *Sexual Behavior in the Human Female,* pp. 452–453.

25. Charlotte Wolff, *Love between Women* (New York: Harper & Row, 1971), p. 64.

26. Ibid., pp. 68–69.

27. Eleanor E. Maccoby and Carol N. Jacklin, *The Psychology of Sex Differences* (Stanford: Stanford University Press, 1974), pp. 63–114.

28. M. C. Shaw and J. T. McCuen, "The Onset of Academic Underachievement in Bright Children," *Journal of Educational Psychology* 51 (1960): 103–108.

29. Judith Stacey, Susan Bereaud, and Joan Daniels, eds., *And Jill Came Tumbling After: Sexism in American Education* (New York: Dell, 1974), pp. 213–223.

30. A. H. Stein and M. Bailey, "The Socialization of Achievement Orientation in Females," *Psychological Bulletin* 80 (1973): 345–366.

31. J. Veroff, S. Wilcox, and J. Atkinson, "The Achievement Motive in High School and College-Age Women," *Journal of Abnormal and Social Psychology* 49 (1953): 108–119.

32. Bardwick, *Psychology of Women,* p. 182.

33. Matina S. Horner, "Toward an Understanding of Achievement-Related Conflicts in Women," in *Women and Achievement: Social and Motivational Analyses,* ed. M. Mednick, et al. (New York: Wiley, 1975), p. 209.

34. Lynn Monahan, D. Kuhn, and P. Shauer, "Intrapsychic versus Cultural Explanations of the 'Fear of Success' Motive," *Journal of Personality and Social Psychology* 29 (1974): 60–64.

35. Frances Cherry and Kay Deaux, "Fear of Success versus Fear of Gender-Inconsistent Behavior: A Sex Similarity" (Paper presented at meeting of Midwestern Psychological Association, Cleveland, 1972).

36. Sandra S. Tangri, "Determinants of Occupational Role Innovation among College Women," in Mednick et al., *Women and Achievement,* p. 270.

37. Ibid.

38. Lois W. Hoffman, "Early Childhood Experiences and Women's Achievement Motives," in Mednick et al., *Women and Achievement,* pp. 129–146.

39. Tangri, "Occupational Role Innovation," p. 271.

40. Maccoby and Jacklin, *Psychology of Sex Differences,* pp. 110–114.

41. Ravenna Helson, "Women Mathematicians and Their Creative Personality," *Journal of Consulting and Clinical Psychology* 36 (1971): 210–220.

42. Anne Anastasi and C. A. Shaefer, "Biographical Correlates of Artistic and Literary Creativity in Adolescent Girls," *Journal of Applied Psychology* 53 (1969): 267–273.

43. Bardwick, *Psychology of Women,* p. 203.

44. Judith A. Birnbaum, "Life Patterns and Self-Esteem in Gifted Family-Oriented and Career-Committed Women," in Mednick et al., *Women and Achievement,* p. 418.

45. Ibid., p. 218.

46. D. Entwistle and E. Greenberger, "Adolescents' Views of Women's Work Role," *American Journal of Orthopsychiatry* 42 (1972): 648–656.

47. Peter Weston and Martha Mednick, "Race, Social Class, and the Motive to Avoid Success in Women," in Mednick, et al., *Women and Achievement,* pp. 231–238.

48. Algea O. Harrison, "Black Women," in *Toward Understanding Women,* ed. Virginia E. O'Leary (Monterey, Calif.: Brooks/Cole, 1977), p. 138.

49. Inge K. Broverman et al., "Sex-Role Stereotypes and Clinical Judgments of Mental Health," *Journal of Consulting and Clinical Psychology* 34 (1970): 1–7.

50. Maccoby and Jacklin, *Psychology of Sex Differences,* pp. 349–366.

51. Elizabeth Douvan and Joseph Adelson, *The Adolescent Experience* (New York: Wiley, 1966), p. 45.

52. R. Carlson, "Stability and Change in the Adolescent Self-Image," *Child Development* 36 (1965): 659–666.

53. Paul S. Rosenkrantz et al., "Sex-Role Stereotypes and Self-Concept in College Students," *Journal of Consulting and Clinical Psychology* 32 (1968): 287–295.

54. D. M. Connell and J. E. Johnson, "Relationship between Sex-Role Identification and Self-Esteem in Early Adolescents," *Developmental Psychology* 3 (1970): 268.

55. R. Monge, "Developmental Trends in Factors of Adolescent Self-Concept," *Developmental Psychology* 8 (1973): 382–393; and M. M. Nawas, "Change in Efficiency of Ego Functioning and Complexity from Adolescence to Young Adulthood," *Developmental Psychology* 4 (1971): 412–415.

56. Kay Deaux, *The Behavior of Men and Women* (Monterey, Calif.: Brooks/Cole, 1976), pp. 38–44.

57. Kay Deaux and Tim Emswiller, "Explanations of Successful Performance on Sex-Linked Tasks: What Is Skill for the Male Is Luck for the Female," *Journal of Personality and Social Psychology* 29 (1974): 80–85.

58. N. T. Feather and J. G. Simon, "Reactions to Male and Female Success and Failure in Sex-Linked Occupations: Impressions of Personality, Causal Attributions and Perceived Likelihood of Different Consequences," *Journal of Personality and Social Psychology* 31 (1975): 20–31.

59. Douvan, "New Sources of Conflict," p. 41.

60. M. Wright, "Self Concept and the Coping Process of Black Undergraduate Women at a Predominantly White University" (Ph.D. diss., University of Michigan, 1975).

61. Joyce A. Ladner, *Tomorrow's Tomorrow: The Black Woman* (New York: Doubleday, 1972), p. 48.

62. Douvan and Adelson, *Adolescent Experience,* pp. 174–228.

63. Ibid.

64. Douvan, "New Sources of Conflict," pp. 31–43.

65. Lenore J. Weitzman, "Sex-Role Socialization," in *Women,* ed. Jo Freeman (Palo Alto, Calif.: Mayfield, 1975), p. 127.

66. Douvan and Adelson, *Adolescent Experience,* pp. 119–173.

67. Gisela Konopka, *Young Girls: A Portrait of Adolescence* (Englewood Cliffs, N.J.: Prentice-Hall, 1976), pp. 64–73.

68. Ibid., p. 61.

69. Ibid., p. 59.

70. Douvan and Adelson, *Adolescent Experience,* pp. 229–261.

71. Ibid.

72. Douvan, "New Sources of Conflict," p. 41.

73. Alexandra G. Kaplan and Joan P. Bean, "Conclusion: From Sex Stereotypes to Androgyny: Considerations of Societal and Individual Change," in *Beyond Sex-Role Stereotypes: Readings toward a Psychology of Androgyny* (Boston: Little, Brown, 1976), pp. 383–385.

74. Ibid.

75. Alice S. Rossi, "Sex Equality: The Beginnings of Ideology," in Kaplan and Bean, *Beyond Sex-Role Stereotypes,* p. 88.

REVIEW QUESTIONS

1. Describe Horner's concept of "fear of success." Explain this concept in terms of recent research concerning fear of sex-role deviation.
2. How does the special nature of the female sexual-reproductive system affect the formation of a stable and positive identity during adolescence?
3. What effects do cultural stereotypes have on female achievement behavior during the high-school years?
4. Describe the ways in which you think society must change to reduce conflicts for the adolescent girl's identity formation. Be specific.
5. The young woman in our society is often described as being oriented toward interpersonal success, placing great emphasis on approval and popularity as a measure of her worth. Describe in detail the various social forces that encourage this kind of orientation.

CLASSROOM EXERCISES

1. Explore all the ways that the double standard operates on a typical date between two adolescents. (Perhaps the instructor will write a list of these on the board.) Now reverse the sex roles on this hypothetical date so that the female behaves as the male usually does and vice versa. What are your reactions to this reversal? Which reversals of behavior seem uncomfortable for you? Which reversals seem

like changes for the better? Now imagine a hypothetical date in which the male and female roles are completely equal. What is your reaction to this situation?

2. Imagine the following: Dr. Susan Brown graduated in the top 10 percent of her class at one of the best medical schools in the country. She then did a year of internship and three years of residency in surgery at a famous New York hospital. She now has a successful practice in surgery and is one of the youngest professors of medicine at the University of Michigan. Now list her personality traits. (Perhaps the instructor will write a list of these on the board.) Do any of the traits reflect fear of success? Is Dr. Brown ever described as not really feminine? Socially rejected? Then look at the traits to see if they explain her success in terms of skill or luck.

3. For female students only: Request that students provide a brief description of their initial reaction to their first menstrual period. Do these descriptions reflect ambivalence about menstruation? In what ways?

4. Did you ever daydream about achieving some kind of personal success but gave up this wish because it seemed unrealistic or impossible, such as becoming a writer, a scientist, or a lawyer? Examine your reasons for abandoning this daydream. (Be honest!) Are any of the reasons linked to your own stereotypes about femininity and achievement?

5. For female students only: Remember your high-school years and recall your best friends. In what ways did these friendships encourage you to conform to social standards of femininity? Were there times when you felt uncomfortable with these standards?

6. For males only: Imagine that you are seriously dating a young woman who is very intelligent and ambitious and will probably choose a career in engineering rather than motherhood. How would her aspirations affect you? Would you consider marrying her? Would there be strains in the relationship? Why?

SELECTED READINGS

Bardwick, Judith M. *Psychology of Women: A Study of Biocultural Conflicts.* New York: Harper & Row, 1971.

Not a feminist book but one of the first attempts to define a psychology of women. Despite a conservative approach, it is valuable reading for provocative ideas about the role of female biological and anatomical characteristics as determinants of personality.

Boston Women's Health Collective. *Our Bodies, Ourselves.* New York: Simon & Schuster, 1973.

A book that should be read by all women to gain further understanding of female sexual and reproductive functions. There is a strong emphasis on health care from a feminist perspective, rather than the traditional physician's viewpoint.

Cox, Sue. *Female Psychology: The Emerging Self.* Chicago: Science Research Associates, 1976.

A collection of writings from many strongly feminist authors, interspersed with lovely illustrations and to-the-point quotations. The final section, "Toward Human Liberation," provides the reader with a lucid and compelling description of the goals of feminist psychology.

Gallatin, Judith. *Adolescence and Individuality: A Conceptual Approach to Adolescent Psychology.* New York: Harper & Row, 1975.

Provides a clear, detailed description of Erikson's concept of identity formation during adolescence. Chapter 12 deals with the unique problem of feminine identity in light of Erikson's theory.

Konopka, Gisela. *Young Girls: A Portrait of Adolescence.* Englewood Cliffs, N.J.: Prentice-Hall, 1976.

This small book is concerned exclusively with adolescent girls and their perceptions of important issues, such as sexuality, adults, goals, friends, school, and political concerns. The author has chosen many beautiful and touching quotations from girls' interviews and journals to illustrate strong feelings about each issue.

McCary, James Leslie. *Human Sexuality,* 2d ed. New York: Van Nostrand, 1973.

Provides superb sex education for the young adult in a straightforward, honest fashion. All aspects of sexuality, male and female, are presented in detail, yet with humanity.

Maccoby, Eleanor E., ed. *The Development of Sex Differences.* Stanford: Stanford University Press, 1966.

A collection of essays from different theoretical viewpoints concerning the development of sex differences during childhood. Two chapters present the social-learning theory model and the cognitive-developmental model, the most popular of theories used in psychology to explain sex differences in behavior.

Maccoby, Eleanor E., and Carol N. Jacklin. *The Psychology of Sex Differences.* Stanford: Stanford University Press, 1974.

This large volume contains a review of all psychological research concerning sex differences in intelligence, achievement, social behavior, and psychological characteristics. It will be a standard reference for anyone interested in sex differences for years to come.

Unger, Rhoda Kesler, and Florence L. Denmark. *Woman: Dependent or Independent Variable?* New York: Psychological Dimensions, 1975.

Contains a large number of original research articles concerning the psychology of women. While some of the articles require an understanding of research methodology, others are easy and informative reading. Of particular interest is a series of four articles concerning women in psychotherapy.

Williams, Juanita H. *Psychology of Women: Behavior in a Biosocial Context.* New York: Norton, 1977

Provides an excellent overall view of the psychology of women, covering all important aspects in a thorough manner. Of particular significance are the chapters concerning myths and stereotypes about women, the effects of hormones on behavior, traditional and new life-styles, middle age, and the aging woman.

CHAPTER 7

Women's Roles in the Family

Gwen Reichbach

As we learned in previous chapters, there is widespread sex stereotyping in our society. The impact of this sex stereotyping upon family life is profound: The father is reinforced in his role as breadwinner and decision maker, and the mother, in her role as nurturer and homemaker.

This chapter considers how and why such stereotypes have endured in the family and their effects on women's identity, unity with one another, and participation in society. Major changes and adaptations of these traditional stereotypes are dramatically influencing both men's and women's roles and the very structure of many families, such as single-parent families, Black families, and blue-collar families.

FACTORS CAUSING CHANGES IN THE FAMILY

The traditional nuclear family of the twentieth century reflects both the tradition of the past and the stamp of the recent demographic shifts, such as smaller family size, increases in female participation in the labor force, and increases in single-parent families. During the Great Depression many marriages were delayed and the average age at marriage rose, both factors contributing to a low birth rate.[1] Lifetime childlessness also edged up toward 20 percent. The extensive dislocations of family life during World War II caused marriage and birthrates to remain low. As men returned from the war, two opposite phenomena occurred simultaneously: Both marriage and divorce rates rose briefly, fell again sharply, and then gradually rose.[2]

The "feminine mystique" of the 1950s was the epitome of the traditional role for women. This concept, described by Betty Friedan, stated that women believed being a housewife and rearing children provided deep and lifelong satisfaction when actually these tasks were often boring and unsatisfying.[3] As evidence of the "feminine mystique," couples were marrying at the youngest ages on record and 96 percent of those at the height of the child-bearing period eventually married. Particularly in the upper socioeconomic groups, where many women had previously remained single, the marriage rate increased. The "baby boom" peaked in 1957 and did not diminish significantly until after 1960. In fact, only about 10 percent of all women in the childbearing ages, and 6 percent of those who married, remained childless.[4] Even with the "baby boom," however, longer life expectancies meant women would be free of child-rearing responsibilities for many of their later years.

The turbulent sixties were marked by a falling marriage rate. By the early 1970s the marriage rate among young single people was as low as it had been at the end of the depression. At the same time, the average age at first marriage rose gradually until by 1974 it was a full year higher (twenty-one years of age for women) than it had been in the mid-1950s. The number of children born was the lowest in U.S. history: 1.9 children per women, as compared with 3.8 in 1957. The Bureau of the Census predicts that this overall low fertility rate will continue through the 1970s.[5] It should be noted, however, that the fertility rate for older women has been increasing in spite of the overall low fertility rate. This indicates that many women who delayed childbearing are now having children, and thus rates may rise again in the future.

Other factors have influenced the traditional nuclear family. So far in the 1970s women have obtained more education and have been awarded about 43 percent of all bachelor's degrees.[6] Their increasing degree of education influences family roles. The more education a woman obtains, the more likely she is to remain single, to hold a professional job, to continue employment outside the home while married and a mother. She is also less likely to be in a family in which members follow traditional sex-differentiated roles.

The women's movement has accentuated these trends toward new roles which were started by changing fertility, educational, and work patterns. In the 1970s these changes in family roles are also reflected in the steadily increasing divorce rate, which is now 5.4 per 1,000 population.[7] In 1977 one in every 2.5 recent marriages was expected to end in divorce, although three out of four women and five out of six men will remarry.[8]

Thus there have been several recent demographic trends influencing family structure and roles which have resulted in a variety of family patterns. Many families still adhere to traditional roles, others have adopted moderate changes, and still others have attempted new structures and new relationships. Let us now look at several types of families and several aspects of families which illustrate points on this continuum.

THE TRADITIONAL WIFE AND MOTHER

In the traditional family the woman's position is essentially the stereotypic one described in the chapter on history. While men are the providers and protectors, women are the nurturers and homemakers. The traditional family usually casts the husband in the role of main authority figure and source of decision-making power. He particularly makes the decisions about transportation, insurance, housing, and major purchases, whereas the wife has greater say in such internal matters as interior decorating, food shopping, and questions concerning the children.

Decision-making power such as this is partly a matter of tradition and partly a matter of the resources that one partner can contribute to a marriage to help the family fulfill its needs. The resources most frequently considered —money, education, and status—are almost always found in greater abundance among husbands in traditional marriages. Women may have such resources as attractiveness, social status, and competencies of many kinds, but these seldom can compete with those of the husband to enable her to gain much decision-making power. Even wives who enter the labor force and gain the resources of money and a possible attractive alternative to their present marriage may not use their power because of traditional beliefs that the husband is the authority figure.[9]

Norms for growing equality and companionship between husband and wife have improved the wife's decision-making position to some degree. However, the division of labor in most traditional families is along stereotypical masculine and feminine lines. The husband is expected to be the breadwinner, and in return for support, the wife is expected to take care of most of the household tasks and his physical needs. A study by Blood and Wolfe of nine hundred couples in the Detroit area shows that in the traditional family tasks are still divided between husband and wife in role-specialized ways.[10] According to Blood and Wolfe, husbands tend to be responsible for "repairs, lawn and walk," and wives, for "food, cleaning and children."[11] There is a somewhat more even division of responsibility on paying bills and grocery shopping, but women predominate in these tasks. Bott's study of twenty London families, and Levinger's examination of sixty Cleveland families, substantiated Blood and Wolfe's findings and further found that marital-role segregation of tasks increases with the addition of children.[12]

In the traditional middle-class family the wife's activities are seen as an adjunct to her husband's career. The addition of her skills to his career position forms a "two-person career," or a shared-role pattern. She assists his advance in his career by taking most of the responsibility for household and family management, serving as his hostess in business, and supporting his decisions. These services are considered essential by both the husband and his employer. When men seek employment, the wives may be interviewed right along with their husbands. In these situations, the wives' satisfaction, status, and prestige are derived from her husband's position and advancement. What professional needs she may have, she fulfills vicariously through her husband's career.

This finding of self-worth through another's actions has strong negative implications for the wife's identity. She is not considered for herself or her own qualities and abilities but rather for how successful her husband is or how pretty her daughter is and how athletic her son is. Such loss of identity has far-reaching ramifications for women's mental and emotional health.

We can better understand these detrimental effects when we look at the traditional marriages described by Jessie Bernard. She believes that the traditional marriage really consists of two separate marriages: the "Her" and "His" marriages. "Contrary to all the charges leveled against it, the husband's marriage . . . is awfully good for him," she says.[13] Married men have consistently scored higher than never-married men on a variety of demographic, psychological, and social indexes.[14] Their mental health is far better and, at middle age and later, so is their physical health; they succeed economically, and almost twice as many married as never-married men consider themselves as "very happy."[15]

For women, marriage is not as beneficial. According to Glick, "being married is about twice as advantageous to men as to women in terms of continual survival."[16] Wives more than husbands report marital frustration and dissatisfaction, marital problems, consideration of separation or divorce,[17] feelings of frequent depression or unhappiness,[18] feelings that they are going to pieces, fear of death, and being bothered by physical pains and ailments.[19] Some critics blame the nature of women for these reported ailments.[20] On the other hand, when unmarried women are compared with unmarried men, single women are superior on education, occupational and income indexes, and experience greater happiness and less discomfort.[21] The never-married woman also tends to be more upwardly mobile and achievement motivated than the single man.[22] Bernard thus concludes that "women start out with an initial advantage which marriage reverses."[23,24]

Let us examine the situation of women in traditional marriage to see what may have caused these problems. A shock which is particularly difficult for educated women to bear is the lowering of status that marriage brings. The legal status of wives, for instance, is lower than both their husbands' and unmarried women. They may be unable to sign contracts in their own names, obtain credit or have full control over income and property. For many women an even worse type of lowering of status is "dwindling" into a wife. This movement involves a redefinition of the self and an active reshaping of the personality to conform to the wishes, needs, or demands of her husband. The results of this Pygmalion effect often are a more negative self-image, a slowing of personal development, and a loss in self-esteem.[25] As we saw in Chapter 4, the loss of personal identity, and society's treatment of women as individuals who cannot think as rationally as their husbands, both contribute to this loss of self-esteem for many wives. Furthermore, wives tend to make more of the adjustments called for in marriage than do husbands. Men maintain their old work routines, leisure-time activities, and friends; but this is more difficult for women. The wife may also feel more guilt in maintaining her previous activities. Women are likely to make more of these changes in life patterns, as they generally give up more on entering marriage and thus in a couples-oriented society have more to lose economically and socially if that marriage fails.

Increasing the shock is the low status of the housewife's work in our society. Housewives are not considered part of the labor force and are not paid for their services, even though the economic value of a homemaker's services has been estimated at more than $14,000 per year.[26] The low status of wives' work has ramifications in the relationship between the spouses, the ways decisions are made, and the distribution of material items. In addition, housework is often isolating, boring, monotonous, and repetitive. Finally, housework is a dead-end, no promotion job. All these characteristics of the housewife role may have negative psychological effects. Housewives have high rates of alcoholism and are heavy users of tranquilizers in an effort to escape their growing frustration.

Another important, and often confusing, aspect of housework is the difference between feelings about housework and orientation to the housewife role. A woman may despise housework while positively identifying with the homemaker role, which is a "whole construction of psychological femininity." Identity as a housewife or homemaker is a deeply rooted facet of being feminine. Thus a woman is told by the culture that to be truly feminine she should enjoy cooking, cleaning, and caring for children. Women may feel they have failed as women if they are unhappy with their domestic role. They blame themselves for their sadness rather than the structure of marriage.

Why do women stay in a situation that causes them such unhappiness? For many women, part of the stereotype of marriage is that it is a safe, secure haven. Women who have lost their confidence may also feel that they cannot succeed at anything but the housewife role, and they want the social security that marriage brings in a couples-oriented society.

Changing norms, the women's movement, the greater participation by women in the labor force, have led many women in largely traditional marriages to attempt to share more household labor with their husbands and to gain more decision-making power for themselves. Probably the most important factor leading to the modification of traditional roles is the increasing participation of wives and mothers in the labor force.

Working Wives

Women are entering the labor force in greater numbers and more rapidly than ever before. Forty million women were working in mid-1977, and the number is projected to rise to about 49 million by 1990.[27] This statistic is particularly remarkable because women who are married, live with their husbands, and have children at home—all factors that have tended to keep women out of the labor force—comprise the majority of this increase.[28] In particular, many of these women are mothers; in 1976, 46 percent of children under the age of eighteen, and 37 percent of children under the age of six, had mothers in the labor force.[29]

Then why are these women working? Sullerot noted that 95 percent of working wives cited the money earned as the major reason for taking a job.[30] They realize that one of the best ways to contribute to their family's economic well-being and to spell the difference between barely "scraping by" and having a few "luxuries" is to become a wage-earner. The income is usually of absolute necessity for 6.2 percent of households headed by single-parent women and for the 20.6 percent that are single-person households. Some homemakers enter the labor force for primarily non-monetary reasons: to escape from the tediousness of housework or the isolation from other women and society, or to satisfy their need for personal and educational fulfillment. In fact, the higher a women's educational attainment, the more likely she is to work, to stay in the labor force longer, and to have more job opportunities open to her.

This rise in working wives and mothers also has significant implications for sex roles in the family. As working wives contribute 25 to 40 percent of their families' incomes, their position as decision makers in the family is usually strengthened.[31] Attractiveness, status, and other intangibles gained from the working situation may also affect the wife's decision-making power. Hoffman found in her studies, however, that working mothers, as compared with a matched group of nonworking mothers, made fewer decisions about routine household matters and were about the same in husband-wife power.[32] This suggests that power relationships are deeply intertwined with psychological needs, such as acceptance and approval, or that a mother's employment is too weak a stimulus to change the power structure a great deal.

The enormous increase in female participation in the labor force is not without its costs. The working wife is usually expected to combine her occupational and housewife roles. Even when other family members help with household duties, working wives still labor between seventy and eighty hours a week.[33] It is also noteworthy that only about 20 percent of the husbands of working wives help at all with the housework, and even when their husbands do help with household tasks, frequently wives continue to have the primary responsibility for running the house. According to the International Labor Organization of the United Nations, employed mothers usually have less than two thirds of the free time that their husbands enjoy. Many women try to be supermom at home while maintaining a difficult career. They feel they must not only balance schedules, secure good, reliable child care, and give their spouses the support and attention they need, but also be a gourmet cook, make the children's clothes, and be cub-scout den mother. Thus in a dual-job marriage the wife holds two jobs; outside the home and at home.

Another problem working wives have is the guilt about leaving children and the difficulty in finding adequate day-care facilities. Nevertheless, recent studies show no evidence of any negative effects on children traceable directly to maternal employment.[34] On the contrary, children of working mothers tend to be taught responsibility and cooperation earlier and are generally more independent. Hoffman concluded that working mothers provide role models that their daughters admire and emulate.[35]

A more difficult problem to resolve is that of finding adequate day-care facilities. Most women do not have money for private care at home, and good institutional care is usually quite hard to find. Many states have no licensing or supervision of day-care facilities or teachers. Two related problems for many working mothers are transporting children to and from day care and caring for sick children. It is generally still the norm in our society that the mother stays home from work if the child is sick. The problem of day care is indicative of the lack of support systems for the working mother. Other similar problems include industries and professions that do not have hours that are convenient for the working mother.

In spite of all difficulties, in an increasing number of families both spouses are heavily committed to their careers and have adapted their family life to better fit this duality. Some couples even live in different places, and one of them commutes on weekends; in some cases wives travel frequently on business. While these situations work out well for some couples, for others they lead to jealousy, child-care problems, and differences in their views of acceptable role patterns.[36]

In the dual-career family where their jobs are a major source of satisfaction and commitment for both spouses, there are also many benefits.[37] Many families have learned the advantages of sharing roles and household responsibilities. Working wives relieve their husbands of the heavy burden of being the sole economic provider. The working wife has better mental health, is less susceptible to the housewife syndrome, and is less likely to become depressed when her children no longer require her full-time attention. Husbands who help with child care get to know their children better and develop closer, stronger relationships with them.

Whether the wife has a career outside the home or is a full-time homemaker, the arrival of the first child is often quite a shock for both parents, leading to changes in schedules, role patterns, relations between husband and wife.

Parenting and Child Care

Contemporary young people have little or no experience that would enable them to bring their conceptions of parenthood in line with reality.[38] Sex and parenting are two areas where the American practical notion of "learning by doing" is not condoned. Women and men having their first babies often lack even basic information about infants.[39] (A notable exception is the childbirth and parenting classes sponsored by the Lamaze Association.) Another influencing factor is the abruptness of the transition to parenting. The birth of a child is not followed by a gradual assuming of responsibility. The new parents immediately start on twenty-four-hour duty.

Prepared or not, most couples do have children, and with the arrival of the first comes an abrupt role transition. Many new mothers experience "cabin fever," a feeling of exhaustion, "postpartum blues," or guilt over blaming the child for problems and inconveniences. New fathers may feel economic stress or undergo a psychological crisis as their needs are no longer the wife's primary priority.[40] Additionally, the relationship between the spouses may be altered by the baby's birth. Changes in division of labor, frequency and satisfaction of sex, and time spent outside the home for social activities often occur. In particular, the couple usually experiences a redividing of chores along traditional lines, even in families where sharing had been the norm.

How severely children affect the marital relationship varies sharply with different couples. Several studies show that marital satisfaction declines with parenthood. In a study of almost 330 couples with young children, Russell found that both spouses reported a slight-to-moderate crisis upon the baby's birth; but the better their general level of marital adjustment, the less serious the crisis developed.[41] In other studies, however, most couples reported their marriage to be either improved or unchanged after the birth of a child. Certainly, attitudes about having children and planned versus unplanned births also affect the relationship.

Changing Aspects of Parenting

Birthrates today are at their lowest level since the late 1930s. In 1972 the fertility rate dropped below the replacement level of 2.10 children per family. The fertility rate in 1973 was 1.9 children per woman.[42] What lies behind this change is a "virtual revolution in our attitudes toward childbearing, supported by vastly improved birth control technology."[43] Greater reliability of birth-control methods has been accompanied by a decrease in the number of children women want and expect to have. There is also greater control over when and whether they have them, as evidenced by the significant upturn in the number of older women deciding to have children.

Only about 5 percent of married couples remain voluntarily child-free. Until recently this group was considered deviant and self-centered,[44] but now their reasons—preservation of energy and time; the notion of marriage as a self-sufficient, fulfilling unit; concern for population pressures and food and energy shortages—are easily accepted by most of society. In one study one third of couples who decided before marriage that they would not have children usually incorporated that decision in an informal marriage "contract."[45] The other two thirds came to their decision through postponement and realization of the rewards of childlessness.

Another new and changing aspect of parenting is the relationship between fathers and children. The role of father in the traditional American family is well defined: His word is final; he is the primary disciplinarian and the role model of physical courage, toughness, competitiveness—in a word, masculinity—for his sons.[46] Many fathers have become detached from the family because of work demands.[47] The executive-professional men's workweek is long, and time is absorbed in commuting and performing civic responsibilities. Middle-class men tend to see fatherhood with the single purpose of providing for the family.[48] Working-class men, although their primary job may not be as time consuming, are separated from the children because of moonlighting, nights out with "the boys," or the notion that childrearing is the wife's domain.

Yet the father-child relationship is changing. Many fathers are making genuine efforts to meet the individual needs of their children. In the preface to *How to Father* Dodson notes that now, more than ever before, the father's role in childrearing is becoming more vital and is being recognized as such.[49] As we saw earlier, in a dual-career marriage the father's greater participation in household chores and childrearing tends to strengthen the father-child relationship, as well as foster a more egalitarian relationship between the spouses.

In addition to the rise in the number of working wives, three adaptations of the basic traditional family are of particular significance today: the blue-collar family, the Black family, and the single-parent family. Each of these will be discussed in terms of its own characteristics and its definition of the role of women as compared with that of the traditional middle-class family.

BLUE-COLLAR MARRIAGES

The working class makes up about 40 percent of the nation's families. Blue-collar marriages are generally traditional marriages that have some very special aspects of their own. Although there are many subdivisions of the working class, certain general patterns can be seen: The men are expected to be the economic providers, and it is preferred by both spouses that the women not work outside the home. Men are often afraid of their wife's involvement at work and do not want their authority threatened by her earnings. However, the pressures of financial strains dictate that 58 percent of working-class wives hold jobs.[50] Many of these are part-time jobs; the wives are likely to move in and out of the labor force depending upon the husband's overtime hours, job stability, and the needs of the family. If possible, they work when the children are in school or when their husband can baby-sit. Unless the father or a relative can baby-sit, they have serious child-care problems because they usually cannot afford to hire someone to come to their home or pay the costs of child-care centers.

Rubin reported that many of these women find the world of work a satisfying place, particularly as compared with the role of housewife.[51] Ironically, the low-status, low-paying dead-end jobs the blue-collar wives hold have conditions similar to those of housework, requiring service, submission, and suppression of intellectual development. Few of the wives expect to do more exciting work or have aspirations for a career. They view their employment as an extension of their household role and expect to work at mundane jobs.

Working-class wives, whether they are in the labor force or full-time homemakers, are much more closely involved with the housewife role and the domestic interests and activities in general than are middle-class wives. The area of housework and the role of housewife are both sources of stress and stability in blue-collar families. Working-class women understand that a highly structured division of labor is typical in their social system, but two major sources of discomfort are the unrelieved responsibility for young children and a feeling of being tied down.[52] However, there is less pressure on the working-class wife; she feels little pressure to be involved in the community, to keep up intellectually, or even to maintain her looks. The women generally accept the traditional segregation of masculine and feminine tasks and do not expect help from their husbands. Nor do they get such help. All agree that housework is the woman's job. "His" masculinity is already threatened by "her" work. Both husband and wife prefer that it not be further threatened by him doing feminine jobs. Although many husbands expect to "help her out" in a pinch, men often resist even when help is obviously needed. For instance;

> One 21-year-old mother of 3 infants (aged 2 years, 1 year, and 3 weeks) complained that her husband won't get up at night to help with the crying baby. He confesses guiltily that he likes to sleep, although he adds with a sheepish smile that even his mother warned him that his exhausted wife might drop the baby out of sheer fatigue unless he relieved her occasionally.[53]

Times are changing, however, and younger working-class men with a high-school education seem to have absorbed norms about helping a little more, especially with child care and shopping.

Childhood and early socialization also strongly influence patterns of social interaction and life-styles in the blue-collar family. The parental family from which men and women consciously or unconsciously acquire their conceptions of marriage roles remains their major reference group after marriage. Both men and women are attached to their mothers. Many of the women visit their mothers daily or several times a week. These parental families play a supportive role for the married couple, but in a traditional way. Older women may try to get the husband to help more; but, as often as not, they counsel the wife to lower her expectations, to resign herself to the situation, to know her place.[54] Husbands and wives maintain separate groups of friends and usually have a limited social life, socializing with relatives more than any others.

In sex, as in other matters, the barriers to communication are high. Women tend to put duty and honor before enjoyment, whereas men reverse these priorities. Woman, socialized from infancy to experience their sexuality as a negative force to be inhibited and suppressed, find it difficult to respond positively to sexual innovation and a loosening of sexual constraints. A "good girl" or "bad girl" ideology is particularly influential in the use of birth control. Many women are pregnant on their wedding day because using birth control would imply that they are "bad girls" who think ahead about sex. Men, more often than women, speak of their desire for sex to be freer and with more mutual enjoyment,[55] but they do not know how to communicate these ideas to their spouses.

What kind of marriage relationships do such diverse and at times conflicting attitudes and feelings engender? Blue-collar marriages in America today are characterized by stress.[56] The stress is a product of the marriage, role segregation, and the consequent widely divergent socialization patterns for men and women.[57] The husbands have been trained to restrain or deny their feelings and not to communicate or express them. The women, on the other hand, learn to express their feelings and to react to situations in an emotional manner. "Thus they talk *at* each other, *past* each other, or *through* each other —rarely *with* or *to* each other."[58]

A particularly sensitive aspect of the gulf in communications is the changing expectations for life and marriage that some working blue-collar wives are experiencing. The women get glimpses of egalitarian marriages in soap operas and at their jobs. Their expectations for proper roles are changing— much to the consternation of their husbands. The women want greater companionship, sharing, and intimacy, but they do not know how to verbalize these needs. While the same changes are being experienced in middle-class families, in blue-collar couples there are not overt changes in roles or much discussion of women's liberation. However, although both men and women tend to reject the women's movement, they are obviously still feeling its influences.

American blue-collar marriages do have strengths which promote stability. Both spouses generally come from traditional backgrounds; from childhood both have developed the ability to meet and survive adversity. They have lower expectations of life and marriage, and their children are strongly socialized for their segregated roles.[59] From the wife's point of view, if the husband is a steady worker, does not drink, and is good to her and the children, that is enough.

Much of the discussion of working-class marriages also applies to lower-class families, except that often in these families the problems are exaggerated. A major characteristic of marital life is fluidity.[60] Economic deprivations, anxiety about the future, feelings of defeat, concern about failure to give children a good start in life, and the bleak existence these families have, have a variety of negative effects on marriages.[61] When the situation becomes intolerable or the man needs to move to find employment, the couple may separate. These and other factors account for the higher divorce rate in this group and the higher incidence of common-law relationships or consensual unions rather than formal commitments or marriage.

Some of the results of this economic pinch can particularly be seen in the life-styles and structure of Black families. However, other factors interact with economics to produce the differentiated pattern of the Black family.

THE BLACK FAMILY

To understand the Black family, one must look at its historical roots in the American culture. Although the structure and function of the Black family were radically altered under slavery, the concept of family was one of the most important survival mechanisms for Black people while in bondage. Families in the slave quarters provided love, companionship, socialization, and affection for their members.

The male role in the Black family is highly disputed. Some argue that the traditional male role so decreased in slave circumstances that a mother-centered, or "matrifocal," family system developed and was reinforced by assigning housing and food rations to the mother-child unit.[62] Others contend that although the male could not perform many traditional husband and father functions, the male was important and respected in the slave family and community, and his role was not subservient to the female's.[63]

With emancipation, two different trends were evident. In families that had achieved stability during slavery, the father acquired more authority.[64] However, families marked by instability tended to break completely under the stresses following emancipation, further emphasizing the mother-child relationship.[65] Additionally, some sociologists believe that the matriarchy did not develop until Black families were settled in the ghettos and the female-oriented job opportunities and social welfare programs came into play. This historical heritage has left its mark in many ways on the modern Black family.

Most contemporary Black families are male-headed, but at the same time a significantly larger percentage of Black families than White are female-headed. The 36 percent of Black families headed by women are primarily a result of socioeconomic forces in the lower economic level. For this and other reasons, Black families were among the first to show the dysfunctional structure of marriage. For many, however, the problems in the Black family arose for very different reasons than did those in the middle class. Thus, applying White middle-class concepts of social class, life-style, or cultural values is difficult and often inaccurate.

Loyalty and responsibility patterns illustrate such differences in cultural values. The Black kinship network is more extensive and cohesive than that among the white population. Thus, among women, there is less loss of unity, although unity with other females is at a price. That price is generally less companionship between spouses. For example, the single parent who takes in other relatives to live with her and her children is quite prevalent among Black families.[66]

Another aspect of social structure is the fluid interchanging of roles. The instrumental role of many Black women has long been known. Less well known is the frequency of Black males engaging in expressive functions in the areas of child care and household tasks. Much of this fluidity derives from the socialization of sex roles during infancy and childhood. Unlike the Euro-American tradition in which many of the traits of maleness and femaleness are mutually exclusive, Black culture does not transmit to the Black child, with equivalent thoroughness, standards that polarize behavioral expectations according to sex.[67] For example, aggressiveness, nurturance, independence, emotional expressiveness, and sexual assertiveness are all behavioral traits to which both males and females in the Black culture are socialized. Birth order and age, rather than sex, are crucial in determining parental and family treatment. Thus Black girls are often well prepared for their instrumental and leadership roles in Black society.

Since E. Franklin Frazier's pioneering study *The Negro Family in The United States,* social scientists have emphasized the central and critical role of the female in Black families. In upper-, middle-, and upper-lower-class Black families wives are far more likely to work outside the home than is the case in White families, owing to lower income, less job security, and stronger norms favoring it. Black women, in the past, could often find jobs in urban areas where their men were unemployed. These women could get jobs precisely because they were women and Black, thus not threatening to the White male community. Moreover, almost two thirds of Black women who head families hold jobs outside the home.[68] Women's instrumental roles are emphasized in urban ghetto situations while the men may be unemployed or underemployed and spending their days on the street corner.[69]

However, many Black families have assimilated the family role patterns of the mainstream culture. Several studies indicate that husband-wife relationships in many Black families are egalitarian.[70] In decision making, Black husbands tend to have more influence than their wives, but most decisions, nevertheless, are made jointly.[71] Many Black husbands share extensively in performing household tasks in many families, and in particular, Black males may share child-care responsibilities.

As with all groups, Black family life is changing, and the changes are not necessarily those found in White, middle-class American society. There is more equality in decision making and division of labor as in White middle-class families. However, these changes do not directly evolve from the women's movement. While Black women want equal employment opportunities and income parity, they often cannot relate to White women's issues as expressed in the women's movement. They may not feel the need to change roles in a household where they already have status and contribute an income. Another reason they may resist the women's movement is that they may have been told that to advance their race they must be subservient to the Black male.

As we noted, a significant proportion of Black families are headed by single parents. This is the third adaptation of the traditional American family which we shall now consider. Although single-parent families result from a variety of situations—death, divorce, adoption, and never marrying—the most prevalent cause today is divorce.

THE SINGLE-PARENT FAMILY

The number of divorces in the United States has been rapidly climbing, totaling over one million in 1975.[72] The number of divorces per 1,000 population almost doubled between 1965 and 1975.[73] Thus both the number and probability of divorce have rapidly escalated. It is now estimated that one out of three marriages will end in divorce. The probability of divorce varies among groups. Divorce rates among Black people, the poor, those who marry young, and those who have low or very high educational levels are significantly higher than those among people who marry late, have moderately high educational levels, and are wealthier.[74]

What are the reasons for divorce? As women move out of the home into the labor force, they develop broader and stronger economic alternatives, meet and interact with more men, fulfill more of their personal needs outside the home, and change their roles within the family. These factors are all influential when spouses decide upon divorce. Another factor leading to a higher divorce rate may be that some people enter marriage with unrealistically high expectations that cannot be met. In addition, that couples are having fewer children or no children to consider, combined with the growing possibility of obtaining the less painful "no-fault" divorce, opens up a broader set of alternatives for those considering the termination of a marriage. No-fault divorce has in some situations made divorce easier, less costly, and less time consuming. It is not, however, always advantageous for women: "No-fault divorce, without concurrent changes in provision for division of property, alimony and child support, has eroded the economic protection of dependent spouses and children."[75] Whether the divorce is on a fault or no-fault basis, it has tremendous ramifications for the future life of the spouses and their children. There are minor children in about three fifths of divorces today. Approximately one child in six is raised for part of his/her life in a single-parent home, and at any one time there are over 3.5 million single-parent families. Although the circumstances when starting single-parent families vary broadly, there is a common range of experiences, functions, and problems that single-parents usually have. As 90 percent of the single parents are women, we shall concentrate on them.[76]

A major area of concern is financial. Divorce and low income are related; research indicates that poverty often follows divorce, and the median income of women-headed families is less than half that of two-parent families.[77] Kriesberg's study of poor mothers indicates that the economic status of women heading families is frequently determined not by their socioeconomic origins but their current circumstances.[78] Thus most divorced women experience downward economic mobility owing to economic discrimination, less job training, concentration in low-paying, less secure jobs, and infrequent or nonexistent support payments.[79]

After a period of adjustment single mothers usually, therefore, get jobs in hopes of solving their economic problems. Although this boosts family income, employment outside the home presents the same problems faced by all working mothers, but made even more difficult for single parents. Employment often conflicts with child care and homemaking activities, thus, for some, necessitating part-time rather than more lucrative full-time jobs. Stein, for instance, found that while 70 percent of the women heading families in his study worked at some time during the year, only 38 percent were able to work full-time all year.[80] The lack of adequate, reasonably priced child-care facilities intensifies the problems of women working and may preclude paid employment for some who head families. For those who do work, lack of funds may intensify the problems of finding competent day care.

Providing for the physical safety and emotional well-being of the children and the physical maintenance of the household is difficult for a single parent. Family needs still tend to be ignored in the structuring of job conditions, mothers tend to be isolated in their domestic tasks, and relatives are less likely to assist a woman (as compared with a man) with housework.

A particularly stressful aspect of being both father and mother is child discipline.[81] Research differs concerning the single parent's authority over her children. There is evidence that because of diminished respect and power in the community, and lack of training in authority roles, the mother has less authority with her children. Recent research has indicated that sons know this and may therefore act in less socially acceptable ways.

Emotional support systems are usually lacking for the single parent. Negative attitudes toward single-parent families and divorced mothers are common in society.[82] Glasser and Navarre found that these women often believe that society sees them as abnormal, and they accept and internalize this label.[83] Possibly because of these feelings and the overload of domestic responsibilities, divorced mothers do not tend to get out of the house for social activities as frequently as they did when married. Reestablishing their social life can be a challenging but frightful experience.[84] Nevertheless, dating activities and boyfriends are often an important part of a divorced mother's social life and emotional support system.

An impressive two-year study found that stress and worry in all these areas were a frequent part of life for a divorced mother. Stresses included practical problems, such as economic and occupational problems and concerns in running a household. Other areas of stress were changes associated with emotional distress and changes in self-concept and identity. Finally, interpersonal problems in maintaining a social life, in developing depth relationships, and in interacting with the ex-spouse and with children were other sources of stress.

However, there is a positive aspect to the role of a single parent. Recent research indicated that many women perceived their divorced state as giving them more independence and power.[85] New identities—though painful—for women (both single parents and others) are evolving. They often include a new pride of accomplishment in supporting a family, holding a job, and fulfilling the material, physical, and emotional needs of the children. Such pride is often accompanied by more self-confidence and positive feelings of self-worth. In addition, as these women assume the responsibilities of both mother and father, they often become more androgynous and in turn may rear more androgynous children. As recent research has shown that such androgyny leads to more flexible behavior and higher self-esteem, this is also a positive aspect of the single-parent situation.

The father who heads a family without a partner will experience some of the same problems as a woman, but also some different ones. The financial situation will probably not be as bleak as for the woman. However, fathers usually have less experience and skill in household management.

The ultimate goal for most divorced persons is remarriage. Eighty percent of divorced persons remarry; 20 to 40 million people who have been divorced are remarried.[86] However, about 60 percent of these second marriages end in divorce, as opposed to 37 percent of first marriages.[87] As with most relationships, there are both advantages and problems with a second marriage. It may help alleviate loneliness, satisfy the need for a depth relationship, and provide reentry into the mainstream, couples-oriented society. Although LeMasters states that a child needs only one competent adult to satisfy her/his emotional and psychological needs, mothers frequently see remarriage as providing a dual sex-role model for the child. Finally, for many divorced persons, remarriage is a chance to erase bad memories, learn from mistakes, and start over.[88]

Many of the disadvantages or problems in remarriage are the difficulty in maintaining ties to old friends and relatives, blending children from one or both families into the new family, and jealousy and rivalry between the first and second spouses. There are likewise resultant strains of integrating many careers, interests, and sets of children. Even with these problems, the fact that five out of six men and three out of four women eventually remarry implies that most people prefer to be married. Furthermore, remarriage provides new opportunities, especially for women. Women tend to keep the stronger identity and pride gained while a single parent, and more equality in decision making and division of labor are likely in the new marriage.

Although most adults prefer to be, and are, married, not all of them are members of traditional unions. Some choose not to marry at all; they prefer what they regard as the advantages of singlehood. Others opt for marital alternatives to traditional marriages, such as "open marriage" or two-step marriage.

ALTERNATIVES TO TRADITIONAL MARRIAGE

In addition to the traditional marriage, other types of relationships may include singlehood, the homosexual relationship, symmetrical shared-role pattern, "open marriage," and two-step marriage.

The symmetrical shared-role pattern is for two people who have settled into a long-term bond with each other. It emphasizes work and obligation and management of dual responsibilities for both work and leisure.[89] These dual-career families have innovative work patterns and conservative, monogamous sexual arrangements. Many of the dual-career marriages we discussed earlier also display the symmetrical shared-role pattern. A variation on the shared-role pattern is the open marriage which emphasizes even more individuality for each of the spouses.

Open marriage is described as an "honest, open relationship between two people, based on the equal freedom and identity of both partners."[90] It involves a total commitment—emotional, verbal, and intellectual—to each other for the right of both members to grow as individuals within and outside the marriage. The relationship is one of equality based on mutual liking and trust, allowing each his/her mental and emotional freedom and promoting the development of the individual.

Many people are attracted by the perceived advantages and excitement of open marriages. However, there are several potential hazards. Our past experiences and our value system may work against establishing an open marriage. A reasonably secure sense of self is a prerequisite to this type of relationship, and people must feel secure enough in their relationship to allow both members to experiment and not need either member's continual presence. These factors may be particularly difficult for women who have been socialized in other directions.

Another possibility for the future would be the two-step marriage. Margaret Mead envisioned one marriage for procreation and the other for companionship and recreation.[91] In this structure one would have a set period for trying a childless, companionate marriage. If this version worked, then the spouses could opt for parenthood.

Perhaps a version of this is the trial marriage or cohabitation. It is becoming a more openly acknowledged practice before marriage and, for some people, is a long-term alternative to marriage. Cohabitation for many years between the same two people is especially popular among middle-aged divorced people who wish to retain child-support payments or perhaps fear being inhibited again by the structure of marriage. Another group that is openly living together is the elderly. In most cases, if they were to marry instead of cohabitating, the size of their Social Security benefits would decrease.

Some people opt not to marry or to live with the opposite sex. An increasingly popular alternative to traditional marriage is singlehood. In the past women married to avoid the stigma of being an "old maid," to have social relationships in a couples-oriented society, and to gain economic security, among other factors. As women move in greater numbers into the labor force and work at better jobs and earn higher incomes, and as the stigma against the single woman dissipates, more women are choosing not to marry or to marry at a later age.[92]

Still another alternative to the traditional family is the homosexual relationship. As homosexuality is becoming more accepted by society, the number of people who are willing to publicly acknowledge their homosexuality is increasing. The Kinsey study and others have reported that about 4 percent of all men and women are exclusively homosexual in their sexual preferences, and for about 18 percent of the adult population one half or more of their sexual experiences are homosexual. More recent studies show that homosexual relationships and a homosexual life-style provide a satisfying alternative to marriage for the majority of those who engage in them.

THE FUTURE OF THE FAMILY

Is "the future of the family" a statement of fact or a question? The alternatives to the traditional family discussed above will increase in numbers and degree of acceptance as the years go by. However, social scientists predict that although the family may change in format, roles played by members, and its relationship to other institutions, it will continue to be the central focus for people throughout life.

In the future women will probably assume a stronger role both within the family and in other institutions, such as the labor force. Such growth in their roles outside the family will have positive effects on their power and decision-making roles inside the family. There will probably be more real sharing of responsibility in the home and on the job. Living arrangements will develop to provide better family support systems and less family isolation. In this respect the development of more unity in help-giving and perhaps some type of communal living may extend Black family kinship patterns to the white community.

Jessie Bernard poignantly makes the point that there are no final solutions
to the problems we presently experience and anticipate in the future.

marriage is the best of human statuses and the worst, and it will continue to be.
And that is why, though its future in some form or other is as assured as anything
can be, this future is as equivocal as its past. The demands that men and women
make on marriage will never be fully met; they cannot be. And these demands
will rise rather than decline as our standards—rightfully—go up. Men and
women will continue to disappoint as well as delight one another, regardless of
the form of their commitments to one another, or the living style they adopt, or
even of the nature of the relationship between them.[93]

NOTES

1. Paul Glick, "A Demographer Looks at American Families," *Journal of Marriage and the Family* 37, no. 1 (February 1975): 15.

2. Ibid., p. 16.

3. Betty Friedan, *The Feminine Mystique* (New York: Dell, 1963).

4. Glick, "Demographer Looks at Families," p. 17.

5. U.S. Bureau of the Census, "Prospects for American Fertility: June, 1974," *Current Population Reports,* ser. P-20, no. 269 (Washington, D.C.: Government Printing Office, 1974), p. 1.

6. Alice S. Rossi, "Discrimination and Demography Restrict Opportunities for Academic Women,"in *And Jill Came Tumbling After: Sexism in American Education,* ed. Judith Stacey, Susan Bereaud, and Joan Daniels (New York: Dell, 1974), p. 366.

7. Delia Ephron, "The State of the Union," *Esquire* (February 1977): p. 63.

8. Glick, "Demographer Looks at Families."

9. David Heer, "The Measurement and Bases of Family Power: An Overview," *Journal of Marriage and the Family* 25 (May 1963): 134.

10. Robert Blood and Donald Wolfe, *Husbands and Wives: The Dynamics of Married Living* (New York: Macmillan, 1960), p. 51.

11. Ibid., p. 51.

12. Elizabeth Bott, *Family and Social Network* (London: Tavistock, 1957); George Levinger, "Task and Social Behavior in Marriage," *Sociometry* 27 (December 1964): 433–448.

13. Jessie Bernard, *The Future of Marriage* (New York: Bantam, 1973), p. 17.

14. Ibid.

15. Norman Bradburn, *The Structure of Psychological Well-Being* (Chicago: Aldine, 1969), p. 9.

16. Paul Glick, "Marital Stability as a Social Indicator," *Social Biology* 16 (September 1969): 158.

17. Bernard, *Future of Marriage,* p. 28.

18. Phyllis Chesler, *Women and Madness* (New York: Avon, 1972), p. 116.

19. Genevieve Knupfer, Walter Clark, and Robin Room, "The Mental Health of the Unmarried," *American Journal of Psychiatry* 122 (February 1966): 842.

20. Chesler, *Women and Madness,* p. 115.

21. Gerald Gurin, Joseph Veroff, and Sheila Feld, *Americans View Their Mental Health* (New York: Basic Books, 1960), p. 110.

22. Richard Klemer, "Factors of Personality and Experience Which Differentiate Single from Married Women," *Marriage and Family Living* 16 (February 1954): 44.

23. Bernard, *Future of Marriage,* p. 35.

24. Ibid., p. 42.

25. Chase Manhattan Bank, Informal Survey, 1974.

26. U.S., Bureau of Labor Statistics, *U.S. Working Women: A Databook* (Washington, D.C.: Department of Labor, 1977), p. 1.

27. Ibid., p. 61.

28. Ibid., p. 1.

29. Ibid., p. 15.

30. Evelyne Sullerot, *Women, Society and Change* (New York: World University Library, 1973), p. 82.

31. David Heer, "Dominance and the Working Mother," in Nye and Hoffman, *Employed Mothers in America* (Chicago: Rand McNally, 1963), p. 261.

32. Lois Hoffman, "Parental Power Relations and the Division of Household Tasks," in Nye and Hoffman, *Employed Mother in America,* p. 229.

33. *New York Times,* January 12, 1975, p. E-7.

34. Alice S. Rossi, "Why Seek Equality between the Sexes: An Immodest Proposal, "in *Confronting the Issues: Sex Roles, Marriage and the Family,* ed. Kenneth Kammeyer (Boston: Allyn and Bacon, 1975), p. 270, 271.

35. Lois Hoffman, in Nye and Hoffman, *Employed Mother in America,* p. 197.

36. Letha Scanzoni and John Scanzoni, *Men, Women and Change* (New York: McGraw Hill, 1976), p. 238.

37. Ibid., p. 239.

38. Reiss, Ira, *Family Systems in America,* 2nd ed. (Hinsdale: Illinois: The Dryden Press, 1976), p. 340.

39. Ibid.

40. Gerald Leslie and Elizabeth Leslie, *Marriage in a Changing World* (New York: Wiley, 1977), p. 268.

41. Candyce Russell, "Transition to Parenthood: Problems and Gratifications," *Journal of Marriage and the Family* 36 (May 1974): 299.

42. Glick, "Demographer Looks at Families," p. 16.

43. Leslie and Leslie, *Marriage,* p. 236.

44. J. E. Veevers, "Voluntarily Childless Wives: An Exploratory Study," *Sociology and Social Research* 57 (April 1973): p. 357.

45. Ibid., p. 358.

46. Jack Balswick and Charles Peek, "The Inexpressive Male: A Tragedy of American Society," *The Family Coordinator* 20 (October 1971): p. 364.

47. David Lynn, "Fathers and America in Transition," *The Father: His Role in Child Development* (Monterey, Calif.: Brooks Cole, 1974), p. 104.

48. Joseph Maxwell, "The Keeping Fathers of America," *The Family Coordinator* 25 (October, 1976): 387.

49. Fitzhugh Dodson, *How to Father* (New York: New American Library, 1974), p. x.

50. Lillian B. Rubin, *Worlds of Pain; Life in the Working-Class Family* (New York: Basic Books, 1976), p. 167.

51. Ibid., p. 169.

52. Mirra Komarovsky, *Blue-Collar Marriage* (New York: Vintage Books, 1967), p. 60.

53. Ibid., p. 54.

54. Komarovsky, *Blue-Collar Marriage,* p. 39.

55. Rubin, *Worlds of Pain,* p. 136.

56. E. E. LeMasters, *Blue Collar Aristocrat* (Madison, Wis.: University of Wisconsin Press, 1975), p. 36.

57. Rubin, *World of Pain,* p. 116.

58. Ibid.

59. Ibid.

60. Hyman Rodman, "Lower Class Family Behavior, "in *Blue Collar World: Studies of the American Worker,* ed. Arthur Shostak and William Gomberg (Englewood Cliffs, N. J.: Prentice-Hall, 1964), p. 68.

61. Komarovsky, *Blue-Collar Marriage,* p. 290.

62. Reiss, *Family Systems,* p. 415; and Gerald Leslie, *The Family in Social Context,* 3rd ed. (New York: Oxford University Press, 1976), p. 315.

63. Robert Staples, *Introduction to Black Sociology* (New York: McGraw-Hill, 1976), p. 118.

64. Leslie, *Family in Social Context,* p. 317.

65. Ibid.

66. Andrew Billingsley, *Black Families in White America* (Englewood Cliffs, N.J.: Prentice-Hall, 1968), p. 21.

67. Diane Lewis, "The Black Family: Socialization and Sex Roles," *Phylon* 36 (Sept. 1975): 228.

68. Leslie, *Family in Social Context,* pp. 332–333.

69. Ulf Hannerz, "Roots of Black Manhood," *TRANS-action* 6 (October 1969): 16.

70. Billingsley, *Black Families,* p. 25.

71. Robert Hill, *The Strengths of Black Families* (New York: Emerson Hall, 1971), pp. 18–19.

72. Reiss, *Family Systems,* p. 305.

73. Leslie and Leslie, *Marriage,* p. 295.

74. Ibid., p. 296.

75. Dee Dee Ahern and Betsy Bliss, *The Economics of Being a Women* (New York: McGraw-Hill, 1976), p. 164.

76. Gladys Jenkins, "The Single-Parent Family—An Overview," in *Proceedings of the Changing Family Conference V* (Iowa City, Iowa: The University of Iowa Press, 1976), p. 11.

77. U.S., Bureau of the Census, *Current Population Reports,* Series P-60, No. 97, January, 1975.

78. Louis Kriesberg, *Mothers in Poverty* (Chicago: Aldine, 1970), p. 29.

79. Ruth Brandwein, Carol Brown and Elizabeth Fox, "Women and Children Last: The Social Situation of Divorced Mothers and Their Families," *Journal of Marriage and the Family* 36 (August 1974), p. 501.

80. Robert Stein, "The Economic Status of Families Headed by Women," *Monthly Labor Review* 93 (December 1970), p. 7.

81. Robert Weiss, "A Preliminary Examination of Potential Contributions of Quality of Life to an Understanding of Single Parenting,"(Springfield, Va.: U.S. Department of Commerce, 1976), p. 8.

82. Brandwein, Brown and Fox, "Women and Children Last," p. 506.

83. Paul Glasser and Elizabeth Navarre, "Structural Problems of the One-Parent Family," *Journal of Social Issues* 21 (January, 1965), p. 101.

84. Leslie and Leslie, *Marriage,* p. 327.

85. Brandwein, Brown and Fox, "Women and Children Last," p. 504.

86. Morton and Bernice Hunt, "The World of the Formerly Married," in *Proceedings of the Changing Family Conference V* (Iowa City, Iowa: The University of Iowa Press, 1976), p. 25.

87. Amitai Etzioni, "Is the Marital Merry-Go-Round Giving Families a Bum Trip?" *Des Moines Sunday Register,* January 11, 1976, p. 4-E.

88. Verne Kelly and Patricia Kelly, "Considering Remarriage?" in *Proceedings of the Changing Family Conference V* (Iowa City, Iowa: The University of Iowa Press, 1976), p. 63.

89. Janet Giele, "Changing Sex Roles and the Future of Marriage," in *Contemporary Marriage: Structure Dynamics and Therapy,* eds. Gruenbaum and Christ (Boston: Little, Brown and Co., 1975), p. 71.

90. Nena O'Neill and George O'Neill, *Open Marriage: A New Life Style for Couples* (New York: M. Evans and Co., 1972), p. 38.

91. Margaret Mead, "Marriages in Two Stages," *Redbook Magazine,* July, 1966.

92. Glick, "Demographer Looks at Families," p. 16.

93. Bernard, *Future of Marriage,* pp. 323–324.

REVIEW QUESTIONS

1. What aspects of traditional roles do you see in your family and in your friends' families?

2. What advantages for men and women do you see in the traditional family and in the contemporary family?

3. Why do you think men are more likely to remarry than women?
4. What are the orientations toward work, marriage, and family of young women today, and how do they compare and contrast with those of their mothers' generation and of women in the nineteenth century? Answer these questions as they apply to men.
5. Describe some of the frequent adjustments faced by new mothers and fathers.
6. What distinguishes a dual-career marriage from other marriages in which the wife works?
7. How can women, and how can men, lessen some of the stress experienced after divorce?
8. In what areas do retired people generally suffer the greatest losses, and how do or might they cope with them?
9. What are some of the strengths of Black families in general and of women-headed families in particular?
10. Hypothetically place yourself in one of the alternatives to traditional marriage. Discuss its advantages, disadvantages, and how you would adjust to this new life-style.

SELECTED READINGS

Bernard, Jessie. *The Future of Marriage*. New York: Bantam, 1972.

Bernard's inquiry into the future of marriage considers the nature and probable future of the commitment that transforms a relationship into a marriage and the nature of the life-styles that are going to accompany it. Of particular interest to the study of women's roles in the family is the discussion of the presence of two marriages in every marital union—his and hers. The husband's and the wife's marriages differ and do not always coincide.

Brandwein, Ruth, Carol Brown, and Elizabeth Fox. "Women and Children Last: The Social Situation of Divorced Mothers and Their Families." *Journal of Marriage and the Family* 36 (August 1974): 498–514.

This review focuses on the mother-and-family unit that remains after the father leaves, with particular emphasis on the consequences of the unit's being headed by a woman. The article evaluates the findings on divorced women as single parents, and the family units they head; it reexamines effects of stigma on these families. The first section considers how four family functions—economic, authority, domestic, and supports—are fulfilled in single-parent families. The second section discusses some of the methodological problems in the studies of father-absent families.

Burden, Susan, Peggy Houston, Eva Kripke, Roger Simpson, and Fred W. Stultz, eds. *Proceedings of the Changing Family Conference V. The Single Parent Family*. Iowa City: The University of Iowa, 1976.

The papers presented in this volume represent a balance of the seven major presentations, thirty-two mini-lectures, and ten workshops held at the conference. As a whole the volume is a good introduction to the varying types of single-parent families, including father-headed families, and to some of the major problems faced in these situations.

Family Coordinator 25 (October 1976): 25.

Deals with all aspects of fatherhood: men's entrance to parenthood, fathers and infancy, and sex-role development of their children. Single-parent fatherhood, stepfathers, father-child communication are also considered.

Hetherington, E. Mavis, Martha Cox, and Roger Cox. "Stress and Coping in Divorce: A Focus on Women." Charlottesville: University of Virginia.

This paper reports part of the findings of a two-year longitudinal study of the impact of divorce on family functioning and the development of children. These findings deal with alterations in family relations and life-style, stresses, and coping by mothers, and how these factors change in the two years following divorce. Includes an extensive review of the literature, references, and several tables of data to supplement the commentary.

Komarovsky, Mirra. *Blue-Collar Marriage.* New York: Vintage Books, 1967.

A major work and one of the first attempts to study working-class families in many aspects of married life. It is based on a study of fifty-eight marriages and utilizes the case-study-interview method. Excerpts from the interviews are utilized throughout the book to support concepts and hypotheses. Considered in depth are such topics as division of labor, power, emotional and psychological attitudes of the spouses, communication, and women working outside the home.

Reiss, Ira. *Family Systems in America,* 2nd ed. Hinsdale, Ill.: Dryden Press, 1976.

This textbook presents an integrated sociological view of the family with the purpose of providing greater sociological understanding of the many patterns of human belief and behavior in family systems. Emphasis is on the importance of the dyadic relationship in the traditional family, the contemporary family, and the many changing elements of families. The five major sections are family system, courtship, marriage, family, and future trends.

Rubin, Lillian B. *Worlds of Pain: Life in the Working-Class Family.* New York: Basic Books, 1976.

The most recent detailed examination of the family life of the white working class in America. Its central concerns are the natures of the strains, the sources of the conflicts, and the quality of the struggles that engage working-class women and men. Most of the material presented is based on an intensive study of fifty white, working-class, intact families.

Skolnick, Arlene, and Jerome Skolnick, eds. *Family in Transition,* 2nd ed. Boston: Little, Brown, 1977.

This collection of readings considers the diversity of family life-styles, including structural, class, and role differences. The widely varying readings are grouped under four headings: the evolving family, sexuality and sex roles, parents and children, and variations in household and life-style. One of the major strengths of this collection over many others is its inclusion of articles on topics often not considered, such as the sociology of the black family, voluntarily childless marriages, working-class families with middle-class incomes, and singlehood.

8

Women's Economic Roles, Problems, and Opportunities

Mary F. McCarthy

Fortune magazine publishes an annual directory of the largest U.S. firms. In one year of the early 1970s *Fortune* found that the big companies paid an annual salary of more than $30,000 each to about 6,500 employees, of whom only eleven were women.[1]

Why have the highest financial rewards in our economy gone almost exclusively to men? One possible answer rests on assumptions that men and women are expected to spend their adult years in different ways. Earlier chapters indicated the long history of such assumptions, their existence in many cultures, and their reinforcement in our society.

This chapter examines the economic roles, problems, and opportunities of the contemporary American woman. It shows how sex stereotyping, search for identity, and other themes discussed elsewhere in this book are reflected in one aspect of women's participation in our society—the economic aspect.

SOME DEFINITIONS AND QUESTIONS

Alternative Uses of Time

Paid work is one of three alternative ways of spending our time as adults. Another is unpaid home production. Leisure is all the time that is not counted in the first two. As we have seen, for generations women have been expected to be responsible for most of the unpaid home production while men work for pay outside the home.

If one spends eight hours a day in the market economy doing something that results in money income, that same eight hours cannot be spent in activities producing goods and services for which money income is not received (such as preparing meals and tending children). Nor can those eight hours be considered leisure. Since both paid work and unpaid work produce goods and services useful to the worker and to others, how do women nowadays actually allocate their working time? Are the long-standing assumptions about how women and men spend their nonleisure time in accord with current reality?

Labor Force Participation Rate

The "labor force" includes only those who work for money income or who are hunting such work. The "labor force participation rate" of a certain group indicates what percentage of that group either has a paying job or is looking for one. This chapter begins with factual information about women in the U.S. labor force in the mid-1970s. To what extent do women participate in the labor force? Are there changes since an earlier period?

WOMEN IN THE LABOR FORCE

The number of women who work for pay or are looking for paid work just about doubled in the United States between 1950 and 1974, while the number of men in the labor force rose about one quarter, as shown in Table 8.1. Why has there been a bigger increase in the number of women workers as compared with men workers? To answer this, we must first find out why women work.

Why Women Work

Women work primarily for money income, the same as men do! The majority of never-married women have to support themselves. Many women who have been widowed, divorced, or separated have to work to support themselves and often their children. The number of women in these categories has been rising, and their rate of participation in the labor force has increased as well. Table 8.2 shows, however, that the largest increase has been among those who are married and living with their husbands.

Nowadays Americans live differently than they did in earlier times. Nearly all of us have television sets, and color ones at that. Two-car families are common. We travel more frequently—and farther—during our vacations. Our children receive more years of education. Even if our wants had not expanded and we were content to live as past generations did, we would still

TABLE 8.1.   Men and Women in U.S. Labor Force, 1950 and 1974

	1950	1974	Percent Change 1950 to 1974
Women	18,412[a]	35,892[a]	+94.9
Men	45,446[a]	57,349[a]	+26.2
Women as percentage of total labor force	29	38	

SOURCE: U.S. Department of Commerce, Bureau of the Census, *A Statistical Portrait of Women in the U.S.*, Current Population Reports, Special Studies, ser. P-23, no. 58 (Washington, D.C.: Government Printing Office, April 1976), p. 27 (hereafter referred to as *Statistical Portrait*).
[a]In thousands of persons 16 years and over.

TABLE 8.2.   Women in the Labor Force and Labor Force Participation Rates by Marital Status, 1950 and 1975

	1950	1975	Percent Change 1950 to 1975
Number (in thousands):			
Single	5,621	8,464	+50.6
Widowed, divorced, separated	3,624	6,932	+91.3
Married, spouse present	8,550	21,111	+146.9
Labor Force Participation Rates:			
Single	50.5	56.7	+12.3
Widowed, divorced, separated	37.8	40.7	+7.7
Married, spouse present	23.8	44.4	+86.6

SOURCE: *Statistical Portrait*, p. 30.
NOTE: The Bureau of the Census provides no explanation for the difference in the women in the 1950 labor force given here and in table 8.1.

be squeezed by inflation. Higher prices and new products require us to have higher incomes. "The workingman breadwinner who doesn't have a wife on a payroll just may wind up not having enough bread."[2]

Women work, therefore, to support themselves and their children and because their husbands do not earn enough to provide for the family. Former Congresswoman Martha W. Griffiths opened the 1973 hearings on the economic problems of women by stating: "Two-thirds of all women in the labor force are either single, divorced, separated, or have husbands who earn less than $7,000 a year."[3] In 1974 the earnings of working wives contributed 26.5 percent of the total family income of all husband-wife families. The 1974 median family income of husband-wife families where the wife was not in the paid labor force was $12,082, and $16,461 when she was.[4] (The median refers to the midpoint. For example, in 1974 half the husband-wife families where the wife was in the paid labor force had incomes at or under $16,471 and half had incomes at or over $16,461.)

Effect of Increased Years of Schooling

Historically, for both men and women, more education has made them more economically productive, has brought the chance for greater annual earnings, and has led to higher labor force participation rates. Although women still are less likely than men to go past high school, college enrollment has increased at a more rapid rate for women in recent years. In 1960, of all men aged sixteen to thirty-four, 11.6 percent were enrolled in college; in 1974, 16.1 percent were. For women aged sixteen to thirty-four, only 5.5 percent were in college in 1960; by 1974, 12.0 percent were.[5]

This increase in years of schooling helps explain the greater number of women in the labor force. Furthermore, the labor force participation rates of these more-educated women have also risen, as shown in Table 8.3. (Note the opposite change for men!)

Additional Influences

Other factors interact with economic ones to raise labor force participation rates. Women now marry for the first time at a later age than they did in the 1940s. Birthrates have dropped dramatically. Divorce rates have soared.

It may be that more women are now in the labor force because they can depend less on a man for economic support than in the past. On the other hand, it may be that marriages have been postponed and dissolved, and women have chosen to bear fewer children because there now is a socially acceptable alternative to being a full-time wife and mother.

Recent Trends

Although labor force participation rates for nearly all women rose between 1950 and the mid-1970s, there are sharp differences in the increases among the various categories of women, as shown in Table A.1 (see Appendix). In 1950 no age-group had even half its women members in the labor force; by 1974 all age-groups between twenty and fifty-four had over half their women members in the work force. Although nonwhite women continue to have a

TABLE 8.3.   Labor Force Participation Rates by Educational Status for Persons 18 Years Old and Over

Education	Women		Men	
	1959	1975	1959	1975
Not high school graduate	31.6	31.6	81.2	65.2
High school graduate, no college	42.8	52.5	92.7	87.6
Four or more years of college	53.3	64.1	92.8	90.4

SOURCE: *Statistical Portrait*, p. 29.

higher participation rate than white women, the gap has narrowed. Married women living with their husbands show a larger rise in labor force participation rates than do other ever-married women. However, women who are widowed, divorced, or separated have higher rates for both years, with one exception: ever-married women without children under eighteen in 1974, who were more likely to be older, less educated, and frequently eligible for Social Security benefits. The most striking change is in the participation rate of mothers, especially those with children under six. The old assumption that the economic role of women with children was to spend all their working time in unpaid home production no longer holds true. As Chapter 7 has shown, the question of how to care for the children of mothers who work outside the home has no easy or simple answer.

Paid Work Experience

Table A.2 of the Appendix summarizes the paid work experience of women and men during two census years, 1950 and 1970.

For both men and women, the total number of those who work during any given year is larger than the average of those in the labor force. Some persons, especially students, hold jobs for only a few weeks or months; graduates often enter the labor force in midyear; still others retire permanently. However, when women leave a job either voluntarily or involuntarily they are far more apt to be counted out of the labor force than men are. If a man under 65 is not working or in school full time, our society expects him to be actively seeking work. He generally considers himself unemployed. Therefore he is included in the labor force, even though he may be engaged in unpaid home production, such as remodeling the interior of his house. Housewives, on the other hand, are not included in the labor force and are not under societal pressure to be job-hunting.

There is a particularly marked rise in part-time paid employment. (Paid employment is judged as part-time when a person works less than thirty-five hours a week.) Whereas male part-time workers outnumbered their female counterparts among teenagers in both periods, by 1970 the adult part-time worker was far more apt to be a woman, which was not the case twenty years earlier. Of the seven million women who entered the labor force from 1967 to 1976, half began with part-time jobs.[6] Later we shall examine more closely the possible implications of such work.

In 1970 about half of women workers held full-time jobs and worked at them the year round, in contrast with two thirds of the men. Yet the ratio of women to men full-time, year-round workers has climbed dramatically. In 1950, for every one hundred male full-time, year-round workers, there were twenty-nine female ones. By 1970 the ratio had risen to forty-three female workers for every one hundred males, and by 1974, to forty-seven.[7] Since both employees and employers think of those who work full time the year round as permanent members of the labor force, a continuation of this trend may bring changes in career planning by women and enhance their employment opportunities, on-the-job training, and chances for occupational advancement.

Unemployment Rates

The unemployment rate of women is higher than that of men, although many women have a socially acceptable alternative to labor force participation—that is, engaging in unpaid home production. Figure 8.1 shows that this holds both for prosperous times and for recessions (except for the 1958 recession). The gap is larger in good times, perhaps because women think there might be jobs for them and actively seek work. Furthermore, the difference in unemployment rates has become wider since the early 1960s.

Earnings from Paid Labor

Whether women work full time or part-time, whether women have much or little education, whether women are young or old, their annual earnings are less than those of men with the same characteristics.[8] Since people earn more if they work full time the year round than if they work part-time or part-year, Table 8.4 compares overall median earnings for women and men who worked full time the year round. In 1974 women college graduates employed full time the year round had median earnings of $10,357, compared with $17,188 earned by their male counterparts. Women with one to three years of college found their median earnings below those of men who had no more than eight years of elementary schooling.[9]

Leviticus, chapter 27, verses 3–4, tells us that women in Old Testament times were to be valued at 60 percent of men: "And thy estimation shall be of the male from twenty years old even unto sixty years old, even thy estimation shall be fifty shekels of silver. And if it be a female, then thy estimation shall be thirty shekels." In spite of the women's movement, in spite of passage of equal pay and equal employment opportunity legislation, in spite of lawsuits and judicial decisions, the ratio of the median earnings of women to those of men has declined and fallen below the biblical precept. By 1975 the dollar gap between the median annual earnings of fully employed men and women was $5,260, or more than $100 a week!

Why, then, has the economic position of women in the work force worsened relative to that of men? The reason lies in the persistent division of jobs into "man's work" and "woman's work."[10] The earnings differential results in large part because female and male workers are segregated into different occupations and industries.

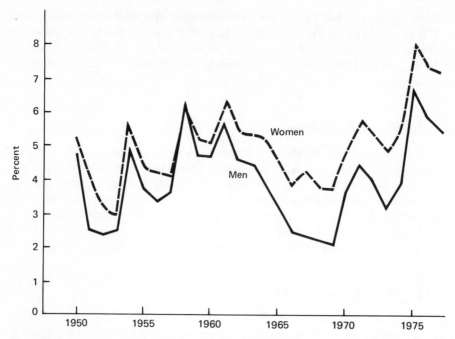

Figure 8.1. Unemployment Rates for Men and Women 20 Years Old and Over, 1950–1977

SOURCE: *Economic Report of the President* (Washington, D.C.: Government Printing Office, January 1978), p. 291.

OCCUPATIONAL AND INDUSTRIAL SEGREGATION

"Occupation" describes the activity that one is employed to do, such as clerical work, or the actual job title, such as machine operator. "Industry" broadly describes the good or service produced, such as mined coal or health care. For instance, the occupations of secretary or electrician could apply to people who work in an industry producing coal or in one producing relief from disease.

Occupational Segregation

Whether women are employed as white-collar workers, blue-collar workers, or service workers, they continue to be clustered in relatively few occupations.

White-collar workers are professionals and technicians, sales workers, and clerical workers. At the time of the 1970 census 14.8 percent of employed women and 13.5 percent of employed men were professional, technical, and

TABLE 8.4. Median Earnings of Year-Round, Full-Time Civilian Workers 14 Years Old and Over by Sex for Selected Years

Year	Median Earnings		Earnings Ratio Women to Men
	Women	Men	
1957	$3,000	$ 4,750	0.63
1960	3,257	5,368	0.61
1965	3,828	6,388	0.60
1970	5,325	8,966	0.59
1971	5,593	9,399	0.60
1972	5,903	10,202	0.58
1973	6,335	11,186	0.57
1974	6,772	11,835	0.57
1975	7,500	12,760	0.59

SOURCE: *Statistical Portrait*, p. 48; and *New York Times*, February 19, 1977, p. 23, and April 3, 1977, p. 35.

kindred workers, such as engineers, lawyers, scientists, teachers, clergy, physicians, dentists, registered nurses, and social workers. These occupations require more education than most others, and generally the earnings are higher. Yet 70 percent of women in this broad occupational grouping were registered nurses and teachers—that is, in the lower-paying fields—whereas less than 20 percent of the men were. Thirty percent of the men were engineers, lawyers, judges, doctors, and dentists, whereas less than 2 percent of women professionals were in this relatively well-paid group.[11]

The 1970 census indicates sex segregation in other types of white-collar occupations. Over one third of all women in the labor force were clustered in merely nine white-collar occupations: bookkeepers, secretaries, stenographers, typists, telephone operators, retail sales workers, registered nurses, and elementary and secondary teachers. These nine occupations employed only about one in every twenty male workers.[12]

In blue-collar work the same pattern prevailed. Less than 2 percent of women in the work force were employed as skilled crafts workers, while about twenty percent of the men were. Out of every six women in the labor force, one was a blue-collar worker and tended to be an unskilled, lower-paid assembler or sewer and stitcher.[13]

Many blue-collar workers must wear safety equipment on the job, otherwise an employer cannot be found liable for an injury under such legislation as the Occupational Safety and Health Act. Yet asbestos suits and safety shoes are seldom manufactured in women's sizes. A woman working at a job requiring quickness in using the hands finds that the only safety gloves available to her are too big.[14]

Among service workers, women were 96 percent of private household workers and 55 percent of other service providers. In the latter group, women tended to hold such jobs as dental assistants, nurse's aids, practical nurses, child-care workers, and beauticians, whereas men were fire fighters, police officers, and security guards.[15]

In the mid-1970s women workers were found in lower-paid jobs within broad occupational classifications.[16] If women and men were equally spread over all jobs within an occupation, one would expect the median earnings of women to be more nearly equal to those of men. Yet even in occupations that are highly paid for women, their median earnings fell below the overall median earnings of men. The median earnings of male sales workers are well above those of all men, but women sales workers were among the lowest paid women (see Table A.3 in the Appendix). Retailing, where many women work, pays less than the male-dominated wholesale trade.

Industrial Segregation

If we look at where people work instead of at what they do, we find industry after industry employing predominantly men or women. If women had been employed in each industry according to their 1970 percentage of the total labor force, we would expect that industries would have had about 61 women workers for every 100 men they hired, or a women/men ratio of 0.61. Yet the construction industry employed only 6 women for every 100 male workers, while department stores hired 217 women for every 100 men. Manufacturers of transportation equipment, such as automobiles and airplanes, had only 15 women for every 100 male employees, while clothing manufacturers had 346 women for every 100 men. (Table A.4 in the Appendix shows a more complete picture of industrial segregation.)

Women tend to be disproportionately segregated into those industries where annual incomes are relatively low, as indicated in Table 8.5. Men employed in industries using a relatively large percentage of women, such as retail trade and personal services, had median incomes considerably lower than those of most other male workers. In all industries women workers earned far less than men.

The earnings gap has widened in recent years. The *increase* in the average weekly earnings of coal miners from October 1973 to October 1976 was $105, or almost as much as the *total* weekly earnings of $117 received by laundry workers in October 1976.[17] The average weekly wage received by workers in the predominantly male transportation equipment industry was $281 in February 1977, while workers in the predominantly female apparel industry averaged $124.[18]

High-wage industries where male employees predominate are often characterized by strong unions. Workers in these industries receive additional fringe benefits, such as employer-financed pensions and health insurance. Workers in the low-wage industries where women tend to work generally have to meet current health-care expenses out of their meager incomes. For most, when they retire there will be no private pension plan.[19]

TABLE 8.5. Median Earnings of Year-Round, Full-Time Workers 14 Years Old and Over by Industry, 1974

Industry of Longest Job	Median Earnings		Earnings Ratio Women to Men
	Women	Men	
Total with earnings	$6,772	$11,835	0.57
Agriculture, forestry, and fisheries	2,503	5,619	0.45
Mining	(B)	13,014	(X)
Construction	7,189	11,552	0.62
Manufacturing, total	6,550.	12,202	0.54
Durable goods	6,988	12,335	0.57
Nondurable goods	5,981	11,945	0.50
Transportation, communication, and other public utilities	8,431	12,773	0.66
Wholesale trade	7,043	12,286	0.57
Retail trade	5,361	9,919	0.54
Finance, insurance, and real estate	6,474	12,975	0.50
Business and repair services	6,954	10,479	0.66
Personal services	3,984	8,068	0.49
Entertainment and recreation services	5,523	8,865	0.62
Professional and related services	7,727	12,801	0.60
Public administration	8,194	13,030	0.63

(B) = median earnings not shown because base is less than 75,000 persons
(X) = not applicable
SOURCE: *Statistical Portrait*, p. 50.

Minority Women

Nonwhite women face racial as well as sex-related employment handicaps. In 1974 a slightly greater percentage of nonwhite women, as compared with white women, worked full time the year round, but they were more concentrated in unskilled blue-collar and service occupations. In addition, unemployment in 1974 was greater for nonwhite women (10.7 percent) than for white women (6.1 percent).

In the decade 1965–1974 the occupational distribution of nonwhite employed women shifted dramatically. Less than 25 percent were white-collar workers in 1965; by 1974 over 40 percent were. In 1965, 55 percent of these women were service workers, and more than 30 percent were private household workers. By 1974, 37 percent were service workers, and slightly over 11 percent were private household workers. As nonwhite women moved out of the lowest-paying jobs as fast as they could, their median earnings when working full time the year round climbed from 75 percent of those of white women working full time the year round in 1967 to 85 percent in 1973 and to 92 percent in 1974.[20]

Table 8.6 compares the 1973 incomes of white males, nonwhite males, white females, and nonwhite females when each group cited worked full time the year round.

Women, whether white or nonwhite, work for the same reason as men—to get money income; but women workers are found in lower-paying occupations and industries to a greater extent than men are. What, then, are the causes of the occupational and industrial segregation?

POSSIBLE REASONS FOR OCCUPATIONAL AND INDUSTRIAL SEGREGATION

Economists cannot agree on any single economic basis for occupational and industrial segregation that leads to lower earnings for women than for men.[21] Much of the economic theory was first developed in an effort to discover why nonwhite males earned less than white males. When it was noticed that the earnings gap between men and women was greater than that between white and nonwhite men, the original theories were broadened to apply to women as well as nonwhite males. Some additional theories were later specifically concerned with differentials in male and female earnings. Yet each theory has been criticized either for being descriptive rather than explanatory or for making unrealistic assumptions.

Taste-for-Discrimination Theory

This explanation can be subdivided according to who is said to have the "taste for discrimination." However, each of these explanations is refuted.

Statement: Employers who are prejudiced against women prefer to hire men, even though they must pay a larger wage to the men. *Refutation:* A competitor who does not discriminate would hire women to do the same work at a lower wage, make a higher profit, and drive the prejudiced employer out of business.

TABLE 8.6.   Median Income of Full-Time, Year-Round Workers by Race and Sex, 1973

	Amount	*As Percentage of Income of White Males*
White males	$11,800	100.0
Nonwhite males	7,953	67.4
White females	6,598	55.9
Nonwhite females	5,595	47.4

SOURCE: U.S. Department of Commerce, Bureau of the Census, *Current Population Reports*, ser. P-60, no. 97 (Washington, D.C.: Government Printing Office, January 1975), p. 49.

Statement: Male employees refuse to work with women. Therefore, even nonprejudiced employers will not risk losing their male labor force by hiring women. *Refutation:* Such behavior may explain occupational segregation but not pay differentials.

Statement: Consumers do not want to deal with nor buy the products of women workers. They do not trust the competence of a female airline pilot or dentist or bus driver. *Refutation:* A relatively large percentage of women are working in the service-providing sector—as, for example, nurses or retail sales clerks—where there is much consumer-worker contact. Product consumers are interested in the price and quality of the product (for example, a sack of potatoes or a can of paint) and seldom consider the sex of the producer relevant.[22]

Statement: Women themselves have a taste for entering low-paying occupations and industries; they prefer "female jobs," whereas men do not want to be nurses or secretaries; and the majority of women have the same preference for "female jobs." *Refutation:* This reasoning merely blames the victim! Earlier chapters indicated that the tracking of girls into preparation for a limited number of adult roles tends to ignore their preferences and talents.

Human-Capital Theory

Statement: Human capital represents an investment in people with the goal of increasing their productivity. Formal education and on-the-job training are types of such investment. This approach to sex segregation assumes that since women have accumulated less human capital, they are not interchangeable with male workers. Women spend fewer years in the labor force and therefore are not so productive for the employer. The conclusion is that women workers are paid less, simply because their productivity is lower.

Some aspects of the human-capital theory are valid. On the whole, women have spent less time in the labor force than men, for women have traditionally been expected to devote much of their working years to unpaid household production. Since young women anticipate spending fewer years in the labor force than men, they frequently enter occupations that they can leave and reenter without penalty (for example, retail sales). Furthermore, since they may not be working enough years for an adequate rate of return on a large expenditure for training, women act rationally when they fail to undertake a long, expensive education (for example, medical school). Employers, expecting women to have a higher quit rate than men, will not provide costly on-the-job training to those they predict will soon leave the firm.

Refutation: Although women on the average can expect to spend twenty-three years in the labor force, compared with men's forty-three years, the average never-married woman remains in the labor force for forty-five years.[23] Employers erroneously assume that all women will permanently leave the labor force after a few years, and thus deny them opportunities for on-the-job training leading to higher-paying work.

Furthermore, this descriptive approach fails to explain sex segregation within skill categories (for example, waitressing and janitorial work); nor does it explain sex segregation within occupations that require about the same long training periods (for example, registered nurses and pharmacists); nor does it explain sex segregation in firm-specific training (as, for example, in the case of executive secretaries and administrative assistants).

The human-capital approach assumes that women have freely chosen to become waitresses, nurses, and executive secretaries; that parental support or institutional scholarships and loans to meet the cost of education have been equally available to female and male students; and that women have a higher quit rate. This theory overlooks the societal factors that steer women toward "female jobs," as well as the unequal funding for the education of females.[24]

Women on the average do have slightly higher rates of turnover and absenteeism than men. According to the Public Health Service, women were absent from work an average of 5.1 days during 1974, whereas the absentee rate for men was 4.8 days. This difference is not statistically significant, for we cannot be certain that it is not due to a sampling error.[25] In any case, women are more apt to be absent from work to care for a sick child than their higher-paid husbands are. It costs the family less if she gives up a day's pay. Men are more apt to be absent from work on the first day of the hunting season than their wives are.

Is the rate of absence from work related to the type of work rather than home responsibilities? There is some evidence that this is so. Women tend to be in jobs that are dead-end, repetitive, boring, and low paid. Men holding jobs with similar characteristics have comparable quit and absenteeism rates.[26] When either men or women in such work take days off or quit, they do not lose out on promotions and pay increases. Even when monotonous work without much opportunity for advancement is highly paid, such as automotive assembly, absenteeism and quit rates are notoriously high.[27] The most lucrative and steady part-time job for college students in the Detroit area is work in the auto plants as roving substitutes for regular, full-time employees who are absent on Mondays and Fridays.

A 1976 study of time-use based on individually kept diaries, interviews, and observations by outsiders shows that working women, in contrast with male workers, take fewer scheduled and unscheduled rest breaks, such as coffee breaks, overstaying lunch hours, and "shooting the breeze" with co-workers. In addition to spending more time on the job, women also expend more effort than men do.[28] These findings contradict the theory that women workers are less productive.

Crowding Theory

Statement: When there are too many workers of a certain type at the prevailing wage, relative to the employer's wish to hire those workers, the wage level drops. High wages are maintained by "crowding" out certain potential workers. This is accomplished through actions on the part of employers and male employees (such as discrimination against women); through non-job-related hiring standards (such as standards requiring that apprentices in the construction trades be 18 to 25 years old); through legislative action (such as laws "protecting" the weaker sex from the perils of certain types of work, such as bartending); or through educational barriers (as in the case of certain vocational courses, such as drafting or automotive mechanics, that are not open to girls). The remaining workers receive relatively high earnings, and those who are excluded seek work elsewhere. As the latter join the workers who, through free choice, are in the more open occupations, wage levels there are forced down. Consequently, since women are crowded out of many occupations, the wages received by both sexes in fields open to women are low. *Refutation:* This theory, however, does not explain why profit-seeking employers in high-wage situations would not resist the crowding mechanisms in order to lower their labor costs.

Demand-and-Supply Theory

Statement: In the years since World War II, as the economy grew, more workers were needed. As demand for labor increased and women found paid work, other women were encouraged to seek it. So many women entered the labor force that the increase in the supply of women workers was greater than the increase in the demand for them. Therefore, although the earnings of women rose, they did not rise as fast as those of men. The earnings gap between men and women widened. *Refutation:* Again the theory is merely descriptive. One questions the distinction between the demand for *women* workers and the demand for *all* workers. Without this distinction, the earning of *all* workers should have changed at the same rate.

Monopsony Theory

Statement: Individual female job seekers are often in a take-it-or-leave-it situation. The "it" is a job offered by the one available employer of her labor, the monopsonist. If she leaves that job, her only alternative is likely to be unpaid home production. Other potential employers are in areas too far away to allow her enough time to fulfill her household responsibilities after the time spent at paid work and in commuting. Or these other employers might be in another area entirely, where there are no jobs for her husband. Therefore, the monopsonist offers to pay a wage less than her worth to him but high enough for her to give up time otherwise spent in unpaid home production or leisure.

Refutation: The major criticism of this theory is that it also applies to men, who are likely to have more choice while seeking work or in the initial period of employment. However, once they have put in several years at a firm, they too are often at the mercy of the employer. The male worker accumulates pension and seniority rights, which he would lose if he sought work elsewhere. He may have received special training, which raises his worth only to the employer providing the training.

Institutional Approach

Statement: Occupational and industrial segregation arises from our economic institutions—that is, our established customs and practices. Employers treat individual job seekers as part of a group or category, and employers' decisions rest on their stereotyped perceptions of group characteristics. Two separate levels of jobs exist in our economy. One type is the entry level, open to those without special skills or training. The other level includes those jobs that are obtained either through advancement within a firm after experience is gained or through specific formal training and education. Entry-level jobs are characterized by a dual labor market. The primary market contains relatively few lower-level job categories. These pay well, the working conditions are good, and there is job security along with opportunities for moving to a better job. In the secondary market are many entry-level occupations, which are low paying and have poor working conditions, little job security, and little, or no, chance for advancement. Workers drift into and out of jobs in the secondary market.

Assume that a firm has two entry-level jobs to fill: The higher-wage job is at the bottom of a long promotion ladder, and the low-wage job is dead-end after one or two advances. Two similarly qualified applicants appear, one female and one male. Each is vague about available jobs and how well suited she/he is for them. The personnel officer assumes that the female applicant will quit in a few years anyway—to get married, to have children, or when her husband is transferred—and that the male applicant will be enticed to remain with the firm by the high pay and advancement opportunities. Each of the applicants is hired to fill a sex-stereotyped job, and ultimately the personnel officer's assumptions are found valid. *Refutation:* This approach, however, does not explain the occupational segregation and earnings differential which exist between the sexes both within relatively well paid labor markets and low-paid, dead-end ones.

Beyond Economic Theory

Two eminent women economists wrote in 1973 that "a proper analysis of discrimination [against women] . . . will have to fuse elements of economics, sociology, psychology, and history."[29] Kenneth Arrow, who was awarded the Nobel Memorial Prize in Economics, agrees:

The basic root is outside the economic realm. . . . Economic arguments of all schools deal with anonymous individuals. The characteristics of sex . . . are not incorporated. It may not be totally surprising that economic theories have nothing to say about the causes of sexual . . . differences.

It is true that economic theories can say something about the effects, given that you have sexual discrimination. . . . They are not in a position to explain why the phenomenon occurred in the first place.[30]

Paul Samuelson, another recipient of the Nobel Memorial Prize in Economics, pointed out that discrimination against women results in lower national productivity and living standards. He called for continued pressure through government action to eliminate discrimination and its immense economic and social costs.[31]

GOVERNMENTAL ACTION

Just as economists paid attention to economic discrimination against women only after considerable empirical and theoretical work on discrimination against nonwhite males, government action on discrimination was originally directed toward overcoming race discrimination.[32]

Equal Pay

Equal pay for equal work is required by the Equal Pay Act of 1963. The U.S. Supreme Court upheld this law in 1974 when determining that women inspectors on a day shift should receive the same base pay as male inspectors on a night shift.[33] It took court decisions to provide equal pay for the same tasks performed under different titles, for example, (female) nurse's aides and (male) orderlies.[34] However, the criteria for determining equal work are not clear if people perform slightly different tasks. Especially in blue-collar jobs, physical effort is typically given twice the weight of mental effort or job responsibility.[35]

Equal Employment Opportunity

The Civil Rights Act of 1964 created the Equal Employment Opportunity Commission (EEOC) to investigate and conciliate complaints of discrimination brought by individuals. Not until 1972 did the EEOC have the power to sue employers and to obtain relief for past discrimination. Even with greater power, the EEOC has been hampered by constant turnover in leadership. In mid-1977 the seventh chairperson in its twelve-year history took office. The case backlog has steadily climbed—25,000 in 1970, 98,000 in 1974, 130,000 in 1977—with complaints being received faster than they can be processed.

An average complainant must wait three years for a decision.[36] By that time, many complainants have left their employers and cannot be located to receive any settlement awarded. Justice delayed is justice denied.

The Office of Federal Contract Compliance in the Department of Labor has had the main responsibility for implementing a 1965 executive order requiring those holding federal contracts to provide equal employment opportunity throughout their entire business operations. Investigators for the General Accounting Office found that after ten years the Labor Department did not even have a list of all covered contractors. Other government agencies have been equally lax. Even when contractors are listed, they seldom have been required to comply with antidiscrimination regulations.[37]

By late 1977, however, Labor Department officials announced their intention to adopt corrective action. The secretary of labor pledged not only to enforce existing law but to require federal contractors to adopt goals and timetables for hiring women. The Labor Department began to provide positive help in qualifying women for work from which they had been barred. For example, the federal government granted $260,000 to the Graphic Arts Union to train one hundred women for work traditionally done only by men in the printing industry.[38]

The extent to which federal legislation to overcome discrimination in employment and in compensation is successful depends not only on executive branch implementation of the laws but also on judicial interpretation of them. The law allows employment on the basis of sex only if sex is a "bona fide occupational qualification" (BFOQ) for that work. Courts have narrowly defined BFOQ, refusing to link it to the assumption that because the average woman perhaps has less physical strength and endurance than the average man, all women are weaker than all men. Additionally, the Supreme Court decided in 1971 that an employer who hired fathers of preschoolers could not refuse to hire the mother of a preschooler without proving that her parental responsibilities interfered with her job performance. On the other hand, in 1976 the Court held that an employer's plan that provided benefits for all temporary physical disabilities except those related to pregnancy was not sex discriminatory, even though the plan paid for time lost for disabilities that could be incurred only by males.[39]

Several months later the same Court ruled that women and others who were subjected to employment discrimination before the 1964 Civil Rights Act and later transferred to better jobs with the same employer could not carry their old unit seniority with them but had to start at the bottom of the new unit seniority list. Although the discrimination from which they had suffered is currently illegal, they continue to be handicapped by its continuing effects. It is not yet clear whether this ruling will stiffen employer resistance to proposed remedies and redress for past discrimination. However, the lawyer who for many years was in charge of EEOC litigation against employers and who switched in 1977 to a law firm defending employers stated: "I never lost a case arguing for the EEOC. And now I don't expect to lose one for the employers, thanks to this decision."[40]

Veterans' Preferences

Veterans receive preferential hiring for many jobs, especially at all levels of government. Since women have had to possess higher qualifications to serve in the armed forces, relatively few women are veterans. If a male veteran gets ten extra points toward a civil service job, he is hired over a female nonveteran whose exam score was nine points higher. This policy was challenged on the ground that there are alternative ways of aiding veterans. However, the U.S. Supreme Court held that preferential hiring of veterans was not unconstitutional discrimination against women.[41] Even in employment that does not involve veterans' preference, federal, state, and local governments have been charged with sex discrimination. Top-level jobs are filled by men, while women are consigned to low-paid, dead-end work. Government itself has not set a good example for the private sector.

Federal Income Taxes

By 1975 about half the husband-wife families had at least two workers; yet federal taxes weigh more heavily on two-earner families.[42] Married couples generally file joint income tax returns whether only one or both are in the labor force. As total taxable income rises, the percentage of the additional income paid in taxes also rises. In 1976 if Mr. A with a nonemployed wife had a taxable income of $18,000 and Mr. and Mrs. B both worked for a total taxable income of $18,000, each couple would have paid an income tax of $3,813. If Mr. A had been single, his tax on $18,000 would have been $4,502. If the Bs were not married, if his taxable income was $10,000 and hers, $8,000, their combined tax would have been $3,668. Mr. A saved $689 in taxes by being married, whereas the B's were penalized $145. However, most two-earner families do not know exactly how much of their additional income from the second job is taken away by greater income taxes. Instead they pay attention to the extra take-home pay resulting from the second job. Only in recent years has Congress granted some partial tax relief to working parents for the cost of child care.

Social Security Taxes and Benefits

The Social Security tax also tends to discriminate against two-earner families. In 1977 the first $16,500 earned by each person was subject to a 5.85 percent tax. If Mr. C earned $25,000, he would pay $965.25 in Social Security tax. That part of his income over $16,500 was not taxable. Mr. D earned $15,000 and his wife earned $10,000. Every dollar of their joint $25,000 earnings was taxed—for a total of $1,462.50.

The benefits received from Social Security are roughly related to the amount paid in. Since women earn less than men, their benefits from their contributions are lower. A wife has the option of drawing benefits as a dependent of her husband or on the basis of her own earnings—not both. Six million women workers had retired by 1971. Of these, about one million were receiving payments as dependents rather than the smaller sum they would have drawn from their own years in the labor force.[43]

Furthermore, the "displaced homemaker"—widowed, separated, or divorced after years of providing unpaid household services and depending on the income of another family member—cannot draw any Social Security until she is sixty if widowed without minor children. If divorced, she must have been married at least ten years and is eligible only when her ex-husband retires.[44]

For many years the Social Security taxes paid by women workers did not buy as much protection for their survivors as did those paid by men. Not until 1967 did the law grant the same benefit status to the child of a deceased working mother as that of a child of a deceased father. Ten years later the Supreme Court held that widowers were entitled to collect benefits on exactly the same basis as widows were.[45] In other ways women's dollars have not been worth as much as those of men.

CREDIT AND INSURANCE

Borrowing for such purposes as buying or improving a home, or for education, or a small business has been more difficult for women. In the case of married couples, the potential lender would partially or entirely disregard the wife's income when determining their ability to pay off the loan. Widows and divorced women find they have no credit rating since all charge accounts have been in the husband's name. The Equal Credit Opportunity Act, designed to correct this situation, took effect in October 1975, but more than a year later women were still finding overt and subtle discrimination against them by creditors.[46]

Women either are denied insurance coverage or must pay higher rates than men for many types of insurance such as health care and disability income.[47] One major insurance company makes the following distinction:

Total disability for males means the inability to perform the duties of his occupation for 60 months, after which it means the inability to perform the duties of any occupation. Females are charged a higher premium and are covered for 24 months after which they are expected to perform the duties of any occupation.[48]

A male surgeon who loses a hand can draw disability benefits for five years, whereas his female counterpart would be expected after two years to obtain paid work that could be done with one hand. A woman pays more for less coverage in the event of disability. No federal legislation has attempted to correct this inequity.

WOMEN AND LABOR UNIONS

Union Membership

Federal laws such as the Equal Pay Act and the Civil Rights Act of 1964 have had an impact on labor unions and their predominantly male membership. If a union has been in any way responsible for discriminatory practices, it can be required to share in the payment of back pay.[49] Equal employment opportunity, by opening jobs to women in unionized plants, has helped to increase the percentage of women among total union membership from 18.1 percent in 1952 to 21.7 percent in 1972. Union members, whether male or female, have higher earnings than their nonunion counterparts. Although the earnings of women union members are considerably lower than those of men union workers, the gap is smaller than that between women and men who do not belong to unions.[50]

One major steel company hired no women to work in a large unionized mill after 1946. During World War II over half the work force had been female, but by 1960 only twelve women remained to work alongside ten thousand men. In 1972 an eighteen-year-old woman applied for a mill job, was refused, and went to the EEOC. She got the job. By September 1976 over two thousand other women had been hired to work in that mill, and one out of every eight blue-collar workers there was female. The union has handled the grievances of female and male members on the same basis. However, only two women were union stewards, the first rung on the ladder of union leadership.[51]

Some women eligible for union membership feel that they would gain nothing by joining, since the unions ignore their needs.[52] Airline flight attendants who believed the male-dominated Transport Workers Union was insensitive to women's issues broke away and formed their own Independent Union of Flight Attendants. In 1977 the new union won the right to bargain collectively with Pan American World Airways on behalf of about four thousand members formerly represented by the Transport Workers.[53]

Union Leadership

Women are conspicuously absent from leadership throughout the union movement. All thirty-three members of the executive council of the AFL-CIO are men. About one of every seven members of the United Automobile Workers is a woman, but only one woman serves on the chief governing board. Unions where women members outnumber men, such as the Communications Workers and the American Federation of Teachers, typically have male high officers. A few unions, including those for auto and electrical workers, have women's departments that vigorously pursue the concerns of women workers.[54] The Coalition of Labor Union Women (CLUW), founded in 1973, had over a thousand delegates from sixty unions and forty-three states at its 1975 convention.[55] Its goals include a stronger voice for women within their unions and the organization of presently unorganized women workers.

Why are working women less likely than men to be union members? And, once they are in a union, why are women less likely to be leaders? As their labor force participation rate rose, women went into white-collar and service occupations, which traditionally have not been organized. Furthermore, part-time workers seldom belong to unions. Women who have household responsibilities cannot devote as much time to forming a labor union and participating in its affairs. They may lack self-confidence, be unfamiliar with union procedures, and require specific encouragement to become more active.

Yet women, especially those employed by government and nonprofit institutions, have since the 1960s formed and joined unions. Registered nurses and other hospital workers, schoolteachers, and clerical workers have been demonstrating a militancy unthinkable a few years ago.

What Women Want from Unions

Women workers are interested in pay but place more emphasis on working conditions than do their male coworkers. The consciousness-raising aspects of the women's movement do not touch these women much and may even seem threatening. They care about equal pay for equal work, about adequate pensions, about doing away with mandatory overtime, and about paid maternity leaves. Those who work nights want well lighted and guarded parking lots and nearby, safe public transportation. Women want clear job descriptions, freedom from sexual harassment on the job, and grievance procedures that protect their right to file complaints without getting fired. They expect to work hard but want to have working conditions that leave them enough energy to fulfill their household responsibilities.[56]

The matter of balancing time and effort between paid work and household responsibilities is important to women. By early 1977 over two thirds of the women in the labor force were members of husband-wife families or were single parents. Most of these women held full-time paying jobs.[57]

WOMEN AS UNPAID HOME PRODUCERS

To keep a household functioning requires much time and effort. Someone has to cook, wash, buy food and other products, do the laundry, clean the house, see that bills are paid, make minor repairs, and do a host of other things. If there are children, they have to be bathed and fed, watched over, helped with their learning, taken to doctors and dentists, and so on. Many services to others are produced in the home. When these services are unpaid, they are not counted in the gross national product (GNP), which attempts to measure the monetary value of the goods and services produced in the economy during a given time period, usually one year. "What is not counted is often not noticed."[58]

Value of Household Production

One of the criteria for the value our society places on individuals is how much they earn, which supposedly reflects how productive they are. Various attempts have been made to estimate the dollar value of a housewife's unpaid services, but none are considered satisfactory.[59] As we shall see, proposals to pay actual salaries to housewives also encounter major problems.

Another criterion is the rating assigned to an occupation by the federal government's 1965 *Dictionary of Occupational Titles.* The rating is based on the complexity of the job in terms of data, people, and things. Each of the three categories is given a number from 0 to 8; for example, if a specific occupation requires synthesizing data, acting as mentor to people, and setting up things on which others can work, its rating would be "000." The lowest possible rating would have to be two 8s and one 7, since all jobs have at least a minimum relationship to data, or to people, or to things. Homemaking is rated at "878," indicating no relationship to data or things but a servant relationship to people. (The same rating is given to child-care attendants, nursery school teachers, practical nurses, home-health aides, nurse-midwives, office boys, rest-room attendants, and baggage checkers, whereas newspaper carriers are rated at "868," showgirls at "848," and animal caretakers at "874.")[60] A new edition of the dictionary, published in the late 1970s, has revised some ratings.

Salaries for Homemakers

Since work within the household produces goods and services useful to a family, some have proposed that there be money payment for such work. Should all homemakers receive the same salary? Responsibilities differ with the number and ages of children in the family. Is there an aged or handicapped family member needing special care? Does the family live in a suburb, and does the husband spend much time commuting to his paid work? If so, the housewife in this family is more likely to mow the lawn, chauffeur the children, and repaint the living room than one who lives in a city apartment near good public transportation. Should a woman who knows just where to kick a balky refrigerator to make it run again be paid more than one who does not?

Even if there were agreement on salary scales, what about compensation for injuries incurred on the job? How about sick pay, paid vacations, and so on? Should government pay homemakers? Would a homemaker have to pass a civil service exam? Or should she be employed by her husband? Where is he going to get the money? What conflicts might arise within the marriage relationship? When one marriage partner hires the other, is love's labor lost?

If a housewife refrains from entering the labor force, evidently she values her time spent at home more highly than that same time spent at paid work.[61] See Table 8.3 for the effect of education on the decision to spend time in the labor force. The time of more-educated women has a greater market price. Therefore, as the level of their education rises, women spend more of their adult years at paid market work than in unpaid household production.

"Women's Work Is Never Done"

Whether or not women hold paid jobs, they still do housework. In spite of labor-saving devices and appliances, women not in the labor force in the 1960s averaged fifty-five hours per week at housework, three hours more than comparable women in the 1920s. Furthermore, fifty-five hours is longer than the average workweek of those in the labor force. Women with paid jobs spent less time on housework but still averaged twenty-six hours a week in fulfilling their household responsibilities.[62]

Not only do homemakers work longer hours at housework than do employed women, but they spend more hours on it over weekends!

> Since the value of household work is not clear, nonemployed women feel pressure to spend long hours at it. Time spent in work, rather than the results of the work, serves to express to the homemaker and others that an equal contribution is being made. Women who work in the labor force contribute income to the family and so do not feel the same pressure.[63]

Once a certain standard of living has been reached, the administration and management of a household's possession and consumption of goods become arduous, complex, and time-devouring tasks. The husband, who is ordinarily the earner of the larger income, usually determines where the household lives and its expenditure patterns. If his policy is to wear a clean shirt every day, his wife gets to determine which kind of detergent and which washer-cycle setting will help keep him supplied with those clean shirts.[64]

In the 1960s women with outside jobs had no more paid help, nor did they receive more help with household chores from their husbands, than women not in the labor force. "Contrary to popular belief, American husbands do not share the responsibilities of household work. They spend only a few hours a week at it, and most of what they do is shopping."[65]

In the decade between 1960 and 1970, as the employment of women climbed by 38 percent, the number of paid private household workers moved in the opposite direction, declining by over 36 percent.[66] This is strong evidence that women, if given a choice, prefer other types of work. Yet housework still must be done. No wonder that women who undertake paid work along with caring for their families' needs have been described as "the original moonlighters."[67]

Effects of Years of Schooling

Differences in how women allocate total time spent in household work are related to the levels of their schooling. Various studies have shown that the more education a mother has, the more time she spends in child care relative to other household tasks—whether or not she is in the labor force.[68]

The educational level of women also affects their husband's earnings. When husbands' education and work experience are taken into account and only the effects of variations in wives' education are considered, the husbands' annual earnings increase by between 3.5 and 4.1 percent for every additional year of the wives' schooling. This holds whether her schooling came before or after marriage.[69] The average husband whose wife is now going to college should find *his* future earnings increasing! Her abilities to function as a helpmate evidently become greater.

Yet our society tends to ignore the positive impact of women's unpaid work on the productivity of other family members and to place little value on homemaking. We noted earlier that the *Dictionary of Occupational Titles* rated it lower than animal caretaking. The 1974 median earnings of year-round, full-time private household workers were $2,676. If we believe that the laborer is worthy of her hire, then household work is not worth much. After all, most of it is done free!

The Homemaker's Dependency upon Others

Those engaged only in unpaid household production are not directly covered under our Social Security system. They are not eligible for compensation for injuries suffered at work. They do not receive paid sick leave and vacations nor time-and-a-half for overtime and premium pay for working Sundays and holidays. Nor does unemployment insurance exist for them. They are dependent for their livelihood on the generosity and thoughtfulness of others. Legislators, employers, and union leaders have focused social and private programs toward meeting the needs of those in the labor force.

Displaced Homemakers

Women who have devoted many years to full-time unpaid work for their families have often found themselves without a job as a result of death, desertion, or divorce. Their children are grown. Society, which had earlier praised these women highly, now places no market value on their skills. They face discrimination on the basis of both age and sex. After long dependency on others, how can these women enter the labor force and become self-sufficient? In 1975 California was the first state to fund experimental centers for counseling and training such women. By mid-1977 eleven other states had enacted Displaced Homemaker Acts, generally providing small appropriations for pilot programs. Similar legislation has been introduced in other states and at the federal level.[70]

WOMEN AND POVERTY

Reasons for Poverty among Women

Since many private and governmental social insurance and compensation programs are directed toward maintaining the incomes of those in the labor force when they become sick, injured, laid off, disabled, or elderly, women who have not engaged in paid work long enough for eligibility in these programs obviously cannot qualify directly. Any program benefits they do receive result from their dependency on another family member. When that other person is no longer present as a result of death, divorce, separation, or desertion, the program benefits either stop entirely or are greatly reduced.

Women who do qualify directly through their own paid employment usually find benefits related to earnings records. The lower the earnings, the lower the benefits. As we have seen, women's earnings are far less than those of men.

Female-Headed Families

Of the more than 56 million U.S. families in 1976, over 13 percent were headed by women. (Until 1977 the Bureau of the Census considered all husband-wife families to be male-headed, even when the wife was the sole earner.) Nearly one out of every six children lived in a family where the father was absent. Of all U.S. families below the poverty level, 46 percent were headed by females. One in eight of all U.S. children under eighteen years old lives in poverty, and well over half of these are in families headed by women. While the number of children under eighteen living in poverty-level, male-headed families was more than halved between 1960 and 1974, the number of those in female-headed families rose by nearly 50 percent.[71]

An income that supported one household adequately often is insufficient for two households after separation or divorce. The Urban Institute made a six-year study of postdivorce support payments.

About 30 percent of mothers from families with pre-divorce incomes over $11,000 reported they had received no child support or alimony at all. . . . When such payments were made . . . , they averaged about $2,000 per year, an amount which went typically to support several children. Only 2 percent of all families received over $5,000 per year.

... Men in income categories over $7,000 allocated only about 12 percent of their before-tax income to their former families. Even fathers with a history of providing some support made payments with great irregularity.[72]

Families headed by females had a 1974 median income of $6,413 from all sources—earnings, support payments from absent fathers, unemployment insurance, public assistance—as compared with $13,788 for families with male heads. Nearly 40 percent of the women who headed poor families worked for at least part of 1974. In 1976 about 281,000 of all families with dependent children were headed by women who earned so little from their full-time, year-round work that the family was nevertheless in poverty. These families are eligible for Aid to Families with Dependent Children (AFDC) in some states.[73]

Welfare Mothers

Most mothers on welfare want to work. However, they realize that in a number of states the benefits to them and their children from AFDC and in-kind programs such as the food stamp program and medicaid are greater than the amount they could earn in the labor force. Even so, a study that followed a sample of welfare mothers from 1967 through 1975 found that most of these women did not stay on welfare for the entire eight years; most were on welfare only once; and most worked each year they were not on welfare. Government assistance programs to provide income to the nonworking poor are sometimes considered the equivalent of unemployment insurance. When a marriage breaks up and the displaced homemaker and her children no longer receive support in exchange for services rendered to *a* man, they can turn to *the* man. Government becomes the primary source of income until the family is supported by its earnings. Between 1966 and 1976 the number of female-headed families eligible for AFDC nearly doubled, and actual participation rose from approximately half of those eligible to about 90 percent.[74]

The basic problem, then, is not that welfare recipients scorn work. Rather they are eager to work, but the jobs are not there (refer to Figure 8.1 on unemployment rates). Federal job-training programs give priority to males. Even when women do enroll in such programs, they are less likely than men to be placed in jobs. Furthermore, if they are placed, their jobs pay less than the men's jobs.[75]

Elderly Women

When we examine the other end of the adult life span, we find that there are three women aged sixty-five and over for every two men in that age-group. Over five million elderly women lived alone in 1975; of these, more than half had an income below the official poverty level. Among all workers who retired in 1969 and 1970, nearly half the men received a private pension, but only 20 percent of the women did so. For those fortunate enough to receive such pensions, the median 1970 pension for men was $2,080, but for women, only $970. In at least one retirement program where male and female employees retire at the same age and where each (or their employer) has contributed the same amount for a single-life annuity, the woman receives about 13 percent fewer dollars each month than the man.[76]

Thus we see that the hardships and indignities of poverty are far more likely to befall women than men. This holds true whether they are single parents trying to meet the material, emotional, and psychological needs of their children, or whether they are among the elderly who have already spent many adult years at work, both paid and unpaid.

WHAT MIGHT THE FUTURE HOLD?

Any projections about the future economic roles and problems of women must be viewed with suspicion. In 1973 Department of Labor experts forecast that it would take until 1985 before women workers were 40.7 percent of the labor force; by 1976 that figure was reached.[77]

Assumptions and Questions

Predictions made now depend upon many assumptions. Will the future bring prosperity or recession? If the latter, blue-collar workers will be hit harder than service-providing ones. If goods-producing industries are cutting back, women will not find jobs there, and those recently hired are likely to be laid off.

What effect will the energy crisis have on employment patterns? The number of jobs in the auto industry may decrease, while those in coal mining increase. How about technological advances? Although the computer industry as a whole is expected to expand, fewer keypunch operators will be needed. As computers become more sophisticated, there may be less call for many types of clerical workers.

What will be the international situation? Will a larger proportion of the federal budget be devoted to defense? Or will a more peaceful world enable an expansion of federal funding of health care, the arts, national parks, and child-care centers?

Has the birthrate stabilized? Or will it shoot back up? There is some indication that many couples continue to want children but are postponing the arrival of the first until the mother is in her late twenties or early thirties and has established a work history.[78] If a society is to survive into the future, it must have children to carry on its values and it must defend itself against outside aggression. Will women receive credits toward job seniority and pension benefits during time spent on maternity leave, just as men have often received such credits for military service? Forecasts about the birthrate affect forecasts about jobs in such areas as baby-food manufacturing, teaching, orthodontics, and recreation.

Education and Retirement

The college enrollment of women aged twenty-five to thirty-five doubled between 1970 and 1976.[79] Are these women trend-setters? As the proportion of the population sixty-five and over rises, will these people pursue the higher education denied them in their youth? Will retirement become voluntary rather than mandatory? If more of the elderly keep on working, will there be fewer jobs for new entrants into the labor force? Or will there be earlier and pensioned retirement after a specific number of years (as, for example, in a policy of thirty and out)?

Official Forecasts

The U.S. Department of Labor periodically attempts to answer many questions such as these and issues projections both for occupations and industries. As of late 1976 the department forecast that overall employment would rise by 20 percent, or about 17.5 million workers, from 1974 to 1985. The occupations expected to grow by 50 percent or more are primarily in the health field, such as registered nurses, practical nurses, dental hygienists, and health administrators. Others among whom a 50 percent or higher increase is expected are surveyors, computer specialists, secretaries, teachers' aides, operators of bulldozers and excavating machines, boiler makers, repairers of data-processing machines, opticians, asbestos and insulation workers, child-care workers, welfare-service aides, and garbage collectors.[80]

Since an occupation with 100 people in 1974 and 150 in 1985 would show a 50 percent growth, we also ought to examine the anticipated number of increased jobs. For all occupations mentioned in the previous paragraph, there will be slightly less than 5 million additional workers in 1985 as compared with 1974. The health field alone will grow by 2,327,000. This sector already employs about three women for every man. The "women's occupations" of secretaries, teachers' aides, child-care workers, and welfare-service aides are expected to employ another 2 million workers. The relatively new fields of computer programming and systems analysis have not yet become sex-stereotyped. All the other occupations listed earlier are primarily male dominated, and the forecast is that they will add only 367,000 jobs by 1985.[81]

Occupations where employment is expected to grow by at least 100,000 between 1974 and 1985 include engineering drafters, elementary school teachers (but secondary school teaching jobs will decrease by 100,000), accountants, lawyers, personnel and labor relations workers, social workers, bank officials, retail trade sales managers, school administrators, retail trade sales clerks, wholesale trade sales representatives, typists, bank tellers, bookkeepers, cashiers, receptionists, shipping and receiving clerks, stock clerks, carpenters, electricians, plumbers and pipe fitters, automobile mechanics and body repairers, heavy equipment mechanics, welders, manufacturing checkers and inspectors, assemblers (except transport), truck drivers, building interior cleaners, janitors and sextons, cooks (except in private households), waiters, hairdressers and cosmetologists, police and detectives, and stock handlers.[82]

This list contains some occupations traditionally filled by men and others traditionally filled by women. Will the new jobs in these fields lead to a lessening of sex segregation? Time will tell.

Additional Influences

The lessening of occupational sex segregation depends on a number of factors. Will women prepare for employment as workers in the skilled trades, such as electricians and automobile mechanics, and in the professions, such as accountants and engineers? They will if they believe there will be job openings. Will government take stronger action toward equal employment opportunity? The Labor Department in 1977 began preparing regulations requiring greater employment for women in the skilled construction trades. The regulations, if implemented, should add at least thirty thousand women annually in these male-dominated and relatively well paid jobs.[83] Enrollment of women in law schools has climbed at a more rapid rate than the increase in total enrollment. Some fear that the nation will soon have more lawyers than jobs for them. However, others point to the inclusion of prepaid legal services as a fringe benefit in some recent labor agreements. They forecast shortages in the legal profession similar to those occurring in the health professions as medical insurance became widespread. Will women more actively seek the responsibilities of leadership in unions and professional organizations, especially in those fields where women are the majority? The number of women members of labor unions and professional associations dropped by fifty thousand between 1974 and 1976, probably owing to heavy unemployment in the predominantly female electronics and garment industries and to low seniority for women in other industries suffering layoffs.[84]

Will the labor force participation rate of women continue to rise and that of men continue to fall? Will there be a continuation of the trend for males to spend fewer years in the labor force and more years in school and to retire earlier? Will the "normal" workweek fall from forty hours to thirty-five? Will there be more paid holidays and longer paid vacations? Answers to these questions will affect job opportunities for women.[85]

Part-Time Work

One clue to a possible major shift in the allocation of time to paid work lies in the growing proportion of voluntary part-time workers. In the early 1960s, 10 percent of the labor force wanted nothing but part-time work; by 1977 nearly 16 percent fell in that category. Several small manufacturers hire only part-time workers. Women work in the morning when their children are in school, whereas students fill a short afternoon shift. Department stores, insurance companies, and restaurants are among major employers of regular part-time workers. Such workers are usually paid at or only slightly above the minimum wage, ordinarily get no fringe benefits (which add to employers' labor costs), and are unlikely to be offered promotions. Yet absenteeism and quit rates are low.[86]

Will the trend toward more voluntary part-time work continue? If so, will part-time workers continue to be relatively unskilled, low paid, and highly vulnerable to layoff? Or will they organize—either independently or as members of the union representing full-time workers—and collectively bargain for higher pay, job protection, and greater opportunity for advancement? If part-time work becomes more attractive, will many of those now working full time choose part-time jobs instead? Or will the part-time job be in addition to a full-time one?

Flexi-time

Some employers, although not many, have adopted flexi-time. Workers still put in a forty-hour week and must be on the job during the peak business hours. However, some may choose to work from seven to three, others from eight to four, nine to five, or ten to six. In some instances, workers may work three eight-hour days, one ten-hour day, and one six-hour day during the week. Employees on flexi-time can then schedule appointments with dentists or their children's teachers, do their shopping when stores are uncrowded, and avoid rush-hour commuting.

Effects on Home Production

As the allocation of women's time has shifted toward paid work so that for women as a whole fewer hours are spent in home production, buying habits have changed. Cake mixes, TV dinners, frozen stew vegetables which need only to be cooked, raisins already boxed for one serving are examples of products not available until recently. Slow-cookers and ovens can be preset to turn themselves on in the cook's absence. In the mid-1960s one of every five dollars spent on food went for restaurant and fast-food takeout meals, and ten years later this ratio was one of every three.[87]

As women participate more and more in the labor force, will men participate more and more in nonmarket work? Many of today's young adults grew up with working mothers. The most recently published studies of household work date back to observations made in the 1960s. Children helped some but not much. Yet many now in their twenties and thirties learned as children to pick up after themselves, wash dishes and clothes, clean, polish, and wax. The formation of one-person households by young adults who move away from parental homes and delay marriage until a later age means that many men gain proficiency in basic household skills.

SUMMARY AND CONCLUSIONS

We have seen that the old assumptions no longer describe the current economic roles of women and men. Only about 6 percent of U.S. households in 1977 fit the traditional image of a family consisting of a husband supporting a wife and two children.[88] In over half the marriages both spouses engage in paid work. Moreover, women without husbands are even more apt to be in the labor force.

Sex segregation in the paid work force is more pervasive than race segregation, and the gap between the earnings of women and men has widened in recent years. Government action to provide equal pay for equal work and to open up employment opportunities may merely have kept the earnings gap from widening even farther. Both income tax and Social Security legislation have discriminated against women, as have insurers and lenders. Women are more apt to live in poverty than are men.

The growing awareness of the rapid and tremendous changes in women's economic roles has recently brought about some legislation to help overcome unjust economic treatment of women. The greater the number who are affected by inequitable opportunities and practices, the greater the pressure to correct the inequities.

Women have always worked. Now they work for money income to an extent never before known. Our society has already moved far from the old model of sole male responsibility for a household's material well-being. The future may bring a fuller sharing between men and women and less specialization in all types of labor—both paid and unpaid. And let us not forget the third use of time. Everybody needs some leisure time, some relaxation, some serenity in which to enjoy life and the people who make it worth living.

APPENDIX

TABLE A.1. Labor Force Participation Rates of Women by Age, Race, and by Presence and Age of Children

	1950	1974	Percent Change 1950 to 1974
Total, 16 years and over	33.9	45.7	+34.8
Age:			
16 to 19 years	41.0	49.3	+20.2
20 to 24 years	46.1	63.2	+37.1
25 to 34 years	34.0	52.4	+54.1
35 to 44 years	39.1	54.7	+39.9
45 to 54 years	38.0	54.6	+43.7
55 to 64 years	27.0	40.7	+50.7
65 years and older	9.7	8.2	−15.5
Race:			
White	32.6	45.2	+38.6
Black and other races	46.9	49.1	+4.7
Presence and age of children:[a]			
Married women, husband present:			
No children under 18	30.3	43.9	+44.9
Children 6 to 17 only	28.3	52.3	+84.8
Children under 6	11.9	36.6	+207.7
Other ever-married women:			
No children under 18	33.7	33.2	−1.5
Children 6 to 17 only	63.6	67.2	+5.7
Children under 6	41.4	55.0	+32.9

SOURCE: *Statistical Portrait*, pp. 28, 31, and 71 (with some computations by author added).
[a]The years compared are 1950 and 1975.

TABLE A.2. Size of Labor Force by Sex and Work Experience, 1950 and 1970 (numbers in thousands)

	1950	1970	Percent Change 1950 to 1970
Total labor force, annual average:	63,858	85,903	+34.5
Women	18,412	31,560	+71.4
Men	45,446	54,343	+19.6
Worked during year:			
Women	23,350	38,704	+65.7
Men	45,526	54,919	+20.6
Worked part-time:			
Women, 14 to 19 years old	371	1,494	+302.7
Men, 14 to 19 years old	724	2,207	+204.8
Women, 20 years and older	2,636	7,372	+179.7
Men, 20 years and older	3,129	4,968	+58.8
Worked 50 to 52 weeks at full-time jobs:			
Women	8,592	15,738	+83.2
Men	29,783	36,295	+21.9
Ratio: women to men	0.29	0.43	(X)
Unemployed, annual average:			
Women	1,049	1,853	+76.6
Men	2,239	2,235	−0.2
Ratio: women to men	0.83	0.47	(X)
Unemployment rate:			
Women	5.7	5.9	+3.5
Men	5.1	4.4	−13.7
Ratio: women to men	1.12	1.34	(X)

SOURCE: *Statistical Portrait*, pp. 27, 31, 32, and 40.
(X) = not applicable

TABLE A.3. Median Earnings by Occupation of Year-Round, Full-Time Civilian Workers 14 Years Old and Over, 1974

Occupation of Longest Job	Median Earnings		Ratio of Women to Men
	Women	Men	
Total, with earnings	$6,772	$11,835	0.57
Professional, technical, and kindred workers	9,570	14,873	0.64
Managers and administrators, except farm	8,603	15,425	0.56
Sales workers	5,168	12,523	0.41
Clerical and kindred workers	6,827	11,514	0.59
Craft and kindred workers	6,492	12,028	0.54
Operatives, including transport	5,766	10,176	0.57
Laborers, except farm	5,891	8,145	0.72
Farmers and farm managers	(B)	5,459	(X)
Farm laborers and farm supervisors	(B)	5,097	(X)
Service workers, except private household	5,046	8,638	0.58
Private household workers	2,676	(B)	(X)

SOURCE: *Statistical Portrait*, p. 49.
(B) = median earnings not shown because base is less than 75,000 persons
(X) = not applicable

TABLE A.4. Ratio of Number of Women to Number of Men in Industry for Employed Persons 14 Years Old and Over, 1970 (with some selections within industry classifications)

Industry	Ratio of Women to Men
Total employed	0.61
Agriculture, forestry, and fisheries	0.12
Mining	0.09
Construction	0.06
Manufacturing	0.39
Durable goods	0.27
Electrical machinery, equipment and supplies	0.62
Transportation equipment	0.15
Nondurable goods	0.62
Textile mill products	0.86
Apparel and other fabricated textile products	3.46
Transportation, communications, and other public utilities	0.27
Communication	0.94
Wholesale and retail trade	0.68
Wholesale trade	0.30
Retail trade	0.82
Department stores (general merchandise)	2.17
Eating and drinking places	1.42
Finance, insurance, and real estate	0.99
Business services	0.67
Repair services	0.13
Personal services	2.46
Private households	8.87
Beauty and barber shops	2.11
Entertainment and recreation services	0.55
Professional and related services	1.70
Health services	2.93
Educational services	1.67
Public administration	0.43
Postal services	0.25

SOURCE: *Statistical Portrait*, p. 37.

NOTES

1. *Ann Arbor News,* March 29, 1973, p. 26.

2. *Wall Street Journal,* February 2, 1976, p. 1.

3. U.S. Congress, Joint Economic Committee, *Economic Problems of Women: Hearings,* 93rd Cong., 1st sess., July 10, 1973, p. 2.

4. U.S. Department of Commerce, Bureau of the Census, *A Statistical Portrait of Women in the U.S.,* Current Population Reports, Special Studies, ser. P-23, no. 58 (Washington, D.C.: Government Printing Office, April 1976), p. 52 (hereafter referred to as *Statistical Portrait*).

5. Ibid., p. 24.

6. *New York Times,* April 12, 1977, p. 56

7. *Statistical Portrait,* p. 40.

8. There is one exception to this: In 1974, the latest year for which data are available, women who worked part-time for 50–52 weeks earned a median income of $2,423, whereas the annual median income of men with the same work experience was $40 less. See *Statistical Portrait,* p. 50.

9. Ibid., p. 48.

10. See Martha Blaxall and Barbara B. Reagan, eds. *Women and the Workplace: The Implications of Occupational Segregation* (Chicago: University of Chicago Press, 1976); Juanita M. Kreps, ed., *Women and the American Economy: A Look to the 1980's* (Englewood Cliffs, N.J.: Prentice-Hall, Inc., for American Assembly, 1976); and Cynthia B. Lloyd, ed., *Sex, Discrimination, and the Division of Labor* (New York: Columbia University Press, 1975).

11. Derived from *Statistical Portrait,* p. 35.

12. Ibid.

13. Ibid.

14. Linda Miller Atkinson, remarks at seminar on Women and the Law, Detroit, Michigan, October 8, 1976.

15. Derived from *Statistical Portrait,* p. 35.

16. See Appendix, Table A.3.

17. *New York Times,* January 26, 1977, pp. D-1, D-5.

18. *New York Times,* May 9, 1977, p. 49.

19. Joint Economic Committee, *Economic Problems of Women,* 93rd Cong., 1st sess., July 25, 1973, pp. 292, 294–299.

20. *Statistical Portrait,* pp. 72, 74.

21. This section relies to some extent on the discussion in Francine D. Blau and Carol L. Jusenius, "Economists' Approaches to Sex Segregation in the Labor Market: An Appraisal," in Blaxall and Reagan, *Women and the Workplace,* 181–199.

22. Janice Fanning Madden, "Comment III," in Blaxall and Reagan, *Women and the Workplace,* pp. 247–248.

23. *Equal Opportunity Forum* 4, no. 10 (1977): 20.

24. Mark R. Rosenzweig, "Child Investment and Women," in Lloyd, *Sex, Discrimination,* pp. 269–270.

25. *Equal Opportunity Forum* 4, no. 10 (1977): 20.

26. Barbara R. Bergmann and Irma Adelman, "The 1973 Report of the President's Council of Economic Advisers: The Economic Role of Women," *American Economic Review* 63, no. 4 (1973): 511; and *New York Times,* August 26, 1973, p. F-3.

27. Emma Rothschild, *Paradise Lost: The Decline of the Auto-Industrial Age* (New York: Vintage Books, 1974), pp. 123–125.

28. Institute for Social Research, University of Michigan, *ISR Newsletter,* summer 1977, p. 8.

29. Bergmann and Adelman, "Economic Role of Women," p. 509.

30. Kenneth Arrow, "Comment I," in Blaxall and Reagan, *Women and the Workplace,* p. 236.

31. Joint Economic Committee, *Economic Problems of Women,* 93rd Cong., 1st sess., July 10, 1973, pp. 59–61. Other economists also are convinced that the cost to society of discrimination is high. See, for example, Michael J. Boskin, "The Effects of Government Expenditures and Taxes on Female Labor," *American Economic Review,* 64, no. 2 (1974): 251–56, who estimated that discrimination in government tax and expenditure policies alone costs at least $20 billion annually.

32. In an effort to complicate, delay, and defeat the passage of the Civil Rights Bill of 1964 banning racial discrimination, a Southern congressman insisted on adding a prohibition against sex discrimination.

33. *New York Times,* June 4, 1974, p. 1.

34. *Wall Street Journal,* August 22, 1973, p. 19.

35. Winn Newman, "Presentation III," in Blaxall and Reagan, *Women and the Workplace,* pp. 271–272.

36. *New York Times,* May 2, 1976, p. 26, and June 6, 1977, p. 45.

37. *New York Times,* May 5, 1975, p. 1, and May 12, 1976, p. 48.

38. *New York Times,* October 1, 1977, p. 25; and *Wall Street Journal,* October 4, 1977, p. 1.

39. Margaret J. Gates, "Occupational Segregation and the Law," in Blaxall and Reagan, *Women and the Workplace,* pp. 61–74; *New York Times,* August 26, 1973, p. F-3; and *Wall Street Journal,* December 8, 1976, p. 3.

40. *New York Times,* June 1, 1977, p. 1; June 2, 1977, p. 1; and June 5, 1977, p. 15.

41. Joint Economic Committee, *Economic Problems of Women,* 93rd Cong., 1st sess., July 26, 1973, pp. 375–376; *New York Times,* April 4, 1976, p. 41; and *Ann Arbor News,* October 11, 1977, p. 1.

42. Howard Hayghe, "Families and the Rise of Working Wives: An Overview," *Monthly Labor Review* 99, no. 5 (May 1976): 12.

43. Joint Economic Committee, *Economic Problems of Women,* 93rd Cong., 1st sess., July 25, 1973, p. 300.

44. Federal employees and elected officials have their own retirement system and are not covered by Social Security. A divorced spouse receives no benefits from a retirement annuity no matter how many years of marriage.

45. Joint Economic Committee, *Economic Problems of Women,* 93rd Cong., 1st sess., July 25, 1973, p. 314; and *New York Times,* March 6, 1977, sec. 4, p. 7.

46. Joint Economic Committee, *Economic Problems of Women,* 93rd Cong., 1st sess., July 12, 1973, pp. 151–220; and *Wall Street Journal,* January 21, 1977, p. 26.

47. Joint Economic Committee, *Economic Problems of Women,* 93rd Cong., 1st sess., July 12, 1973, pp. 151–220.

48. Ibid., p. 170.

49. For a survey of the practices held discriminatory by courts and regulatory agencies and of the decreed remedies, see Jane Goldman, "Unions, Women and Economic Justice: Litigating Union Sex Discrimination," *Women's Rights Law Reporter* 4, no. 1 (Fall 1977): 3–26.

50. Virginia A. Bergquist, "Women's Participation in Labor Unions," *Monthly Labor Review* 97, no. 10 (October 1974): 3; and Edna E. Raphael, "Working Women and Their Membership in Labor Unions," *Monthly Labor Review* 97, no. 5 (May 1974): 27.

51. Douglas E. Brooks, "A Case Study of the Effect of Government Action on the Employment of Women" (Paper prepared for Economics 328, Eastern Michigan University, 1976).

52. Louise Kapp Howe, *Pink Collar Workers* (New York: G. P. Putnam's Sons, 1977), chaps. 2, 3, 4, and 5.

53. *New York Times,* October 14, 1977, p. A-14.

54. Bergquist, "Women's Participation," pp. 5–8; Raphael, "Working Women," p. 32; and *New York Times,* February 19, 1977, p. 10.

55. *Ann Arbor News,* December 8, 1975, p. 12; and *New York Times,* December 8, 1975, p. 39.

56. Nancy Seifer, *Absent from the Majority: Working Class Women in America* (New York: National Project on Ethnic America, 1973), pp. 1–3, 29–32, 56–60; and Howe, *Pink Collar Workers.*

57. Janet L. Norwood, "New Approaches to Statistics on the Family," *Monthly Labor Review* 100, no. 7 (July 1977): 33–34.

58. John Kenneth Galbraith, *Economics and the Public Purpose* (Boston: Houghton Mifflin Company, 1973), p. 33.

59. See, for example, *New York Times,* January 13, 1976, p. 39; Juanita M. Kreps, *Sex in the Marketplace: American Women at Work* (Baltimore: Johns Hopkins University Press, 1971), pp.

66–75; and Statements for the Record, Joint Economic Committee, *Economic Problems of Women,* 93rd Cong., 1st sess., pt. 3, pp. 443–445.

60. *New York Times,* April 3, 1977, p. 35; and U.S., Department of Labor, Manpower Administration, *Dictionary of Occupational Titles,* vols. 1, 2 (Washington, D.C.: Government Printing Office, 1965).

61. Kreps, *Sex in the Marketplace,* p. 66; Reuben Gronau, "The Intrafamily Allocation of Time: The Value of the Housewives' Time," *American Economic Review,* 63, no. 4 (September 1973): 634–635; and Arleen Leibowitz, "Women's Work in the Home," in Lloyd, *Sex, Discrimination,* p. 227.

62. Joann Vanek, "Time Spent in Housework," *Scientific American* 231, no. 5 (November 1974): 116–118.

63. Ibid., p. 120.

64. Galbraith, *Economics and the Public Purpose,* pp. 29–37.

65. Vanek, "Housework," p. 118.

66. Derived from *Statistical Portrait,* p. 35.

67. Elizabeth Janeway, *Man's World, Woman's Place* (New York: Dell Publishing Co., Inc., 1971), p. 166.

68. Arleen Leibowitz, "Education and Home Production," *American Economic Review* 64, no. 2 (May 1974): 243–250.

69. Lee Benham, "Nonmarket Returns to Women's Investment in Education," in Lloyd, *Sex, Discrimination,* pp. 292–307.

70. Laurie Shields, "Displaced Homemakers Win New Laws," *Women's Agenda* 2, no. 7 (September 1977): 9–10.

71. Norwood, "New Approaches," pp. 31–34; and *Statistical Portrait,* p. 53.

72. *New York Times,* September 24, 1977, p. 20.

73. *Statistical Portrait,* p. 52; *New York Times,* September 26, 1976, p. 36; and U.S., Congress, Congressional Budget Office, *Welfare Reform: Issues, Objectives, and Approaches* (Washington, D.C.: Government Printing Office, July 1977), p. 21.

74. Isabel Sawhill, "Discrimination and Poverty among Women Who Head Families," in Blaxall and Reagan, *Women and the Workplace,* pp. 201–211; Elizabeth Durbin, "The Vicious Cycle of Welfare: Problems of the Female-Headed Household in New York City," in Lloyd, *Sex, Discrimination,* pp. 313–345; "Do the Poor Want to Work?" *The Brookings Bulletin,* Summer 1972, pp. 1–3; *New York Times,* September 29, 1976, p. 25, and May 31, 1977, p. 28; and Congressional Budget Office, *Welfare Reform,* p. 22.

75. Joint Economic Committee, *Economic Problems of Women,* 93rd Cong., 1st sess., July 26, 1973, pp. 340, 371–373.

76. U.S. Congress, House of Representatives, *Congressional Record: Extensions of Remarks,* 95th Cong. 1st sess., January 11, 1977, p. E139; Martha W. Griffiths, "Can We Still Afford Occupational Segregation? Some Remarks," in Blaxall and Reagan, *Women and the Workplace,* p. 12; and Daniel Halperin, "Should Pension Benefits Depend upon the Sex of the Recipient?" *AAUP Bulletin* 62, no. 1 (April 1976): 43.

77. *New York Times,* September 12, 1976, p. 49.

78. A Rand Corporation study predicts that the level of fertility is likely to remain low now that so many women are in the labor force. It is too expensive for these women to take time out from paid work to bear and raise large families. See *New York Times,* October 8, 1977, p. 10.

79. *Chattanooga News–Free Press,* May 4, 1977, p. A-10.

80. Max L. Carey, "Revised Occupational Projections to 1985," *Monthly Labor Review,* 99, no. 11 (November 1976): 10–22. More recent estimates by the Urban Institute of the overall labor force are higher, primarily because of larger projections of participation rates of women. See *New York Times,* October 1, 1977, p. 25.

81. Derived from Carey, "Revised Projections," pp. 13–14.

82. Ibid.

83. *New York Times,* August 11, 1977, p. 1, and August 21, 1977, sec. 3, p. 15.

84. *New York Times,* September 3, 1977, p. 28.

85. The labor force participation rate of men aged 25 to 54, the "prime" working age, dropped from 96.6 percent in 1966 to 94.2 percent ten years later. See *Wall Street Journal,* June 21, 1977, p. 1.

86. *New York Times,* April 12, 1977, pp. 1, 56.

87. *New York Times,* April 10, 1977; p. 1.

88. Less than one out of every six U.S. families in 1976 consisted of a husband in the labor force, a wife not in the labor force, and one or more children under 18. See Norwood, "New Approaches," p. 31.

REVIEW QUESTIONS

1. Women tend to have higher unemployment rates than men, are more apt to work part-time, and are more likely than men to have intermittent participation in the labor force. Discuss (*a*) the reasons behind these differentials and (*b*) how these differentials lead to additional economic problems for women.

2. Comment on this conversation, which actually took place in 1974:

    MAN (aged about sixty): I've had two wives and neither one of them ever wanted to work. Tell me, *why* do women want to work nowadays?

    WOMAN (aged about fifty-five): For the same reason men do—money!

    MAN: But women have such lousy jobs!

    To what extent was each participant in the conversation correct?

3. While the majority of voluntary part-time workers aged twenty or over are women, a rising number of such workers are men, especially in two groups: those in their twenties who have completed their formal schooling and reject what they term the "rat race," and those aged fifty to sixty-five who receive private pensions from previous full-time employment. Discuss the implications of the trend toward voluntary part-time work by both men and women in terms of *(a)* the allocation of time, *(b)* the total output of the economy, and *(c)* specialization in and division of work according to sex.

4. Housewives' labor does not now make them eligible for Social Security coverage nor for unemployment insurance. Do you think it should? If so, how would you finance the program(s)? If not, what protection against displacement from their (unpaid) job should they receive?

5. Does the large rise in AFDC case loads in the past ten or fifteen years represent rational economic behavior on the part of women? Explain your answer.

CLASSROOM EXERCISES

1. Update the data found in tables in this chapter by using more recent U.S. government sources such as the latest *Economic Report of the President* (tables are in back); recent issues of the *Monthly Labor Review* (look at articles as well as tables in

back); and the *Current Population Reports* issued by the Bureau of the Census. Do you see any changes since the dates of the tables in this chapter? If not, why not? If so, what might have brought them about?

2. Interview a woman family member or neighbor who has held a job for at least ten or twenty years. Ask her to describe any discrimination she has met; what, if anything, she did about it (or alternatively, why she did not do anything about it); and what success she had in correcting the situation. Next pretend that you are her employer or union representative. What case could you make that no sex discrimination occurred? Finally, pretend that you are a judge and summarize your findings about her charge of sex discrimination.

3. If you live at home and have a working mother (or are a student-wife or student-worker-wife), keep a record for one week of how much time each family member spends on which type of unpaid home production.

4. Ask to see the affirmative action plan of your college or university and reports on the institution's progress in eliminating sex segregation in student aid and athletic programs and in the hiring, promotion, pay, and fringe benefits for the top administrative officers, faculty, clerical workers, custodial and maintenance workers, and other staff.

SELECTED READINGS (For the Instructor)

U.S. Congress. Joint Economic Committee. *Economic Problems of Women: Hearings.* 93rd Cong., 1st sess. Pt. 1: July 10, 11, and 12, 1973; pt. 2: July 24, 25, 26, and 30, 1973; pt. 3: Statements for the Record.

Then Congresswoman Martha W. Griffiths chaired these hearings, which dealt with all facets of discrimination against women. Testimony was given by federal government officials, academics, women active in welfare rights and other women's organizations, insurance commissioners, and so on. Ms. Griffiths and other members of the committee interrogated many witnesses sharply. Some witnesses brought prepared statements which are included in part 3. Other witnesses were asked to get additional information for committee use, and this material is also in part 3. The actual hearings make for lively reading. This source is now out of print but should be available in a library with a government documents section.

U.S. Department of Commerce. Bureau of the Census. *A Statistical Portrait of Women.* Current Population Reports, Special Studies, ser. P-23, no. 58. Washington, D.C.: Government Printing Office, April 1976.

The first census ever devoted entirely to American women is an indispensable source for any research on the changing social and economic status of women in the United States. It provides otherwise unobtainable data not only on women's labor force participation, occupations, work experience, and income status, but also on population growth and composition, longevity and mortality, residence and migration, marital and family status, fertility, education, voting and public office holding, and crime and victimization. There are special chapters on black women and women of Spanish origin.

Blaxall, Martha, and Barbara B. Reagan, eds. *Woman and the Workplace: The Implications of Occupational Segregation.* Chicago: University of Chicago Press, 1976.

Most of the chapters were presented in a preliminary form at a May 1975 workshop on occupational segregation. The participants were drawn from various social science disciplines, from the legal profession, and from the staff of labor unions. The usefulness of the papers is uneven, but in general they provide much insight.

Kreps, Juanita M. *Sex in the Marketplace: American Women at Work.* Baltimore: Johns Hopkins University Press, 1971.

The data are now out of date, but the interpretations of trends and forecasts are not. A most thoughtful study.

Kreps, Juanita M., ed. *Women and the American Economy: A Look to the 1980's.* Englewood Cliffs, N.J.: Prentice-Hall, Inc., for American Assembly, 1976.

This book was distributed as advance reading for the 1975 program of the American Assembly, a nonpartisan public affairs forum whose trustees are for the most part members of the white male establishment. The papers in this volume are by a variety of authors and examine the broad social forces affecting the economic roles of women in the past and present. Some predictions about the future are made. A valuable interdisciplinary source.

Lloyd, Cynthia B., ed. *Sex, Discrimination, and the Division of Labor.* New York: Columbia University Press, 1975.

The seventeen economists who contributed papers to this volume are mostly young. Many of the essays are based on material from recent Ph.D. dissertations. There is no better source of research findings in the field indicated by the book's title.

Madden, Janice Fanning. *The Economics of Sex Discrimination.* Lexington, Mass.: D. C. Heath & Company, 1973.

A rather technical analysis of the various theories of sex discrimination in the labor market. Various economic models are presented. The book would be difficult for anyone not a professional economist.

Vanek, Joann. "Time Spent in Housework." *Scientific American* 231, no. 5 (November 1974): 116–120.

Although this article appeared in a popular magazine, it is based on material contained in Ms. Vanek's doctoral dissertation. The article gives a more careful analysis of empirical studies, done over time, of the allocation of time to housework, and of the implications of changes or lack of changes, than any other source used on this subject.

Monthly Labor Review. Published monthly by U. S. Department of Commerce, Bureau of Labor Statistics.

An indispensable source of current data, which can be found in a section toward the back called "Current Labor Statistics." Signed articles by bureau staff members and other labor economists and labor lawyers are found each month, and many of these articles deal specifically with women. Most college and university libraries subscribe to this publication.

New York Times. A careful reading of a daily newspaper is required for those interested in recent economic developments affecting women. The *New York Times* is the unofficial "newspaper of record" in the United States.

CHAPTER 9

Women in American Politics

Marjorie Lansing

> Thus far women have been the mere echoes of men. Our laws and constitutions, our creeds and codes, and the customs of social life are all of masculine origin. The true woman is as yet a dream of the future. (Elizabeth Cady Stanton, aged seventy-two, speaking to the International Council of Women in the year 1888)

Increasingly, women are challenging the traditional male-dominated world of American politics. Feminists have realized that the goals of the women's movement cannot be achieved outside the political power structure, and have seen the importance of change in the political role of women. The evidence suggests that their political role will change. Social scientists have found that women's perception of their political role is influenced by a field of forces, including, for example, their socialization, their education, and their economic status.[1] All of these forces are changing. Women are increasing their entry into the paid work force, enrolling in greater numbers in colleges and professional schools, and transforming family structure and life-style.

Why have women traditionally been second-class citizens in politics, and what forces will affect the outlook for a new politics? This chapter explores the political participation of women by looking briefly at the history of the fight for suffrage and the socialization of women, and it looks in detail at women's active involvement in politics: their voting history, elite participation, activism, and effect on public policy.

THE HISTORY OF WOMEN'S SUFFRAGE

In the eighteenth century when the United States won its independence the prevailing body of law governing the legal status of women was English common law. Common law barred women from voting, holding public office, or serving on juries, and denied them legal control of their children and property. Colonial America inherited her legal system from England where the jurist, Sir William Blackstone, had stated in his influential *Commentaries:* "The husband and wife are one, and that one is the husband."[2]

The main movement for the rights of women began in the early nineteenth century, with the experience of women, many of them Quakers, who were working for the abolition of slavery. Women quickly learned that they could not function as equals with male abolitionists who rebelled at allowing them positions on committees or permitting them to speak in public or sit as delegates at the World Anti-Slavery Convention held in London in 1840. Two of the women relegated to the gallery at the convention, Lucretia Mott and Elizabeth Cady Stanton, returned home to America and organized the first women's rights convention, held in Seneca Falls, New York, in the summer of 1848. One statement adopted at the convention asserted "that all men and women are created equal," and demanded that women be given equal status with men in educational, economic, and political matters. However, many nineteenth-century feminists did not consider political participation to be appropriate behavior for women. The issue of granting the right to vote to women provoked the greatest controversy at Seneca Falls; the issue continued to divide women until the vote was finally won in 1920. Although abolition (until the Civil War) and suffrage were the dominant themes in the women's movement, some women pursued other reforms apparently regarded as more respectable. Women worked to enlarge opportunities for education and to improve prison conditions, labor conditions, and treatment for the insane. Thus one of the best means of understanding the role of women in politics is to study the history of the women's movement itself. It seems clear that nineteenth-century feminists perceived the link between their political activity and their larger social role.[3]

The surprising fact about the achievement of the goal to give women the right to vote in 1920 is that it accomplished very little change. As O'Neill summarized in *Everyone Was Brave:*

It took seventy-two years for women to get the vote. Generations wore out their lives in pursuit of it. Some women went to jail, many picketed, marched, and protested their deprived state in other ways. In the last stages of the fight for equal suffrage, literally millions of women contributed something to the cause. Yet when the vote was gained it made little difference to the feminine condition. A few women were elected to office, political campaigning became more refined, and the sex-lives of candidates were more rigorously policed. The ballot did not materially help women to advance their most urgent causes; even worse, it did not help women to better themselves or improve their status. The struggle for women's rights ended during the 1930's, leaving men in clear possession of the commanding places in American life.[4]

POLITICAL SOCIALIZATION

As we have seen, girls are conditioned to be passive and dependent, whereas the young boy is encouraged to be aggressive and independent. The chief agents of this learning process (the family, school, peers, and media, among others) have taught females personality traits that run counter to the models of successful politician and activist citizen. There are a host of studies on sex-role learning and political socialization; in general they have found that the agents of socialization "channel women into lower occupational expectations and willingness to play a marginal role in the economic, political, and social aspects of society."[5] In effect, the early feminists were right: The vote would be meaningless without a larger program of women's rights, which they called for in their declaration at Seneca Falls.

Other factors which contributed to the decline of feminism in the 1920s undoubtedly related to the concentration in the late years of struggle on the single, narrow issue of suffrage. It was plausible for women to concentrate on a single issue, the rights of citizenship, including the vote, as a constitutional guarantee. It was a very different issue for women to join political clubs and organizations, which in the 1920s were male precincts. It was not irrelevant that country courthouses in America, which have been the locus of political power at the local level, did not provide toilet facilities for women until recent decades. For women to become candidates and powerful figures in politics, it would have been necessary for them to compete rigorously with men. For the most part the avant-garde, which supplied the leadership for the suffrage movement, represented women of the upper-income leisure class who had not competed with men in business, industry, science, university, or any other arena.

Another major cause for the decline of feminism after 1920 may well be that there was no ideology with a clearly defined theoretical position to rally women. Suffrage had provided the women's movement with a major issue around which women's organizations cutting across class lines could flourish. There was no rallying point after the vote had been obtained. The lessons of this era may well be learned by the feminists today, namely, that one legislative gain, one leader, or one issue is not sufficient to sustain a dynamic movement.

Another element of the post-1920 era of the political history of women deals with their voting performance.

THE WOMEN'S VOTE

In fact, only a minority of women exercised their right to vote. One objection of politicians to the enactment of the amendment granting suffrage to women had been the fear that if women had the vote, they would clean up politics. This fear was undoubtedly generated by the position of women of the leisure class during the nineteenth century. The so-called Madonna-image notion prevailed: Women were pure, refined, innocent, and possibly humanitarian, and their impact on the ballot box would be to end political corruption, scandal, and graft.

Contrary to expectation and congressional fear, women did not clean up politics; in fact, they barely voted at all. Exact figures do not exist, because voting statistics only rarely are recorded by gender. However, the best estimates are that roughly one third of the women who were eligible by age and citizenship actually went to the polls in the presidential election of 1920, the year that women voted for the first time in all the states in a federal election.[5] Men voted in that election at considerably higher rates than women and continued to do so until the 1960s.

A case history adds meaning to the statistics. The city of Chicago classified election statistics by gender in 1920. Two professors of political science at the University of Chicago, Merriam and Gosnell, conducted pioneer survey studies in the neighborhoods of Chicago. Their report commented on the women's vote:

> The first outstanding fact to notice is that nearly three-quarters of these non-registered adult citizens were women. Women were allowed to register for local elections in Chicago as early as 1913; yet ten years later not half of the adult female citizens of the city had established voting habits.[6]

More important than women's low turnout was the fact that they did not seize the opportunity to vote as a bloc. Women did not materially advance their most important causes. Suffrage did not help women to upgrade their status.

If feminists could rewrite history, the flashback would show that it would have been more profitable if women had recognized the women's vote as a bloc. That realization might well have resulted in significant legislation improving the social and economic conditions for women long before the 1960s. The enlightenment in Congress in the 1960s, which brought approval of the Equal Pay Act of 1963, approval of Title VII of the 1964 Civil Rights Act, and other similar legislation, followed the militancy of the civil rights movement of the 1950s. Women, however, have not followed the example of the Black population in voting as a bloc and thus electing members of their group to positions of political power. Former member of Congress, Martha Griffiths, who steered legislation for the Equal Rights Amendment (ERA) through the House of Representatives, noted the significance of the bloc concept:

Women have the right to vote. They must learn to use it for themselves rather than being distracted by highly idealistic slogans such as "peace in our time," "food for the hungry world" or other equally worthy pleas; to vote for those men and women who propose a course of action that will promote the equality of women; to vote against those who do not support such equality. A woman voter, for a while at least, will need to let her party line count less, and the candidate's position on the rights of women more, than any other single issue.[7]

Just how do women vote? What factors influence their decisions? Scholars have drawn on survey research to examine electoral behavior in considerable detail. It is possible to document differences among women in relation to their voting turnout which lends understanding to their voting record.[8]

The first picture that emerges from the survey analyses of the late 1940s and 1950s was that women voted less than men. Further, their sense of political efficacy—that is, their sense of personal political worth in influencing the political system—was less than that of men.[9] During those years women had less interest in politics than men, and were generally less well informed. It was generally held by researchers in the 1950s that gender was not as influential in voting determinants as other variables, such as level of education, income, occupation, or social class.

Table 9.1 displays the overall record of voting by women and men from 1948 through 1976. Women lagged behind men about ten percent in voting from 1948 through 1960. By 1964 the gap between female and male voters narrowed to a few percentage points. Moreover, although a smaller percentage of women (two percent) than men voted in 1972, more votes were cast by women than by men because there are more women than men in the population (53 percent). Women voted at roughly the same rates as men in 1976.[10]

With comparisons across time, it is possible to locate tendencies and trends in voting performance. There are specific indicators which can be examined to learn more about the relationship of political behavior to background characteristics of individuals.

Education has always been a prime indicator of whether persons will vote and how they will cast their ballots. Further, education appears to make a

TABLE 9.1.   Percentages of Men and Women Voting in Elections, 1948–1972

	1948	1952	1956	1960	1964	1968	1972	1976
Men	69	72	80	80	73	69	64	54
Women	59	62	69	69	70	66	62	53

SOURCE: Center for Political Studies, University of Michigan, 1972. Data were obtained from U.S. Department of Commerce, Bureau of the Census, *Current Population Reports, Population Characteristics*, "Voting Participation in November, 1972," ser. P-20, no. 244, December, 1972; "Voting and Registration in the Election of November, 1976," ser P-20, no. 322, March, 1978.

slightly greater difference in the political behavior of women than of men. It seems clear that recent increases in the levels of education attained by women are closely associated with the increase in voting by women. Thus, change in the general educational levels of women serves as a weathervane of change in their overall role and status. Over time, the discrepancy in education between the sexes has served as an obstacle to women's political performance.

Education for women in the early nineteenth century was restricted to the daughters of the wealthy and was limited in scope, with the curriculum weighted in the areas of music and needlework. After the Civil War primary education for both sexes became free, public, and almost universal for white citizens. However, the doors to most colleges were closed to women. A few women's colleges were founded, beginning with Mount Holyoke in 1837, and three coeducational colleges existed before the Civil War. But college education remained for the most part a privilege for the sons of the family; the daughters were intended for marriage.

The picture changed dramatically in this century. Since 1900, women have been more likely to graduate from high school than men. There has been a steady increase in the level of education for both sexes.

Young women as a group are much better educated than their mothers. It is the college-educated, younger women who can be expected to consider organizing to vote as a women's bloc and to seek positions among the political elite.

The relationship of education to voting is shown in Table 9.2 which compares men and women by three levels of education for the national elections from 1948 through 1964. Women who attended college voted seven percentage points less than men in 1948 and four percentage points less than men in 1956. In three elections these women voted at the same rates as men of comparable education. Thus the difference in voting rates between men and

TABLE 9.2. Relation of Education to Sex Differences in Voting for President (in percentages)

	Grade School			High School			College		
Year	Men	Women	M to W	Men	Women	M to W	Men	Women	M to W
1948	57	48	+9	72	58	+14	77	70	+7
1952	66	47	+21	74	69	+14	80	80	0
1956	70	52	+18	80	68	+12	88	84	+4
1960	74	52	+22	80	66	+14	84	84	0
1964	64	59	+4	73	70	+2	80	80	0

SOURCE: Center for Political Studies, University of Michigan.
NOTE: Figures in this table are based on a combination of data from the national election samples. The primary percentage entries in each cell represent a simple subtraction within the category of the proportion of women voting for president from the same proportion among men. Positive percentages indicate that the percentage of men voting was higher than the percentage of women voting.

women who have attended college was erased in three of the five elections and declined over the period. This comparison of women and men shows the differential effects of education on voting that can be related to gender.

These trends continued in the most recent election. Figure 9.1 shows the years of education completed in relation to the percentage of women voting in the 1964, 1968, and 1972 elections. As the figure demonstrates, the relationship is stable. Moreover, the proportion of women in the higher-educated categories increased during this period, while the number of poorly educated women declined. In general, since voting tends to increase as education in-

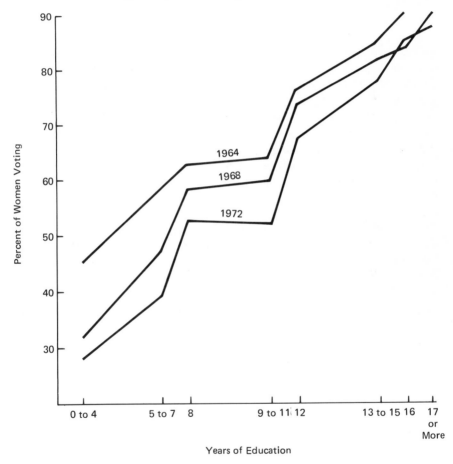

Figure 9.1. Relationship of Years of Education to Voting for President by Women, for 1964, 1968, and 1972 Elections.

SOURCE: U.S. Bureau of the Census, *Current Population Reports, Population Characteristics*, ser. P-20, no. 143 (Washington, D.C.: Government Printing Office, October 1965); no. 192 (December 1969); no. 253 (October 1973).

creases, and since the level of education of women is rising both absolutely and relatively in relation to men, we may expect that voting rates for women (again both absolute and relative to men) will increase as the proportion of educated women grows.

In general, the politically apathetic, uninvolved, and poorly informed woman found in the survey data of the 1950s is disappearing. The new generations of women have shown more interest in politics than their grandmothers, and among the college-educated, ability to influence politics on a personal level is higher. This is the group which has become active in political campaigns and organizations.

In addition, specific factors such as the region in which a woman lives have been found to be of considerable influence in voting turnout. This relationship of turnout to region also pinpoints an important discovery, namely, that women found in traditional environments, that is, where role and status conform to the old-fashioned concept of womanhood, are less inclined to vote. Women who live in the South, considered to be the most traditional region, have voted consistently at lower rates than women in all other regions. Younger Southern women, however, are providing some evidence that they differ from their grandmothers.

College-educated women are not the only women who have been voting in greater numbers in recent elections. Only about 20 percent of the women in the labor force have attended college, yet working women as a group vote at significantly higher rates than nonworking women.

One of the most important recent changes in the status of women was the entry of large numbers of married women into the paid work force during World War II. The majority of women without husbands had always worked, but until 1940 few married women were employed. As Chafe observed, the war broke up the traditional housewife-breadwinner division of labor as it became a national imperative that women join the labor force. Almost seven million women went to work, three quarters of them married. And they remained in the work force after the war. These women have been joined by others, with the percentage of married women in the labor force increasing from 34 percent in 1950 to 44 percent in 1972.[11]

Table 9.3 compares voting rates of working and nonworking women in three national elections. In 1964 and 1968 the difference between the two groups was 8 percent. In 1972 it was 7 percent. Women in better-paying jobs are compared with women who are not in the work force. In 1972, 80 percent of the women working for the government voted, whereas 59 percent of nonworking women voted. Younger women who were not in the work force voted at somewhat higher rates than older women who were not working. Women who were in nonagricultural employment voted at considerably higher rates than those who were in agriculture. Self-employed workers voted at higher rates than those who were employed as wage and salary workers in both agriculture and nonagriculture. The overall observation can

TABLE 9.3.   Relation of Employment Status to Voting, for Women Voting in Presidential Elections, 1964, 1968, 1972

Employment Status	Women Voting Election Year 1964 %	1968 %	1972 %
Employed in civilian labor force, total	72	71	66
Agriculture	54	64	62
Self-employed workers	65	72	71
Wage and salary workers	33	45	45
Nonagricultural industries	73	71	67
Private wage and salary workers	69	67	62
Government workers	85	83	80
Self-employed workers	76	76	69
Not in labor force, total	64	63	59
Under 65 years old	66	47[a] 67[b]	44[a] 63[b]
65 years and over	59	59	57

SOURCE: Bureau of the Census, *Current Population Reports, Population Characteristics*, P-20, no. 143 (October, 1965); no. 192 (December, 1969); no. 253, (October 1973).
[a] Voters under 25
[b] Voters aged 25–64

be made that women who are in the paid work force vote at considerably higher rates than women who are not in the labor force, with variations depending on the kind of employment.

In summary, it can be said that when women are well educated, when they are in the work force, when they live in environments that are undergoing changing perceptions of the appropriate roles for women, voting is increasing.

WOMEN AS POLITICAL ELITES

Although women in the 1970s have become the voting equals of men, very few women are found in elite positions. And yet women represent more than half of the population. What explains this disparity in representation?

The most common answer found in social science literature is that cultural norms have prevented women from attempting to achieve, or actually achieving, elite status. Women have had a predefined place in society—primarily to serve as homemaker and caretaker of children. The political arena was also seen as corrupt and not the place for a "nice" woman. There are a host of notions or theories that can add to this explanation. An interesting Freudian explanation has been that women are unsuited physiologically and psychologically for the rigorous decision-making pace of political life. For example, medical doctors in the recent decade have suggested that women's changing hormonal patterns make them temperamentally unsuited to carry the burdens of office-holding!

Another theory is that the male-dominated political process in America somehow has excluded women. Although more and more women are graduating from college, they are just beginning to enter the occupations and professions that lead to political careers. Women are still concentrating in the professions traditionally dominated by women: teaching, nursing, social work. Yet more than half of the members of Congress have always been lawyers. A law degree has been the entrée for successful male candidates and officeholders. The young lawyer serves a form of apprenticeship, enters politics at the local level, then runs for the state legislature and eventually for a congressional seat. The candidates who lose return to their successful law practices or business ventures. Often appointments to high places in the federal or state government agencies have been made because the recruited persons aided the successful president or governor in his race at election time. Appointments to the Supreme Court are also made partially on the basis of political credentials. Thus far no woman has served on that Court.

There is some evidence that women have been entering this network in the 1960s and 1970s. Admission of women to law schools has tripled in the last five years. Women are demanding equal representation on the policymaking boards of political parties and at national conventions where the vice-presidential and presidential candidates are chosen. Recruitment and apprenticeship for political office are undergoing change. In the wake of the Vietnam war and Watergate episode, which have exposed the corrupting influence of political tenure, self-starters, both men and women, are running successfully for office for the first time. The influence of political parties is declining.

A further obstacle for female candidates is described in a growing body of personal biographies and research.[12] A major constraint for women seeking high posts in state government or in Congress has been the inability to raise the funds necessary for victory. An aspirant in a competitive House district in a major state must spend $100,000 to win. To win a post in the U.S. Senate, successful candidates in an advanced industrial state spend a million dollars or more. The evidence is that women have more difficulty raising campaign funds than do men. Women do not have the business connections and credit that men have. More importantly, people give money to candidates expected to win.

The outlook, however, is improving slightly. A new type of woman is going to the halls of Congress. Until the most recent past, women eased into Congress on the coattails of a father or husband from whom they inherited the position. This is not the case with the new breed of woman in the House of Representatives. (Barbara Jordan is prominent for her questions on the House committee investigating the Nixon impeachment and for her keynote speech at the 1976 Democratic National Convention.) Although political roles demand a great deal of time, there are women who are combining familiar roles, even prègnancy (as in the case of Yvonne Braithwaite), with membership in the House of Representatives. There are an increasing number of women entering state legislatures. There are two female governors of states: Ella Grasso in Connecticut and Dixie Ray in Washington. The walls are slowly falling, and prospects may well improve if the new wave of political campaign ethics and finance laws are enacted by state legislatures and Congress. The financing of the presidential campaigns in 1976 from the federal treasury is generally seen as a model to be emulated at other election levels. Turnover in Congress, for example, is more often achieved today by death or retirement of a member. Federal financing of campaigns for congressional posts would undoubtedly be more helpful to women and other minorities than to the traditional white, male, well-educated, high-income professional. The same is true of elite posts in state government.

The long-run history has been that one or two women have been highly visible in presidential administrations, but the overall percentage of female administrators has been extremely low. The women's caucus at the Democratic National Convention in 1976 extracted more promises from the nominee, Jimmy Carter, than from any previous president.

In summary, to accelerate the trend for women to receive appointment or election to high political office, it will be necessary for women to enter the professions that serve as connecting links to recruitment and election. It may also be necessary for women to realize more than ever before that an organized bloc support for qualified female candidates is required.

WOMEN AS POLITICAL ACTIVISTS

Political scientists who have studied the era of the old-fashionéd urban political machine describe a party organization which involved few women. Porter and Matasar in 1972 studied one of the last of the machine organizations, the Chicago Democratic party under the leadership of the late Mayor Daley. They concluded that the role and status of women had remained relatively unchanged for forty years, that "the Daley women are like children as far as influence in the Cook County Democratic Party goes—they are to be seen and not heard."[12]

As a party organization emerged in the 1950s that included amateurs who were not so interested in personal favor for their party vote or work, women apparently joined parties in greater numbers. The sociologist James Q. Wilson wrote that a new type of activist appeared after World War II: "For the most part they are young, well-educated, professional people, including a large number of women. In style of life they are distinctly middle- and upper-class, in mood and outlook—products of a generation that came of age after World War II."[13] These women were generally underrepresented in influential party positions. Women served primarily as unpaid volunteers who, as one analyst observed, "remain traditional hewers of wood and drawers of water; doorbell ringers, raffle vendors, telephone recruiters, and stamp lickers."[14] Women had been represented on a 50 percent basis on the national committees of the two major parties since the 1920s, and in some states women were represented in equal numbers with men on the highest policy-making central committee, but the stereotypical woman was the volunteer who wielded very little power.

As the women's movement sought legislative victories in the 1960s, two major groups representing women's rights were organized: the National Women's Political Caucus (NWCP), with 35,000 members in fifty states, and National Organization of Women (NOW), with a membership close to a million. The NWCP was instrumental in helping to increase the number of women delegates attending the national party conventions in 1972, as well as the number of women elected to public office that year. The percentage of women attending the Democratic National Convention increased from 13 percent in 1968 to 38 percent in 1972 but dropped to 34 percent in 1976. The most controversial issue at the Democratic National Convention in 1976 was the proposal from the women's caucus to the rules committee that women should attend the 1980 convention in equal numbers with men. That proposal lost to a more moderate compromise that the states chould have cross-sectional representation on a voluntary basis.

NOW also encourages women to be involved in politics but is more inclined to concentrate on supporting issues and lobbying legislatures to upgrade the status of women.

There is scanty empirical research on the activism of women. No more than 10 percent of the population, including men, can be counted as party or candidate workers. An exception in terms of women's involvement is found in Jeane Kirkpatrick's research on women who attended the national conventions in 1972:

> The principal hypothesis of this study is that there were among the delegates to the two conventions of 1972 political types whose personal and political goals, resources, and styles differed in identifiable ways from those of the political actors who have dominated presidential politics in the past decades, that these distinctive traits were associated with sex, political generation, candidate preference, and social structure; and that they have important political implications for the future of the presidential parties.[15]

Her hypothesis was confirmed and is reinforced by the data which describe the women who attended the International Women's Year Conference in Houston, Texas, in 1977. At a minimum, it can be stated that the patterns of behavior for women in activist politics are undergoing fundamental change from the passive volunteer to a more articulate participant.

THE INFLUENCE OF WOMEN ON PUBLIC POLICY

Women have always had influence as lobbyists in voluntary groups and organizations, such as the League of Women Voters. A host of related women's organizations has been energized at local, county, and state levels to press for causes that pertain to upgrading the status of women. A most helpful development has been the broadening of the support for many of the goals of women's groups to include men and women in all walks of life. A key factor indicative of the increasing political awareness and support is found in the Equal Rights Amendment (ERA). Since 1975 public opinion polls have found support for this controversial legislation among the majority of women and men.

The swift enactment of the ERA by Congress was testimony to the acceptance of the concept of female equality by an articulate majority of the public. Jo Freeman, in her account of the origin of the women's liberation movement, makes the important point that legislative support to upgrade the status of women followed closely on the heels of the passage of civil rights legislation when the country and Congress seemed to be in a mood to legislate for equality.[16]

The importance of the ERA cannot be overestimated. The crucial point is simply that women in America have always been discriminated against on the basis of the law and by the courts. The legal status of women has heavily influenced their economic and social roles in society. Speaking to an undergraduate course in 1971 at Eastern Michigan University, Congresswoman Griffiths stated that she hoped to live long enough to see the Supreme Court recognize a woman as a person. Her statement attests to the importance of the passage of the ERA by Congress and the final ratification needed from the states. The amendment reads:

Section 1. Equality of rights under the law shall not be denied or abridged by the United States or by any State on account of sex.

Section 2. The Congress shall have the power to enforce, by appropriate legislation, the provisions of this article.

Section 3. This amendment shall take effect two years after the date of ratification.

There have been legislative acts, Supreme Court decisions, and programs such as affirmative action in the 1960s and the 1970s which have made possible actual improvement in the status of women. However, many programs lag: Thousands of cases languish in courts; business, industry, governmental bureaucracies, universities, and other institutions have often been slow to carry out the provisions of acts of legislatures or the courts.

The principal adversaries to the ERA have been women's organizations of conservative ideologies and antiabortionists both in and outside various church groups. Despite the opposition of well-organized, well-financed groups that went to the International Women's Year Conference in Houston, Texas, in 1977 to kill the ERA, the conference went on record at its first voting session to approve state ratification of the ERA. The action at Houston was well supported in public opinion polls which found that the majority of the citizens in the United States favored improving the status of women and specifically supported the ERA.

The cutting edge of the ERA is that its final ratification by the states gives a legitimacy to actions by the women's movement to place new pressures on state legislatures, the Congress, and the state and federal courts to provide equity for women in enforcing existing legislation and in removing barriers of inequality and injustice for men and women.

GENDER DIFFERENCES ON ISSUES

A key question which is only partially answered is whether or not women and men differ sufficiently in political behavior and attitudes to make a difference in outcome if more women voted as a bloc and if more women were elected to high political office. This analyst has published in other research that women differ somewhat on issues pertaining to military force and involvement in wars. Survey data from the 1950s indicated that women were more likely than men to oppose sending troops to Korea, and in the 1960s women were more likely than men to take dovish positions regarding the war in Southeast Asia. Women also seem somewhat more tolerant on civil rights–libertarian issues.[17] However, research on legislative behavior has been limited by the low numbers serving in elected positions. The columnist Clayton Fritchey commented on this question in relation to the women's caucus in the House of Representatives:

> There is not much wrong with America that couldn't be cured if the majority of the population [women] was fairly represented in Congress. Also, with a woman in the White House the country might avoid war, if for no other reason than that women are seldom afflicted with machismo, the most dangerous vice of male Presidents.
>
> The belief that women officeholders tend, more than men, to oppose a belligerent foreign policy and extravagant military spending is borne out by a study of the 1975 voting records of women members of Congress, the first such analysis ever made. There are now 19 women in the House and they voted unanimously against U.S. involvement in the Angolan war, including the five women Republicans who had the courage to go against the policy of their own party leader.
>
> Large majorities of the 19 women also opposed the leaders of both major parties in voting against the costly new B-1 bomber. They balked at providing

arms or security aid to the Chilean military dictatorship; they supported a ban on using U.S. funds to plan assassinations or to influence foreign elections.

All but two of the group voted to override President Ford's vetoes of a bill controlling strip-mining and legislation creating a public works jobs program. A majority of the women of both parties had voting records more liberal than their party leaders'.[17]

CONCLUSIONS

Partly because of the development of the women's movement in the early 1960s, women have made actual gains in the political life of America. Women today are voting at higher rates than in the 1950s and are becoming more active in political campaigns and in lobbying for issues crucial to improving women's life-styles and legal status. These gains are significant because they represent a political reawakening for women.

There are also some trends that suggest that women may eventually achieve more power as political elites. This dramatic change, however, will depend on a continuing transformation of cultural attitudes which have previously viewed politics as belonging to the world of men. It will also depend on women's entering the network of training and occupations for recruitment to political office. Most important, for women to join the mainstream of political power in America, there will have to be a recognition that a cohesive female bloc vote must be organized. If these conditions are met, women may indeed achieve equality in the legal and political processes.

NOTES

1. The literature on voting behavior is vast. See, for example, Angus Campbell, Philip Converse, Warren Miller, Donald Stokes, *The American Voter* (New York: John Wiley & Sons, Inc., 1964). See Sidney Verba and Norma H. Nie, *Participation in America: Political Democracy and Social Equality,* (New York: Harper & Row, Publishers, Inc., 1972). See Marjorie Lansing, "The American Woman: Voter and Activist," in *Women in Politics,* ed. Jean Jaquette (New York: John Wiley & Sons, Inc., 1974).

2. Mary R. Beard, *Women as a Force in History* (New York: The Macmillan Company, 1964), Chap. 5.

3. For the history of the women's rights movement in the United States, see Eleanor Flexner, *Century of Struggle* (New York: Atheneum Publishers, 1974).

4. William L. O'Neill, *Everyone Was Brave: The Rise and Fall of Feminism in America* (Chicago: Quadrangle, 1969), p. 269.

5. Stuart A. Rice, *Quantitative Methods in Politics* (New York: Alfred A. Knopf, 1929), pp. 246–247. Since voting statistics are not generally recorded by gender, the vote by women before academic surveys (1948) is estimated.

6. Charles E. Merriam and Harold F. Gosnell, *Non-Voting: Causes and Methods of Control.* (Chicago: University of Chicago Press, 1925), p. ix. This study included women in the data.

7. Conference of leaders of the American Assembly of Columbia University: "Women and the American Economy: A Look at the 1980's," Martha Griffiths, Columbia University, (Englewood Cliffs, N.J., Prentice-Hall, Inc., 1976), pp. 146–147.

8. The data are from the studies of the national electorate made by the Center for Political Studies at the University of Michigan, which bears no responsibility for this analysis.

9. The Center for Political Studies developed a Scale of Political Efficacy as a measurement and has used the same questions, so that trend data are available from 1956 through 1976.

10. Data are also included from the Bureau of the Census analyses of national elections, as noted with the tables.

11. William H. Chafe, *The American Woman; Her changing Social, Economic and Political Role, 1920–1970* (New York: Oxford University Press, 1972), chap. 6.

12. Mary Cornelia Porter and Ann B. Matasar, "The Role and Status of Women in the Daley Organization," in Jaquette, *Women in Politics,* pp. 85–108.

13. *The Amateur Democrat: Club Politics in Three Cities* (Chicago: University of Chicago Press, 1962), p. 13.

14. Nancy Reeves, *Womankind* (Aldine/Atherton, 1971), p. 76.

15. Jeane Kirkpatrick, *The New Presidential Elite* (Russell Sage Foundation, Twentieth Century Fund, 1976), p. 16.

16. Jo Freeman, *The Politics of Women's Liberation* (New York: David McKay Co., Inc., 1975).

17. Clayton Fritchey, column in *Los Angeles Times,* April 25, 1976.

REVIEW QUESTIONS

1. Write a short essay in which you describe how you were politically socialized.
2. Can you think of examples from your personal experience of the ways in which the agents of socialization affected your values or attitudes concerning politics?
3. Prepare an argument for and against this proposition: Women are psychologically unsuited for the rigors of office-holding.
4. Evaluate the role of campaign financing in relation to the success or failure of women candidates who have run for political office.
5. Social scientists have found from analysis of survey data of national elections that there is a strong link between the level of education of the individual woman and her voting performance. Can you explain this relationship?
6. As women continue to enter the paid work force in greater numbers, what is likely to be the effect on the turnout of women at the polls?
7. Compare the old-style female member of Congress who entered on the coattails of a husband or father with the new type exemplified by more recent elected members, such as Shirley Chisolm or Elizabeth Holtzman.
8. What is the importance of the increasing enrollment of women in professional schools, such as law school, in relation to the recruitment of political candidates?
9. The French have a saying, *"Vive la différence."* In your opinion, what difference would it make if more women were elected to elite political positions in terms of policy outcome? Is there empirical evidence on this question?
10. Do you aspire to run for political office? What is your motivation? What are the possibilities for your success?

CHAPTER 10

The Future of Sex Roles

Meda Rebecca and Robert Hefner

The future of sex roles, especially the idea that future sex roles may be very different from sex roles today, is of interest to everybody. Many people from all segments of society are unhappy about sex roles as they are today. Both the stereotypes and the actuality of roles for women are seen as limiting and destructive to women, to marriage, and to society. A long string of actions, beginning with the Civil Rights Act of 1964, have attacked these limitations through legislation, judicial decisions, executive orders of various presidents, and constitutional amendments. One wing of the women's liberation movement places primary stress on these requirements for legal equality.

Another wing of the women's movement stresses instead a feminine takeover of society, maintaining that only women know how to run things—only women have the right values and therefore only women can get us out of the mess that men have made of the world.

Gay liberation adds another set of criticisms of conventional heterosexual patterns, male dominance, female submissiveness, and rampant homophobia (an excessive and irrational fear of homosexuality on the part of "straight" people).

Of course, all these movements also bring out a backlash from those who loudly assert that sex roles indeed present a problem—but that problem is in the breakdown of the stereotype. They say we need to return to marriages of the dominant-male-and-submissive-female type so that women can once again be happy serving men and so that men will not feel threats to their masculinity and potency. From this perspective it is the liberation movements themselves that represent a danger.

When we look at the rapidly growing literature on sex roles, we find little basis for an analysis of all these diverse positions; each new book or article seems to have a new complaint, another area to discuss (who asks whom for a date? what about women in "male" careers? what is happening to virile men?). In order to develop a systematic analysis, we have attempted to reduce the conflicting opinions to a common framework—a common basis on which they can be compared. In other words, what we are presenting here is a systematic analysis of various political positions (ideologies) about how women and men should interact in the future.

We shall also present examples from the contemporary debates: Should women accommodate to male definitions of success, develop new definitions for both men and women, or pursue goals different from those pursued by men? Should women seek maximum interaction with men in integrated schools and colleges, heterosexual couples, heterosexual communes, or common political organizations; or should they seek minimal interaction in separate schools and colleges, lesbian couples, women's communes, separate businesses, and separate women's political organizations? We are, in short, addressing the questions of what is (and will be) a woman's identity; how this identity is influenced by unity with other women; and what this identity means for participation in society.

TRADITIONAL SEX ROLES AND BEYOND

Before we discuss the possibilities for where women and society will go, we shall review some of the ideas about sex-role socialization (as presented in Chapter 5) and discuss two important theories of change in sex-role behavior: androgyny and sex-role transcendence.

The *traditional* beliefs and studies about masculinity and femininity assume that at the end point of sex-role development a person should display exclusively either masculine or feminine characteristics. These studies further state that these characteristics are opposite to each other in quality, that every "normal" person of a particular sex should display the "appropriate" characteristics, and that once these characteristics are learned, no further change is necessary or desirable. Thus the "typical" or "normal" or "ideal" woman is nurturant, dependent, expressive, emotional at adolescence—and stays that way throughout her adult life—and *every* woman should be described in this way. If a woman does not fit the ideal, she should strive toward it. As we learned in Chapters 4 and 6, stereotypes are strongly embedded in our thinking and in society and are very restrictive to identity formation in adolescence.

Consider your own life: Do the stereotypes of sex-role behavior seem reasonable? Does sex-role development end at adolescence? Are masculinity and femininity opposites, which is to say that you cannot possess one if you have the other? Can all women be put in one category and all men in another?

The literature on androgyny has attempted to correct the major shortcomings in the studies of sex roles and opens the way to thinking about identity without the restrictions of stereotypes.[1] Androgyny is the belief that sex-role behavior may extend beyond the narrow stereotypes prescribed by both the scientific literature and society. In the androgynous vision of the world a person may want, and need, to combine masculine and feminine characteristics. Thus, if a person is androgynous, she or he could be assertive during an argument and nurturant when interacting with a child. Whereas traditional theories identify women in terms of their femininity, androgyny identifies women in terms of both femininity and masculinity. The new ideal is a blend of feminine and masculine characteristics in the same person.

The concept of androgyny includes the following beliefs:

1. Present ideas of "feminine" and "masculine" are legitimate concepts and perhaps valuable for certain purposes. However, the rigid division between them (including the fixed linkage to biological sex) is quite artificial and damaging to individual women and men who do not perfectly fit the stereotypes. Thus the division is not functional for the society as a whole.

2. One can accept the concepts of "masculinity" and "femininity," but it is still possible to see the concepts in much broader light—perhaps as ladders on which individuals may vary from low to high.[2]

3. Androgyny also includes the ideas that behaving in a way different from one's biological sex (or in cross-sex manner) is not deviant or sick behavior.

4. Heterosexuality is not necessarily the expectation that will be held for a person's affectional or sexual choice; people may be homosexual, bisexual, or asexual.

5. The new ideal for both males and females would be a blend of masculine and feminine characteristics. As Kaplan and Bean have written:

> When we use the word *androgyny* . . . , we mean flexibility of sex role. We refer not to individuals with male and female sex organs, but to individuals who are capable of behaving in integrative feminine and masculine ways, who are assertive and yielding, independent and dependent, expresssive and instrumental.[3]

Although the work on androgyny is a major advance in our view of sex roles, we still do not know if this abstract concept captures all the different ways that people behave in real life. We do not know how a person becomes androgynous, if androgyny has a distinct place in the development of sex roles, or if, indeed, androgyny is itself an end point. The sweeping societal changes in roles for women and men that are already occurring remind us that we must not be content with any one concept of the nature of people. This is why we have thought out a developmental model of sex-role transcendence which tries to capture the emerging possibilities—possibilities that might be quite different from the way of life we now know.[4] Transcendence means to go beyond what we know. In the area of sex roles it means to go beyond the rigid definitions of masculinity and femininity so that these terms lose their meaning. The basic questions are: How did we get to be the way we are? Where are we going in the future?

Briefly, in Stage I of our theory children have no knowledge of sex roles. In Stage II people behave according to the polarized stereotypes of masculinity and femininity. Sex-role transcendence occurs in Stage III. Sex-role transcendence is an idea involving choices of behavior which are in no way related to biological sex or even to the concepts of masculinity or femininity. Additionally, sex-role transcendence provides for the possibility of new behaviors or combinations of behaviors in relation to different situations and personal desire. It is thought of as a goal to be reached, and not as an end to development. The basic assumption in this model of sex-role development is that a person can continually change and develop across the entire life span. In this model, androgyny is thought of as a transitional development between the polarized roles of Stage II and the transcendence of Stage III.

Transcendence involves both situational flexibility and personal flexibility. When confronting a particular situation a person can adapt to the situation by behaving appropriately to the situation (being assertive, passive, independent, nurturant, as the *situation* requires). This is situational flexibility. Alternatively, he/she can change the situation to suit his/her needs (he/she feels more comfortable being nurturant, assertive, so he/she rearranges the structural aspects of the situation to accommodate his/her personal requirements). This is personal flexibility.

As an example, consider a woman who has entered a premed curriculum. This woman may have been socialized to be cooperative, sensitive, nurturant, and nonassertive. She enrolls in chemistry, biology, and other required courses and finds the environment competitive. Although there are several solutions to this problem, it would probably be proposed that the woman either adjust to the situation or drop out of the program. The tendency (even for those hoping for her success), then, would be to blame the woman and perhaps suggest ways for her to adapt to the situation. At the individual level, the woman may be able on her own to learn how to behave in such a way as to succeed in these classes. Or she may enlist the help of various programs such as assertiveness training.

But this is only one alternative. She may also decide *not* to adapt to the situation by being competitive herself; rather she may opt to change the structure of the classes by setting up collectives of women in each class who are committed to work *cooperatively* in order to help each other. In this way the student is engaging in much more far-reaching change. Rather than adjusting to a situation defined by male clues, she would be undercutting this culture and creating alternative solutions.

Transcendence, then, involves several levels of change. It has to do with going completely beyond (transcending) present gender specific behavior, personality, and expectations. This is something quite different from a mere time-sharing of masculine and feminine characteristics in the same person, nor is it a mere freeing of both females and males to be both masculine and feminine. It requires the invention of new ways of being that are not merely fusions of what we already know, as in the medical school example.

The cumulative impact of individual and group changes happening in this way in many different places in society would be a genuine cultural change —a redefinition of what we understand as success. At the very least, we would have a pluralism in which alternative models of success are accepted, not only those male values that are currently dominant.

AN ANDROGYNOUS, OR TRANSCENDENT, FUTURE

As mentioned earlier, according to traditional theories of sex roles, a woman's identity is defined by rigid adherence to the "feminine" stereotype. Therefore her participation in society is limited to the roles and activities of wife and mother within the family system. Owing to the nature of the nuclear family, she is isolated from other women and indeed from peers of both sexes. In an androgynous conception of sex roles a woman's identity is defined by both feminine and masculine characteristics. She may be both passive and assertive or dependent and independent depending on the situation. Thus the woman would no longer be restricted to family roles; she could also participate in the public sphere of society (for example, by being employed) without being considered deviant or destructive to the family. In this way there is an increased opportunity to interact with peers or colleagues outside the family. The idea of sex-role transcendence encompasses the options available with androgyny. However, even more options will be available when people and society no longer think in terms of gender. A woman will be nurturant not because it is feminine but because she needs or wants to be nurturant. She will have the option of a multiplicity of roles, but without the requirement that she engage in just one particular role. She may want to raise a family or have a career or do both. She may want to remain single or to marry but not have children. No role or activity will be denied her because of biological sex, nor will any role be considered better or more worthy than others.

INDIVIDUAL DEVELOPMENT AND SOCIETAL ORGANIZATION

Obviously there are many ideas about what sex roles should be like. Everyone is not going to change suddenly to androgyny or sex-role transcendence. Some people will not accept the *idea* of moving beyond traditional sex roles. Other people want to change but are not able to because their jobs and their families, among other factors, hold them back.

The possibilities of androgyny or sex-role transcendence at the individual level are very much dependent on the whole network of interaction at the societal and cultural levels. Androgynous or transcendent beliefs will foster new ideas about interaction at the societal level. Likewise, different societal systems will facilitate or inhibit sex-role development beyond the traditional stereotypes.

There are a number of different possibilities of how men and women will interact in the future. We are talking about ideas of different forms of societal organization which correspond to different levels of individual sex-role development. We can arrange different positions along a neat one-dimensional continuum* by considering the *degree* of power and control over the terms of the interaction exerted by the dominant group or, conversely, by the subordinate group (see Figure 10.1).†

Positions at both ends of this continuum represent extremes that are highly unlikely, given the fairly even population split between females and males and the fact that both groups are now educated, articulate, and consciously aware of at least some of the consequences of extreme oppression. Open support for the extreme position is voiced by only a tiny fraction.[5] Therefore for most of the discussion here we will confine ourselves to the five positions in the middle that seem to be the focus of most discussions for change.

Table 10.1 presents a brief positive statement of each position, that is, a noncritical statement from the perspective of a sincere believer of the position. Clearly each of these ideologies of societal organization has implications for the way individual women and men should be and behave and, therefore, for their individual sex-role socialization. In terms of the concepts described earlier:

1. Exclusion of females and male supremacy require hyperpolarized, nonoverlapping roles (traditional sex roles).
2. The melting-pot concept requires an androgynous merger of masculine and feminine roles.
3. Conservative pluralism requires a reaffirmation of the distinctiveness and value of both feminine and masculine roles.
4. Emergent pluralism requires a transcendence of sex roles, with the emergence of differentiated, multiple ways to be, not based on sex.

There is no agreement inside or outside the women's movement about what the desired future is. Therefore, there are groups pushing for a variety of changes. Sometimes these groups have overlapping goals. For example, even conservatives agree that women who are doing the same work as men deserve equal pay for equal work. Sometimes the groups have directly conflicting goals. For example, some groups want to take women into already existing

---

*This is not to say that it is really so simple; there are other differences in ideology also. For example, some people supporting the "melting-pot" ideology assume that feminine values will predominate; others assume that the common values will be mostly masculine.

†We assume at the outset that women are a subordinate group in our society.

structures, even if these structures continue to be dominated by men for the time being. Other groups want women to stop interacting with men and to form, for example, their own businesses, political parties, even if these groups are less effective than existing male-dominated groups for the time being.

But that is not all. There are also groups who do not want any change or who want changes returning to the alleged "good old days." The well-financed resistance to the constitutional amendment banning sex discrimination, the ERA, is but one example of this no-change orientation. In part such resistance is clearly related to the economic advantage conferred on certain groups by the present position of women in our society. One estimate is that equal pay for equal work in the present work force (that is, not assuming the emergence of new opportunities for employment or advancement of women) would cost American businesses about $90 billion per year. If a requirement of equal pay for equal work is a real result of the ERA (presumably it would also require explicit congressional action based on the ERA), then it is easy to imagine how opposition to the ERA can get funding from business organizations.

Therefore the present situation is presumably the net result of these conflicting political pressures as well as changes in individual sex-role development.

In spite of many changes at the individual and societal levels, why is it that we (individually, organizationally, and societally) seem to be stuck in a hyperpolarized, stereotyped way of thinking about sex roles? To put it another way: Everyone used to assume that people developed to traditional sex roles and then stopped; that assumption defined the ideal, the goal, and the healthy state for normal adults. But the myth of sex-role stereotypes has now been shattered by the many people who do not fit the pattern, by the political impact of a new women's consciousness, and by those who actively imagine new futures.

And yet, in spite of shattered myths, many of us still find our lives molded in the old familiar stereotypes. Even among those whose lives have changed drastically, there are times when the old stereotypes dominate. Why are traditional sex roles so persistent and how will change come about? The next section of the chapter describes some of the conservative patterns that inhibit change and then attempts to describe a variety of possible strategies for change.

INHIBITIONS TO CHANGE, STRATEGIES FOR CHANGE, AND RESTRICTIVE PATTERNS THAT INHIBIT CHANGE

One of the critical shortcomings of traditional approaches to socialization is that socialization implies continuation of the status quo. However, this idea

Figure 10.1. Ideologies of Societal Organization

Position	Underlying Continuum		Subcategories	Examples
	0%	100%		
1. Revolution and female supremacy			a. Total male genocide b. Partial male genocide c. Control	SCUM (Society for Cutting Up Men) High risk for males (e.g., birth control)
2. Separatism			a. Total b. Partial c. Temporary	Feminist separatist communes One-sex religious communities
3. Emergent pluralism	Degree of control over the terms of the relationship exerted by the *dominant* group	Degree of control over the terms of the relationship exerted by the *subordinate* group		Sex-role transcendence
4. Conservative pluralism				Equal valuation but traditional role divisions
5. Melting pot				Unisex identity Androgyny
6. Assimilation to male model of success	50%	50%	a. Total b. Partial	Antidiscrimination laws Program for teaching women "male" skills
7. Exclusion of females			a. Partial b. Total	Catholic education Toilets and showers Purdah
8. Male supremacy	100%	0%	a. Control b. Partial female genocide c. Total female genocide	High risk for females (e.g., birth control) Female infanticide

TABLE 10.1.   Five Ideologies of Societal Organization

Emergent pluralism

A pluralistic society where all options are open to everyone and where true equality is afforded to all ways of living. However, it is fruitless to talk of this ideal arising out of present conceptions of masculinity and femininity. These positions are already defined as different and unequal, and each is hopelessly contaminated by the master-slave game now going on. We must develop opportunities to create multiple new concepts.

Conservative pluralism
Present masculine and feminine roles are preserved.

Both masculine and feminine values and roles are important, functional, and necessary to society. The tasks of society in the family, the home, the economy, the government, must all get done, and we must see to it that all roles are equally valued and rewarded. All people must be guaranteed the right to participate fully in the larger society without discrimination.

Melting pot

In order to bring about a society with unisexual human values, there should be a cultural merger of the sexes—the complete disappearance of sex differences. This will produce a new society in which neither "masculine" nor "feminine" roles are valued, but new ideas combining the best of both are developed. When this is accomplished, past differentiations will be gone and men and women will have identical androgynous roles.

Assimilation to male model of success

The present criteria for success in our society are clear-cut and functional. Women have sometimes been discriminated against in their attempts to join the masculine world. Women who want to do so should be given the opportunity to meet these criteria by relinquishing those feminine values that are opposed to success in the real world. Full participation is available to any woman who can meet the requirements, and there should be equal pay for equal work and no discrimination based on sex.

Female exclusion
The traditional pattern in our society.

Because women are biologically different from men, they perform less effectively in many areas of life. Therefore, for the benefit of both men and women, women need to be physically separated from men in various areas of our society, such as industry and schools. In other areas women interfere with the productivity and satisfaction of men engaged in the activities of these areas (athletics, bars, clubs); therefore they should be excluded from them.

that people learn static lessons from a culture does not have to be true. Several people have offered concepts of socialization that do take into account historical change. In Bengston and Black's definition, socialization is a bilateral process in which the parent generation and the child generation influence *each other* by negotiating those factors leading to change or to traditional behavior.[6] The idea of parent-child conflict causing rethinking and change can also be seen in larger, somewhat more theoretical terms.

Change and Growth as Part of Socialization

Our ideas about sex-role transcendence focus on conflict, contradiction, and change. The emphasis is on movement instead of equilibrium. Sex-role socialization is not accounted for solely by piecemeal learning or by thinking through changes in behavior. For example, a woman may be psychologically prepared to enter a male-dominated field, but she receives no cultural support. This is a conflict between her psychological development and the culture. How the woman resolves this conflict—by giving in, changing herself, and/or helping to change society—will affect the direction of her growth and societal change.

To clarify this, let us look at several additional examples pertinent to sex roles. Conflict occurs between the physical capacity of women and employment laws governing how much women are allowed to lift. Women can easily lift far more than the thirty pounds they are allowed under some laws. Indeed, some women with children lift much heavier loads many times every day. Conflict also occurs when a woman socialized to traditional feminine roles receives messages from the women's movement that there are alternative life-styles possible now in the society. For a married couple, conflict may occur over the man's career development and the woman's career development. Conflict occurs when an economic recession (meaning no new jobs) comes at a time of "required" affirmative action in employment. The important point in all of these examples is that conflict pushes the individual, group, and/or society to change. An imbalance exists which forces adaptation, change, and (ideally) growth. From the resolution of conflict comes a new stage of balance and new interaction.

It is apparent from this approach that balance or equilibrium is not the most interesting or useful state to study; to study merely the resolution of a conflict, and not its sources and further consequences, obscures the process by which people develop. Thus we must study the changes, not just the equilibrium. This approach also stresses that change involves both individuals and cultural practices, not one without the other.

Change at the Individual Level

We believe that proposals for change based on changing women as individuals are almost certain to fail, if practiced alone, and consequently that failure is seen as "proof" that real change is not possible.[7] (Many of these blame the victim and are fundamentally politically reactionary.)[8] Note that we are *not* saying that individuals do not need to change. We think that strategies for individual change are an important (vital) *part* of overall strategies for change that focus upon societal, institutional, and organizational change *in addition to* changing the "victims" of past and present practices.

As a concrete example, suppose someone suggests training junior-high-school girls in skills required for baseball, basketball, and football so that they can more equally participate with boys in sports. By itself, without other changes, this is a blame-the-victim program. It asserts that there is something wrong with junior-high girls, which has prevented full integration of sports activities, and proposes to remedy the situation by changing the girls. You will probably agree that such a program is bound to fail (that is, to result in few or no girls being accepted on varsity teams in these sports). However, such a training program, if combined with a number of other changes, might be positive, beneficial, and successful. You might, as an exercise, try to design such a program for change. It might include, for example, shifting the emphasis in athletics from interschool competition to individual development and widespread participation. It might be necessary to change the rules of the state interscholastic athletic association concerning mixed-sex participation, and also competition of limited groups (e.g., football for those under 120 pounds, basketball for those shorter than five feet six inches). Maybe you need to look at recruitment and training of women coaches and also at sensitization of male coaches to special problems in coaching girls. Another approach would be to train boys in traditionally female athletic participation (e.g., dance, field hockey). Outside the school itself changes in community groups like the Little League and in recreational hockey—which would include ending exclusion of girls and emphasizing participation instead of competition—are also needed. Media coverage of sports needs to change from its present tendency to focus on male superstars to greater coverage of women and recreational and individual development activities, among other things. You can probably think of many more approaches. Thus we must have cultural and institutional change as well as individual change.

Change in Science

Scientific studies are part of our *mis*understanding of sex roles. We have seen that traditional socialization tries to keep the equilibrium or status quo and does not admit the role of change. A further problem is that support for traditional sex roles is frequently based on biased scientific studies which prescribe what one should be or do. The traditional social science literature perpetuates a view of women, and of women's capacities, as inferior to men and to men's roles. Although traditional scientists believe that science is value-free and that scientific conclusions are based on reliable results obtained by valid research, these beliefs about science are false. Assumptions and value judgments underlie approaches to scientific theory and research design and lead traditional science to a picture of women as inferior to men, thus justifying sex discrimination.

As we have seen, one of these scientific assumptions about sex roles is based on the two-sided view of sex roles in which women are childbearers and rearers in the private sphere and men are creators and controllers in the public sphere. These views are only taken from the larger society; but the scientists who believe them make them appear more valid by claiming that they are scientific observations, not merely personal biases. The studies systematically set out to prove scientifically the differences between roles. Studies that document overlaps and similarities between the sexes are rare, either because they are not designed or because they are not published (see note 4 for documentation). Areas of female superiority or uniquely female characteristics are also inadequately treated in the professional literature. This value bias in favor of traditional roles is usually ignored or denied in the traditional views of science.

We must recognize how important these scientific values are for social change. We then need to attempt to develop a vision of social change that will direct the course of scientific research as well as grow out of it. If scientists believe in the possibility of sex-role transcendence, and design research accordingly, the results can have far-reaching effects in many sectors of society. It shows people that there are alternative ways of development. Thus we know that we need scientific research and change strategies based on the idea of transcendence of sex roles and not just an explanation of traditional socialization.

Change at the Cultural Level

There are also problems when one focuses on institutional and cultural change. Different concepts about change make fundamentally different assumptions about what is required. Many programs suggested clearly presume the goodwill and good intent of all involved to end sex discrimination as soon as possible. Thus many timetables for change assume that problems of sex-role stereotyping and sex discrimination will all be cleared up in just a few years. For example, the Women's Educational Equity Act, in the U.S. Office of Education, was set up by Congress for a three-year period expiring in 1978. Many public service organizations have set up programs with foundation funds that clearly will not be available for more than a few years at most, with no provision for alternative funding. School districts, businesses, and government agencies frequently set up short-term (e.g., two-day) training programs, perhaps with a brief follow-up after one year. We need to recognize that changes will need long-term support.

On the other hand, some people expect programs for change to require a major social revolution, including overthrow of the present form of government and establishment of a different form of society, following which there would be a sudden (or, perhaps, gradual) end to problems of sex discrimination. Others speak of working within the present framework but giving up on those people already (mis)socialized, putting off a complete solution to sex discrimination until there is an essentially complete population turnover (after perhaps eighty years). This view is just as unrealistic. We must begin change now.

Probably the most important difference between those who see short-term solutions to the problem and those who take a much longer time perspective has to do with the perception of resistance to change. Are both men and women ready to change if some advantages are demonstrated for more flexible sex roles (in which case changes could occur rapidly)? Or is there a fundamental threat to the entrenched, privileged position of men in any program for change (in which case men will resist the changes, and thus change will come about much slower)? It seems that there are clearly elements of both. The question is, How can we emphasize the advantages of sex-role change rather than its threatening aspects?

SCENARIOS FOR THE FUTURE

The utopian ideal for the future that guides efforts to effect social change is one of a completely nonsexist society. That future might be perceived in terms of a unisex melting pot, with a complete absence of sex-role differentiations. On the other hand, the ideal future might be seen as a pluralistic society with sex and gender differentiations (or perhaps other differentiations no longer linked to sex) but with complete equality for men and women. Figure 10.2 indicates some of the possible changes that might take place in the spiral of historical changes in sex roles and provides a way to look at the dynamics of these changes as they proceed (or might proceed) over time. The positions indicated are those presented earlier in Figure 10.1 and Table 10.1.

Various groups urge and work toward different changes, depending on their perspective and ideology. Feminist revolutionaries argue for a female takeover, with a temporary shift to female domination (G in Figure 10.2) mirroring the present male domination. This requires that women unify in order to carry out such a revolution, becoming the dominant groups in the postrevolutionary society, with men in distinctly subordinate roles. It does not require that a female-dominated society has to be just like a male-dominated society, however. For one thing, there is an explicit ideology that the female domination would be temporary—a step on the way toward a future egalitarian society. It is a necessary step (to enable women to develop the knowledge and skills needed for the egalitarian society and to enable men to develop the motivation needed to move on to the new society) but not a *permanent* view of what society should be like. Also, women have a long history of oppression, which should give them some insight into, and empathy for, the newly oppressed men.

A DIRECT MOVE TO SEX-ROLE TRANSCENDENCE

Others who view the present male holders of power as more neutral (and/ or as also disadvantaged by their present dominant role,[9] and willing to give up their present dominance voluntarily) argue instead for moving to emergent pluralism or sex-role transcendence (H) from our current situation (D). One

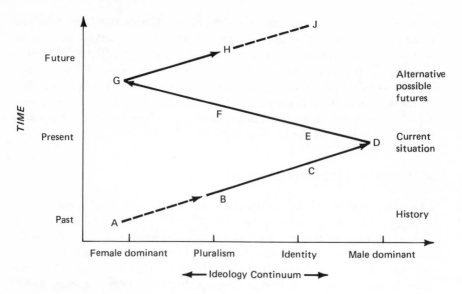

Figure 10.2.   Spiral of Sex-Role Changes

A = Alleged ancient "primitive" matriarchy.

B = Ancient "primitive" egalitarian division of labor, all roles equally valued.

C = "Primitive" attempt at identical sex roles: does not work when childbearing is a dominant feature of most women's lives.

D = *Present* male domination, devaluing of women's separate roles.

E = Assimilation to male model of success—all alike, *according to present male model*; not the most preferred position of presently dominant males, but the compromise, and attempted cooptation, by males faced with threat of change to F, G, H, or J.

F = Conservative pluralism, as defined in Table 10.1; equal valuation of distinct male and female roles.

G = Female domination, *reversal* of present patterns, reached through revolution.

H = Emergent pluralism of future, reachable because both males and females (after G) have interest and motivation to get there through their historical experience.

J = Genuine melting pot (not assimilation), a unisex combining best of masculine and feminine characters.

would break both the restrictions in "masculine" and "feminine" life-styles and the linking of styles to biological sex (that is, any person could choose any style, without regard to sex). Still others want to move to a melting-pot, unisex future with identical roles for women and men (J). In this view, people would adopt the best of each of their past roles into one common, universal life-style.[10]

Of course, the dominant masculine society also has a concept of a sex-differentiated future (in effect, a return to the "good-old-days"). One version of this theme resists any change at all, or even argues for *negative* change, that is, turning back the clock to an alleged historical period when sex roles were presumably clearer and unquestioned. In those days women supposedly

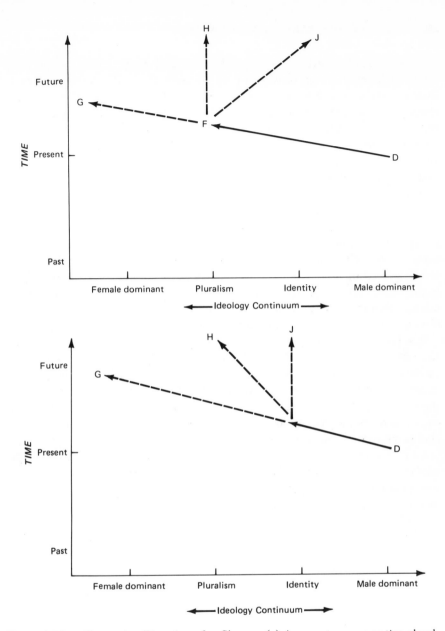

Figure 10.3. Alternative Directions for Change. (a) A move to conservative plural-ism (F) results in continued dissatisfaction with restricted roles; but women have more economic power (from such programs as pay and retirement benefits for house-work); so further changes occur to female domination (G), (H), or melting pot (J). (b) Assimilation of some women to the male model of success (E) results in contin-uing dissatisfaction as well as many women who have decision-making and economic power; they use this power to move on to more desirable alternatives (G, H, J). Assimilation is the most common pattern at the present time.

achieved gratification by serving, and vicariously participating in the successes of, powerful men to whom they were attached. (This version argues that we are now somewhere between D and E on the spiral of sex-role changes and should move back to D.)[11] The literature propounding this view often blames most faults of the modern world on the blurring of distinctions between men and women.[12] In the second sentence of *The Feminized Male* the author remarkably manages to blame mixed-up sex roles for the assassinations of John and Robert Kennedy.[13]

A quite different theme suggests accommodation to pressures for change by making minimal changes, coopting* the leadership of the challenging groups, using divide-and-conquer strategies with the contending change groups—in general, bringing to bear all of the conventional political machinations to deal with challenges to established authority. Since cooptation involves admitting *some* women into male-dominated and male-defined roles in this society, strategy requires at least partial assimilation (E). A few women are accepted in what remains a male-dominated world. These women must identify with male values and male colleagues in order to succeed.

It is important to see that such accommodation seldom completely stems the tide of pressures for change. When assimilation to the male model of success persists as the main strategy, not every woman will be "bought off" in this manner and change her private views. In the long run this may mean the creation of a substantial number of women who do have the power and the skills to change society more to their own liking and who can unify with similar women to bring about these changes.

Thus, for example, the very few women in top positions in the federal government were traditionally believed to be docile and content with their own positions in the male-dominated hierarchy. But, angered by the refusal of other federal officials to enforce the provisions of the 1964 Civil Rights Act which prohibited sex discrimination in public accommodations (the men in charge of enforcement said the act was just a joke in Congress, and they did not intend to enforce it), these women became the core of a new lobby to compel compliance with the law, the National Organization for Women.[14]

Therefore these women may use their power (in decision making, in financial control, in political influence) to achieve concrete gains in other areas of importance to women: for example, passage of the ERA and the creation of equal employment opportunities for many women (instead of just a few token women). The changes are often far beyond what is intended when they are first introduced (consider our total failure to predict or understand the consequences for the entire society of the introduction of the automobile or

*To coopt is to take over or buy off individuals. Through financial and career incentives, the women who are the leaders of groups challenging the male establishment can be encouraged to join the establishment, rather than continue the challenge. Of course, joining the establishment is only possible if one gives up wild ideas and adjusts one's views so that one fits in comfortably.

effective birth-control procedures). It seems clear that the entering wedge of newly liberated women will have equally broad (and equally unexpected) impacts on our society as a whole. It is an exciting challenge to try to anticipate these societal movements (see Figure 10.3).

In summary, we note that people who want to change the role of women in the society have many different goals. Some want women and men to be exactly the same in a unisex society. Some want to return to traditional differences such as they were "when men were men." Still others want to assimilate some women into occupations that are traditionally male, while preserving the options of traditional roles and marriages for women and men who choose that route.

And there are also strong disagreements about the tactics for changing society in the desired direction. Some tactics focus on individual women. Assertiveness training or career preparation helps some women move into areas that were once almost entirely male. Or programs aimed at the "Total Woman" train women to accept and exploit a subordinate position in marriage and society. Other tactics focus on institutional change. Legislation and administrative orders require affirmative action in opening jobs or education to women. Pressure groups seek new legislation, like the ERA, and medical and vacation benefits for pregnant employees. And the advocates of the most drastic changes claim that only a complete revolution of oppressed women can change the society.

It is important for each of us to clarify our own personal ideas about the future and to relate them to this larger picture. What identity do you want for yourself in the future? Is this identity freely chosen, or is it a result of limited available options, restrictive socialization, and sexism in society? Would you want the same identity for your daughter? Your son? Everyone? Or, is your choice of identity just for yourself, with the expectation (and perhaps hope) that other people will be quite different in a pluralistic society?

We all have ideas about what contemporary women and men are like (or should be like). Some of these ideas reflect publicly held stereotypes, while others reflect the variability that exists in everyday interaction. We are more inclined to think of others in terms of stereotypes and rather less inclined to think of our own lives in that way. We also have ideas about what the future will be or should be like. This may sound like so much common sense, but once we think consciously about sex roles, it is easier to confront the stereotypes and deal realistically with future options. The mere proposal of sex-role transcendence as a stage of human development that replaces the stereotypic end point of rigid sex roles gives us another alternative. For example, consider two different mother-daughter interactions: On the one hand, a mother reinforces her little girl for rigid, typically female behaviors when she considers these the ultimate in development; on the other hand, a mother interacts more flexibly with her little girl who is behaving in a "typically feminine" way when she believes that this is merely a "stage" her daughter is going through on her way to a more flexible life-style.

In relating this to broader societal change, we must be clear about what kind of future we personally anticipate and knowledgeable about the ways likely to get us there. No matter how important sex roles are for a person, transcendence will continue to be difficult if it is not reinforced by change in society. We must allow for emerging possibilities which will come, in part, when women define who they are, independently of male definitions of them, and incorporate this self-definition into the world with which they interact. This implies that there will be new ways for women to interact with men, with women, and with their environment, which are not mere reversals of roles or combinations of roles (although these might be included among the options) but genuinely creative alternatives. The purpose of this chapter has been not to present utopian ideas of the future, but to stimulate all of us to think creatively and openly about future possibilities. We must unearth our common understandings so that they can be challenged. In the long run, society, and those of us who constitute that society, will inevitably change. Let us all be conscious of what kinds of changes we would like and how we can help bring them about!

NOTES

1. C. Heilbrun, *Toward a Recognition of Androgyny* (New York: Alfred A. Knopf, Inc., 1973); S. Bem, "The Measurement of Psychological Androgyny," *Journal of Consulting and Clinical Psychology* 42 (1974): 155–162; idem, "Sex-Role Adaptability: One Consequence of Psychological Androgyny," *Journal of Personality and Social Psychology* 31 (1975): 634–643; idem, "Probing the Promise of Androgyny," in *Beyond Sex-Role Stereotypes: Readings Toward a Psychology of Androgyny*, ed. A. Kaplan and J. Bean (Boston: Little, Brown and Company, 1976); J. T. Spence, R. Helmreich, and J. Stapp, "The Personal Attributes Questionnaire: A Measure of Sex-Role Stereotypes and Masculinity-Femininity," *JSAS Catalog of Selected Documents in Psychology* 4, 43, (Ms. No. 617).

2. Spence, Helmreich, and Stapp, "Questionnaire"; and Bem, "Probing."

3. Kaplan and Bean, *Beyond Sex-Role Stereotypes.*

4. R. Hefner, M. Rebecca, and B. Oleshansky, "Development of Sex-Role Transcendence," *Human Development* 18 (1975): 143–158; see also C. Heilbrun, "Further Notes toward a Recognition of Androgyny," *Women's Studies* 2 (1974): 143–149.

5. V. Solanas, *SCUM Manifesto* (New York: Olympia Press, Inc., 1968), excerpted in *Sisterhood Is Powerful,* ed. R. Morgan (New York: Random House, Inc., 1970).

6. V. Bengston and K. Black, "Intergenerational Relations and Continuities in Socialization," *Life-Span Developmental Psychology: Personality and Socialization,* ed. P. Baltes and K. Schaie (New York: Academic Press, Inc., 1973).

7. B. Oleshansky, M. Rebecca, V. D. Nordin, and R. Hefner, "Institutional Sexism," Report prepared for N.I.E. (Contract NIE-C-74-0144), 1974, National Institute of Education.

8. W. Ryan, *Blaming the Victim,* rev. ed. (New York: Vintage Books, 1976). A most interesting and provocative book that examines blaming the victim as a general concept about social divisions, how they occur, and how they are perpetuated. Briefly, Ryan asserts that blaming the victim is a social control mechanism designed to prevent social change, preserve the privileges of the presently dominant group, and force the subordinate group to bear most of the costs. One crucial issue in the operation of the mechanism is that the victim (through educational experiences and political socialization) shares the ideologies that place the blame on the victim instead of the larger society.

9. W. Farrell, *The Liberated Man* (New York: Random House, Inc., 1975).

10. K. DeCrow, "The Future of Sex Roles." Address delivered at the University of Michigan, January 29, 1976.

11. See, for example, M. Morgan, *Total Woman* (Old Tappan, N.J.: Fleming H. Revell Company, 1973).

12. G. Gilder, *Sexual Suicide* (New York: Quadrangle, 1973).

13. P. C. Sexton, *The Feminine Male* (New York: Vintage Books, 1969). For an excellent summary of this point of view, see C. Tavris and C. Offir, *The Longest War: Sex Differences in Perspective* (New York: Harcourt Brace Jovanovich, 1977).

14. J. Freeman, "1973, The Origins of the Women's Liberation Movement," in *Changing Women in a Changing Society,* ed. J. Huber (Chicago: University of Chicago Press, 1973).

EXERCISES

1. Describe your own daily life as you imagine it will be fifteen years from now.
2. Describe your own beliefs about sex-role development and where you are now, and will be fifteen years from now, in sex-role development.
3. Describe your own beliefs about ideal interaction between women and men and the roles they should play.
4. Discuss any contradictions between your response to question 1 and your responses to questions 2 and 3.
5. Following the model used in the chapter for junior-high-school athletics, consider a blame-the-victim analysis of women's problems in becoming physicians (or lawyers, politicians, truck drivers, engineers, managers, crane operators; select an area that is of interest to you) and attempt to restructure the situation and the possible remedies from a broader individual and societal perspective.
6. Write down your projections for a date (year) for attainment of each of the following:

	Earliest Possible Date	Most Likely Date
First woman president of U.S		
10% of members of U.S. Congress women		
25% of U.S. Senators women		
51% of U.S. Senators women		
Women's average earnings 75% of men's earnings		
Women's average earnings 100% of men's earnings		
49% of nursery school teachers male		
Men do 50% of child care in the home		

Compare your answers with those of other members of the class. Discuss where and why discrepancies occur in your projections.

CLASSROOM EXERCISE

Sex is a major organizing device that we use to see other people, judge their behavior, and plan our own reactions. Following are brief sketches of four people as they describe themselves. Their sex and relationship to each other are unidentified. However, two are women and two are men, representing two married couples. First, just read through the descriptions.

A is an attorney who values competence, openness, nurturance, and confidence. A free spirit yet serious, A likes open space and outdoor activities. Work is of primary importance to A; A's extracurricular activities are centered in the political arena.

B is an assistant professor of English whose major avocation is music. Competence and positive social relationships are central aspects of B's belief system. B strives continually for competence but dislikes pressure. Outside the work area B is a humanitarian characterized by warmth, friendliness, compassion, and sensitivity. B likes interacting with children, raises many plants, and might want to become a historical librarian in the future.

C works as a photographer, and although this is an outlet for creativity, there is no commitment to the job as a lifelong career. C values material things, likes privacy, and has a general *joie de vivre*. C is very concerned with the general quality of life and cares deeply about the happiness of other people. The education and career of C's spouse are limiting to the couple in the short run but will open up opportunities for them in the long run. C gave up a prestigious job which would have required a move, focusing instead on other aspects of life including the marriage. C does needlepoint as a hobby and is very involved with a number of pets.

D always wanted to be a doctor and is now a professor in the medical sciences. Work concerns and social relations are very important. D is both conventional and unconventional, independent and dependent; competent, intellectual, competitive, and dominant at work. In general, D is strongly influenced by the Protestant work ethic. D feels pressured at work, especially when assuming administrative responsibilities. D cooks the meals and cleans the house. D considers the spouse as a balancing influence in life and is very concerned with family and friends.

The table below lists twelve sets of two couples that you could make up from the four individuals described:

	Couple 1		Couple 2	
	Female	Male	Female	Male
	A	B	C	D
	A	C	B	D
If A is a	A	D	B	C
woman	A	B	D	C
	A	C	D	B
	A	D	C	B
	B	A	C	D
	C	A	B	D
If A is a	D	A	B	C
man	B	A	D	C
	C	A	D	B
	D	A	C	B

Which combinations would make "good" marriages? Why? Which combination do you think might represent the real situation of the four people described? Why? If you are having difficulty deciding, why is this?* These are current descriptions of four real people. If sex is used as a major organizing device, and if you had seen these people before reading about them, would you have come to different conclusions?

It should be obvious now that people depart from stereotypes even when science and society define them according to stereotypes, which prevent us from recognizing humanity as it exists today and possibilities for the future. Change is already happening, but we need a new consciousness in order to see and understand this change as well as changes that might occur in the future.

SELECTED READINGS

Bem, S. "Probing the Promise of Androgyny." In *Beyond Sex-Role Stereotypes: Readings Toward a Psychology of Androgyny,* edited by A. Kaplan and J. Bean. Boston: Little, Brown and Company, 1976.

A good summary of both the theoretical and the empirical work that Bem has done on androgyny. It includes experiments done to operationalize androgyny and explore the consequences of androgyny. The anthology itself is an excellent resource for information on what psychologists have done with the concept of androgyny and includes both critiques of the traditional sex-role literature as well as applications to several areas of psychology such as clinical practice.

Chicago, J. *Through the Flower.* New York: Doubleday & Company, Inc., Anchor Books, 1977.

Although this book was not cited in the chapter, it is a good personal account of the process an artist goes through to come to terms with her feelings as a woman and the male definition of what it is to be an artist.

Chodorow, N. "Family Structure and Feminine Personality." In *Women, Culture and Society,* edited by M. Rosaldo and L. Lamphere. Stanford: Stanford University Press, 1974.

Although Chodorow takes a psychoanalytic perspective, she introduces new twists on the traditionally male-oriented position and tries to explain the secondary status of women in terms of universal socializing experiences. The book as a whole is a good collection of mainly anthropological articles on women.

Constantinople, A. "Masculinity-Femininity: An Exception to a Famous Dictum?" *Psychological Bulletin,* 80, 1973, 389–407.

A good critique of the literature on the psychological assessment of masculinity and femininity, including an exploration of assumptions, methods, and interpretation of results.

Heilbrun, C. *Toward a Recognition of Androgyny.* New York: Alfred A. Knopf, Inc. 1973.

A detailed discussion of the concept of androgyny and its presentation through three thousand years of myth and literature. Good reading!

*See page 00 for the correct identification of A, B, C, and D (after you do the exercise!).

Mao Tse-tung. "On Contradiction." In *Selected Works,* pp. 311–345. Peking: Foreign Language Press, 1975. (Also included in nearly every other collection of his writings.)

The modern statement, in the Chinese revolutionary context, of the Hegelian-Marxist-Leninist concept that contradiction, conflict, and change are universal and essential aspects of all situations.

O'Brien, P. *Woman Alone.* New York: Time Books, 1973.

Very readable account of interviews with women who are alone for various reasons: divorce, widowhood, singlehood. Explores how these women come to terms with their own identities.

Riegel, K., ed. *Development of Dialectical Operations.* Basel: Karger, 1975.

A selection of readings that addresses the application of a particular critique of psychology to several different areas including sex roles. A major feature of this critique is that psychology has not looked at concrete, real-life events, a situation which leads to the perpetuation of the status quo including stereotypes. It also calls for a scientific prescription for social change.

Ryan, W. *Blaming the Victim,* rev. ed. New York: Vintage Books, 1976.

A very readable analysis of how the ruling elite redefines every situation of oppression so that the oppressors, the victims, and third parties all agree that it is the "fault" of the victim. Includes a new chapter but is in all other respects the same as the original published in 1976.

Sherfey, M. J. *The Nature and Evolution of Female Sexuality.* New York: Random House, Inc., 1972.

Sherfey is a psychoanalyst who took seriously Freud's request to revise his theory as new biological information became available. The result stands Freud on his head: Females are the primary sexual beings (what we see in society today is the repression of female sexuality, required for male domination and stable nuclear families); female development is consistent, whereas male development is a deviation and tends to be unstable. Rather turgid medical writing; a popular interpretation of the sexual implications may be found in Barbara Seamen's *Free and Female* (Greenwich, Conn: Fawcett Publications, Inc., 1972).

Index

Abortion laws, 89
Absenteeism, 198
Achievement motivation and
     performance, 122, 142–147
Activists, political, 237–238
Adam, 73
Adams, Laura, 59–61
Adams, Margaret, 87
Addams, Jane, 18, 19
Adelson, Joseph, 148, 150, 151, 154
Adolescence, 34, 133–162
  biological aspects of identity,
       135–141, 157–158
  identity solutions, 154–155, 157
  intellectual aspects of identity,
       141–147
  psychological aspects of identity,
       147–150
  social aspects of identity, 150–154
Advertising, 81, 114
Affirmative action, 258
Aged women, 59, 211–212
Aggression, 102, 120–121
Aid to Families with Dependent
     Children (AFDC), 211
Albee, Edward, 51, 53
Alther, Lisa, 59, 61
American Federation of Labor–Congress
     of Industrial Organizations
     (AFL–CIO), 205
American Federation of Teachers, 206
American Psychiatric Association, 139
American Revolution, 11
Ambivalence, 135
Analytic performance, 101
Anastasi, Annie, 145–146
Androgens, 98, 99, 102
Androgyny, 156–157, 245, 247, 248

Anthony, Susan B., 17
Anthony and Cleopatra (Shakespeare),
     51
Antislavery societies, 16
Antiwar movement, 22
Approaching Simone (Terry), 56
Approval, need for, 86–87
Arapesh culture, 29–30
Archetypes, 50–52
Aristotle, 2, 22
Arrow, Kenneth, 200–201
Art, 79–80
Assertiveness training, 88, 258
Aurora Leigh (E. Barrett Browning), 62
Austen, Jane, 56
Authority figure, husband as, 165
Autonomy, 145, 146

Bacharach, Burt, 79
Bardwick, Judith M., 135–136, 139, 146
Barton, Clara, 17
Be a Woman (Baker), 81
Bean, J., 245
Beauvoir, Simone de, 33
Behaviors, male–female differences in,
     102–103
Bellini, 79
Bem, Sandra, 82–83, 122
Bengston, V., 251
Bennet, Susan M., 83
Bernard, Jessie, 73, 76, 166, 181
Bettelheim, Bruno, 36–37
Biological aspects of identity, 135–141,
     157–158
Birnbaum, Judith A., 146
Birth-control methods, 170
Bishop, Nadean, 48–70
Black, K., 251

Blacks, achievement motivation and
    performance, 146–147
  civil rights movement, 22
  divorce rates, 176
  in drama, 54–55
  employment, 175, 190, 195–196
  families, 174–176
  female networks in economic
    exchange, 41
  in fiction, 58–59
  parental expectations, 110–111
  self-esteem, 150
  slavery, 15, 16
  voting performance, 230
Blackstone, Sir William, 11, 228
Blanche of Castile, 3
Bloc voting, 230–231
Blood, Robert, 165
Blue-collar workers, 171–174, 193, 212
"Blues," 135–136
Body Parts of Margaret Fuller, The
    (Broner), 56
Bona fide occupational qualification
    (BFOQ), 202
Books, sex-role learning and, 117–118
  See also Literature, women in
Boothe, Clare, 53–54
Bossen, L., 42
Bowen, Elizabeth, 59
Brackney, Barbara, 133–162
Brahmins, 38
Braithwaite, Yvonne, 237
Broner, E. M., 56
Brontë, Charlotte, 56
Brontë, Emily, 56
Brooks, Gwendolyn, 64
Broverman, Inge K., 86, 147
Brown, Rita Mae, 59
Browning, Elizabeth Barrett, 62
Bundu culture, 40

Call Me Ishtar (Lerman), 61
Calvin, John, 8
Campaign funds, 236
Care preparation, 258
Career choice, 120
  See also Employment
Carlson, R., 148

Carter, Jimmy, 237
Caste status, 74
Chafe, William H., 21–22, 234
Change, 251–255
Charlemagne, Emperor, 3
Chekhov, Anton, 57
Child bearing, 29, 33, 34, 36
Child care, 21, 33, 34, 187, 190
  in blue-collar families, 172
  changing aspects of, 170–171
  father–child relationship, 171
  role transition, 170
  single parents, 177, 178
  tax relief, 203
  traditional mother role, 169
Child-care centers, 21, 169, 172
Childbirth, 37
Children's Hour, The (Hellman), 55
Childress, Alice, 55
Christian Era, 2–4
Chromosomes, 97–98, 99, 102–103
Civil Rights Act of 1964, 201, 202, 205,
    230, 243, 257
Civil rights movement, 22
Clitorectomy, 40
Colonial America, 10–12
Church participation, 3–4
Clothing, 11–12, 115
Coalition of Labor Union Women
    (CLUW), 206
Cognitive abilities, 100
Cognitive-development theory,
    106–107, 134
Cohabitation, 180
Cole, Claudia, 84
College-educated women, 234
Commentaries (Blackstone), 11, 228
Communications Workers, 206
Compassion rap, 87–88
Competition, 120–122, 144
Concept mastery, 101–102
Congressional posts, 236–237
Congressional Union, 19
Consciousness-raising groups, 88
Conservatism, 19
Contamination, 33, 35–37
Contemporary Women Novelists (Spacks),
    58

Cooptation, 257
Cornell, D. M., 149
Cottage industries, 7
"Councils" (Piercy), 65–66
Courtier, The (Castiglione), 5
Courtly love, cult of, 4, 5
Creativity, 145–146
Credit, 89, 204, 236
Crowding theory, 198–199
Cultural change, 254–255
Cultural influences on sex-role
    behavior, 111–118

Dating, 138, 151–152
David, Hal, 79
Day-care centers, 21, 169, 172
"Dear God, the Day Is Gray" (Halley),
    64
Decision-making power, 89, 165, 168,
    175–176, 257
Declaration of the Rights of Woman
    and of the Citizen, 9
Degas, Edgar, 80
Delayed marriages, 89
Delta Wedding (Welby), 58
Demand-and-supply theory, 199
Democratic National Convention, 237,
    238
Dennich, B., 36
Devaluation of women, 33, 35–37
Devouring Mother, 50, 51
Dickinson, Anna, 17
Dickinson, Emily, 62–63
Dictionary of Occupational Titles, 207,
    209
Displaced Homemaker Acts, 210
Divorce, 9, 87, 164, 176–179, 189
Dix, Dorothea, 17
Dodson, Fitzhugh, 171
Dolls, 113
Doll's House, A (Ibsen), 49, 52
Domesticity, ideal of, 15, 20
Dominance behavior, 102, 121
Double standard, 138
Douvan, Elizabeth, 148, 150, 151, 154,
    155
Dowries, 6
Drama, 49–56

Draper, Patricia, 39
Dual-career family, 85
Duffy, Maureen, 54
Dutchman (Jones), 53

Earnings, 168, 186
    divorce and, 177
    of the elderly, 212
    of female-headed families, 210–211
    occupational and industrial
        segregation and, 192–196
    from paid labor, 191–192
    program benefits and, 210
    by race and sex, 196
    of union members, 205
    of working wives, 188
Economic roles and opportunities
    achievement motivation and
        performance, 142–147
    of Blacks, 146–147
    in colonial America, 10–11
    credit, 89, 204, 236
    in early twentieth century, 20–21
    earnings (*see* Earnings)
    employment (*see* Employment)
    future, 212–216
    insurance, 194, 204–205
    in Middle Ages, 4, 7
    post-Civil War era, 17–18
    post-World War II, 21
    poverty, 210–212
    in primitive societies, 42–43
    in Renaissance, 6–7
Education, 213
    in colonial America, 12
    employment and, 168, 189, 213
    family roles and, 164
    housework and, 209
    in nineteenth-century America, 13
    Protestant Reformation and, 7–8
    in Renaissance, 5
    sex, 89, 137
    sex-role behavior and, 118–120
    voting performance and, 231–234
*Effect of Gamma Rays on Man-in-
    the-Moon Marigolds, The* (Zindel),
    51
Elderly women, 59, 211–212

Eleanor of Aquitaine, 3
Elementary school, 119
Eliot, George, 56
Elites, political, 235–237
Elizabeth I, Queen of England, 5, 51
Emergent pluralism, 248–250
Employer-financed pensions, 194
Employment, 186–226
  of Blacks, 175, 190, 195–196
  discrimination, 21, 192–201
  education and, 168, 189, 213
  flexi-time, 215
  future, 212–216
  governmental action, 201–204
  labor force participation, 167–168,
    187–192, 217–219, 234
  labor unions, 205–206
  of married women, 21–22
  occupational and industrial
    segregation, 192–201, 214
  paid work, 186, 187, 190–192
  part-time, 190, 215
  of single mothers, 177
  unemployment, 191–192, 195, 211,
    218
  unpaid home production vs.,
    186–187, 206–210
  voting performance and, 234–235
  working conditions, 18
  working wives, 167–169, 172, 188,
    206
English Common Law, 10
Entwistle, D., 146–147
Environment versus heredity argument,
    96–97
Equal Employment Opportunity
    Commission (EEOC), 201–203
Equal Pay Act of 1963, 201, 230
Equal Rights Amendment (ERA), 19,
    20, 230, 239–240, 251
Erikson, Erik, 133
Estrogens, 99, 102, 103, 136
Euripides, 50
Eve, 51, 73, 75, 79, 80, 81
Eve–Madonna image, 78
Everyone Was Brave (O'Neill), 228–229
Exclusion-of-females ideology, 248–250

Factory work, 18
Family, 163–185
  adolescent relationships in, 152–154
  alternatives to traditional marriage,
    179–180
  Black, 174–176
  blue-collar marriages, 171–174
  factors causing changes in, 163–164
  female-headed, 210–211
  future of, 180–181
  single-parent, 176–179
  traditional wife and mother, 165–171
Fascinating Womanhood (Andelin), 81
Fashion, 11–12
Father, The (Strindberg), 52
Father–child relationship, 171
Fear of Flying (Jong), 61
Federal income taxes, 203
Female-domination ideology, 255, 256,
    259
Female-headed families, 210–211
Female Man, The (Russ), 61
Female solidarity, 40–41
Female Woman, The (Stassinopoulous),
    81
"Feminine mystique," 164
Feminine Mystique, The (Friedan), 22
Femininity, definition of, 86–87
Feminist presses, 50
Feminized Male, The (Sexton), 257
Ferguson, Mary Anne, 57
Fertility rate, 164, 170, 189
Fiction, 56–62
Finishing Touches (Kerr), 56
Firestone, Shulamith, 22
Flexi-time, 215
Fluidity of marital life, 174
For Better, for Worse: A Feminist
    Handbook on Marriage and Other
    Options (Fleming and Washburn),
    82
Fortune, 186
Foster, Abbey Kelly, 17
Fourteenth Amendment, 18
Fox, Greer Litton, 75
Frazier, E. Franklin, 175
Freeman, Jo, 239

French Revolution, 8–9
Freud, Sigmund, 54, 106, 107, 133–134
Friedan, Betty, 21, 164
"Friend, The" (Piercy), 64
Friendships in adolescence, 150–151
Fringe benefits, 194, 209–210, 212, 215
Fritchey, Clayton, 240–241

Games, sex-role behavior and, 114–115
Games Mother Never Taught You, 82
Gay liberation, 243
Gender, 97–104
Gilman, Charlotte Perkins, 22
Glasser, P., 178
Glick, Paul, 166
Goddard, Mary Katherine, 10
Godwin, Gail, 60
Goffman, Irving, 85, 112
Goldberg, Philip, 84
Goldberg, S., 109
Golden Notebook, The (Lessing), 58
Gompers, Mrs. Samuel, 21
Good Mother, 50–51
Goodman, P., 114
Gosnell, Harold F., 230
Governors, female, 237
Grahn, Judy, 65
Grasso, Ella, 237
Great Awakening, 15
Great Mother, The (Neumann), 50
Greece (ancient), 2, 49, 50–51
Green, Adolf, 79
Greenberger, E., 147
Griffiths, Martha W., 188, 230–231, 239
Grimké, Angelina, 16, 54
Grimké, Sarah, 16, 22
Growing-up-female novels, 60
Guilds, 4, 6, 7

Hacker, Helen, 74, 85–86
Hafter, Daryl, 1–27
Hammerstein, Oscar, II, 78, 79
Hampson, J. L., 104
Hansberry, Lorraine, 54–55
Harper, Edward, 38
Harrison, Algea O., 147
Health insurance, 194, 204–205

Hedda Gabler (Ibsen), 52
Hefner, Robert, 243–264
Hellman, Lillian, 55
Helson, Ravenna, 145
Heredity versus environment argument,
    96–97
History of women, 1–27
    American Revolution, 11
    Christian Era, 2–4
    colonial America, 10–12
    French Revolution, 8–9
    Greece (ancient), 2, 49, 50–51
    in nineteenth-century America, 13–18
    Protestant Reformation, 7–8
    Renaissance, 4–7, 49, 51–52
    suffrage, 18–20, 228–229
    World War II, 21
Hoffer, Carol, 40–41
Hoffman, Lois W., 145, 168, 169
Hogbin, Ian, 37
Homemakers, dependency upon others,
    209
    displaced, 209–210
    See also Housework
Homophobia, 243
Homosexuality, 59, 61, 139–141, 180,
    245
Hormones, 98–99, 102, 135–137
Horner, Matina S., 142–143
Housekeeping toys, 113
Housewife role, 76–77, 85, 165–167,
    168, 172
Housework, in blue-collar families,
    172
    education and, 209
    salaries for, 207–208
    shift toward paid work, effect on,
        215–216
    single parents and, 177–178
    status of, 167
    as unpaid home production, 186–187,
        206–210
    value of, 207
    working wives and, 168–169
How to Become an Assertive Woman
    (Taubman), 82
How to Father (Dodson), 171

How to Save Your Own Life (Jong), 59, 61
Howe, Florence, 62
Hull House, 18
Human capital theory, 197–198
Hunting and gathering societies, 28, 32, 39–40

Ibsen, Henrik, 49, 52
Identity, 133–162
    biological aspects of, 135–141, 157–158
    intellectual aspects of, 141–147
    psychological aspects of, 147–150
    psychosexual, 104
    social aspects of, 150–154
    solutions, 154–155, 157
    of traditional wife role, 165–166
    See also Sex role socialization
I'm Glad I'm a Boy, I'm Glad I'm a Girl (Darrow), 118
Images of Women in Literature (Ferguson), 57
Imitation, 105, 106, 107
Income (*see* Earnings)
Income taxes, 203
Independence, 109, 110–111, 145, 146
Independent Union of Flight Attendants, 205
Individual development, 247–251
Individual level, change at, 252–253
Industrial segregation, 194–201
Inheritances, 4
Initiation, ritual process of, 36–37
Institutional approach, 200
Institutional change, 253
Institutional reinforcers of sex roles, 118–120
Insurance, 194, 204–205
Intellectual aspects of identity, 141–147
Intelligence, 141
International Labor Organization of the United Nations, 168
International Women's Year Conference, 238, 240
Isabel of Spain, 5
Ivey, M. E., 135–136

Jacklin, Carol, 96, 100, 102, 110, 119, 121, 122, 148
James, Henry, 57
Jefferson, Thomas, 13
Johnson, J. E., 149
Jones, LeRoi, 53
Jong, Erica, 59, 61, 63
Jordan, Barbara, 236
Jung, Carl Gustave, 50
"Just Anger, A" (Piercy), 65

Kaplan, A., 245
"Kathe Kollwitz" (Rukeyser), 63
Kaufman, Shirley, 64
Kerr, Jean, 55–56
Kinflicks (Alther), 59, 61
King Lear (Shakespeare), 51
Kirkpatrick, Jeane, 238
Kohlberg, Lawrence, 106, 134
Kollwitz, Kathe, 63
Konopka, Gisela, 152–153
Kopit, Arthur, 53
Kriegel, Harriet, 51, 53
Kriesberg, 177
Kuhn, D., 143
!Kung bushmen culture, 39

Labé, Louise, 5
Labor, division of, 30, 31, 39
Labor, U.S. Department of, 202, 213
Labor force participation, 167–168, 187–192, 217–219, 234
Labor unions, 18, 205–206
Labouvie-Vief, Gisela, 84
Ladner, Joyce A., 150
Lamaze Association, 170
Lamphere, Louise, 32, 39
Language, sex-role behavior and, 111–112
Lansing, Marjorie, 227–242
Last Judgment, The (Rubens), 80
Law schools, 236
League of Women Voters, 20
Learning abilities, 100
Leavitt, Ruby, 29
Left Hand of Darkness (LeGuin), 61
Legal status of wives, 166
LeGuin, Ursula, 61

LeMasters, 178
Lerman, Rhoda, 61
Lesbian Image, The (Rule), 59
Lesbianism, 59, 61, 139–141
Lessing, Doris, 58
Lever, E., 114
Levertov, Denise, 65
Lewis, I. M., 41–42
Lewis, M., 109
Lindner, Richard, 80
Literary Women (Moers), 57
Literature, women in, 48–70
  drama, 49–56
  fiction, 56–62
  poetry, 50, 62–66
Literature of Their Own, A (Showalter),
  56
Little Foxes, The (Hellman), 55
Locker-room syndrome, 89
Loesser, Frank, 79
Logic, male–female differences in,
  101–102
Lowell, James Russell, 63

Macbeth (Shakespeare), 51
McCarthy, Mary, 186–226
Maccoby, Eleanor E., 96, 100, 102, 110,
  119, 121, 122, 148
Mad and/or miserable wife novels,
  60–61
Madonna, 74, 75
Mae Enga culture, 35–36
Magazines, 80–81
Mailer, Norman, 57
Major Barbara (Shaw), 53
Male bonding, 32
Male inferiority, 37
Male supremacy, 36, 248–250, 255–257,
  259
Marguerite of Navarre, 5
Marriage, alternatives to traditional,
  179–180
  blue-collar, 171–174
  delayed, 89
  in nineteenth-century America, 13
  Protestant Reformation and, 8
  rates, 164
  Saint Paul on, 3

Marriage *(cont.)*
  sexuality after, 76
  traditional, 165–171
  See also Family
"Marriage" (More), 62
Martineau, Harriet, 13
Mary, Mary (Kerr), 55
Mary, Virgin, 51
Masturbation, 137
Matasar, Ann B., 237
Material instinct, 123–124
Mathematical ability, 101
Matriarchy, 29
Matrifocal family system, 174
Mead, Margaret, 29–31, 37, 105, 180
Medea (Euripides), 51
Mednick, Maratha, 147
Meggitt, M. J., 35, 36
Melting pot ideology, 248–250, 256,
  259
Memoirs of an Ex-Prom Queen
  (Schulman), 60
Men in Groups (Tiger), 32
Menarche, 135
Menstruation, 33, 35, 37, 135–137
Mental health of housewives, 85
Merriam, Charles E., 230
Middle Ages, 2–4, 7
Military issues, gender differences on,
  240
Millay, Edna St. Vincent, 63
Miller, Isabel, 59
Minority group, treatment of women
  as, 74–75
Minority women, employment
  handicaps, 195–196
  See also Blacks
Moers, Ellen, 57
Mommies at Work (Merriman), 118
Monahan, Lynn, 143
Money, John, 104
Monopsony theory, 199–200
"Monster" (Morgan), 65
Moods, male–female differences in,
  102–103
Moore, Marianne, 63
Moral guardianship of society, 14–16
More, Sir Thomas, 49
Morgan, Maribel, 81–82

Morgan, Robin, 65
Morrison, Toni, 58
"Mother, The" (Brooks), 64
Mother–child bonding, 32
Mother role, traditional, 165–171
"Mothers, Daughters" (Kaufman), 64
Mott, Lucretia, 16, 228
Mundugumor culture, 29–30, 105
Munichen, Patricia, 109–110
Music, 78–79
Muslim Africa, 41

Napoleon I, Emperor, 9
Napoleonic Code, 9
Narcissism, 134
National Confederation of Business and
    Professional Women's Clubs, 19
National conventions, 237, 238
National Organization of Women
    (NOW), 238, 257
National Woman's Party, 19, 20
National Women's Loyal League, 17
National Women's Political Caucus
    (NWPC), 238
National Women's Suffrage
    Association, 18, 19, 20
Nature, identification of women with,
    33
Navarre, E., 178
Negro Family in The United States, The
    (Frazier), 175
Neumann, Eric, 50
New Deal, 21
Nice girl, image of, 75–76
Nin, Anais, 66
Nineteenth Amendment, 19
Noblewomen, 2, 3–5
No-fault divorce, 176–177
Nuclear family, 163–164
Nuns, 3–4
Nupe culture, 37–38
Nurturance, inherited versus learned
    nature of, 123–124

O'Brian, Patricia, 89
Occupational segregation, 192–201, 214
Ochs, Phil, 79
Odd Woman, The (Godwin), 60

Oden, M. H., 120
Oedipal period, 50
Office of Federal Contract Compliance,
    202
Olsen, Tillie, 58, 59
Olympe de Gouges, 9
O'Neill, Eugene, 53
O'Neill, William L., 228–229
Open marriage, 179–180
Organized labor, 18, 205–206
Orgasm, 137
Ortner, Sherry, 32–34, 43

Paid work, 186, 187, 190–192
Paige, Karen, 136
Parent, Gail, 60
Parents, of adolescent children, 152–154
    as reinforcers of sex-role behavior,
        107–111
    working mothers, 167–169
    See also Child care
Parker, Dorothy, 58
Part-time work, 190, 215
Passivity, 15, 134
Pasternak, Boris, 63
Patience and Sarah (Miller), 59
Paul, Alice, 19
Paul, Saint, 3, 73
Penis envy, 134
Pensions, 194, 203–204, 206, 212,
    213
Petry, Ann, 58
Petting, 137
"Phantasia for Elvira Shatayev" (Rich),
    65
Physically inherited factors, 97–104
Picasso, Pablo, 80
Piercy, Marge, 59, 61, 64, 65–66
Piety, ideal of, 15
Pillars of Society (Ibsen), 52
Pinckney, Eliza Lucas, 10
Plato, 2, 49
Playgirl, image of, 75
Please Don't Eat the Daisies (Kerr),
    55–56
Pluralism, 248–250, 255, 256, 259
"Poem as Mask, The" (Rukeyser), 63
Poetry, 50, 62–66

Politics, 89, 227–242, 257
  activists, 237–238
  élites, 235–237
  gender differences on issues, 240–241
  public policy, 239–240
  socialization, 229
  suffrage, 18–20, 228–229
  voting performance, 19–20, 230–235
Popular music, 78–79
Porter, Mary Cornelia, 237
Possession, 41, 42
Poverty, 210–212
Power relationships, 168
Premarital sex, 138–139
Premenstrual syndrome, 135–136
Preschool, 118–119
Presidential administrations, women in, 237
Progressive Movement, 18
Protestant Reformation, 7–8
Psychological aspects of identity, 147–150
Psychosexual identity, 104
Puberty, 135
Public policy, 239–240
Purification, ritual of, 34
Purity, ideal of, 15
Pygmalion (Shaw), 53

"Queen Bee" syndrome, 84
Quit rates, 198

Rachel (Grimké), 54
Raisin in the Sun, A (Hansberry), 54–55
"Rape" (Rich), 65
Ray, Dixie, 237
Reasoning, male–female differences in, 101–102
Rebecca, Meda, 243–264
Reichbach, Gwen, 163–185
Reisman, David, 79
Remarriage, 178
Remy, D., 42
Renaissance, 4–7, 49, 51–52
"Renascence" (Millay), 63
Renée of Ferrara, 8
Renoir, Pierre Auguste, 80

Retirement, 212, 213
Rich, Adrienne, 48, 62, 64–66
Richardson, Dorothy, 57
Richmond-Abbott, Marie, 71–132
Rise of the Novel, The (Watts), 56
Rites (Duffy), 54
Rodgers, Richard, 78, 79
Rodin, François Auguste René, 80
Role innovators, 144–145
Roosevelt, Eleanor, 21
Rosaldo, Michelle, 31–34, 36, 39, 43
Rose, Ernestine, 17
Rosenblat, J. S., 123
Rosenkrantz, Paul S., 149
Rossiter, Margaret L., 1n.
Rubens, Peter Paul, 80
Rubin, Gail, 40
Rubin, Lillian B., 172
Rubyfruit Jungle (Brown), 59
Rukeyser, Muriel, 63, 65
Rule, Jane, 59
Russ, Joanna, 61
Russell, Candyce, 170

Sackville-West, Vita, 59
Saint Joan (Shaw), 52–53
Saints, 8
Salaries for homemakers, 207–208
Samuelson, Paul, 201
Sarton, Mary, 59
School, sex-role behavior and, 117–120
Science, change in, 253–254
Self-concept, 147–148
Self-esteem, 122, 146, 148–150, 166
Self-fulfilling prophecy, 86
Self-hatred, 85–86
Seniority, 202, 213
Senses, male–female differences in, 99–100
Sensuous Woman, The ("J"), 81
Service workers, 193–194, 195
Sex chromosomes, 97–98, 99, 102–103
Sex education, 89, 137
Sex hormones, 98–99, 102–103
Sex-role identification, 154
Sex-role socialization, 96–132, 244
  change and growth as part of, 252
  cultural influences, 111–118

Sex-role socialization (*cont.*)
  heredity-versus-environment
    argument, 96–97
  institutional reinforcers, 118–120
  parental expectations and actions,
    107–111
  physical inheritance, 97–104
  stereotypic behavior as learned
    behavior, 120–124
  theories of learning sex roles,
    105–107
  See also Stereotypes
Sex roles, cross-cultural perspectives
  on, 28–43
Sex roles, future of, 243–264
  androgyny, 245, 247, 248
  change, 251–255
  individual development and societal
    organization, 247–251
  scenarios, 255, 256, 259
  traditional sex roles, 244–247
  transcendence, 245–248, 255–260
Sex and Temperament (Mead), 105
Sexual intercourse, 137, 138–139
Sexual Politics (Millett), 82
Sexuality:
  adolescent, 137–141
  in blue-collar marriages, 173
  contamination associated with, 33,
    35–37
  restrictions related to, 75–78
Sforza, Caterina, 5
Shaefer, C. A., 146
Shakespeare, William, 49, 51
Shauer, P., 143
Shaw, George Bernard, 52–53
"She Leaves" (Piercy), 65
*Sheila Levine Is Dead and Living in New
  York* (Parent), 60
Showalter, Elaine, 56, 57
Sinclair, Karen, 28–47
Single life, 89, 180, 190
Single parents, 176–179, 206
Sisterhood Is Powerful (Morgan), 82
Slavery, 15, 16
Slocum, Sally, 32
Small Changes (Piercy), 59
Snake in the Carpool, The (Schlein), 118

Sociability, inherited versus learned
  nature of, 122–123
Social aspects of identity, 150–154
Social-learning theory, 105, 107
Social Security, 190, 203–204, 221
Socialization, 32
  political, 229
  sex-role (*see* Sex-role socialization)
Societal organization, 247–251
Songs, 78–79
Sonnets from the Portuguese (E. Barrett
  Browning), 62
Soto, Debbie Halon, 84
Spacks, Patricia, 58
Spaeth, Sigmund, 78
Spirit possession, 41, 42
Sports, 252–253
Stanton, Elizabeth Cady, 16, 17, 227,
  228
Stein, Gertrude, 59, 62
Stereotypes, 71–95, 186, 191, 200
  in advertising, 81
  agreement on, 82–84
  in art, 79–80
  combating, 88–90
  "ideal" man, 72, 74
  "ideal" woman, 72–74
  influences of, 84–86
  learning and, 120–124
  lesbian, 140
  in literature, 49–50, 57
  in magazines, 80–81
  perpetuation of feminine behavior
    by, 86–88
  persistence of, 78–82
  in popular music, 78–79
  sexuality of women, restrictions
    related to, 75–78
  treatment of women as minority
    group, 74–75
  See also Sex-role socialization
Stone, Lucy, 17, 18
Stowe, Harriet Beecher, 66
Street, The (Petry), 58
Stress, 173, 178
Strikes, 18
Strindberg, August, 49, 52
Strongin, Lynn, 64

Success, competitiveness and, 122
  fear of, 142–144
Suffering-single novels, 60
Suffrage, 18–20, 228–229
Sullerot, Evelyne, 168
Summer before the Dark, The (Lessing),
  58
Support groups, 88–89
Support payments, 210–211
Supreme Court, 201, 202, 203, 236, 239
Symmetrical shared-role pattern, 179

Tangri, Sandra S., 144
Taste-for-discrimination theory,
  196–197
Tavris, Carol, 84, 85
Taxes, 203–204
Tchambuli culture, 29, 31, 105
Teachers, 119
Television, sex-role behavior and,
  115–117
  views of women on, 56
"Tell Me a Riddle" (Olsen), 59
Terman, L. M., 120
Terry, Megan, 56
Testosterone, 103
Tiger, Lionel, 32
Time, uses of, 186–187, 197–198, 199,
  206, 208–209
Titian, 79
Tocqueville, Alexis de, 13, 72, 73
Tooley, Kay, 137
Total Woman, The (Morgan), 81
"Total Woman" programs, 258
Toulouse-Lautrec, Henri de, 80
Toys, 113–114
Traditional marriage, 165–171
  alternatives to, 179–180
Traditional sex roles, 244–247
Transcendence, sex-role, 245–248,
  255–260
Transport Workers Union, 205
Trial marriage, 180
Trojan Women, The (Euripides), 50
True womanhood, cult of, 14–15
  role of, 20
Truth, Sojourner, 16
Tubman, Harriet, 16

Turnover rates, 198
Two-step marriage, 180

Uncle Tom's Cabin (Stowe), 66
Unemployment, 191–192, 195, 211, 218
United Automobile Workers, 205–206
Unpaid home production, 186–187,
  206–210
Urberg, Kathryn A., 84

Value system, 72, 73, 75–78
"Van Gogh" (Strongin), 64
Venus, 79
Veterans' preferences, 203
Visual–spatial performance, 101
Voting, performance, 19–20, 230–235
  suffrage, 18–20, 228–229

Walker, Alice, 58
Walker, Mary Edwards, 17
Walum, Laurel, 112
Watts, Ian, 56
Weil, Simone, 56
Welfare, 192–193, 195, 206, 212
Welfare mothers, 211
Welter, Barbara, 14
Welty, Eudora, 58
Western industrialization, 42–43
Weston, Peter, 147
Wharton, Edith, 59
White-collar workers, 192–193
Whitman, Walt, 63
Who's Afraid of Virginia Woolf (Albee),
  51
Williams, John E., 83
Williams, Tennessee, 53
Wilson, James Q., 237
Wilson, Woodrow, 19
Wine in the Wilderness (Childress), 55
Witchcraft, 37–38
Wives, traditional, 165–171
  working, 167–169, 172, 188, 206
Wogeo culture, 37
Wolf, Margery, 40
Wolfe, Donald, 165
Wolff, Charlotte, 140–141
Wollstonecraft, Mary, 22
Woman Alone (O'Brian), 82, 89

Woman on the Edge of Time (Piercy), 61
Women, The (Boothe), 53–54
Women in Drama (Kriegel), 51, 53
Women's Bureau, 19
Women's Educational Equity Act, 254
Women's International League for
    Peace and Freedom, 19
Women's rights movement, 134, 243
    antislavery movement and, 16
    beginnings of, 15–17
    Civil War and, 17
    family roles and, 164
    political power structure and, 227
    Seneca Falls declaration, 16

Women's Trade Union League, 18
Woolf, Virginia, 57, 59
Work (*see* Employment)
Workday, 18
Working class, in late Middle Ages, 4
    marriages, 110, 171–174
Working conditions, 18
World Anti-Slavery Convention,
    228
World War I, 19, 29
World War II, 21
Wright, M., 150

Zindel, Paul, 51